# Austerity, Youth Policy and
## of the Youth Service

"Bernard Davies's commitment to tracing the details of the deconstruction of the Youth Service in England is exemplary. To read the account, as an informed and passionate insider, is devastating. It strengthens my view that a comprehensive re-visioning of an alternative practice is now needed, strong enough to create a sense of mutual respect and belonging, connection and solidarity in these increasingly divided, fragmented and impoverished times."
—Janet Batsleer, *Reader in Education, Principal Lecturer Youth and Community Work, Manchester Metropolitan University, UK*

"In these challenging times for young people and their services, there is an urgent need for detailed critical analysis of recent youth policy. There is no one more qualified for this task than Bernard Davies."
—Tania de St Croix, *Lecturer in the Sociology of Youth and Childhood, Kings College London, UK*

"This book is an essential read for anyone who wants to fully understand the impact so called 'austerity' has had on youth work. Its comprehensive review and detailed critique provide the reader with numerable insights."
—Jon Ord, *Associate Professor, Plymouth Marjon University, UK*

"In this timely publication, Bernard Davies continues his long-standing commitment to understanding the past as a crucial guide to the future. Viewed through the prism of youth work and the youth service he unravels painstakingly the damaging consequences for young women and men of the last decade of neoliberal economic and social policy. Letting the facts speak almost for themselves he documents, in particular, the destructive impact of outcome-obsessed, individualising neoliberal ideology upon open-ended youth work, pondering in conclusion whether the tide is turning in favour of a renewed emancipatory and democratic practice."
—Tony Taylor *has been involved in youth work across five decades, most recently as a Chief Youth Officer [1989–1998], a Senior Lecturer [1998–2000] and In Defence of Youth Work Coordinator [2009–2018], UK*

"Bernard Davies' previous volumes on youth service history have been an essential feature on reading lists for youth work and youth studies programmes, and an engaging read for students, practitioners and academics. This latest work reflects critically on the last couple of decades, offering a nuanced and well informed analysis of both the New Labour years and post-2010 austerity era on youth work and youth services. He offers a convincing critique of the impact of neoliberalism over the last few decades and how this now leaves not just youth work and youth services, but young people themselves, facing an uncertain and precarious future. Davies writes with his usual flair, bringing to light the challenges, distortions and pressures imposed on youth services under the political ideologies of recent years as well as an 'insider' account of the movements to respond and defend youth work. A must-read for students, academics and practitioners."

—Naomi Thompson, *Lecturer in Youth and Community Work, Goldsmiths, University of London, UK*

Bernard Davies

# Austerity, Youth Policy and the Deconstruction of the Youth Service in England

palgrave
macmillan

Bernard Davies
Warkwickshire, UK

ISBN 978-3-030-03885-4       ISBN 978-3-030-03886-1   (eBook)
https://doi.org/10.1007/978-3-030-03886-1

Library of Congress Control Number: 2018961181

This Palgrave Macmillan imprint is published by the registered company Springer Nature Switzerland AG
The registered company address is: Gewerbestrasse 11, 6330 Cham, Switzerland

# Preface

With England as its prime focus, this book provides an account and analysis of how UK state and voluntary sector policy-makers responded after 2007 to an age group flexibly defined as 13–19 year olds. After being located within the legacies of the wider New Labour 'modernisation' strategy for public services, the youth policies which resulted are throughout examined critically in relation to the dominant ideological, political and economic priorities of the period. Key aims include tracing both how and why, at the time, these policies were conceived and implemented, perceived and received and their longer-term impacts on young people and the services provided for them.

Where relevant, consideration is given to policies for education, child care and child protection, youth justice and health including mental health. However, primary critical attention is given to policies designed to reach and influence young people in their out-of-school, out-of-work hours, using local authority Youth Services in England as appropriate to illustrate and clarify their 'on-the-ground' impacts. (The parallel state structures for providing youth work in the other UK administrations have developed along very different lines and so are not considered.) As well as full- and part-time paid and volunteer 'open access' youth workers, the book will be relevant to students, practitioners and trainers involved in educational, care, justice and health work with children and young people and to teachers and students on academic child and youth studies courses.

The book is divided into six parts.

- *Part I* examines the legacies for youth policies overall and for the local authority Youth Service and youth work specifically of New Labour's efforts to build a 'new model of public services'.
- *Part II* analyses post-2010 governments' economic policies and the consequences of 'austerity' for youth policies and Youth Services, nationally and locally.
- *Part III* considers:
  - a range of wider government policies—'The Big Society', 'Localism', 'early intervention', the 'troubled families' initiatives—which helped shape its youth policies;
  - policies and initiatives specifically aimed at re-moralising young people by 'instilling character', nurturing 'wellbeing' and 'preventing terrorism';
  - the 2011 Commons Education Select Committee reports and the government's responses to them;
  - the development and key messages and impacts of the Coalition's own *Positive for Youth* policy; and
  - the implications of these policy interventions for local authority Youth Services.
- *Part IV* gives critical attention to:
  - the development, operation and impacts of the National Citizen Service, the Step Up To Serve youth volunteering programme, the increased government financial support for uniformed youth organisations including cadet forces, and the OnSide youth building programme;
  - other less high-profile government initiatives;

- the growing reliance on philanthropic giving for providing youth facilities;
- the ways in which the voluntary youth sector responded to these wider policy developments.
- *Part V* analyses the consequences of the shifts in youth policies and provision for the training and qualifications of volunteer, part-time and full-time ('professional') youth workers.
- *Part VI*
  - evidences the resistance to the deconstruction of the Youth Service by young people and wider national alliances and organisations; and
  - considers the state of policies and services for young people by mid-2018 and, in this context, the future prospects for state-supported provision of open access youth work.

Where relevant, the book draws on academic studies and reports of surveys and enquiries conducted for or by, for example, Parliamentary committees, policy institutes and consultancies. Some of these are included in the 'further reading' suggestions at the end of each chapter—though many of these have also been included to reflect and illustrate changes in thinking, policy and action which have occurred over the period covered by the book.

By far the most frequently quoted sources, however, listed in chapter footnotes, are newspaper and periodical articles and reports, particularly from the daily news emails of *Children and Young People Now* (*CYPN*).

To facilitate the book's use as a reference text, chapter cross-references have also been included.

Warkwickshire, UK  Bernard Davies
September 2018

# Acknowledgements

In writing this book, I have had invaluable support, including critical comments on draft sections and documents providing important additional information and evidence, from Graham Bright, Janet Batsleer, Jean Spence, Jon Ord, Mae Shaw, Martha Davies, Mike Geddes, Sue Atkins, Tania de St Croix, Tony Ransely and Tony Taylor—as well as, in more general ways, from my In Defence of Youth Work colleagues.

Above all, my thanks go to Sally Davies, not only for her unwavering encouragement overall, but especially for reading every word of every draft with such a sharp eye for an overlong sentence, an over-complicated phrase and an obscure reference.

For all the remaining defects and gaps I of course take full personal responsibility.

September 2018                                              Bernard Davies

# Contents

1  Mapping and Contextualising the Territory: 2007–2018      1

Part I   The New Labour Legacies

2  Towards a New Model of Youth Services      23

3  Practice Under Pressure: From Youth Work to 'Positive Activities'      45

Part II   Austerity Bites

4  The National Picture: From 'State Monopolies' to 'New Providers'      67

5  The Local Youth Service Experience      89

Part III    Wider Youth Policy Agendas

6    Remaking 'The Broken Society'                            109

7    Remoralising the Young                                   127

8    Parliamentary Scrutiny                                   141

9    Government Policy: How Positive for Youth?               157

Part IV    Youth Policies in Action

10    Towards a National Service for Youth                    181

11    Implementing a National Citizen Service                 195

12    Youth Volunteering—The New Panacea                      217

13    Plugging 'Youth Services' Gaps                          237

14    Beyond the State: How 'Voluntary' Is the Voluntary
      Youth Sector?                                           255

Part V    Training and Qualifying for Work with
          Young People

15    'Modernising' Vocational Qualifications                 281

16    Higher Education Routes in Transition                   303

Part VI    Beyond Deconstruction

17    Defending the Youth Service: Defending Youth Work    327

18    What Future for Youth Policies? What Future
      for the Youth Service?    353

Index    371

# Abbreviations

| | |
|---|---|
| ACEVO | Association of Chief Executives of Voluntary Organisations |
| ADCS | Association of Directors of Children's Services |
| APYCO | Association of Principal Youth and Community Officers |
| BAME | Black, Asian and Minority Ethnic |
| BLF | Big Lottery Fund |
| BYC | British Youth Council |
| CAMHS | Child and Adolescent Mental Health Services |
| CBI | Confederation of British Industry |
| CETYCW | Council for Education and Training in Youth and Community Work |
| CHYPS | Confederation of Heads of Young People's Services |
| CSN | Children's Services Network |
| CWDC | Children's Workforce Development Council |
| CYI | Centre for Youth Impact |
| CYPN | *Children and Young People Now* |
| CYPW | Children and Young People's Workforce |
| CYWU | Community and Youth Workers Union |
| DCLG | Department for Community and Local Government |
| DCMS | Department for Culture, Media and Sport |
| DCSF | Department for Children, Schools and Families |
| DDCMS | Department for Digital, Culture, Media and Sport |

| | |
|---|---|
| DDYP | Delivering Differently for Young People |
| DES | Department for Education and Science |
| DfE | Department for Education |
| DFES | Department for Education and Skills |
| DMU | De Montfort University |
| DWP | Department of Work and Pensions |
| ECM | *Every Child Matters* |
| EDM | Early Day Motion |
| EIF | Early Intervention Fund |
| EMA | Education Maintenance Allowance |
| ETS | Education and Training Standards Committee |
| HE | Higher Education |
| HEFC | Higher Education Funding Council |
| HLF | Heritage Lottery Fund |
| IDYW | In Defence of Youth Work |
| IMF | International Monetary Fund |
| IYW | Institute for Youth Work |
| JNC | Joint Negotiating Committee |
| LGA | Local Government Association |
| LGiU | Local Government Information Unit |
| LLUK | LifeLong Learning UK |
| MoJ | Ministry of Justice |
| NAO | National Audit Office |
| NCB | National Children's Bureau |
| NCIA | National Coalition for Independent Action |
| NCS | National Citizens Service |
| NCVQ | National Council for Vocational Qualifications |
| NCVYS | National Council for Voluntary Youth Services |
| NPI | New Policy Institute |
| NSPCC | National Society for the Prevention of Cruelty to Children |
| NUS | National Union of Students |
| NVQs | National Vocational Qualifications |
| NYA | National Youth Agency |
| OCS | Office for Civil Society |
| OFSTED | Office for Standards in Education, Children's Services and Skills |
| ONS | Office for National Statistics |
| OU | Open University |

| | |
|---|---|
| PALYCW | Professional Association of Lecturers in Youth and Community Work |
| QAA | Quality Assurance Agency for Higher Education |
| RAMPs | Regional Accreditation and Monitoring Panels |
| REYS | *Resourcing Excellent Youth Services* |
| TAG | Training Agencies Group |
| UKCES | UK Commission for Employment and Skills |
| UYSAF | United Youth Social Action Fund |
| VCSE | Voluntary, Community and Social Enterprise |
| YAT | Young Adult Trust |
| YCF | Youth Capital Fund |
| YOF | Youth Opportunities Fund |
| YUF | Youth United Fund |

# List of Tables

Table 5.1    Youth service budget cuts in the Yorkshire region—2010        91
Table 5.2    Selection of youth service budget cuts—2010                    91
Table 11.1   NCS recruitment 2011–2016                                     199
Table 11.2   Actual, forecast or planned spending
             on NCS—2011–2016                                              204
Table 11.3   Cost per NCS place—2011–2016                                  204

# 1

# Mapping and Contextualising the Territory: 2007–2018

The starting date for this book's account and analysis of youth policies in the UK is 2007—the year of a global financial crisis which over the following months came close to bringing the world's banking system to collapse and whose impacts on those policies were felt throughout the following decade.

Three 'contextual' features here were particularly critical: a neo-liberal ideology which, in often taken-for-granted ways, defined most of the policies' goals; a reinforcement of the historic power balances already embedded within the society's political structures and processes; and— particularly high-profile after the crisis—an increasingly unequal access to that society's economic resources. Directly and indirectly, these markers of the post-2007 period went far to determining what eventually came to be labelled as 'youth policy'. This included how 'youth' was seen and its needs and problems defined; the kind of adults young people were expected, even required, to become; and the ways in which the services and programmes mandated to 'deliver' those aims were conceived and set up, funded, managed and eventually evaluated. In this period, policies became increasingly preoccupied, too, with how young people viewed and used the newly developing forms of information technology.

© The Author(s) 2019                                                                                    **1**
B. Davies, *Austerity, Youth Policy and the Deconstruction of the Youth Service in England*, https://doi.org/10.1007/978-3-030-03886-1_1

This chapter, with commentary, outlines the crucial features of these formative conditions. In particular it seeks to clarify how and why the state, increasingly in collaboration with civil society and for-profit organisations, responded as it did to young people.

## The Neo-liberal Context: Via 'Market Freedoms' to 'Self-Regulation'

Though with a longer pre-history,[1] it was the assumptions and prescriptions of the ideology labelled 'neo-liberalism' which, since the 1980s, had shaped the public discourse on young people and government and non-government organisations' responses to them. Even though the roots of the 2007–2008 financial melt-down lay in the largely uncritical ways in which these ideas had been understood and applied, by those in power they continued to be treated until late in the period as largely self-evident and unchallengeable 'truths'.[2]

What then were their defining features and how did they help shape youth policies?

Neo-liberalism's foundation premise has been that 'the market'—the supply of goods and services traded for profit—has an in-built and unlimited capacity to generate the wealth that a nation and its population need. To ensure that this potential is fully exploited, the main actors within it—banks and other profit-making institutions—must be allowed to 'self-regulate': given maximum freedom from external and especially state direction or even guidance on how they should act. Only then can the market's presumed intrinsic benevolence be fully realised.

The rationale for these 'market freedoms', however, was not just to ensure that businesses had maximum room for making their profits. They were seen as essential, too, for releasing the competitive energy and drive essential to fully realising the market's wider wealth-creating possibilities—a process which would in turn, it was assumed, ultimately benefit all citizens including the poorest via a built-in 'trickle down effect'.

Underpinning all these propositions was a further core premise: that, as Margaret Thatcher put it in the 1980s, 'there is no such thing as society, only individuals and families'. Certain personal qualities were then seen as particularly (and again self-evidently) ones which all citizens needed to display in their daily lives and which therefore merited (demanded) special nurturing and reward, including, somewhat contradictorily, via public policy. These, understood in entirely de-contextualised ways, included self-reliance and (emotional) resilience, personal confidence and ambition. Also systematically resurrected within Conservative educational policies after 2015 and given strong intellectual support by one of Prime Minister David Cameron's closest advisors Paul Oginsky[3] was the notion of 'character'.

Within neo-liberal thinking, the corollary of this affirmation of the individual and individual responsibility was an at least implicit but sometimes quite explicit denial of wider and deeper structural inequalities and their impacts on those individuals' life chances. In this analysis, the ways in which those lives continued in often crucial ways to be determined by class, gender, race, sexual orientation and (as so many young people discovered) age remained largely unacknowledged. Indeed, the possible <u>consequences</u> of these inequalities—of poor educational achievement, failures to get a well paid job and, for up to a third of those born between 1980 and 1996, the prospect of living in rented accommodation all their lives[4]—were often rebranded as evidence of inadequate individuals or, at its widest, dysfunctional family relationships.

The neo-liberal promotion of individualistic, privatised and competitive values also delegitimised a collective pursuit of shared goals, not least because such collectivities were seen as obstructing the market's freedoms. This was perhaps exemplified particularly starkly by increasing restrictions on trade union action and by legal constraints imposed on charities' pre-election campaigning and lobbying.[5]

All this also indicated another of the far-reaching consequences of neo-liberal policies: the systematic weakening of the independence of those charities—of that 'ungoverned space' within civil society which constitutes a defining feature of democracy in action. Starting under New Labour, these organisations increasingly found themselves pressured (even contractually required) to work in the 'corporate' ways favoured by neo-liberalism. This could include developing 'business plans', adopting 'new managerialist' staff structures and redesigning themselves as 'social enterprises' generating profits to fund their activities. In return for getting what state funding remained, more of them also to took on policies and agendas with government-defined priorities including requirements to 'measure' their 'impacts' in statistical ways.[6]

A powerful negative driver of these policies was the assumption that state bodies were intrinsically bureaucratic and hidebound and so operationally inefficient and not cost-effective—or, as a House of Commons Education Select Committee put it in 2011, that 'the Government as default provider … stifles competition and innovation …'[7] The Coalition government, in its first Treasury Spending Review in October 2010, made it clear that, for a wide range of social, health, justice and youth services, it would '… look at setting proportions of appropriate services across the public sector that should be delivered by independent providers.…'[8] As well as applying these perspectives directly, the period's 'austerity' policies, though repeatedly explained as unavoidable for economic reasons, also acted as cover for reducing the role of the state. With philanthropic bodies expected to fill many of the resultant gaps in services, these as a citizen's right were thus replaced, implicitly if not always explicitly, by a growing entitlement presumption by the wealthy and powerful that it was for them to decide who was 'deserving' and of what. Though governments made much of the need for 'partnership' and 'collaboration', a key corollary of this was their insistence that competitive procedures such as 'commissioning', 'procurement', 'outsourcing' and 'contracting' must be used to allocate whatever state resources were still available.

These neo-liberal premises were never applied in the purest form. Where major profit-making interests judged restriction of market freedoms to be necessary, this happened openly through international trade agreements as well as through behind-the-scenes arrangements. When these same interests required a 'strong' state—for example, as in 2007–2008, to bail out banks that couldn't be allowed to fail, and to carry out crucial security functions—these tasks got taken-for-granted endorsement from even the most committed of free-marketeers.

It turned out, too, that often substantial amounts of state money could be found for approved policies. Between 2011 and 2016, for example, £863 million was made available to pay for 175 sites (often above their market value) for the free schools which for largely ideological reasons the government was setting up across the country. (A further anticipated £2.5 billion was also allocated up to 2022 for acquiring additional land).[9] When something as important to Prime Minister Cameron as the National Citizen Service (NCS) was struggling to meet its target numbers, not only did the state again promise billions of pounds of funding. It also did what it had consistently refused to do for local authorities' Youth Service: it made the scheme 'statutory'.

It was only after the political upheaval of the European Union (EU) referendum vote in June 2016 that neo-liberal thinking and its effects were subject to wider critical debate. In what one commentator called 'a new ideological spectrum',[10] some of this focused on the extent to which class and age[11] inequalities had shaped the vote. Even the Governor of the Bank of England expressed concerns about the 'growing sense of "isolation and detachment" among people who feel left behind by globalisation'.[12] By the time the campaign for the 2017 general election got under way, some political and media recognition was also being given to the neo-liberal drivers of young people's 'bleak lifetime of economic realities'.[13]

By mid-2018, this critique of neo-liberalism and its ways of operating[14] had been further sharpened by two other events. One was the revelations that a Conservative-led county council, Northamptonshire—a 'pioneer' in contracting out public services—was bankrupt, and that other local authorities were also on the brink.[15] The other was the collapse of Carillion, the second largest UK construction company holding major government contracts. Both these forced into the public (including the political) debate some acknowledgement of the inherent risks of outsourcing public services to organisations which ultimately prioritised their profits, dividends for share holders—and bonuses for managers—over the quality and reliability of services often crucial to their users' everyday living.[16]

## The Political Context: What 'Youth Voice'?

Though young people's political interventions in this period did eventually contribute to the challenge to the dominant wisdoms of the period, these started from a position of historic powerlessness. This was demonstrated concretely by an electoral system which continued to exclude all those under 18 with efforts to lower the voting age to 16 repeatedly being blocked.[17] In this period, too, a voter registration process was adopted which was seen by many as putting younger voters at a disadvantage.[18]

Despite these obstacles, in the two months after Prime Minister Theresa May called the 2017 general election 1.05 million 18–24-years-olds registered to vote. Their turn-out was estimated by the polling firm Ipsos Mori to have been 64% and by YouGov, for registered 18–19 year olds, 57%. Though still low in comparison to overall turn-out, this was significantly higher than the 43% at the 2015 general election.[19]

Nonetheless young people remained a low priority for national and indeed local politicians and were even seen by one commentator in 2017 as the government's 'victims by design'.[20] This was exemplified by the government's continuing protection of pensioners' incomes and benefits at a time when it was setting a lower minimum wage for under-21s and threatening to abolish the right of 18–21 year olds to housing benefit[21]—a proposal which was withdrawn in March 2018 because of the risk of more young people being made homeless.[22] Excluded still from voting in the 2016 EU referendum, and with a result tipped by the votes of older people against what many under-18 year olds saw as their age group's long-term interests, despite a high turn-out[23] their powerlessness this time was experienced in very personal ways.[24]

To a significant degree, however, this underdog status stemmed from a wider and long-standing political and indeed cultural perception of 'youth'. This focused overwhelmingly on their 'transitions'—on their need (and indeed obligation) to become productive workers, responsible parents and law-abiding and 'contributing' citizens. The result was a policy-making view of the young as merely citizens-in-the-making with reduced rights. This assumption operated even in youth policy areas which governments regarded as key such as dealing with youth unemployment, where 'too often young people have had to fit into a bureaucratic system, rather than have that system fit around them'.[25]

Such perspectives were applied even more bluntly, even brutally, to the young's here-and-now concerns as they would define them—including, for example, as young women, as gay or lesbian, as disabled or as working class. A particularly high priority were safe and independent spaces for meeting friends and clarifying and expressing individual and shared identities. As a 2012 report put it '…children deserve consideration in their own right and a level of discourse above and beyond the current focus on families and parenting'.[26] For policy-makers, however, as for much of the media, such expectations were at best low priority and at worst highly suspect, with Muslim young people particularly being seen increasingly through the lens of 'violent extremist'.

Over the years, governments rarely got beyond talking the talk when it came to addressing the powerlessness of young people. As one of its first 'austerity' acts for example, in 2010 the Coalition government closed down the Youth Opportunities and Youth Capital Fund programmes which Labour had established to give young people an, albeit limited, role in allocating public money. Nonetheless, within a year this same government was proclaiming its intention of 'promoting youth voice' and asserting young people's 'right to have their views taken into account in all decisions that affect their lives'.[27] In practice, even on the most generous interpretation, this amounted at most to a commitment to consultation—ranked only half way up (or down!) the 'participation ladders' against which 'youth participation' has often been tested and well below procedures defined as 'young people-initiated and directed'.[28] Indeed, in line with the later conflation of 'social action' with 'youth volunteering' (see Chapter 12), by incorporating more winnable members of the generation into safe 'establishment' decision-making structures and roles, the government's approach could even be interpreted as diverting young people from a genuinely independent exercise of power.

## The Economic Context: A New 'Youth Precariat'

For many young people, one of the other defining experiences in this period was material deprivation and inequality—issues to which youth workers had long given specific attention.[29] In the face of neo-liberalism's claims of 'trickle-down' wealth, these in fact worsened during the decade after 2007, particularly as governments' 'austerity' policies after 2010 took hold and levels of poverty generally rose in the UK above those of many other developed countries.[30]

Between 2009 and 2014 for example the wages of 22–29 year olds fell by 12.5%—in comparison to a 3.7% fall for the over-60s. A 2015 report by the New Policy Institute found that some 30% (approximately 2.7 million) of UK 14–24 year olds were living in poverty—a higher proportion than for any other age group—with 1.9 million having incomes considerably below the poverty threshold.[31] Even before under 21 year olds lost their right to housing benefit, one 2014 survey reported that 8% of 16–24 year olds had been homeless in the previous five years.[32]

The Coalition's abolition of the Education Maintenance Allowance (EMA) was also felt very directly by many post-16 year olds struggling to stay in education, while even Chancellor George Osborne's introduction of what he called a 'living wage' had the effect for many of further disadvantaging them in the labour market.[33] Between April and June 2018, with a 16–24 year old unemployment rate of 11.7% compared to 4% nationally,[34] over half a million young people were anyway without jobs. To escape this situation, many were also increasingly having to negotiate a 'gig' economy offering non-contracted zero-hours work, no sick-pay and no holiday entitlement.

Even those with degrees—in the past regarded as a privileged cohort with a secure future—felt the impacts with, by 2018, one in four graduates working in jobs not requiring a degree.[35] Often carrying large debts from their student years,[36] the 'career path' of many was exemplified by one Alex Regan:

(Age) 23, … graduated … with a 2:1 in history from King's College London… had had 10 short-term roles in the clerical and catering sectors. He now works for Pret a Manager to finance a masters in journalism.[37]

More broadly, as one researcher noted

… a new kind of working life is emerging… For many it is a life in which they do not know from one week, day or even hour to the next when or whether they will work, so they keep their smartphone always to hand, ready to hit 'accept' at a moment's notice.[38]

All of which, in response to his own rhetorical question 'Are you in your twenties?', led the *Guardian's* Money Editor to admit:

> … you are paying a colossally high price so that people in my age bracket – 40-plus – can enjoy a rather pleasant recession…'[39]

Nor for this post-crisis generation was the damage only material. A 2013–2014 World Health Organisation report on 42 countries provided an early global perspective on the mental health effects: that 15 year olds in England and Wales were amongst the least likely to express high levels of satisfaction with their lives.[40] By 2017 a Prince's Trust survey was reporting that 28% of the 2200 16–25 year olds questioned felt 'trapped by their circumstances' and 'out of control' of their lives. Eighteen percent believed that they had no way of changing their situation while, according to other research, only 22% believed things would get better.[41]

As young people came to see getting poor grades at school as a sign of 'failure'[42] and as more of them concluded that they weren't making the most of their personal talents at work,[43] other evidence accumulated on how they were dealing with the resultant pressures. Between 2010–2011 and 2014–2015, the number of 18 year olds diagnosed in A&E departments with mental health problems more than doubled (from 7000 to 15,000)[44] while the number of under 18 year old patients identified there as having self-harmed rose by over 20%. Hidden within these findings, too, was evidence of young women often being significantly more seriously affected than young men[45]; of ethnic minority young people also finding life disproportionately difficult[46]; and, within communities left behind in post-industrial Britain, of white 16 year old working class boys as the lowest academic achievers for any socio-economic group.[47]

## The 'Virtual' Context: Young People in a Digital World

What also increasingly pressed hard on young people in this decade were the realities of living in an all-encompassing digital world. Though evidence was emerging of some disillusion with social media,[48] these were often used in positive ways—to keep in touch with peers and others important in their lives; to expand their experience and their understanding of the wider world; to find fun things to do and share. Precisely because this new technology and its applications were part of their taken-for-granted everyday world in the ways that printed and even broadcast matter had been for the generations before them, these young people did much to pioneer their acceptance and wider use. Indeed, youth workers began to argue that an important way forward for youth work—even perhaps its best hope for its survival—was to work not just with but through 'digital practice'.[49]

Here too however, at the very least, strong contradictory pressures were at work—and not only because of the growing evidence of the bullying, exploitation and abuse carried out through social media. For an age group focused on clarifying and taking confident ownership of emerging personal identities, the expanded possibilities which the new social media brought also came with exposure to a much wider, more complicated and more complicating range of personal choices, expectations and demands which, via social media, could again be experienced, at least in part, as highly individualised, privatised and even isolating.

# Boundaries and Definitions

## 'Young People'

The young people considered in the book are normally assumed to be aged between 13 and 18/19, though, for specific groups—for example young people with disabilities—the age range may be extended to the mid-twenties. In references to or quotations from source documents, especially official reports, 'young people' are also sometimes hidden within the category of 'children'—defined for example in a 2018 House of Commons Briefing paper as including 'people … aged 16-19, not married or co-habiting and in full-time non-advanced education'.[50]

## Open Access Youth Work

In seeking to describe and account for the impact on youth work of the youth policies on which this book concentrates, the practice is defined not by its values or aims but by its distinctive features.[51] It thus proposes that youth work is taking place when:

- (crucially) the practice is being implemented in facilities and projects which are 'open access' and to which young people choose to come;
- the young people are perceived and received <u>as</u> young people and not through the filter of adult-imposed labels;
- the practice starts from the interests and concerns <u>these</u> young people bring with them to their encounters with the adults in these setting— not least their expectation of being able to relax, meet friends and enjoy themselves;
- in responding to these interests and concerns, the practice seeks to open up informal educational opportunities which encourage young people to develop their personal potential and to be critical and creative in their responses to their experiences and their wider society;
- while keeping the young person as an individual as a key focus, the practice respects and works with and through her or his peer and wider community and cultural networks and supports young people in seeking collective (group) outcomes;
- the practice seeks proactively to tip balances of power in young people's favour; and
- it is as concerned with how they feel as with what they know and can do.

As this definition's emphases on working with and through young people's wider networks, seeking collective outcomes and tipping balances of power towards them make clear, rooting the practice in 'community'—defined by identity as well as geography—is seen as one of its core features. However, in what follows the labels 'youth and community work' and 'Youth and Community Service'—widely used in the past and still current—have not been adopted. Within the limits of a single text, the priority has been to focus on a population group, young people, which during the time this book was being written was increasingly marginalised, economically and politically; and on a practice which throughout that period struggled to be recognised, not least by policymakers, as a distinctive way of engaging purposefully with that group.

## The Local Authority Youth Service: History and Definition

This practice—known initially as 'youth leadership'—was by the mid-to late nineteenth century being offered to young people in their leisure time in open access facilities created by a range of voluntary organisations and implemented face-to-face mainly by volunteers. Though the state subsequently made some tentative interventions, it was the wartime conditions after 1939 which, raising new concerns about 'youth', eventually lead to the inclusion in the 1944 Education Act of broadly expressed clauses purportedly giving statutory recognition to local authority Youth Services' provision of this practice. However, as later chapters will show, throughout the Services' history in England—this 'statutory base' was so open to interpretation that local authorities increasingly observed it in the breach to the point where, after 2010, most felt free to close down their Services altogether.[52]

This book's analysis of the Youth Service in England does not start, however, from a presumption that it is or has ever been one-dimensional. Across the country, it has often taken different organisational forms, with what has actually been provided and how this has been done often changing. For example, despite their often determined campaigning to improve—even save—the Service, those involved in it in the 1940s and 1950s could hardly have imagined that within a decade, in the aftermath of the Albemarle Report,[53] it would have been guaranteed local and national budgets, a growing network of purpose-designed buildings and an expanding trained and qualified workforce. Nor probably would most of those 1960s practitioners have anticipated how the gender and, in some areas, the ethnic balance amongst staff would shift; how 'detached' work would move from an 'experimental' to an established way of working; or that some provision would be very specifically focused on young women, young people from 'BME' communities and gay and lesbian and disabled young people. By the 1970s some were also having to adjust to working in renamed Youth and Community Services.

Some of this post-Albemarle 'progress' was not sustained. Some of it over time anyway left a difficult legacy—such as the need to find money from reducing budgets to maintain and run buildings which might no longer be in the right locations for or even particularly attractive to a new generation young people. The local authority structures in which the Youth Service was embedded increasingly adopted bureaucratic forms of decision-making and control which fitted uncomfortably with a practice often defined by its improvised and innovative face-to-face exchanges with young people. These changes also tipped power further away from practitioners to managers sitting within elusive hierarchies who were increasingly expected—indeed, required—to enforce 'measured' forms of accountability.[54] As these neo-liberal's ideas took hold, an often unacknowledged but nonetheless demanding national youth policy developed which insisted on a central government role in determining what these services did and how they should do it.[55]

Despite the emerging challenges to it, neo-liberalism's critical view of state provision generally[56] led increasingly to assumptions, including often by influential interests within the youth sector itself,[57] that no longer would or even should the state have an involvement in directly providing youth work. What were needed instead, it was asserted, were social enterprise-type organisations, shaped by those 'business models' of funding and delivery outlined above and focused on developing in young people the preferred individualised characteristics. In the process, any more open-minded re-imaging of how the state's role might be played was in effect delegitimised.

As a result, organisational boundaries became increasingly blurred—not just between the 'traditional' voluntary youth sector and the state (both local and national) but also between both of these and for-profit businesses, some with very doubtful ethical records.[58] These organisational changes in turn brought significant shifts in the overall purposes of 'youth work provision' and its more specific aims, prompting a move from 'open access' to 'targeted' and its (implicit or explicit) redefinition as almost any 'work with young people'. This weakened, even eliminated, key commitments within its historic practice—particularly to young people's freedom to choose whether to attend (or not) and how to use the facilities and adult relationships when they did.

Always contested territory, youth work's meaning and methodology thus became increasingly blurred to the point where, within the structures state policy-makers were willing to fund or at least endorse, its distinctive features were masked, denied, dismissed as no longer relevant—or changed radically.

## Notes

1. Stephen Sedley, 2018, 'Be Careful What You Wish For', *London Review of Books*, Vol. 40, No. 16, 16 August.
2. Tony Taylor, et al. 2018. 'The Impact of Neo-liberalism on the Character and Purpose of English Youth Work and Beyond', in Alldred, Pam, et al. (eds), *The Sage Handbook of Youth Work Practice*, London, Sage.
3. Adam Offord, 2016, 'Assessing Character Development', *CYPN*, 25 October.
4. Neil Puffett, 2018, 'Daily Roundup … Renting …', *CYPN*, 17 April.
5. Sam Burne James, 2014, 'Analysis: Has the Lobbying Act Caused Charities to Tone Down Their Campaigning in the Election Period?', *Third Sector*, 23 April; Liam Kay, 2017, 'Five Charitable Bodies Register with Electoral Commission as Election Approaches', *Third Sector*, 31 May.
6. National Coalition for Independent Action, 2015, *Fight or Fright: Voluntary Services in 2015*, January, http://www.independentaction.net/wp-content/uploads/sites/8/2015/02/NCIA-Inquiry-summary-report-final.pdf.
7. House of Commons Education Select Committee, 2011, *Services for Young People: Third Report of Session 2010–2012, Volume 1*, London, Stationery Office, 23 June, para 72.
8. HM Treasury, 2010, *Spending Review 2010*, Cm 7042, October.
9. www.parliament.uk, 2017, *Capital Funding for Schools*, House of Common Public Accounts Committee, https://www.publications.

parliament.uk/pa/cm201617/cmselect/cmpubacc/961/96102.htm, April 2017, paras. 12, 14; Joe Lepper, 2017, 'MPs Criticise Government's Free School Expansion Programme', *CYPN*, 25 April.

10. Chris Anderson, 2017, 'Geopolitics: A New Ideological Spectrum', *Guardian*, 3 January.
11. Lynsey Hanley, 2017, 'What Do We Mean When We Say "White Working Class"?', *Guardian*, 23 March; Toby Helm, 2016, 'EU Referendum: Youth Turnout Almost Twice as High as First Thought', *Observer*, 10 July.
12. Katie Allen, 2016, 'Mark Carney: We Must Tackle Isolation and Detachment Caused by Globalisation', *Guardian*, 6 December.
13. *Guardian*, 2017, 'Generation Inequality: In This Election, Britain Must Seek a Common Path for Old and Young', 24 April.
14. For example Nikal Saval, 2017, 'The Great Globalisation Backlash', *Guardian*, 15 July; Andy Beckett, 2017, 'How Britain Fell Out of Love with the Free Market' *Guardian*, 5 August; Stephen Metcalf, 2017, 'The Big Idea That Defines Our Era', *Guardian*, 18 August.
15. Patrick Butler, 2018a, 'Tory County Council Runs Out of Cash to Meet Obligations: Northampton Is First to Admit Financial Disaster for Two Decades of £10 Million Shortfall', *Guardian*, 3 February; Patrick Butler, 2018b, 'Northampton's Cash Crisis Is a Taste of Things to Come for Councils', *Guardian*, 6 February.
16. Lorna Finlayson, 2018, 'Carillion and Other Parasites', *London Review of Books*, 17 January; Polly Toynbee, 2018, 'It's Not Just Carillion: The Whole Privatisation Myth Has Been Exposed', *Guardian*, 22 January; Grace Blakeley, 2018, 'Carillion's Missing Millions', *Red Pepper*, May, pp. 20–21
17. Adam Offord, 2016, 'Government Dismisses Fresh Bid for Votes at 16', *CYPN*, 7 November.
18. Ellie Mae O'Hagan, 2018, 'Voter ID Is Just the Latest Tory Ruse to Deplete the Labour Vote', *Guardian*, 6 May.
19. Ambition Policy Bulletin 26, 2017, June; Alan Travis, 2017, '"Youthquake" Behind Labour Election Surge Divides Generations', *Guardian*, 20 June.
20. Owen Jones, 2017, 'The Tory Policy for Young People in Britain Is Victimisation by Design', *Guardian*, 12 January.
21. James Derounian, 2012, 'The Grey Side of Localism: Handing Power to Older Residents', *The Guardian*, 15 November.

22. Rob Merrick, 2018, 'Housing Benefit to Be Restored to 18–21 Year Olds After Fears Young People Will Be Made Homeless', *Independent*, 29 March.
23. Sam Wolfson, 2017, 'How Do You Solve Britain's Youth Voting Crisis?' *Guardian*, 18 May.
24. Louise Ridley, 2016, 'EU Referendum Results: Young "Screwed by Older Generation" as Polls Suggest 75 Per cent Backed Remain' *Huffington Post*, 24 June; Jessica Elgot, 2016, 'Young Remain Voters Came Out in Force, But Were Outgunned', *Guardian*, 24 June; Rhiannon Lucy Cosslett, 2016, 'I Can Barely Look at My Parents', *Guardian*, 28 June.
25. Matt Grist, et al. 2011, *Youth Labour's Lost*, Demos, p. 9.
26. Howard Reed, 2012, *In the Eye of the Storm: Britain's Forgotten Children and Families*, Action for Children/The Children's Society/NSPCC, https://www.childrenssociety.org.uk/what-we-do/resources-and-publications/publications-library/eye-storm-britains-forgotten-children-and, January.
27. HM Government, 2011, *Positive for Youth: A New Approach to Cross-Government Policy for Young People Aged 13 to 19—Executive Summary*, p. 4, https://www.gov.uk/government/publications/positive-for-youth-executive-summary.
28. Roger Hart, undated, 'Roger Hart's Ladder of Young People's Participation', https://minorityinclusion.files.wordpress.com/2016/02/roger-hart_s-ladder-of-young-people_s-participation.pdf.
29. See for example Tony Jeffs and Mark Smith, 1990, *Young People, Inequality and Youth Work*, Basingstoke, Macmillan.
30. UNICEF, 2007, *Child Well-Being in the UK, Spain and Sweden: The Role of Inequality and Materialism*, www.unicef.org.uk/childwellbeing; Larry Elliott, 2010, 'Poor Families Bear Brunt of Coalition's 'Austerity' Drive', *Guardian*, 25 August; Joe Lepper, 2016, 'Number of Children Affected by Working Poverty Hits 2.6m', *CYPN*, 7 December.
31. Theo Barry Born and Hannah Aldridge/StreetGames, 2015, *Poverty Among Young People in the UK*, New Policy Institute, http://npi.org.uk/files/7114/2892/2456/Poverty_among_young_people_in_the_UK_FINAL.pdf.
32. Emma Jackson, 2016, 'We Are on the Brink of a Homelessness Crisis Among Young People', *Guardian*, 9 February.

33. Rys Farthing, 2016, 'The National Living Wage Makes a Bad Situation for Young People Even Worse', *Guardian*, 31 March.
34. www.parliament.uk, 2018, 'Youth Unemployment Statistics', 14 August, https://researchbriefings.parliament.uk/ResearchBriefing/Summary/SN05871; Larry Elliott and Julia Kollewe, 2018, 'Pay Rises Slow Despite Fall in Jobless…', *Guardian*, 15 August.
35. Sally Weale, 2018, 'Quarter of Graduates in Low-Skill Jobs, Says Report', *Guardian*, 12 September.
36. Laurie Penny, 2014, 'Sorry Students, I Lied to You: University Is About Desperation, Not Aspiration', *Guardian*, 21 April.
37. Nigel Morris, 2014, 'Overqualified and Underemployed: Britain Faces "Youth Talent Crisis" as New Figures Reveal More Than a Million Young People Working Menial Jobs', *Independent*, 18 March.
38. Ursula Huws, quoted in Larry Elliott, 2016, 'Each Generation Should Be Better Off Than Their Parents? Think Again', *Guardian*, 15 February.
39. Patrick Collinson, 2011, 'Britain's Shameful Generation Gap', *Guardian Money Blog*, 19 August.
40. Sally Weale, 2016, 'British Teenagers Amongst the Least Satisfied in Western World', *Guardian*, 15 March.
41. Neil Puffett, 2017, 'One in Four Young People "Don't Feel in Control of Their Life"', *CYPN*, 6 January; Owen, 2017, op. cit.
42. *CYPN*, 2014, 'Call for Action on Pressures Faced by Young People', 11 October.
43. Nigel Morris, 2014, 'Overqualified and Underemployed: Britain Faces "Youth Talent Crisis" as New Figures Reveal More Than a Million Young People Working Menial Jobs', *Independent*, 18 March.
44. Samuel Osborne, 2016, 'Rise in Number of Children Admitted to A&E for Self-Harm and Mental Illness', *Independent*, 10 February.
45. Young Women's Trust, 2015, *Scarred for Life?* http://www.young-womenstrust.org/assets/0000/1702/Scarred_for_Life_Final_Report_March_2015.pdf; Jess Brown and Adam Offord, 2016, 'Daily Roundup', *CYPN*, 15 March; Young Women's Trust, 2016, 'Vocational Education', http://www.youngwomenstrust.org/what_we_do/campaigning/voca-tional_education_and_apprenticeships; Denis Campbell, 2017, 'NHS Struggling to Cope with Mental Health Crisis Among Girls', *Guardian*, 23 September.

46. Matthew Taylor, 2015, '50 Per cent Rise in Long-term Unemployment for Young Ethnic Minority People in UK', *Guardian*, 10 March; Mhemooda Malek, 2011, 'Mental Health Provision Is Failing Black and Minority Ethnic Young People', *Guardian*, 7 July.
47. Harris Beider, 2011, 'White Working-Class Views of Neighbourhood Cohesion and Change', Joseph Rowntree Foundation, November; Mary Clare-Travers, 2017, 'White Working Class Boys: Teachers Matter', BERA, 31 August, https://www.bera.ac.uk/blog/white-working-class-boys-teachers-matter.
48. Siri Kale, 2018, 'Screen Break', *Guardian*, 29 August.
49. Jane Melvin, 2015, 'Youth Work in Digital Spaces', in Bright, Graham (ed), *Youth Work: Histories, Policy, Contexts*, London, Palgrave, pp. 216–236.
50. House of Commons Briefing Paper 7096, 2018, *Poverty in the UK: Statistics*, Published 23 April, p. 11.
51. Bernard Davies, 2015, 'Youth Work: A Manifesto for Our Times—Revisited', *Youth and Policy*, No. 114, April. See also IIDYW, 2009. 'The Open Letter', https://indefenceofyouthwork.com/the-in-defence-of-youth-work-letter-2/.
52. For brief outlines of the development of the parallel Services in Wales, Scotland and Northern Ireland see Jon Ord and Bernard Davies, 2018, 'Youth Work in the UK (England)', in Ord, Jon, et al. (eds), *The Impact of Youth Work in Europe: A Study of Five European Countries*, Helsinki, Erasmus+/Humak University of Applied Publications, pp. 33–36.
53. Ministry of Education, 1960, *The Youth Service in England and Wales*, London, HMSO.
54. See Bernard Davies, 2015, 'Whatever Happened to the Youth Service? A Brief and Critical Look at Its Development—And Demise', IDYW, https://indefenceofyouthwork.files.wordpress.com/2015/07/ysprocon.pdf.
55. Bernard Davies, 1986, *Threatening Youth: Towards a National Youth Policy*, Milton Keynes, Open University Press.
56. Taylor, et al., 2018, op. cit.
57. See for example Ross Watson, 2010, 'Youth Service Chiefs Back Plans for Shake-Up', *CYPN*, 13 July; Lauren Higgs, 2011, 'NCVYS Appeals for Organisations to Trial Big Society', *CYPN*, 12 August; Tony Taylor, 2012, 'Driven to Market: Youth Work's Sheepish Response?', IDYW, https://indefenceofyouthwork.com/2012/03/07/

driven-to-market-youth-works-sheepish-response/; Joe Lepper, 2018, 'UK Youth Sets Out Plans to Attract Investment in Sector', *CYPN*, 2 March.

58. See for example Corporate Watch, 2012, 'How to Beat Up Refugees, the Serco Way', 30 March, http://www.corporatewatch.org/?lid=4264.

# Further Reading

Batsleer, Janet. 2008. *Informal Learning in Youth Work*. London: Sage.

Brent, Colin. 2018. 'Embracing Chaos in Youth Work'. *Youth and Policy*. 10 September. http://www.youthandpolicy.org/articles/embracing-chaos-in-youth-work/.

Brent, Jeremy. 2004. 'Communicating What Youth Work Achieves'. *Youth and Policy*. No. 84. Summer, pp. 69–73.

Davies, Bernard. 2015. 'Youth Work: A Manifesto for Our Times'. *Youth and Policy*. No. 114. May, pp. 96–117.

Fusco, Dana, et al. 2018. 'Conclusion', in Alldred, Pam et al. (eds), *The Sage Handbook of Youth Work Practice*. London: Sage, pp. 623–628.

In Defence of Youth Work. 2009. 'The Open Letter', https://indefenceofyouthwork.com/the-in-defence-of-youth-work-letter-2/.

Jeffs, Tony. 2015. 'What Sort of Future?', in Stanton, Naomi (ed), *Innovation in Youth Work: Thinking in Practice*. London: George Williams College, pp. 11–17 (Extended version at *Youth and Policy*. No. 114. May 2015, pp. 75–95).

Jeffs, Tony and Smith, K. Mark. 2010. *Youth Work Practice*. Basingstoke: Palgrave Macmillan.

Lanchester, John. 2010. *Whoops! Why Everyone Owes Everyone and No One Can Pay*. London: Penguin Books.

Lanchester, John. 2018. 'After the Fall'. *London Review of Books*. Vol. 40, No. 13. 5 July, pp. 3–8.

Melrose, Margaret. 2012. 'Young People, Welfare Reform and Social Insecurity'. *Youth and Policy*. No. 108. March, pp. 1–19.

Melvin, Jane. 2015. 'Youth Work in Digital Spaces', in Bright, Graham (ed), *Youth Work: Histories, Policy & Contexts*. London: Palgrave, pp. 216–235.

Prince's Trust. 2011. *Broke, Not Broken: Tackling Youth Poverty and the Aspiration Gap*, https://www.princes-trust.org.uk/searchresults?searchParam=youth+index+2011.

Reed, Howard. 2012. *In the Eye of the Storm: Britain's Forgotten Children and Families*, Action for Children, The Children's Society, NSPCC, https://www.childrenssociety.org.uk/what-we-do/resources-and-publications/publications-library/eye-storm-britains-forgotten-children-and (January).

Rose, Celia. 1998. *Touching Lives: A Personal History of Clapton Jewish Youth Centre*. Leicester: Youth Work Press.

Taylor, Tony, et al. 2018. 'The Impact of Neo-liberalism on the Character and Purpose of English Youth Work and Beyond', in Alldred, Pam, et al. (eds), *The Sage Handbook of Youth Work Practice*. London: Sage, pp. 84–97.

Woolley, Liz. 2015. 'Anti-oppressive Youth Work with Young People with Disabilities', in Stanton, Naomi (ed), *Innovation in Youth Work: Thinking in Practice*. London: George Williams College, pp. 34–37.

Wright, Ellie and Ord, Jon. 2015. 'Youth Work and the Power of "Giving Voice": A Reframing of Mental Health Services for Young People'. *Youth and Policy*. No. 115. December, pp. 63–85.

Young Women's Trust. 2015. *Scarred for Life?* http://www.youngwomenstrust.org/assets/0000/1702/Scarred_for_Life_Final_Report_March_2015.pdf.

Young, Kerry. 2008. *The Art of Youth Work* (2nd edition). Lyme Regis: Russell House Publishing.

# Part I

## The New Labour Legacies

# 2

# Towards a New Model of Youth Services

## From Blair to Brown—So What Changed?

In two somewhat contradictory ways the overall perspectives shaping youth policies during Gordon Brown's three years as Prime Minister remained largely unchanged from those of previous New Labour governments. One was their reliance on explanations of young people's problems as stemming mainly from individual and family dysfunction rather than from any embedded structural inequalities. The other was to insist that, insofar as causes did lie beyond individual and family, they stemmed from defects in the services mandated to support the young and in their relationships with each other. In this latter scenario, the local authority Youth Service, though never a major player, attracted particularly sharp criticisms, with ministers repeatedly expressing scepticism about its willingness and ability to reach out to the young people who for them were the priority.

This and the following chapter trace from the Blair into the Brown eras how, often by seeking radical institutional change, New Labour governments addressed both these issues and outline the resultant legacies for youth policies overall and for local authority Youth Services and their youth work practice.

© The Author(s) 2019
B. Davies, *Austerity, Youth Policy and the Deconstruction of the Youth Service in England*, https://doi.org/10.1007/978-3-030-03886-1_2

## Changing 'Agendas': From 'Respect' to 'Targeted Support'

Across the period, New Labour's positive goals for these policies included, for example, nurturing young people's personal qualities of 'resilience'[1] and self-reliance—with the Brown government particularly declaring its recognition of young people's potential. Overall, however, a predominantly deficit model of the young predominated, with the highest priority repeatedly identified as 'targeting' those seen as 'vulnerable' and 'disadvantaged' and 'at risk'.

Indeed, for Blair and his key ministers the 'youth problem' seemed at times to be indistinguishable from 'anti-social behaviour'. ASBO's, 'acceptable behaviour contracts' and local curfews emerged as some of their highest profile policy responses, aimed at containing and controlling that small minority of the age group who were at odds with the law or causing trouble locally. By 2005 this approach had very publicly been enshrined in a 'Respect Action Plan', to be implemented by a specially created task force located in the Home Office.[2] A dedicated guide to 'targeted youth support' was published in April 2008[3] with government-funded research recommending improvements in its strategic development and management.[4]

When first considering the Action Plan's implementation, Education Secretary Ed Balls proposed that it be launched in March 2008 in collaboration with 'local partners' such as 'children's services, the police, schools and community safety teams'. Notable by their absence here were local authority Youth Services, with youth workers getting just one mention, in a case study on reducing tensions between young and old in a local community.[5] Perhaps helping to explain their low profile was the conclusion of a joint Treasury/Department of Children, Schools and Families (DCSF) 'discussion paper' published a year earlier—that 'a very weak positive relationship' existed between what local authorities spent on their Youth Services and 'an area's deprivation index', with the Services' performance in addressing this deprivation thus deemed 'not clear cut'.[6]

Brown presented his decision in March 2008 to replace the Respect Action Plan with his own Youth Taskforce Action Plan as part of a significant shift in his government's view of and plans for young people.[7] Flagged up nine months earlier when the newly created DCSF had, jointly with the Treasury, published *Aiming High for Young People*, this had acknowledged that the 'widespread negative perceptions of youth ... sometimes ... have been the unintended consequence of Government policies...'[8] Located within an over-arching 'Children's Plan' published six months later,[9] what therefore was to be offered in future was a 'triple track' protection framework against 'poor outcomes' based on its declared 'positive vision of youth development'.

Despite the positive rhetoric, targeted youth support remained the top priority. In June 2009, for example, the newly appointed children's minister Dawn Primarolo declared herself 'proud to be associated' with an initiative focused on early intervention with young people at risk which, she announced, had been implemented by more than 95% of local authorities.[10] Also contrasting with the positive spin, three months later the Youth Task Force director prompted local authorities to review their targeted services in order to identify those deemed to be 'struggling' to fulfil their remit.[11] Concerns about young people's 'unacceptable or illegal' and 'poor' behaviour and about the 'serious difficulties' in their lives were also still prominent in two of the elements of the protection framework—'tough enforcement' of 'the boundaries of acceptable behaviour'; and the offer of 'non-negotiable' support.

## Implementing Policy: From Connexions...

For eradicating the perceived in-built weaknesses of the relevant services, particularly through Blair's Respect programme and Brown's Youth Task Force, their governments sought to fulfil a much wider New Labour commitment: to create a 'new model of public services'. A paper published in 2008 described the youth policy route for achieving this as 'a programme of systemic change' designed to 'improve outcomes for every child'.[12] By inserting into them private sector methods of management and 'delivery', the new institutions particularly aimed to re-energise all those state bureaucracies which were viewed through the neo-liberal lens as inherently inefficient and innovation-averse.

New Labour's first major 'modernisation' initiative came in 2000 with proposals for a new Connexions Service with the 'important role in ensuring that all youth service activity is effectively co-ordinated, coherent, and that gaps in provision are filled'. This pursuit of the holy grail of 'joined up government'—described in the youth policy context as 'integration' and 'seamless provision'—came also with a significant shift in language. Though increasingly a range of facilities aimed specifically at the older age group were described generically as 'youth services', the restructured services overall were badged as for 'children and young people' This undifferentiating description not only masked— even implicitly denied—differences of class, gender, ethnicity, disability and sexual orientation with potentially crucial implications for both policy and practice. Encompassing an age group which within the policy frameworks could stretch from birth (or even pre-birth) into the early twenties, and at a time of justifiable concerns about the abuse of young children, it also led to the title's contraction to 'children's services' in some subsequent legislation and by some local authorities. It thus threatened to marginalise differences within the age range and, in particular, the distinctive concerns and expectations of those in their teens.[13]

Blair's first 'youth minister' Kim Howells made clear very early that the thinking underpinning the Connexions initiative was to be applied directly to local authority Youth Services, announcing in February 1998 that they would in future be expected to take 'a full part in achieving our wider educational and social objectives for young people'. Though initially it was suggested that local authorities would retain overall control of the Services, in January 2000 the government also confirmed that 'much of existing (local Youth Services') provision for 13 to 19 year olds will be integrated with the new service'.[14] Despite later evidence that key policy-makers were far from clear what the workers did,[15] the first state paper outlining the Connexions strategy also insisted that

> … local authorities will be expected to incorporate their outreach and detached youth workers within the multi-disciplinary (Connexions) teams of Personal Advisers created at local level.

This, the paper explained was because these workers were

> ... active on the streets and in places where young people congregate, working to establish rapport (outside the confines of 'officialdom') with young people who may have had a negative experience of school or other formal contacts.[16]

By 2002–2003 it was becoming clear, however, that the government was backing away from its more radical Connexions aspirations. Local authorities had from the start particularly resisted the proposal to move some of their services into a 'national unit' and convert key staff such as careers advisors into the new Connexions 'personal adviser'. Connexions Services anyway struggled in many areas to achieve even the more modest aims set for it. As well as 'operating with less resources than originally anticipated',[17] the new service faced conflicting aims: to be both 'universalist'—available to all young people by choice and in non-stigmatising ways—and (ultimately its highest policy priority) to openly target 'the disadvantaged', now relabelled 'not in education, employment or training' or 'NEET'.

## ... via *Every Child Matters*...

Despite these setbacks, New Labour remained set on radically restructuring local services for children and young people. This was again demonstrated by *Every Child Matters* (ECM), published in September 2003—the first of a series of linked policy documents which, into the Brown era, sought to implement the main provisions of two Children Acts passed in 2004 and 2006. Described by the then Secretary of State for Education as 'the most far-reaching reform of services for 30 years', their overall aim remained that they 'worked together much more effectively to design and deliver integrated services around the needs of children and young people'.[18]

Ways of doing this were to include early interventions into the lives of 'vulnerable' children in order to support parents and carers, and organisational changes designed to make services more accountable, break down barriers between them and improve staff training. All this was to be underpinned by computerised data collection—eventually labelled ContactPoint—requiring staff to share clients' personal information across agencies. However, not only was the scheme's implementation repeatedly delayed by technical problems.[19] Its threatened deep intrusions into clients' personal privacy also raised serious ethical questions. (Detached youth workers for example regarded it as a form of undeclared surveillance which would threaten their step-by-tentative-step approach to building relationships outside formal organisational structures with young people liable to see all 'authorities' as suspect.[20]) Even before the scheme was formally launched in November 2009, the Conservatives had thus committed themselves to abandoning it[21]—a pledge which the Coalition fulfilled in 2010 in order, it said, 'to reverse the substantial erosion of civil liberties under the Labour Government and roll back state intrusion.'[22]

In seeking the wider implementation of the ECM aspirations, however, the Brown government clearly sought to apply some of the lessons from the Connexions Service initiative. Local authorities were this time made key players—first by being encouraged and then, by 2008, required to set up 'children's trusts' to be run by a 'director of children's services' and with a designated 'lead member' responsible for both education and children's services.[23] A high priority, too, was that local authorities work with 'partners'—for example by producing overall Children and Young People's Plans and creating Local Safeguarding Children Boards.

At first sight the proposed ECM changes seemed to have few direct implications for Youth Services. However, as the ContactPoint experience showed, their overall aim of reshaping all 'youth services' in an ECM mould inevitably had its impacts. The 2003 paper, in drawing attention to that year's 5.9% increase in the Youth Service budget, highlighted its provision of 'personal development opportunities' and named it as one of the 'key' services for integrating into the new children's trusts.[24]

The paper assumed, too, that Youth Services would reformulate their aims to reflect some at least of the specified 'five outcomes' which eventually became one of ECM's constantly repeated mantras: 'being healthy', 'staying safe', 'enjoying and achieving', 'making a positive contribution' and 'economic well-being'. Though local authorities ' commitment to applying these could often seem stronger in the rhetoric than within youth workers' actual practice,[25] they became an important focus for the Office for Standards in Education (OFSTED)'s 'measurement' of their Youth Services.[26]

Increasingly driving the practice agendas of these emerging 'children and youth' services, too, was a more negative set of motivations. These stemmed from the moral panics prompted by key agencies' failures to prevent the death in 2000 of 8-year-old Victoria Climbè and of other abused young children.[27] For all the constituent agencies within the new structures, social work-defined concerns framed as 'child protection' thus became a dominant preoccupation. In the process this marginalised other agencies' historic priorities and practices including youth work's informal education objectives and approaches. This priority also limited their access to resources which after the 2007 financial crisis anyway became increasingly constrained.

In addition, one lesson from the Connexions experience which the ECM strategy did not apply had particular relevance for youth work—how to convince young people that a service was 'universal' and non-stigmatising when it was widely promoting itself as targeting 'at risk' individuals and groups? This dilemma re-emerged in *Youth Matters*, an ECM paper specifically focused on Youth Services (see Chapter 3), which appeared in the context of the Treasury's explicit view that 'a relatively high proportion of local authority Youth Services—one quarter— have been found to perform inadequately'.[28] Framed overall within ECM's preoccupation with child protection, this laid down that, in addressing young people's deficits and problems, youth workers would 'strike the right balance between (their) rights and responsibilities'.[29]

## ... to *Aiming High for Young People*

In typically New Labour style, within weeks of Brown coming to power *Aiming High for Young People* (see above) defined a new 'mission' for these services. Its priority was signalled by the immediate allocation for

2008–2011 of £184 million of new money, to be added to the £495 million of continuing funding and supplemented by unclaimed assets in bank accounts.[30] Sub-titled *A ten-year strategy for positive activities*, it came to have particular significance for local authority Youth Services as, in its very first paragraph, it set as its overall aspiration 'to transform leisure-time opportunities, activities and support for young people in England'.[31]

For the defined target groups, *Aiming High's* core brief was to reform three specific elements of youth provision: access, quality and empowerment. For young people, the first two of these were to be allocated £60 million over three years for establishing a 'dynamic and attractive' 'youth-led' MyPlace centre in every constituency in England[32] (see Chapters 3 and 13). In support of the 'empowerment' theme, a commitment was also made to extending to 2011 the Youth Opportunities Fund (YOF) and the Youth Capital Fund (YCF) which gave young people control of some of the revenue and capital allocated by the Treasury for spending locally.[33]

'Targeting' remained a core aim of many of these extra resources. Those channelled through YOF and YCF, for example, were for projects in 'disadvantaged communities'.[34] Voluntary youth organisations—particularly those with a track record of engaging the 'hardest-to-reach'—were to be offered additional funding to help young people set up leisure' opportunities.[35] Twenty five million pounds was also to be allocated to local authorities for a new 'national programme'—'year-round highly personalised Positive Activities for Young People (PAYP) provision'—focused on 'the most disengaged young people'. Youth offending teams (YOTs) and primary care health trusts—criticised for 'not always demonstrate(ing) the necessary commitment and shared investment to enable preventative work with young people'—were also expected in future to pool their resources with local youth support services.[36]

Overall, too, organisational structures were becoming increasingly 'joined up'[37] with, by November 2009, OFSTED reporting that each of the eleven local authorities inspected during the year was in the process of introducing 'new integrated youth support arrangements'. It concluded from these inspections that 'the local authority landscape is changing quickly with long-established service boundaries fading in favour of multi-agency working or locality teams of which youth workers are members'. Though the *Aiming High* policies brought some new emphases, the organisational cultures inherited from the Blair era's *Every Child Matters* regimes remained substantially unchanged with 'prevention' continuing to be prioritised over the education-focused approaches which characterised youth workers' practice.

## Via 'Commissioning' to 'Contestability' and 'Outsourcing'

In significant ways, too, assumptions under New Labour also changed about how responsibilities for these 'children and young people' services would be allocated, how they were to be funded and run ('delivered'), and by whom. Since the 1940s the state (local and/or national) had primarily taken on these roles, albeit sometimes 'in partnership' with charitable organisations. Though much of the funding was still to be provided out of taxes, New Labour's 'new model' increasingly expected if not required state agencies to withdraw from directly providing the services and instead develop mechanisms for passing those responsibilities to other often non-state bodies.

As they did for subsequent governments, financial pressures, as well as helping to drive the 'outsourcing' of services, also gave cover for imposing this anti-state, market-oriented ideology. An August 2006 report for the Department for Education and Science (DfES) from the private consultancy firm PricewaterhouseCoopers, 'The Market for Provision of Positive Activities for Young People', thus took it largely as given that in this area of provision 'measures could be taken to grow the market through supporting voluntary and community sector bodies to make an increased contribution to delivery'.[38] For-profit businesses—already said to be running a range of leisure facilities for young people—were also seen as potentially acceptable providers of 'positive activities', not least because they could be more cost-effective[39] and so help reduce spending.

For activating and tapping into this expanded 'market', elaborate and time-consuming 'commissioning', 'contracting out', 'tendering' and 'procurement' procedures were devised and often imposed, aimed at prompting bids from 'any suitable provider'. Within often reduced and time-limited budgets, 'targets' were also usually set for 'outcomes to be 'delivered', many to be validated periodically by forms of statistical 'measurement'.

One of the regular briefing papers from the National Youth Agency (NYA), though focused on youth work, illustrated some of the wider implications of the moves to 'joint planning and commissioning'. To support its acknowledgement that 'moving to a commissioning service represents a fundamental change in how services are delivered', it quoted two senior officers of Cumbria County Council who had worked through such changes—that 'Embarking on commissioning youth work involves a very steep learning curve and massive cultural change…' With the aim of offering practical advice on how to acquire the learning needed to negotiate this change, the briefing paper included a diagram of a nine stage process followed by nine bullet points setting out the essential 'procurement approaches'. Bidders' attention was also drawn to three 'groupings' of evidence which they should be ready to provide: 'of outcomes for young people, including what young people say has changed'; of 'standards in organisational processes and structures'; and of 'the active involvement of young people'.[40]

Despite such guidance, a 2009 OFSTED report concluded that since 2005 progress in 'the commissioning of youth provision from existing or alternative providers… was generally slow'.[41] Nonetheless, by mid-2007 Northamptonshire, Buckinghamshire and Gloucestershire councils were all considering or actually taking steps to outsource their Youth Service.[42] Between 2007 and 2009 Lambeth, Redbridge and Hackney Councils, through newspaper advertisements, invited 'Expressions of Interest to Tender for Universal Services for Young People (14-19)'— described as 'an exciting business opportunity'; offered a 'Contract for the delivery and management of (the) Youth Service' through a 'restricted tendering procedure'; and promised 'a new allocation of funding, by contractual agreement' for providers willing to run… its 'Positive Activities three year programme …'.[43]

Yet in itself the strategy did not necessarily bring the gains which the Blair and Brown governments were seeking or promising. A 2010 research report for the DCFS did conclude that 'on balance ... providers were optimistic about the sustainability of their services'. However, it also suggested that 'principal commissioning bodies—local authorities and schools—had some way to go to achieve both a level playing field and the involvement of providers in service design'. It also judged third sector providers (New Labour's re-badging of voluntary sector organisations) as '...most likely to perceive that their own sector was disadvantaged'. It also identified 'mixed views among providers about their experience of the (actual) commissioning process'.[44]

Within this process, too, were embedded two other, contradictory, expectations: that after competing locally with other organisations for the usually limited funds available, once the new 'providers' had won the contract they would then, as a high priority, 'work in partnership' with these same organisations to ensure a high quality cost-effective service.

## What Statutory Guidance?

Both the Blair and Brown governments also made gestures to strengthen the statutory base of local authority Youth Service. Though this was supposed to have existed for over sixty years, the relevant legislation had never actually named youth work until the 2006 Education and Inspections Act placed an obligation on councils to offer some leisure-time activities 'using youth work methods and approaches'.[45]

Here as elsewhere the (at best) contradictory nature of New Labour's attitude to the Service quickly became clear. Not only did the youth work field have to lobby hard to get the necessary insertions into the Act, with Howells declaring in 1998 that he'd 'become less inclined to do it the more (he'd) discovered about how patchy and unsatisfactory the cover is throughout the country'.[46] When the government did concede, it added a qualifying phrase which local authorities subsequently used repeatedly as a get-out clause: that the youth work activities were to be provided only 'so far as reasonably practicable'.[47]

These mixed policy messages, evident in the 2007 Blair government's Statutory Guidance on the 2006 Education Act, remained in the Brown government's revised version published in 2008. Though again endorsing 'youth work methods and approaches' and explicitly recognising 'its contribution ... in securing positive outcomes',[48] it also drew on an over-simple interpretation of research findings on young people's use of 'unstructured' youth clubs in the 1980s—that 'the future outcomes of attendees ... were significantly worse than for those that went to youth clubs offering structured activities'.[49,50] The guidance which was eventually agreed laid down that the leisure-time provision specified by the 2006 Act must take the form of 'positive activities'[51] (see Chapter 3) which, as well as offering 'a range of safe and enjoyable places in which to spend time', had to operate within national standards. These required contributions to young people's 'personal, social and spiritual development', an offer of 'recreational, cultural, sporting and enriching experiences' and their 'positive contribution to their community'.[52]

For the Youth Service's core practice, the statutory protection offered by New Labour was thus not only deeply flawed in itself. It further embedded requirements which constrained or marginalised the informal educational approaches which had long been central to Youth Services' practice.

## From 'Community Cohesion' to 'Preventing Terrorism'

One section of the youth population seen during the Blair-Brown period as particularly 'vulnerable' and so in need of dedicated attention were Muslim young people. Prompted by the July 2005 bombings in London, the Blair government expressed deepening concerns about the risks of 'home-grown' 'Al-Qaida-influenced' terrorism. The 'Contest' strategy set out in a July 2003 paper *Countering International Terrorism* described its four component element as 'Prevent, Pursue, Protect, and Prepare'[53] with at that stage 'Prevent' increasingly impacting on Muslim young people. This was explained as:

- Tackling disadvantage and supporting reform—addressing structural problems in the UK and overseas that may contribute to radicalisation, such as inequalities and discrimination;
- Deterring those who facilitate terrorism and those who encourage others to become terrorists—changing the environment in which the extremists and those radicalising others can operate; and
- Engaging in the battle of ideas—challenging the ideologies that extremists believe can justify the use of violence, primarily by helping Muslims who wish to dispute these ideas to do so.

By October 2007 the newly created Department of Communities and Local Government (DCLG) was supporting the Strategy with funding of £45 million for 2008–2011, with £12 million of this going in the first year to seventy-nine 'priority' local authorities.

The Brown government spelt out its own intentions in considerable detail in May 2008 in a cross-departmental paper *The Prevent Strategy: A Guide for Local Partners*, sub-titled *Stopping people becoming or supporting terrorists and violent extremists*.[54] As well as 'partners' in England, the paper was aimed at a range other public bodies including 'the devolved administrations' in order, it said, to help them 'develop and implement effective actions that will make their communities safer'. In addition to the money announced by the Blair government, for the financial years 2008–2010 a further £3.5 million was allocated to Youth Offending Teams and young offender institutions for preventing violent extremism, to be focused on 'those individuals who have had contact with the criminal justice system'. Both the level of the funding and the number of authorities 'where it (was) most needed' would, it was assumed, continue to grow, with 'the size of local Muslim communities' being an explicit consideration.

Very quickly 'Prevent' began to override the 'community cohesion' strategy which had become the Blair government's framework for responding to ethnic minority, including Muslim, communities. The term had been introduced into the public discourse by the Cantle report on the serious 'disturbances' in a number of northern cities in the summer of 2001.[55] It quickly became 'a key pillar of government's efforts aimed at addressing what were seen as serious race and ethnic divisions and inequalities within British society'. Regarded by anti-racist campaigners as risking pathologising ethnic minorities, it was far from uncontested. By the early 2000s, however, some research findings were suggesting that youth workers working under the community cohesion label were helping to break down some racial and ethnic community barriers between young people as well as enabling youth work practice itself to develop in new ways.[56]

From the beginning, however, the burgeoning Prevent's element of the new strategy attracted fundamental criticism, particularly because it was seen and widely experienced by Muslims as stigmatising and even demonising them and their communities. This was reflected in a House of Commons Communities and Local Government Select Committee report published in March 2010 which questioned whether, with its responsibility for 'promoting cohesive communities', the DCLG was the appropriate location for interventions which, for Muslim communities, it described as 'potentially alienating'. It also reported the claim of a number of witnesses that Prevent was being 'used to "spy" on Muslims'—allegations which it concluded, 'despite rebuttals … retain widespread credibility within certain sections of the Muslim community'. Evidence from a number of sources also suggested that the extremism and violence of right-wing groups was not only not being addressed but may even have been encouraged by the Strategy's exclusive and high-profile focus on Muslims.[57]

The Select Committee was particularly scathing about Prevent's impacts on work with young people. It for example concluded that:

> … an approach to preventing violent extremism which seeks to promote 'legitimate' interpretations of Islam and decry others, may not be the most effective. The need to debate ideas from a range of perspectives, and not drive the more 'radical' voices underground, was a concern of much of the evidence we received'.

In dismissing the dominant policy focus on 'behaviour modification', some of this evidence, not least from young people themselves, also highlighted the absence of, and the need for, institutional arrangements which were genuinely empowering for the young people involved.[58]

In their responses to what were clearly real and often serious threats, subsequent governments repeatedly adjusted—which often meant toughened—the Prevent strategy, ultimately making its operation feel even more oppressive for Muslim communities and for practitioners working in and with them. The Brown government further embedded perspectives and assumptions into the analysis of the problems and required responses which were often highly discriminatory and counter-productive. In the process it contradicted the more positive and 'asset-based' perspectives on young people which *Every Child Matters* had claimed would guide its youth policies overall.

Despite politicians' and policy-makers' perception of young people in these communities as at high risk of 'radicalisation' and of being drawn into terrorist activity, most of the Prevent strategy's references to 'youth services' were largely low key. The Brown 2008 guidance paper did strongly emphasise the need for local authorities to

> … ensure that their youth provision is sensitive to both culture and faith, and helps to bring young people of different backgrounds together. Youth workers can also be both mentors and role models for young people. Local authorities should take steps to raise the awareness and confidence of youth workers to be able to discuss issues around faith and identity openly with young people, and to know who to turn to if they have particular concerns or need advice.

It made reference, too, to

> … the award-winning work done by Barnet via their Madrassah Citizenship Programme, which has trained local youth workers to deliver a 10-week course to teenagers highlighting the links between Islamic sacred texts and good citizenship, and will be delivered to madrassahs, youth centres and supplementary schools in the borough.[59]

In a sub-section on the role of 'Statutory and voluntary youth services' spelling out specific 'Prevent' concerns and expectations, the guidance paper also revealed some strong echoes of New Labour's wider youth policy thinking, stressing for example the role of 'youth services' in 'help(ing) to build resilience and be a mechanism for supporting vulnerable young people through more targeted support and mentoring'.

Meanwhile, for youth workers working in these communities, implementing the strategy posed serious on-the-ground dilemmas which could leave them 'in a precarious position'.[60] Not only did many of the young people and adults within the Muslim communities forcefully reject the government's conceptions of 'extremism'. Much more immediately and practically, the Prevent programme's expectation that workers would notify the authorities when young people were purportedly demonstrating 'extremists views', together with the threat of being taken to court if they did not, clashed head-on with a central tenet of their youth work practice: to win young people's trust that 'the worker is not going to report them to the police, their parents or their school'. Some evidence was also suggesting that '… youth workers employed by the Youth Offending Service Youth Inclusion Programmes were particularly prone to pressure from the police to reveal names of young people they were working with'. Muslim youth workers, many deeply embedded personally as well as professionally within their communities, thus found themselves negotiating highly ambiguous roles, some of whose demands were at best confusing, at worst irreconcilable.[61]

# Notes

1. For example, Beverley Hughes, 2008, 'Letter to Directors of Children's Services', 8 April, pp. 1, 2.
2. Bernard Davies, 2008, *The New Labour Years: A History of the Youth Service in England, Volume 3, 1997–2007*, Leicester, The National Youth Agency, p. 90.
3. DfES, 2007a, *Targeted Youth Support: Integrated Support for Vulnerable Young People—A Guide*, DfES, April, http://webarchive.nationalarchives.gov.uk/20090810173419/http://www.dcsf.gov.uk/everychildmatters/resources-and-practice/IG00206/.
4. John Roger, Helen Palmer, and James Mahon, 2007, *Targeted Youth Support Pathfinders: Interim Evaluation*, DCSF, December, http://dera.ioe.ac.uk/7424/1/DCSF-RR016.pdf.

5. DCSF, 2008a, *Youth Taskforce Action Plan: Give Respect, Get Respect*, DCSF, pp. 2, 28.

6. HM Treasury/DCSF, 2007a, *Policy Review of Children and Young People: A Discussion Paper*, Norwich, HMSO, January, paras. 4.51, 4.52, http://dera.ioe.ac.uk/6553/1/cyp_policyreview090107.pdf.

7. DCFS, 2008a, op. cit.

8. HM Treasury/DCSF, 2007b, *Aiming High for Young People: A Ten Year Strategy for Positive Activities*, London, HM Treasury, July, paras. 1.11, 1.12.

9. DCSF, 2007, *The Children's Plan: Building Brighter Futures—Summary*, December, http://webarchive.nationalarchives.gov.uk/20130103053027/ https://www.education.gov.uk/publications/eOrderingDownload/ Childrens_Plan_Summary.pdf.

10. Janaki Mahadevan, 2009a, 'Targeted Youth Support in Place in Nearly All Areas', *CYPN*, 18 June.

11. Janaki Mahadevan, 2009b, 'Councils Asked to Review Targeted Services', *CYPN*, 17 September.

12. https://www.education.gov.uk/consultations/downloadableDocs/ Childrens%20Trust%20Statutory%20Guidance.pdf, 2008, para. 1.1.

13. Bernard Davies, 2008, op. cit., p. 37; Bob Cole, 2005, 'Youth Policy 1995–2005: From "the Best Start" to "Youth Smatters"', *Youth and Policy*, No. 89, Autumn, pp. 7, 17.

14. Bernard Davies, 2008, op. cit., 20; 24; 35–35; Chapter 2.

15. Jon Ord, 2016, *Youth Work Process, Product and Practice: Creating an Authentic Curriculum in Work with Young People*, London, Routledge, p. 125.

16. DfEE, 2000, *Connexions: The Best Start in Life for Every Young Person*, London, Department for Education and Employment, pp. 52, 32.

17. National Audit Office, 2004, 'Department of Education and Skills— Connexions Service for all Young People', 31 March, https://www.nao. org.uk/report/department-of-education-and-skills-connexions-service-for-all-young-people/.

18. HM Treasury, 2003, *Every Child Matters*, Norwich, Stationery Office; DfES, 2004, *Every Child Matters: Next Steps*, Nottingham, DfES Publications.

19. Janet Murray, 2008, 'Why the Delay in Launching Database?' *Guardian*, 4 September; Liz Lightfoot, 2009, 'At Risk from the

Register?' *Guardian*, 24 March; Neil Puffett, 2009, 'Security Firm Finds Failings with ContactPoint System', *CYPN*, 30 July.

20. Alison Bennett, 2008, 'Detached Youth Workers Angry Over Information-Monitoring Demands', *CYPN*, 20 November; Tania de St Croix, 2009, 'Swimming Against the Tide? Detached Youth Workers Talking About Information Sharing', in Belton, Brian (ed), *Developing Critical Youth Work Theory*, Rotterdam, Sense Publishers, pp. 119–130; Jon Ord, 2016, op. cit., pp. 126–128; Tania de St Croix, 2010, 'Youth Work and the Surveillance State', in Batsleer, Janet and Davies, Bernard (eds), *What Is Youth Work*, Exeter, Learning Matters, pp. 140–152.

21. *CYPN*, 2009, 'Conservatives Will Shut Down ContactPoint Database', 29 September.

22. David Hoyle, 2010, 'ContactPoint: Because Every Child Matters?', *The Encyclopaedia of Informal Education*, www.infed.org/socialwork/contact-point.htm.

23. DCFS, 2008b, *Children's Trusts: Statutory Guidance on Inter-Agency Co-operation to Improve Well-Being of Children, Young People and Their Families*, https://www.education.gov.uk/consultations/downloadable-Docs/Childrens%20Trust%20Statutory%20Guidance.pdf.

24. HM Treasury, 2003, op. cit., paras. 2.30, 4.30, 5.14; HM Treasury/DCSF, 2007b, op. cit., accessed 25 August 2016.

25. Jon Ord, 2016, op. cit., 122–123.

26. NYA, 2008, '2007 Annual Performance', 24 January.

27. HM Treasury, 2003, op. cit., paras. 1–4.

28. HM Treasury/DCSF, 2007a, op. cit., para. 4.1.

29. DES, 2005, *Youth Matters*, Norwich, DES, para. 8.

30. NYA, 2007, Electronic Youth Policy Update, 'Briefing: Aiming High for Young People…', July, p. 1; Davies, 2008, op. cit., pp. 172–177.

31. HM Treasury/DCSF, 2007b, op. cit., para. 1.1.

32. HM Treasury/DCSF, 2007b, op. cit., para. 4.29.

33. NYA, 2007, op. cit., p. 1, para. 3.6.

34. NYA, 2007, op. cit., p. 1.

35. 'Ten Year Youth Strategy—Key Points', *The Edge*, Autumn 2007.

36. HM Treasury/DCSF, 2007b, op. cit., paras. 3.6, 4.5, 4.81, 5.22, 5.23.

37. OFSTED, 2010, *Supporting Young People: An Evaluation of Recent Reforms to Youth Support Services in 11 Local Areas*, July.

38. DfES, 2006, *The Market for Provision of Positive Activities for Young People*, http://webarchive.nationalarchives.gov.uk/20080620110409/http://www.dfes.gov.uk/research/programmeofresearch/projectinformation.cfm?pro-jectid=14974&resultspage=1, p. 3.

39. NYA, 2006, 'Every Child Matters: Change for Children—Joint Planning and Commissioning for Local Youth Service Briefing', *Spotlight*, No. 36, September, p. 4.
40. NYA, 2006, op. cit., p. 4.
41. OFSTED, 2009, *Engaging Young People: Local Authority Youth Work 2005–08*, OFSTED, March, para. 35.
42. Ross Watson, 2007, 'News Insight: Inside Outsourced Youth Services', *CYPN*, 4 May.
43. *Guardian* Advertisement, 17 October 2007; *Guardian* Advertisement, August 2008; *Guardian* Advertisement, 17 June 2009.
44. DCSF, 2010, *Commissioning—A Survey of the Views and Experiences of Providers of Services to Children, Young People and Families'*, Executive Summary, Research Report RR199, pp. 4–5.
45. DCSF, 2008b, *Statutory Guidance on Section 507B Education Act 1996*, DCFS, March, para. 19; DfES, 2007b, *Statutory Guidance on Section 6 of Education and Inspections Act*.
46. Kev Henman, 1998, 'Yes Minister! I'm Dazed and Confused', *Rapport*, March, p. 7.
47. DCSF, 2008b, *Statutory Guidance … op cit*, para. 19; DfES, 2007b, op. cit., para. 17.
48. DCSF, 2008b, *Statutory Guidance … op cit*, paras. 47.
49. L. Feinstein, J. Bynner, and K. Duckworth, 2005, *Leisure Contexts in Adolescence and Their Effects on Adult Outcomes*, London, Institute of Education, p. 20.
50. DCSF, 2008b, *Statutory Guidance … op cit*, para. 46.
51. DfES, 2007c, *Positive Activities for Young People*, DfES, 5 January.
52. DCSF, 2008b, *Statutory Guidance … op cit*, p. 9.
53. HM Government, 2006, *Countering International Terrorism: The United Kingdom's Strategy*, July, p. 1, https://assets.publishing.service.gov.uk/government/uploads/system/uploads/attachment_data/file/272320/6888.pdf.
54. HM Government, 2008, *The Prevent Strategy: A Guide for Local Partners in England Stopping People Becoming or Supporting Terrorists and Violent Extremists*, May, http://webarchive.nationalarchives.gov.uk/20121004145409/https://www.education.gov.uk/publications/eOrderingDownload/Prevent_Strategy.pdf.
55. T. Cantle, 2001, *Community Cohesion—A Report of the Independent Review Team*, London, Home Office.

56. Paul Thomas, 2006, 'The Impact of "Community Cohesion" on Youth Work: A Case Study from Oldham', *Youth and Policy*, No. 93, Autumn, pp. 41–60.

57. House of Commons CLG Select Committee, *Preventing Violent Extremism*, 2010, 6th Report of Session 2009–2010, London, House of Commons, March 2010, https://www.publications.parliament.uk/pa/cm200910/cmselect/cmcomloc/65/65.pdf, pp. 3–4; evi 112: paras. 5.3, 19, 129.

58. House of Commons CLG Select Committee, *Preventing Violent Extremism*, 2010, op. cit., paras. 91, 93, 37.

59. HM Government, 2008, *The Prevent Strategy*, op. cit., pp. 46, 22.

60. M. G. Khan, 2013, *Young Muslims, Pedagogy and Islam: Contexts and Concepts*, Bristol, Policy Press, p. 170.

61. M. G. Khan, 2013, op. cit., pp. 170–171.

# Further Reading

Cole, Bob. 2005. 'Youth Policy 1995–2005: From "the Best Start" to "Youth Smatters"'. *Youth and Policy*. No. 89, Autumn, pp. 7–19.

Davies, Bernard. 2008. *The New Labour Years: A History of the Youth Service in England, Volume 3, 1997–2007*. Leicester: The National Youth Agency.

Davies, Bernard and Wood Emily. 2010. 'Youth Work Practice Within Integrated Youth Support Services', in Batsleer, Janet and Davies, Bernard (eds). *What Is Youth Work?* Exeter: Learning Matters, pp. 73–89.

de St Croix, Tania. 2009. 'Swimming Against the Tide? Detached Youth Workers Talking About Information Sharing', in Belton, Brian (ed), *Developing Critical Youth Work Theory*. Rotterdam: Sense Publishers, pp. 119–130.

de St Croix, Tania. 2010. 'Youth Work and the Surveillance State', in Batsleer, Janet and Davies, Bernard (eds), *What Is Youth Work*. Exeter: Learning Matters, pp. 140–152.

Feinstein, L., et al. 2005. *Leisure Contexts in Adolescence and Their Effects on Adult Outcomes*. London: Institute of Education.

Gilchrist, Ruth, et al. (Eds). 2005. *Youth and Policy*. No. 89, Autumn.

Khan, M. G. 2013. *Young Muslims, Pedagogy and Islam: Contexts and Concepts*. Bristol: Policy Press.

Lehal, Raj. 2010. 'Targeting for Youth Workers', in Batsleer, Janet and Davies, Bernard (eds), *What Is Youth Work?* Exeter: Learning Matters, pp. 90–103.

Ord, Jon. 2016. *Youth Work Process, Product and Practice: Creating an Authentic Curriculum in Work with Young People*. London: Routledge, pp. 115–132.

Sercombe, Howard. 2015. 'In the Service of the State: Youth Work Under New Labour', in Bright, Graham (ed), *Youth Work: Histories, Policy & Contexts*. London: Palgrave, pp. 38–57.

Thomas, Paul. 2006. 'The Impact of "Community Cohesion" on Youth Work: A Case Study from Oldham', *Youth and Policy*. No. 93, Autumn, pp. 41–60.

Tyler, Mary. 2009. 'Managing the Tensions', in Wood, Jason and Jean, Hine (eds), *Work with Young People*. London: Sage, pp. 233–246.

# 3

# Practice Under Pressure: From Youth Work to 'Positive Activities'

As outlined in the last chapter, driving New Labour's efforts to reform 'youth services' was a critique of their internal structure, how they were managed and how they related to each other. The resultant emphasis on market-oriented ways of operating and on instrumental purposes and practices affected a wide range of youth provision,[1] leaving local authority Youth Services and its youth work practice especially vulnerable.

## Youth Work: 'Pockets of Good Practice'

Initially New Labour's reservations about youth work were relatively measured. *Transforming Youth Work*, the Blair government's first state paper on the practice published in March 2001, described youth work as a 'learning process' for young people which could open up a 'wide range of personal development opportunities'. It also acknowledged 'pockets of excellent examples of good practice',[2] with, as we saw in the last chapter, detached workers particularly regarded as potentially valuable recruits to the new Connexions Service.

© The Author(s) 2019
B. Davies, *Austerity, Youth Policy and the Deconstruction of the Youth Service in England*, https://doi.org/10.1007/978-3-030-03886-1_3

*Resourcing Excellent Youth Services* which followed in December 2002 pledged to provide 'a safe, warm, well equipped meeting place within reasonable distance of home, accessible to young people at times defined by young people'.[3] Two later documents, the green paper *Youth Matters* and the paper spelling out its implementation *Youth Matters: Next Steps*, also found reasons for praising local Youth Services. The former, for example, acknowledged that 'where Local Authorities value and prioritise the Youth Service, it can be excellent.'[4] *Next Steps*, as well as conceding that 'over recent years the *Transforming Youth Work* agenda has strengthened the contribution which youth work can make', endorsed 'youth work skills' which, it said, were

> ... central to engaging with young people, to (their) personal, emotional and social development ... and to ensure that young people's voices are heard in shaping both the demand and supply sides of provision.[5]

As we also saw in the last chapter, youth workers working with Muslim young people were seen as having an important contribution to make to implementing the Prevent strategy.

The Treasury's 'discussion paper' on children and young people's services published in January 2007 identified more nuanced features of youth work practice. It talked for example of 'a key tension (that) lies between ensuring that provision offers young people the opportunities for positive engagement, while still remaining attractive to them'. It also included young people's own testimony on support by youth workers 'who inspired and motivated them'.[6]

Published six months later, *Aiming High* (see Chapter 2) was again positive about the youth work role, seeing it as 'crucial ... in supporting and challenging young people to try different things'. It also acknowledged workers' ability 'to build relationships with young people that other professionals may find challenging'. To recognise young people's positive qualities, it proposed 'pilot' events for celebrating their transition to adulthood and a possible 'youth week' to celebrate their achievements. Implicitly their capacities were recognised, too, by proposals that by 2010 5% of decisions on spending on youth activities (rising to 25% by 2018) would be devolved to young people.

## Youth Work: 'Down-at-Heart' and 'Can't Do'

Increasingly, however, these endorsements were overshadowed by Ministers' expressions of doubt about open access youth work and the Services providing it. Early in 1998—that is, within months of becoming 'youth minister'—Howells was characterising the Youth Service as 'the patchiest, the most unsatisfactory of all the services I've come across', calling it both 'down-at-heart' and 'can't do' and indicating even at this stage the need for 'a more coherent youth service policy'.[7] The 'patchiness' theme—repeated later in the year by Howells' successor, George Mudie—then appeared repeatedly in ministerial statements and in key policy papers[8] until, in due course it was used to justify re-shaping not just youth work's organisational base but its core practice.

Despite the more affirming comments quoted earlier, some of this ministerial scepticism was evident in both *Transforming Youth Work* and *Resourcing Excellent Youth Services*. The former for example described the Service as both 'patchy and all too often not integrated into mainstream provision' and quoted an OFSTED judgement that it was 'at best variable'.[9]

Though some of these criticisms were not new,[10] at work here also was New Labour's wider critique of public services. *Resourcing Excellent Youth Services*, with its strong focus on the specifics of the practice, thus laid down that each local authority should produce a 'clear curriculum statement' for its youth work and 'standards for (its) youth work provision'. Presented by the then Education Secretary as 'a landmark document', it set a 'reach' target of 25% of the 13–19 age group and 'performance measures' defined by the number of 'accredited and recorded outcomes' young people achieved.[11] Despite an OFSTED acknowledgement that 'assessing the impact of youth work can be problematic',[12] many managers and some workers continued to use these 'measurable outcomes' even after they were no longer a central government requirement. Often still widely taken for granted, too, was the need for youth work to, as one senior manager put, 'have open access in order to target'.[13]

Though *Youth Matters*[14] did make <u>its</u> strategic goal 're-invigorat(ing) youth work by building on the ideas set out in *Transforming Youth Work*', Ministers remained largely negative about the Service. A year before the paper appeared, in July 2004, Minister for Children and Young People Margaret Hodge had demanded that youth workers stop 'working in silos' and start 'think(ing) children and young people, not services'.[15] In seeking to locate youth work within 'services integrated around young people's needs' and *ECM*'s 'five outcomes' (see Chapter 2), *Youth Matters* quoted another OFSTED finding—that Youth Services were offering 'highly variable levels of provision and quality'.[16] Three months later, junior education minister (and former youth worker) Phil Hope declared that '… in that 60s sense youth services are not part of the agenda and they've been proved not to work'.[17]

One of the bluntest of these public interventions had come in January 2005 when Hodge, drawing on the research on young people's use of youth clubs in the 1980s, suggested publicly that '… (the young people) would have been better off at home watching television than spending their time with others in this way'.[18] This reading of the evidence contrasted sharply with the researchers' own more nuanced interpretation—that

> Success in this area depends on the very great skill of the youth workers who have to make day to day judgements about the appropriate levels of risk and support, autonomy for challenging and challenged young people and directive management of group dynamics.[19]

Interviewed two years later, lead researcher Leon Feinstein added:

> …youth workers, youth work and provision of space and buildings for young people outside school (is)… important and under-funded.[20]

Hodge's soundbite also ignored two other pieces of research published a few months earlier (one sponsored by the DCSF itself) whose conclusions on youth work's potential and impact, while also cautious and complex, were overall more positive.[21]

By March 2006, when *Youth Matters: Next Steps* set out the government's plans for implementing the green paper proposals, ministers were acknowledging that there had been 'improvement in youth services which will enable more young people to undertake wider activities and to overcome barriers to their achievement'. This was backed by a promise of £1.6 billion for 'youth services and opportunities with a direct focus on *Youth Matters*' and £200 million for the paper's implementation, including £1.15 million to be spent via the YOF and YCF (see Chapter 2).[22]

Somewhat late in the process, *Youth Matters; Next Steps* also acknowledged that, as well as needing 'something to do and somewhere to go', young people might also welcome having 'someone to talk to'. This was specifically endorsed in the paper's strap line and then in a section headed 'Supporting Choices: Information, Advice and Guidance'. This was described as one of the 'challenges' to which, via 'a national offer based on national standards', all *ECM* services would be expected to respond in much more 'integrated' ways. A paragraph on staff training also talked of 'the skills needed to work with young people rather than children'.[23]

As revealing for youth workers, however, were the structures—for example, 'one-stop shops and drop-in facilities'—which were seen as central to providing the 'information, advice and guidance'.[24] Implicitly, these assumed that all the young people needing 'someone to talk to' would be both willing and confident enough to seek them out via a pre-defined formal route. Not recognised as a potential for finding such individual support were the supportive conversations with trusted adults which could emerge out of youth work's self-chosen settings and its young people-led processes.

## Youth Work: 'Not Informal Education' but 'Positive Activities'

New Labour's increasingly embedded negative view of local Youth Services largely shaped its policies for them through to 2010, with impacts on youth work practice which persisted long afterwards. Where this practice wasn't just sidelined or ignored, ministers moved beyond just seeking to 'transform' it to imposing on it a radical redefinition.

Most specifically, it insisted that what young people needed were leisure environments and regimes which were much more 'structured' than the traditional open youth club and that these were to be achieved by introducing what became New Labour's new catch-all methodology—'positive activities'.

The term made its first official appearance in 2003 in *ECM's* announcement of the PAYP programme (see Chapter 2). As presented then, this had clear boundaries. It was to be offered in school holidays, to those 'most at risk of anti-social behaviour, offending and truanting', and—with indications of a possible two year extension—with one-year funding of £25 million.[25]

By December 2005, however, Beverley Hughes, Hodge's successor as Minister for Children, Young People and Families, was decreeing that for Youth Services generally youth work was to be:

> … primarily … about activities rather than informal education. Constructive activities, things … to enhance young people's enjoyment and leisure.[26]

Moreover, far from being an off-the-cuff intervention, this 'ruling' had a year-long back-story shaped by the ministerial embrace of, for them, the most useful of the Feinstein research findings outlined above. By the time Hodge referred to these in January 2005, their publication had been scheduled to appear 'alongside' the *Youth Matters* green paper.[27] By then, too, as part of its efforts to make the ideological as well as the pragmatic case for 'positive activities', the DfES had commissioned the PriceWaterhouseCoopers enquiry into 'Market Provision of Positive Activities for Young People'.[28]

From then on, 'positive activities' became a matter-of-fact feature of youth policy initiatives. Underpinned by the consumerist ideas indicated by the PriceWaterhouseCoopers brief, it was, for example, integral to the proposal for a 'youth opportunity card'. This was intended to give credits ('rewards') 'to be spent on sports and other constructive activities' to young people who volunteered or 'contributed' in other ways.[29] (Those 'who (did) not respect the opportunities they are given, by committing crimes or behaving anti-socially', were however explicitly excluded.[30])

Though by January 2007 Hughes was claiming 'good progress' in implementing the card, two months later it was shelved because of technical problems.[31] An alternative £14.5 million scheme, 'Empowering Young People', was piloted later giving £40 a month for 'positive activities' to young people (some aged 9–12) who were eligible for free school meals or in care. Though an evaluation published in November 2008 found that the pilots had avoided stigmatising the participants and had opened up some valued experiences for them, take-up was lower than planned because not all the eligible young people had responded.[32]

As we saw in Chapter 2, 'positive activities' redefinition of youth work was also given a central place in *Aiming High's* sub-title.[33] By 2008, 'participation in positive activities' had also become one of 198 national indicators within a new local authorities' 'performance framework', with the accompanying 'Handbook of definitions' insisting that:

> The key is that the activities are structured, good quality, adult led and support development towards the Every Child Matters Outcomes'.[34]

That year too, after commissioning research into 'potential solutions to the problem young people faced using public transport ... to access "positive activities"', the NYA published 'Accessing Positive Activities: Innovative solutions to young people's bus travel'. This was followed a few months later by a 'Transport Guidance' paper aimed at local authority children's trusts.[35]

In a letter to Council leaders and senior officers, Hughes had by then 'contextualise(d) the commitment to expand positive activities programmes' within a requirement that local authorities make 'a comprehensive offer of opportunities and integrated, preventative services that respond to young people's needs'. She also made clear her expectation that money coming to local authorities through an Area Based Grant scheme would be spent on what it had been allocated for—positive activities.[36]

With this as the over-arching policy framework, under both the Blair and Brown governments positive activities were located within a wide range of other New Labour youth policies, reports and programmes. These included:

- The March 2008 draft of the Statutory Guidance on the 2006 Education and Inspection Act (see Chapter 2) which included a sub-section on 'The duty to secure access to positive activities' and explained 'positive activities' as the way 'so far as is reasonably practicable' of giving young people 'access to sufficient educational …. and recreational activities'.[37]
- The 'Youth Taskforce' Action Plan paper (see Chapter 2).[38]
- A paper highlighting how 'positive activities' could contribute to creating safer communities'.[39]
- References in the government's 'Prevent' strategy to the role 'positive activities' could have in dealing with the perceived radicalisation of Muslim young people (see Chapter 2).
- A 'quality standards' paper, 'aimed at commissioners and providers … including volunteering/community service providers' and intended to 'influence local inspection decisions'.[40]
- A scheme to promote 'positive activities' through the then emerging social media.[41]

## Youth Work: Where Is the Process?

Early on in its advocacy of 'positive activities' the DCSF carried out a consultation exercise with six groups of young people whose findings were reported in an NYA 'Briefing' paper pointedly entitled 'Cutting the cake'. Though the forty six participants rated activities as 'important', they did not unambiguously identify them (positive or otherwise) as their first priority. For many, 'often vital' for enabling them to become involved in activities, 'support from skilled adults (was) the crucial building block'[42]—a conclusion mirrored by youth workers' own explanations going back decades of the complex and inter-dependent links between activity and relationships.[43] A study commissioned by the Home Office into how sports activities could help connect 'marginalised' young people with local services also suggested that a 'cornerstone' of such work was 'using the relationships established with young people to aid their personal and social development'.[44]

Though ministers did occasionally acknowledge the need for such 'strong supportive adults',[45] they largely treated these 'process' dimensions of the work as givens. Using as their rationale their reductionist 'take' on the Feinstein research findings, they instead seemed to assume that, via some unexplained process of spontaneous combustion, the activity itself could and would generate beneficial 'impacts' on the young person. Policy papers and ministerial statements thus gave little dedicated attention to other Feinstein conclusions—such as that 'success in this area' depended on workers' 'directive management of group dynamics'.[46] Unaddressed, therefore, were such often challenging questions as how these human processes were affecting—even perhaps shaping—the activity and its tasks and what skills the 'supportive adults' needed, especially if they found themselves having to turning participants' 'negative' behaviours into something personally and collectively 'positive' for the young people as well as for 'society'.

One effect of policy-makers' failure to give any explicit attention to these process elements of the leisure-time provision they were offering was thus to further marginalise a defining feature of youth work and so of the defining practice of local authority Youth Services. As a result, opportunities for achieving one of New Labour youth policies' key 'modernising' objectives may have been missed: reaching those judged to be 'vulnerable', 'at risk' and 'anti-social', even 'alienated' and 'excluded'. It was precisely these young people who often struggled to engage with 'services' whose more formalised 'intervention' procedures and processes got in the way of their connecting with where an incoming young 'client' might be starting. Well before post-2010 'austerity' policies, open access youth work's potential contribution to young people's <u>educational</u> development was also being marginalised, including again for those defined as vulnerable and at risk.

# A 'Youth' Building for Every Constituency

'Positive activities' were also seen as important for implementing another of New Labour's high profile youth initiatives—its 'MyPlace' programme. Its stated aspiration was that

All young people would have access to a diverse and attractive local offer of purposeful, exciting and engaging positive activities and places to go that respond to their needs and supports their personal development, including providing routes into more dedicated support and guidance for those who need it.[47,48]

A strong impetus for the programme came from visits to the United States by the director of Bolton Lads and Girls Club and the chief executive of the Salmon Youth Centre in south London—both used as home-grown models for the new initiative. Significantly, included in the latter's list of 'the distinctive features of club work in the USA' which he felt worth transposing to the UK were two which fitted comfortably into New Labour's neo-liberal thinking. One was a 'culture with expectations of philanthropy and giving to the community (encouraged by the tax system) among individuals, families and business'; the other, a 'focus on structured programmes... operating alongside leisure and recreational activities'.[49]

First announced in *Aiming High* in July 2007[50] and launched in April 2008,[51] the MyPlace vision was for a 'state of the art' youth facility in every constituency in England[52]—the most ambitious 'youth centre' building programme since the 1960s. It was to be implemented in three phases over three years with £240 million of government funding supplemented by money from unclaimed bank assets. Following three competitive bidding rounds, the programme was to be completed by 2013 with capital grants worth between £1 million and £5 million having been made for sixty three centres (some multi-site) in 'some of the most deprived areas of England'.[53]

The government's commitment to this 'new programme of capital investment' was reiterated by Hughes in April 2008 in a letter to senior council officers and members. Headed 'MyPlace – Major new investment in places to go for young people', this also included the promise of an 'enhancement' of £23m for the 'Youth Capital Fund to support a more ambitious and strategic approach to improving places for young people to go in our most deprived neighbourhoods'. According to Hughes, the MyPlace funding, to be delivered via the Big Lottery Fund (BLF), would be 'building on the success of the Youth Opportunities and Youth Capital Funds' in order 'to deliver world class youth facilities driven by the active participation of young people and their views and needs'.[54]

Despite needing a bail-out package of £500 billion in 2007, the banks' unclaimed assets initially remained on offer. Doubts were raised subsequently, however, about whether all the money originally promised would be available[55] and about long-term revenue funding,[56] with plans for at least one centre being abandoned when delays occurred in accessing the finance.[57] Within a year of the programme's announcement, the DCSF/NYA paper was nonetheless highlighting a range of positive if often deficit-reduction-type 'outcomes' such as 'increasing young people's employability' and 'offering an alternative to drink and alcohol'.[58]

Three years later (in 2011), with grants to some 70 projects already made,[59] an external evaluation also reported a range of achievements. The buildings themselves were considered 'excellent' by those using them. The programme was judged 'good value for money' and seen as addressing 'a spectrum of priority' ranging from leisure facilities and 'positive activities' to 'problem and issue-based work', with most centres 'fall(ing) between the extremes'. Evidence was identified, too, of the 'empowerment of young people involved' and of the activities on offer appealing to them. The report also highlighted the opportunities for young people to get the information, advice and guidance they needed or were seeking through informal youth work approaches as well as through more structured provision.

Even at this early stage of the programme's development, however, the evaluation report raised some carefully phrased concerns with potentially longer-term implications. Given that the centres were designed to serve a wide geographical areas, one was about their location, especially where—as in rural areas—public transport was limited. Another focused on whether, after involving young people in a building's design, participation practices were being embedded in the centres' day-to-day running. The report also concluded that, in spite of the government's overriding focus on the 'disadvantaged'—with disability identified as the disadvantage most often being addressed—'in some circumstances the (centres') widening use has meant increased involvement of young people who are structurally advantaged'.

Indeed, as early as December 2007 the Chief Executive of the NYA, Fiona Blacke, was asking whether 'the notion of a "youth centre in every town" is the answer to the perceived problem of getting young people "off the streets"'. She even warned that the 'Pizza Hut approach just ain't going to work' and urged that at that stage the policy should be 'more about dialogue with young people about what is needed' and that it might even include 'using a local café two nights a week as a communal space'.[60]

By the time the NYA's joint paper with the DCSF appeared in July 2009, her doubts about the programme seem to have been resolved.[61] Her comments, however, contained challenges which remained pertinent throughout this period and indeed, as we shall see in Chapter 13, beyond. Such as: Might these substantial resources have had wider and longer-lasting impacts if they had been used to refurbish and re-energise the many neighbourhood-based buildings built in the 1960s? And/or: could the money have been invested in new versions of such locally-based facilities for a new teenage generation in new locations?[62]

Such questions may have been implicit, too, in some of the DCSF/NYA paper's findings on why young people valued the MyPlace facilities. Though welcomed both for 'the high quality provision' and for offering young people 'a powerful message about how they were valued', at least as important for them again were 'the relationships they developed with youth workers - as people they trusted, who treated them with respect and who actually liked young people'.[63]

Such responses confirmed that, from a Youth Service/youth work perspective, implementing the MyPlace programme was far from straightforward. Not only again, as *Aiming High* demanded, were 'positive activities' defined as an integral requirement of all the new facilities. More fundamentally, such large-scale and costly facilities could not be planned or developed as neighbourhood-based spaces which, with youth worker inputs, could be at least partially responsive to the existing or emerging interests of the young people who actually came through the doors.[64] Rather, as was suggested by the outcomes most valued by the DCSF/NYA paper, they were designed as multi-purpose, multi-function 'integrated' 'hubs', structured to meet the high priority

New Labour expectations—particularly to provide pre-scheduled structured programmes of 'positive activities' and formalised routes into support and guidance for those who needed it.

## Open for the Weekend: 'Hoovering Young People off the Streets'

One of the other ways in which ministers sought to make the potential gains of 'positive activities' more widely available to young people was by tackling the problem that 'young people often get into trouble on Friday and Saturday nights when youth services are most likely to be closed'. First outlined in December 2007, by the following October discussions at the annual conference of the Association of Principal Youth and Community Officers (APYCO) indicated that the issue was becoming an explicit government demand on—and a major challenge for—many local authority Youth Services. As well as concerns over costs, staffing and 'safety risks during unsocial hours',[65] there was criticism of an initiative described as seeking '... just (to) keep "hoovering young people off the streets"'.[66]

Nonetheless, by April 2009 Hughes was pushing ahead with an 'Open Drive' programme. Again writing to all Children Services' directors and lead councillors, she explained that, on the back of the claim that 'positive activities' had helped reduce weekend anti-social behaviour in some areas by as much as 50%, a key aim was now to 'help the police and local councils avoid the costs associated with youth crime and antisocial behaviour at these times'. Hughes' letter also quoted the response of sixty-six per cent of young people to a recent consultation—that 'more activities would do the most to keep them out of trouble'. Hughes thus called it 'shocking' that a mere 2.5% of Youth Services' 'positive activities' were available on Saturday evenings.[67]

Funding—some of it additional to what had previously been announced—was therefore to be made available through PAYP, the YCF and the MyPlace buildings programme, with a further £15 million for supporting the involvement of small voluntary organisations.[68]

An 'Open for the weekend' supplement appeared in the trade magazine *Children and Young People Now (CYPN)*, followed in July 2009 by a series of local 'Open Weekend' events heavily promoted by the DfES. Local authorities were asked to open their youth clubs and projects on the designated Friday and Saturday evenings as a prompt to 'look again at your activities, involve young people further in its development, and promote this very strongly in communities'—all with a view to determining whether local young people wanted more weekend activities and, if so, how to provide these in the future.[69] With the support of the Confederation of Heads of Young People's Services (CHYPS— formerly APYCO) local authority officers were contacted by phone and a round table event held prior to the publication of a 'briefing paper' on promoting and publicising '"positive activities" and associated facilities in their area'. While acknowledging the need for these to be 'promoted as an entitlement for all young people', it again made clear that 'Friday and Saturday night provision specifically aims to reach vulnerable or disadvantaged young people'.[70]

In a speech to a Local Government Association (LGA) conference in March 2009, Hughes claimed success for the Open Drive initiative, reporting that local authorities had already provided '1,000 extra youth services' (sic) used by more than 15,000 young people.[71] A year later, however, the reliability of these figures and indeed the validity of the whole exercise were being questioned. Research by Wiltshire County Council suggested that young people preferred clubs to be open on weekday evenings, with only just over a third (37.7%) opting for Saturday evening openings compared with 81.4% for their first choice, Wednesday evening. By then, too, CHYPS' Chief Executive was calling for 'a national debate' on the whole exercise, including that 'a larger sample of young people (be) surveyed to inform policy directions'.[72]

Some of the conclusions of DCSF/NYA briefing paper, however, at least raised questions not just about the drive for more weekend openings but about aspects of wider New Labour policies in this area. Amongst the conclusions of *Positive activities for young people— Expanding Friday and Saturday night provision*, published in July 2009, were that:

Young people appear to want less structured, more recreational activities on weekend evenings...

Even apparently unstructured and recreational activities offer opportunities for non-formal education and personal and social development...

The least popular provision (with young people) was structured activities with accredited outcomes...[73]

# The End of New Labour, the Beginning of the End of the Youth Service?

Far from developing in a policy vacuum, local authority Youth Services were directly and often in fundamental ways affected by the prescriptions of major New Labour youth policy papers such as *Every Child Matters* and *Aiming High*. A 'modest' De Montfort University enquiry into eight local authority Youth Services in the summer of 2010[74] acknowledged that managers of these Services 'had found creative ways of responding to government policies ... (and) had stayed true to tried and tested principles'. While warning against 'grand generalisations' from a 'sample and random sample', it however also concluded that, as New Labour youth policies took hold:

- ... the independence of the voluntary and community sector is jeopardised by its dependence on limited funding from the national and local state;
- In (the even then) harsh financial climate policy-makers are bound to turn more to supporting services that target identified individuals, groups, localities and issues.
- Educational principles and purposes are likely to become increasingly hard to safeguard as ones in favour of 'child-saving' and youth control are increasingly prioritised.
- Spontaneous and 'on the wing' interventions and the preventative properties of open access youth work are likely to be harder to defend.

- The demand for evidence of positive impact … tends to encourage a narrow focus on those interventions that lead to immediately demonstrable outcomes.[75]

As well pointing to the longer-term legacy of New Labour youth policies for local authority Youth Services and their open access youth work practice, these conclusions also carried broader messages about future youth policies and the likely priorities and ways of working they would impose on 'youth services' generally.

# Notes

1. See for example Stefan Collini, 2017, *Speaking of Universities*, London, Verso.
2. Connexions/DfEE, 2001, *Transforming Youth Work: Developing Youth Work for Young People*, Nottingham, DfEE publications, pp. 8, 5.
3. Bernard Davies, 2008, *The New Labour Years: A History of the Youth Service in England, Volume 3, 1997–2007*, Leicester, The National Youth Agency; Connexions/DfES, 2002, *Transforming Youth Work: Resourcing Excellent Youth Services*, Nottingham, DfES, p. 22.
4. DfES, 2005, *Youth Matters*, Norwich, HMSO, para. 59.
5. DfES, 2006, *Youth Matters: Next Steps—Something to Do, Somewhere to Go, Someone to Talk To*, Nottingham, DfES Publications, para. 8.24.
6. HM Treasury/DfES, 2007A, *Policy Review of Children and Young People: A Discussion Paper*, paras. 4.16, 4.33, 4.37, available at http://dera.ioe.ac.uk/6553/1/cyp_policyreview090107.pdf.
7. Kev Henman, 1998, 'Yes Minister! I'm Dazed and Confused', *Rapport*, March, p. 7.
8. Bernard Davies, 2008, op. cit.
9. Connexions/DfEE, 2001, op. cit., pp. 5, 8.
10. Bernard Davies, 2015., 'Whatever Happened to the Youth Service? A Brief and Critical Look at Its Development—And Demise', *IDYW*, https://indefenceofyouthwork.files.wordpress.com/2015/07/ysprocon.pdf.
11. Connexions/DfES, 2002, op. cit., pp. 11, 16.
12. OFSTED, 2009, *Engaging Young People: Local Authority Youth Work 2005–08*, OFSTED, March, para. 4, p. 7.

13. Bernard Davies and Bryan Merton, 2010, *Straws in the Wind: The State of Youth Work in a Changing Policy Environment* (Phase 2), De Montfort University, October, http://www.dmu.ac.uk/documents/health-and-life-sciences-documents/research/strawsinthewind-finalreport-october2010.pdf.
14. DfES, 2005, op. cit.
15. Tristan Donovan, 2004, 'Green Paper Will Aim to Create Integrated Services for Youth', *CYPN*, 14 July.
16. DfES, 2005, op. cit., p. 26, para. 59.
17. Bernard Davies, 2008, op. cit., 16.
18. IPPR, 2005, 'The Youth of Today', 19 January, https://www.theguardian.com/society/2005/jan/20/childrensservices.politics.
19. L. Feinstein, et al., 2005, *Leisure Contexts in Adolescence and Their Effects on Adult Outcomes*, London, Institute of Education, p. 20.
20. Alison Bennett, 'Big Interview: The Youth Work Examiner', *CYPN*, 26 June 2007.
21. Bob Cole, 2005, 'Youth Policy 1995–2005: From "The Best Start" to "Youth Smatters"', *Youth and Policy*, No. 89, Autumn, pp. 7, 17.
22. DfES, 2006, op. cit., paras. 2.4, 2.7.
23. DfES, 2006, op. cit., paras. 8.9, 8.20.
24. DfES, 2006, op. cit., para. 6.6.
25. HM Treasury, 2003, *Every Child Matters*, Norwich, Stationery Office, para. 2.40.
26. *CYPN*, 2005, 'Youth Matters', 7 December.
27. IPPR, 2005, op. cit.; NYA Briefing, 2004, 'Cutting the Cake: Things to Do, Places to Go and Someone to Talk To', *NYA*, Issue 4, January, p. 6.
28. DfES/PriceWaterhouseCoopers, 2006, *The Market Provision of Positive Activities for Young People*, London, DfES.
29. DfES, 2005, op. cit., para. 13.
30. DfES, 2005, op. cit., July, p. 1.
31. *CYPN*, 2007, 'Analysis: Policy—Youth Opportunity Card—Outcomes of Youthcard's Collapse', *CYPN*, 7 March.
32. Sue Learner, 2008, 'Spending Schemes Prove Popular with Disadvantaged Teenagers', *CYPN*, 6 November.
33. HM Treasury/DCSF, 2007b, *Aiming High for Young People: a ten year strategy for positive activities*, July.
34. Louise Barnfield, 2008, The Contribution of Non-formal Learning to Young People's Life Chances: Executive Summary, NYA/Fabian Society, pp. 4, 6.

35. John Barker, 2008, *Assessing Positive Activities: Innovative Solutions to Young People's Bus Travel*, NYA, http://nya.org.uk/dynamic_files/research/transport.pdf; NYA, 2009, 'Transport Guidance: Supporting Access to Positive Activities: Executive Summary'.
36. Beverley Hughes, 2008, Letter to Directors of Children Services/Chief Executives/Lead Member for Children Services, 3 April, pp. 2, 3.
37. DFES, 2007, *Positive Activities for Young People, DfES*, 5 January; DCSF, 2008a, *Statutory Guidance on Section 507B Education Act 1996*, DCFS, March, paras. 15, 17.
38. DCSF, 2008b, *Youth Taskforce Action Plan: Give Respect, Get Respect—Youth Matters'*, *A Commitment from the Children's Plan*, Nottingham, DCSF Publications.
39. DCSF, 2009, 'Positive Activities, Safer Communities', DCSF, Summer.
40. DCSF, 2010, 'Quality Standards for Positive Activities (Draft)', DCSF.
41. Charlotte Goddard, 2010, '"Boredometer" to Tell Young People About Positive Activities', *CYPN*, 2 February.
42. NYA Briefing, 2006, 'Cutting the Cake: Things to Do, Places to Go and Someone to Talk To', *NYA*, Issue 4, January, para. 2.1.
43. See for example Don Feasey, 1972, 'Why Activities?', in Bernard Davies and Jennifer Rogers (eds), *Working with Youth*, London, BBC, pp. 17–24.
44. Tim Crabbe, et al., 2006, 'Knowing the Score: Positive Futures Case Study Research—Final Report', Manchester, Substance, 2006, p. 20.
45. Beverley Hughes, 2009, Speech to LGA, 28 April, p. 2.
46. Feinstein, et al., op. cit., p. 20.
47. HM Treasury/DCSF, 2007, op. cit., Box 1.3, p. 15.
48. DCSF, 2007, *The Children's Plan: Building Brighter Futures*, para. 6.2, Norwich, Stationery Office, para. 29.
49. DCFS/NYA/*myplace*, 2008, *Investing in Youth Facilities: Findings from Recent Experience*, November, para. 5.6.
50. Janaki Mahadevan, 2009, 'Winners Announced for the Final Round of Myplace Funding', *CYPN*, 16 December.
51. GOV.Uk, 2014, 'Myplace Programme', available at https://www.gov.uk/government/publications/myplace-programme, accessed 14 February 2018.
52. HM Treasury/DCSF, 2007, op. cit., para. 4.3.
53. GOV.Uk, 2014, 'Myplace Programme' Information, available at https://www.gov.uk/government/publications/myplace-programme/myplace-programme-information, accessed 14 February 2018.

54. Beverley Hughes, 2008, 'Myplace—Major New Investment in Places to Go for Young People', DCSF, 3 April.
55. Tristan Donovan, 2008, 'Dormant Accounts to Fund Youth Projects Despite Banking Crisis', *CYPN*, 16 October; Janaki Mahadevan, 2009, 'Youth Sector Fears Impact of Unclaimed Assets Delay', *CYPN*, 7 April.
56. *CYPN, 2008*, 'Youth Facilities Lack Long-Term Funding', *CYPN*, 16 October.
57. Jon Ord, 2016, *Youth Work Process, Product and Practice: Creating an Authentic Curriculum in Work with Young People*, London, Routledge, pp. 126, 131; Andy Hillier and Joe Lepper, 2009, 'Flagship Youth Centres Delayed', *CYPN*, 26 November.
58. DCFS/NYA/*myplace*, 2008, op. cit., para. 4.1.
59. Jean Spence and Mark K. Smith, 2011, *Myplace Evaluation—Final Report*, Department for Education, April, p. 3.
60. Annie Kelly, 2007, 'High Ambition', *Guardian*, 5 December.
61. NYA/DCSF, 2009, *Positive Activities for Young People—Expanding Friday and Saturday Night Provision*, NYA/DCSF, July.
62. Ord, 2016, op. cit.
63. DCFS/NYA/*myplace*, 2008, op. cit., para. 4.1.
64. Daisy Ritchie and Jon Ord, 2016, 'Making the Case Through Research for Open Access Youth Work', *Journal of Youth Studies*, Vol. 20, No. 3.
65. *CYPN*, 2008, 'Analysis: Youth Services—The Gap in Weekend Youth Services', *CYPN*, October 2008.
66. Andy Hillier, 2008, 'Weekend Activities Need Structure, Says Youth Chief', *CYPN*, 11 December.
67. Andy Hillier and Joe Lepper, 'Flagship Youth Centres Delayed', *CYPN*, 26 November; Beverley Hughes, 2009, Speech to LGA, 28 April, p. 2; Beverley Hughes, 2009, Letter to Directors of Children Services/Lead Member for Children Services, April; *CYPN*, 2009, 'Open Weekend to Get Under Way', *CYPN*, 1 July, p. 82.
68. Andy Hillier, 2009, 'Hughes Calls for More Weekend Youth Activities', *CYPN*, 30 April; DCSF, 2009, 'Open' (Press Release), 30 April; Beverley Hughes, 2009, op. cit.
69. *CYPN*, 2009, 'Open Weekend to Get Under Way', *CYPN*, 1 July.
70. NYA/DCSF, 2009, op. cit.
71. Beverley Hughes, 2009, op. cit., p. 5.
72. Ross Watson, 2010, 'Young People Lukewarm About Weekend Opening', *CYPN*, 2 February.
73. NYA/DCSF, 2009, op. cit., pp. 1, 5.

74. Bernard Davies and Bryan Merton, 2009, *Squaring the Circle?* De Montfort University, April.
75. Bernard Davies and Bryan Merton, 2010, op. cit., p. 63.

# Further Reading

Cole, Bob. 2005. 'Youth Policy 1995–2005: From "The Best Start" to "Youth Smatters"'. *Youth and Policy*. No. 89, Autumn, pp. 7–19.

Davies, Bernard. 2008. *The New Labour Years: A History of the Youth Service in England, Volume 3, 1997–2007*. Leicester: The National Youth Agency.

Davies, Bernard. 2015. 'Whatever Happened to the Youth Service? A Brief and Critical Look at Its Development—And Demise'. IDYW. https://indefenceofyouthwork.files.wordpress.com/2015/07/ysprocon.pdf.

Davies, Bernard and Merton, Bryan. 2009. *Squaring the Circle? Findings of a "Modest Enquiry" into the State of Youth Work in Some Children and Young People's Services*. De Montfort University. April.

Feasey, Don. 1972. "Why Activities?", in Davies, Bernard and Rogers, Jennifer (eds), *Working with Youth*. London: BBC, pp. 17–24.

Feinstein, L., et al. 2005. *Leisure Contexts in Adolescence and Their Effects on Adult Outcomes*. London: Institute of Education.

Ord, Jon. 2016. *Youth Work Process, Product and Practice: Creating an Authentic Curriculum in Work with Young People*. London: Routledge, Chapters 13, 14.

Ritchie, Daisy and Ord, Jon. 2016, "Making the Case Through Research for Open Access Youth Work". *Journal of Youth Studies*. Vol. 20, No. 3. https://www.tandfonline.com/doi/full/10.1080/13676261.2016.1212162.

Sercombe, Howard. 2015. 'In the Service of the State: Youth Work Under New Labour', in Bright, Graham (ed), *Youth Work: Histories, Policy & Contexts*. London: Palgrave, pp. 38–57.

Tyler, Mary. 2009. 'Managing the Tensions', in Wood, Jason and Jean, Hine (eds), *Work with Young People*. London: Sage, pp. 233–246.

# Part II

## Austerity Bites

# 4

# The National Picture: From 'State Monopolies' to 'New Providers'

## 'Breaking the State Monopolies'

Though many young people raised their voices in protest (see Chapter 17), few of them at the time were likely to have made the connection between the sudden boarding-up of their local youth club and sacking of their youth workers and the Treasury's year-on-year cuts to their local council's Revenue Support Grant. Yet from the moment the Coalition government came to power in May 2010, it was these, in the name of 'austerity', which increasingly helped shape all youth policies. Their stated overall goal was to reduce (even eliminate) what was presented as a given: an unacceptably high budget deficit. Though constantly masked by ministerial comments on Labour's financial irresponsibility, its main cause lay in the need in 2007–2008 to inject large amounts of public money into banks whose unregulated and often irresponsible behaviour had prompted a major financial crisis—but which could not be allowed to fail.

As outlined in Chapter 1, however, the Coalition's decision to radically reduce public expenditure was also—perhaps mainly—a cover for a core neo-liberal objective: to eradicate the perceived in-built

© The Author(s) 2019
B. Davies, *Austerity, Youth Policy and the Deconstruction of the Youth Service in England*, https://doi.org/10.1007/978-3-030-03886-1_4

inefficiencies of public services by as far as possible removing the state from directly providing them or where feasible even paying for them.[1] This often came, too, with a commitment to open these services (including some 'youth services') to private for-profit companies.[2] As Prime Minister David Cameron made clear only months after coming into office and then spelt it out in some detail in September 2015, there would be no increases in public spending even when (if?) the deficit was paid off. Because, he claimed, 'many of our country's efforts to extend opportunity have been undermined by a tolerance of state failure', the state now needed to run more like a business, including by 'breaking state monopolies (and) bringing in new providers…'[3]

For services for young people overall and for local authority Youth Services specifically these policies were pursued in two ways which proved particularly damaging. As part of his commitment to eliminating the budget deficit by 2015, Chancellor of the Exchequer George Osborne announced in his first Spending Review in October 2010 that over the following four years the overall amount allocated by the Treasury to the government's Revenue Support Grant for local councils would be reduced year-on-year by 7.1%. Central government funding for all youth services was also to be merged into a single non-ring fenced Early Intervention Grant.[4]

In October 2012 figures from the International Monetary Fund (IMF) revealed just how single-mindedly these goals were pursued. These showed UK government spending was planned to fall from 45% of Gross Domestic Produce in 2012 to 39% in 2017, resulting by 2014 in an estimated 490,000 fewer public service jobs.[5]

# In Search of 'New Providers': Commissioning, Outsourcing and Contracting Out

As significant in the long run as the funding cuts, however, were the main ways in which ministers claimed public services could and would in future be provided, albeit usually on much reduced budgets. Given the continuing grip of neo-liberal ideas, the inescapable first resort, nationally and locally, was Cameron's 'new providers', identified by a variety of 'commissioning', 'outsourcing' and 'contracting out' procedures. In principle these involved four stages: assessing the needs of the potential service users; drawing up plans for the services needed to meet those needs; 'procuring' these services, usually through a public bidding process; and then monitoring the services' quality and outcomes to ensure that that brief was being achieved and the providing organisation was giving value for money.

Under New Labour and increasingly after 2010, a wide range of health, education, social care and other services came to be 'delivered' through these processes. For neo-liberal policy-makers they were particularly attractive because the competitive bidding process concentrated organisational minds on the 'brutal logic' of keeping proposed costs as low as possible and therefore of doing more for less.[6]

As these procedures were to be applied to organisations serving often needy and vulnerable individuals and communities, efforts were made to soften some of their sharper edges. The 2012 Public Services (Social Value) Act required commissioners to take 'social value' into account when awarding contracts. This was introduced as a private member's Bill which, under pressure from ministers, was amended during its passage to limit its scope.[7] Its sponsor, Conservative M.P. Chris White, nonetheless claimed that what he was trying to achieve was an acceptance that the aim was 'not about the cheapest goods or service, but what is going to do something for the community ... What is going to be responsive to local people's needs?'[8]

The Bill was more specifically presented as seeking to prevent this 'market' from being accessible only to private businesses or voluntary sector bodies with the infrastructure capacity to negotiate the often complex bidding procedures. Some of these, too, having used small local projects as 'bid-candy', were said then to be sub-contracting to them elements of a contract most difficult for an 'in-comer' to implement.[9] To address these inequalities and ensure they got more of the estimated annual £236 billion 'public service procurement spend', White wanted 'social enterprises, charities, worker-owned mutuals and "socially responsible businesses" (to) … play a key role in delivering his vision'.[10]

Even as the Bill was going through Parliament, however, evidence was emerging that that year's local government financial settlement had already 'devastated social enterprise and charity budgets'. Confidence among social businesses working in the public sector was described as 'pitifully low', with the opportunities the Act offered likely to 'be quickly filled by large, private companies'.[11] Within a year, Social Enterprise UK was calling for 'creating social value' to be made a legal requirement.[12] Five years later, in May 2016, though it found councils of all political persuasions were using the Act to, for example, support 'community groups', it still had no hard evidence on the number of public bodies in England taking account of the social, environmental or economic impact of their commissioning, with returns from over 350 English councils suggesting that only one in three councils were adopting its requirements in proactive ways.[13]

While the Coalition was in power multi-national private companies were awarded large public service contracts. In its first year, half of its spending on the UK Border Agency and the National Offender Management Service (£383 million) went to G4S and Serco.[14] The latter, whose profits in 2012–2013 rose by 27%,[15] was initially also a leading NCS provider (see Chapter 10). However, with evidence also emerging of both these organisations' questionable ethical practices,[16] in 2012 the founder and chairman of another major recipient of government money, A4E, was forced to resign as David Cameron's 'family tsar' when staff working on a government contract to help job-seekers into employment were arrested. Ten were eventually found guilty of defrauding taxpayers of nearly £300,000 and six were jailed.[17]

By 2014 even the business-friendly *Financial Times* was thus suggesting that 'the government must control its temptation to outsource on all fronts'—not least because its growth 'has outstripped the capability of the civil service to keep providers on their toes'.[18] As early as 2011, the investment organisation Social Finance also pointed out that 'social investment in any form is not a replacement for the revenue that the youth sector is currently losing.'[19]

# Downward Pressure: Local Services Unravelled

Despite such warnings, major cuts to state funding for the sector continued. According to a November 2014 Audit Commission report, support for local services since 2010 was expected to have fallen by 37% by 2015–2016.[20] By 2017 the LGA was predicting that over the following three years that cut would rise to 77% with almost half of local authorities no longer getting any financial support from central government.[21]

As a result, by mid-2018 it was being predicted that in the mainly Conservative-controlled county councils the gap between income and costs by 2020 would be £3.2 billion[22] and for all local authorities it could total £12.4 billion.[23] As early as 2014 council leaders were warning that the £4.1 billion a year black hole in their budgets could mean not only that they might have to close every children's centre, library, museum and park[24] but that even their statutory duties could be at risk.[25] An LGA report published that year also suggested that many councils were being pushed to a financial tipping point. By early 2018 this had become a reality for Northamptonshire,[26] the council which in 2006 had been the first to 'outsource' the whole of its Youth Service, make most of its youth work staff redundant and cut its budget by 66%.[27] By then, too, reports were suggesting that some fifteen other councils were at risk of going bankrupt[28] and that by 2020–2021 two-thirds would struggle to balance their budgets.[29]

Nor were these policies applied equitably across the country. In November 2016, for example, the leaders of 24 local authorities with a total population of 2.4 million children pointed out that if a proposed new schools' funding formula were adopted, 'England's 30 most deprived local authority areas face a net loss of £245 million a year, while the 30 least deprived areas gain £218 million'.[30] All of which seemed to bring closer to realisation a Joseph Rowntrees Foundation prediction made as far back as January 2012—that local government might need to remake the relationship between citizens and government.[31]

# A 'Smoothie Approach' to the Youth Service: The National Picture

These huge reductions in the money available for local authority services impacted very quickly and with accelerating effects on youth services overall and on local Youth Services in particular. For the 2011–2012 financial year, the DfE's own returns showed that Councils' spending on 'services for young people', which included programmes focused on excluded pupils, teenage pregnancy and drug and alcohol support, had reduced since the previous year from £1184 million to £877 million[32] and fell again in 2012–2013 to £791 million—a total cut of 36%.[33] Two months later DfE figures predicted that total spending on these services would fall further between 2013–2014 and 2014–2015 from £712 million to £627 million,[34] with expenditure planned to drop to £447.5 by 2016–2017—a cut of 15.2% from the previous years and £41.99 million less than the spending figure the councils had given the Department three months earlier. For the following year, 2017–2018, the prediction was another reduction to £415.8 million.[35]

The consequences for the Youth Service of the overall cuts were particularly severe. Barely eight months into the Coalition government, in December 2010, a 'snapshot survey' of CHYPS members found that, during that financial year 83% of the respondents had already made savings of £50,000 with 11% losing over £500,000. With budget cuts averaging 14%, the survey suggested that 10% of front-line staff had already been lost, 30% of Services had reduced their centre- and club-based provision and 20% their detached work. During 2010 the government also halved (to £13 million) its YCF allocations (see Chapter 2), leaving councils to find the money to complete projects in progress.[36]

These trends were mirrored in a follow-up CHYPS survey of developments in 2011–2012. Thirty three per cent of the Services responding were expecting to have to make savings of over £500,000, with the average anticipating a funding cut of 28%—double that of the current year. The resultant 28% loss of youth work posts which this indicated[37] had by the following February translated into up to 3000 local authority workers losing their jobs with the total estimated reduction in Youth

Service budgets by March 2012 reaching £100 million.[38] A *CYPN* analysis of local authority returns in January 2013 also showed spending on youth services falling by 26%, from £1.18 billion in 2010–2011 to £877 million in 2011–2012.[39]

Some of the most telling evidence of the Youth Service cuts came from the trade union Unison in two reports published in July 2014 and August 2016. The first revealed that by then nationally at least 350 youth centres had closed, 41,000 youth service places and 35,000 hours of outreach work had been lost and more than 2000 youth worker jobs had been abolished. Two years later, drawing on returns from 180 of the 210 relevant authorities, updated figures revealed that over 600 youth centres had closed, nearly 139,000 places for young people had been lost and 3652 youth worker jobs abolished.[40] In May 2018 a YMCA report added to this evidence, revealing that English local authorities' spending on youth services had fallen from £1.18 billion in 2010–2011 to £448 million in 2016–2017, with the West Midlands and the North West being particularly affected.[41] Significantly, in one of these financial years (2014–2015 to 2015–2016) total local authority spending on 'safeguarding' for children rose by £104.5 million to £2.22 million while spending on 'youth services' fell further by £99.1 million.[42]

Within these overall local cuts were some significant post-code variations. Even before the Coalition took over—between 2009–2010 and 2010–2011 when half of the local authorities were still increasing expenditure on youth services—nearly 61% of Conservative-controlled local authorities had reduced those budgets compared with 48% of Liberal Democrat and 39% of Labour councils.[43] By 2015—that is five years into the Coalition—these variations had become sharper, even though after 2011 richer mainly Conservative-run authorities had had their income boosted by being allowed to keep substantial proportions of their business rates.[44] Nonetheless, one survey of 105 local authorities in 2015 revealed that Conservative-led councils had since 2010 closed down 411 of their 811 youth centres (49%), compared with only half that proportion in Labour-controlled areas which had experienced far deeper cuts in central government support.[45]

The cuts also had significant consequences for how the Youth Services which did survive operated and what they offered. A Cabinet Office analysis showed that as early as 2011 the proportion of local authority 'youth services' spending committed to open access provision had dropped from 55.25 to 47.5%. Seventy five per cent of the 97 respondents also predicted that, within three years, between 75 and 100% of their budget would be allocated to 'targeted work'[46] so that by 2013–2014 the £353 million allocated to targeted programmes was about to overtake the £360 million spent on open access provision.[47]

As we saw in Chapters 2 and 3, these budget pressures came end-on to a decade of New Labour demands that local authorities refocus their 'children and young people's services' on 'the deprived' and 'the disadvantaged'— expectations reiterated as a Coalition priority in its 2011 policy paper *Positive for Youth* (see Chapter 9).[48] In particular, most local authorities argued that, given the new financial realities, they had to give precedence to their statutory duties on 'child protection'. By 2014 at least 58% of the 97 local authorities responding to a Cabinet Office survey were thus admitting that they were at best only partly fulfilling their still weak legal obligation to provide a Youth Service.[49]

This combination of top-down policy priorities and extreme financial constraints provided more and more councils with additional grounds for radically re-shaping their services for young people. As early as October 2012 Fiona Blacke was pointing to

> … a move towards a "smoothie approach" to staffing youth services, so that rather than having distinctive roles for youth social workers, youth workers and others, people are moving toward having generic staff roles.[50]

An NYA report two years later reinforced this view, concluding: 'There is no longer a common form of youth service across England'. It particularly noted that, as Services were reshaped, qualified youth workers—for example in Wigan and Sefton—were being redeployed into social care support roles with the focus on 'the vulnerable and the at risk'.[51] As well as further threatening the existence of stand-alone local authority Youth Services and its open access youth work, these developments also had serious consequences for how that practice was managed, with local authority managers being less and less likely to have had front-line youth work experience.

It was in this context that in September 2015—five years into 'austerity'—David Cameron wrote to the Conservative leader of the Council in which his constituency was located, Oxfordshire, to express his disappointment at how it was dealing with its reduced government grant. He pointed particularly to '… the long list of suggestions to make significant cuts to frontline services' including 'the unwelcome and counter-productive proposals to close children's centres across the county'. Instead, he advised, Oxfordshire should 'be following the best practice of Conservative councils … in making back office savings and protecting the frontline'.

In response, denying that there were any 'easy' back office savings left to make, the council leader pointed out that Oxfordshire had already lost more than 2800 staff; that the sale of assets to fund revenue costs 'is neither legal nor sustainable in the long term'; and that government funding support for his authority since 2010 had been reduced, not by the £204 million Cameron quoted, but by £626 million—that is, by 37%.[52]

# 'Philanthropy to the Rescue'?

In February 2011, the Scout Association's Chief Executive warned that, far from the voluntary youth sector being able to fill the gaps left by local authority cuts, a 'mixed bag' of provision was still going to be required involving both voluntary and statutory sector organisations.[53] Nonetheless, many councils insisted that voluntary organisations would be taking over provision they would no longer pay for, with some—for example Camden and Brighton—initially trying to protect their grants to the sector.[54]

Nonetheless, even before 'austerity' took hold, it too was feeling the effects of the cuts in councils' income. In February 2010, Birmingham City Council told forty voluntary youth organisations that their grants totalling £800,000 would stop in March 2011[55]—a decision apparently challenged successfully in the courts a year later.[56] In October 2010, however, a *CYPN* report revealed that 37% of the 130 youth charities surveyed were anticipating budget cuts of between 10 and 20% with

7% expecting to lose more than 90% of their funding. As a result, 82% were considering stopping some projects.[57]

The December 2010 CHYPS survey quoted earlier confirmed that these anxieties were justified. Thirty nine per cent of councils had by mid-year reduced their support to the voluntary sector, with 5% expecting this to end altogether in the next year.[58] At the same time a National Council for Voluntary Youth Organisations (NCVYS) enquiry revealed that 'almost 70 per cent of organisations (were) seeing a drop in income over the last year (and) 75 per cent (were) cutting projects'.[59]

Local reports quickly provided examples of what this meant for the voluntary sector youth work locally. Between 2010 and 2016 Birmingham[60] and Hampshire talked of cutting their support completely, with the latter in 2014 suggesting 'replacing (it) with a needs-based offer'.[61] At least partial cuts also seemed likely in, amongst other authorities, Bexley,[62] West Sussex[63] and Bracknell Forest.[64]

Starting from the premise that 'youth work look(s) likely to lose public funding completely', this drift back to 'philanthropy … to the rescue of the service' was seen by one former full-time practitioner as youth work going 'full circle' back to its Victorian roots.[65] How far and how quickly that circle was being closed was illustrated by two unconnected 2017 news items—one reporting that eleven young people had raised £500 through the Prince's Trust to renovate a disused cabin in Trowbridge in Wiltshire for use as a 'youth centre'[66]; the other that someone had made a 'secret donation' of £10,000 towards a £50,000 appeal to renovate Yatton Youth Centre in Somerset.[67]

By then, too, one Conservative group was also suggesting that some councillors' allowances be reduced to release money for shoring up the council's Youth Service budget which the Labour-controlled council was proposing to cut by £645,000.[68]

# 'Explain the Difference You Make'

For public services, including many focused on young people, the problem of coping with these growing budget pressures was often exacerbated by funders' hardening demands that 'deliverers' provide evidence of 'measured' outcomes. Moreover, this expectation—deeply embedded in neo-liberalism's market-based preoccupation with getting 'value for money'—was not only adopted by state 'commissioners' of services (local as well as national). Many private and philanthropic funders also made it a taken-for-granted requirement.

For a practice like youth work such expectations posed a particular challenge. This had earlier been demonstrated by the 'performance measures' New Labour introduced in *Resourcing Excellent Youth Services* (REYS) and then in the broader ECM framework of 'five outcomes' (see Chapter 2). By June 2010—that is, well before the Coalition's 'austerity' cuts were being felt—one report on the work of voluntary organisations in two regions of England was warning that these 'data' demands on children and young people's services were already 'excessive'.[69]

Though often diverting youth workers from what they saw as their core purposes and ways of working, the REYS and ECM measures were often flexible enough to be negotiable by imaginative practitioners and managers. The Coalition's 'measures', however, turned out to be much more stringent. Expectations that they be applied got renewed and influential endorsement in 2011 when the Chair of the Commons Select Committee enquiring into youth services (see Chapter 8) accused the chief executives of four national youth organisations of 'an extraordinary failure ... (to) make a better fist at explaining the difference you make' and so of failing to make the case for government funding.[70] Similar reservations about the sector were expressed again in 2015 when the Chief Executive of the Early Intervention Foundation (see Chapter 6) described youth work as struggling to deal with the 'evidence challenge'.[71]

Though the four sector 'leaders' rejected the original charge, they were seen by many in the field as having conceded too much ground.[72] Coming as the criticism did from such high profile and apparently authoritative sources, it anyway embedded as a common sense expectation that, in line with all public services, youth workers could and should provide statistical evidence of their 'outcomes'. Particularly significant in reinforcing this was the Young Foundation's *Framework of Outcomes for Young People*, published in July 2012 with the aim of 'help(ing) the youth sector prove the impact of youth work'.[73] The paper proposed 'a model of seven interlinked clusters of social and emotional capabilities that are of value to all young people', to be 'measured' by 'a matrix of available tools'. It was supported a year later by a NCVYS website, 'Youth Report', available to both commissioners and providers of youth services as a hub for 'evidence on what works'. Its rationale was explained by NCVYS's Chief Executive as making 'a case for more targeted investment … Every penny of spending has to be spent to provide the best possible solutions for young people'.[74] A Cabinet Office *Outcomes Framework* to guide providers and commissioners of youth services also appeared in December 2014.[75]

This approach to accountability gained additional traction as both government and voluntary sector interest grew in alternative business-oriented ways of financing these services. As early as 2011, for example, the senior Labour MP seen as 'the champion of early intervention' was calling payment-by-results 'the only game in town'.[76] His view was still, if implicitly, being endorsed five years later by the Cabinet Office when it created an £80 million fund to pay for improved life chances for vulnerable children and young people based on a payment by results model.[77]

Also attracting increasing attention were social investment and social impact bonds[78]—described by one sceptical commentator as 'Britain's tycoons … looking for ways the rich can make money out of the poor'.[79] These committed public funders to pay private or voluntary sector 'providers' retrospectively for any improved 'social outcomes' which could be shown to have saved public money. In 2012—a year before evidence began to emerge that youth organisations were unprepared for this kind of funding[80]—a NCVYS-led Catalyst consortium (see Chapter 14) published a 'guidance document' on the bonds.

A demand also grew for evidence of impacts expressed in 'monetised' terms. This was exemplified by a 2015 report by NEF Consulting ('helping organisations in the transition to a new economy') on a Prince's Trust's programme for unemployed 16–25 year olds. This concluded that £2.99 of 'social worth' had been generated for every £1 spent, creating in just one year a total of £90 million of social return across the UK. For the over 9000 participants this included the equivalent of £3600 'gross investment' in their communities made up, for example, of an average of £300 through fundraising and about

500 hours of work valued at the minimum wage. The social return also took into account the value of helping some 75% of the young people to move into work, training or education within three months of completing the programme and reductions in the number who were on welfare benefits or in trouble with the law.[81] Some of the annual NCS evaluations also put this form of evidence at the heart of their claims for its impacts (see Chapter 11).

By the end of the period, a national brief for bringing greater coherence and rigour to such 'measurement' had been given to a Centre for Youth Impact (CYI). Though not officially launched till September 2014, government plans for such a body had been flagged up three years earlier in two of its *Positive for Youth* commitments (see Chapter 9). One was to fund a 'Centre for the Analysis of Youth Transitions' to develop standards for evidence'; the other, 'to publish annually a positive set of national measures to demonstrate progress in improving outcomes for young people'.[82]

According to the 'youth minister' at the time, the CYI—initially government-funded with the intention that it eventually become self-supporting—was to provide 'national leadership' by becoming 'the leading voice for the importance of evidence and impact in work with young people'.[83] However, with its predominant emphasis on statistically demonstrated outcomes, it attracted continuing criticisms from the youth work field.[84] Efforts to demonstrate the validity of alternative ways of demonstrating youth work's value to young people were made—for example by an EU-funded research study in five Europe countries led by Plymouth MarJon University whose overall aim was to 'identify the authentic impact of youth work by ... getting to the heart of what's important to young people'.[85]

Over time the CYI encouraged debates on such alternative ways of evaluating a process-led practice like open access youth work.[86] However, the collection of 'data' remained a high priority as, in neo-liberal world, the most credible way of 'demonstrating impact'. In combination with a dominant government policy discourse which treated the removal of state funding from public services as both necessary and desirable, this added significantly to the struggles of youth services generally to gain credibility and, in the case of local Youth Services, even to survive.

# Notes

1. Patrick Wintour, 2010, 'Francis Maude Drives the Pace of Coalition's Deep Spending Cuts', Guardian.co.uk, 30 July.
2. HM Treasury, 2010, *Spending Review 2010*, Cmd 7042, October, para 1.87.
3. Polly Toynbee, 2010, 'Loyal, Public Service Merits More Than Cold Thrashing', Guardian.co.uk, 24 August; Neil Puffett, 2015, 'Cameron Earmarks Children's Services as Priority Reform Area', 11 September.
4. BBC, 2010, 'Spending Review 2010: Key Points at a Glance', 21 October, http://www.bbc.co.uk/news/uk-politics-11569160; *Guardian*, 2016, 'Spending Review 2010: Key Points at a Glance', 20 October, https://www.theguardian.com/politics/2010/oct/20/spending-review-2010-key-points; House of Commons Education Select Committee, 2011, *Services for Young People*, London, Stationery Office, para. 54.
5. BBC, 2010, op. cit.
6. Patrick Butler, 2011, 'MP Paves the Way for More Social Enterprises to Deliver Public Services', *Guardian*, 18 October.
7. Vibeka Mair, 2011, 'Government Seeks to Remove "Social Enterprise" from Social Value Bill', *Civil Society*, 18 October, https://www.civilsociety.co.uk/news/government-seeks-to-remove--social-enterprise--from-social-value-bill.html.
8. Patrick Butler, 2011, op. cit.
9. Michael Bell, 2012, 'From Co-operation to Competition and Fragmentation', *National Coalition for Independent Action*, http://www.independentaction.net/2012/11/22/from-co-operation-to-competition-and-fragmentation/, posted 22 November 2012; Zoe Williams, 2012, 'Public Sector Outsourcing: Finally, an Unfairness We Can Do Something About', *Guardian*, 20 June.
10. Patrick Butler, 2011, op. cit.
11. Patrick Butler, 2011, op. cit.
12. Neil Puffett, 2013a, 'Call for Talks as Social Value Act Shakes Up Commissioning', *CYPN*, 31 January.
13. Peter Holbrook, 2016, 'One in Three Councils Consider Social Value When Awarding Contracts', *Guardian*, 31 May.
14. Centre for Crime and Justice Studies, 2012, 'UK Justice Policy Review', Volume 1, 26 November, https://www.crimeandjustice.org.uk/publications/uk-justice-policy-review-volume-1.

15. Simon Bowers, 2013, 'Serco Reports 27% Rise in Profits', *Guardian*, 5 March.
16. See Corporate Watch, 2012, 'How to Beat Up Refugees, the SERCO Way', 30 March, http://www.corporatewatch.org/?lid=4264; Neil Puffett, 2013b, 'Police to Probe Serco Prisoner Contractor Fraud Claims', *CYPN*, 29 August; Felicity Lawrence, 2013, 'Private Health Contractor's Staff Told to Cut 999 Calls to Meet Targets', *Guardian*, 23 January; Felicity Lawrence, 2013, 'Private Contractor Fiddled Data When Reporting to NHS, Says Watchdog', *Guardian*, 7 March; Neil Puffett, 2016, 'Seven Staff Suspended Over Claims of Abuse at Youth Custody Unit,' *CYPN*, 8 January.
17. Daniel Boffey, 2012, 'Who Is Making Money as Private Firms Move in on the Public Sector?', *Guardian*, 25 February; Sam Marsden and Gemma Mullin, 2015, 'Government Back-to-Work Contractors Who Forged Signatures to Con Taxpayers Out of £300,000 Jailed for Total of 15 Years', 1 April, http://www.dailymail.co.uk/news/article-3020303/Government-work-contractors-forged-signatures-taxpayers-300-000-jailed-total-15-years.html.
18. *Financial Times*, 2014, 'Outsourcing Meets Its Outer Limits', 26 June.
19. House of Commons Education Select Committee, 2011, *op cit*, para. 60.
20. Tom Crewe, 2016, 'The Strange Death of Municipal England', *London Review of Books*, Vol. 28, No. 34, 15 December, pp. 6–10; National Audit Office, 2014, *The Impact of Funding Reductions on Local Authorities*, November, para 11, https://www.nao.org.uk/wp-content/uploads/2014/11/Impact-of-funding-reductions-on-local-authorities.pdf.
21. Andy Bounds, 2017, 'Local Councils See Funding Fall by 77% by 2020', *Financial Times*, 4 July, https://www.ft.com/content/9c6b52 84-6000-11e7-91a7-502f7ee26895.
22. Patrick Butler, 2018a, 'County Councils Face £3.2bn Spending Gap', *Guardian*, 28 June.
23. LGA, 2014, *Future Funding Outlook 2014: Funding Outlook for Councils to 2019/20*, LGA, p. 21, http://www.local.gov.uk/documents/10180/5854661/L14-340+Future+funding+-+initial+draft.pdf/185442 0d-1ce0-49c5-8515-062dccca2c70.
24. Robert Booth, 2015, 'Local Councils Warn of Critical Funding Crisis as £18bn Grant Is Scrapped', *Guardian*, 25 November, https://www.theguardian.com/society/2015/nov/25/local-government-councils-funding-gap-critical-budget-cuts-social-care-spending-review.

25. Rowena Mason, 2014, 'Public Service Cuts Deepen as Councils Near Financial Tipping Point', *Guardian*, 11 May.
26. Patrick Butler, 2018b, 'Tory County Council Runs Out of Cash to Meet Obligations', *Guardian*, 3 February.
27. Bernard Davies, 2008, *The New Labour Years*, Leicester, NYA, p. 95.
28. Patrick Butler, 2018c, 'Northamptonshire's Cash Crisis Is a Taste of Things to Come for Councils', *Guardian*, 6 February; Rajeev Syal, Patrick Butler, and Will Tilbrook, 2018, 'Stretched Councils Raid Reserves to Cope with Social Care, NAO Warns', *Guardian*, 8 March.
29. Patrick Butler, 2018d, 'County Councils Face £3.2bn Spending Gap', *Guardian*, 28 June.
30. *Guardian Letters*, 2016, 'A Flawed Plan for Our Deprived Schools', 19 November.
31. Annette Hastings, et al., 2012, *Serving Deprived Communities in a Recession*, York, Joseph Rowntrees Foundation, pp. 64–65.
32. Neil Puffett, 2013c, 'Councils Slash Youth Services Spending by a Quarter', *CYPN*, 29 January.
33. Tom Barton and Tom Edgington, 2014, 'Youth Services Spending Down by One-Third', BBC News UK, 25 March; Darren Hayes, 2014, 'Daily Roundup: Youth Services, Asylum Seekers and Smoking Ban', *CYPN*, 26 March.
34. DfE, 2014, *Expenditure by Local Authorities and Schools on Education, Children and Young People*, DfE, September; Jess Brown, 2014, 'Council Children's Centre Funding Cuts Double in a Year', *CYPN*, 10 December.
35. Neil Puffett, 2017a, 'Early Years and Youth Services Spending Continues to Fall', *CYPN*, 26 September; Neil Puffett, 2017b, 'Youth Service Cuts "Deeper Than Predicted"', *CYPN*, 18 December.
36. Ross Watson, 2010a, 'Councils to Foot Capital Youth Projects Bill After Government Withdraws Funds', *CYPN*, 27 July.
37. David Wright, 2011, 'Keeping the Youth Work Flame Alive', *The Edge*, January, p. 8.
38. Andy Hillier, 2011a, 'True State of Council Youth Service Jobs Revealed', *CYPN*, 8 February.
39. Neil Puffett, 2013d, 'Children's Centres and Youth Sector Hit, but Care Services Escape Cuts', *CYPN*, 19 February.
40. Unison, 2014, *The Damage: UK Youth Services—How Cuts Are Removing Opportunities for Young People and Damaging Their Lives*,

London, Unison, p. 5; Unison, 2016, *The Damage: A Future at Risk— Cuts in Youth Services*, London, Unison, p. 5.

41. Darren Hayes, 2018, 'Charity Calls for "Drastic Action" to Protect Youth Services', *CYPN*, 4 May.

42. Joe Lepper, 2016, 'Council Spending on Child Protection and Care Surges by £280m', *CYPN*, 16 December.

43. Neil Puffett, 2011a, 'Analysis of Youth Cuts Uncovers Party Differences', *CYPN*, 2 December.

44. Patrick Wintour, 2011, 'Free Councils to Keep Bulk of Cash Raised Through Business Rates', *Guardian*, 23 February.

45. Jack Blanchard, 2015, 'Tory Councils Shut HALF Their Youth Centres Since David Cameron Came to Power', *Mirror*, 4 September, http://www.mirror.co.uk/news/uk-news/tory-councils-shut-half-youth-6383808, accessed 12 November 2016.

46. HM Government, 2011, Youth Service Expenditure in England 2011– 12, Cabinet Office.

47. Neil Puffett, 2011b, 'Young People's Services Undergo Major Change as Cuts Deepen', *CYPN*, 7 August; Neil Puffett, 2013e, 'DfE Data Shows Funding Shift from Universal to Targeted Services', *CYPN*, 15 October; Laura McCardle, 2014a, 'Councils Slash Youth and Children's Spending by 3200m', *CYPN*, 12 December.

48. HM Government, 2011, op. cit., paras. 4.14–4.27.

49. Laura McCardle, 2014b, 'Youth Funding and Services Cut as Councils Overlook Legal Duty', *CYPN*, 22 July.

50. Neil Puffett, 2012, 'Specialist Youth Work Roles Under Threat, Claims NYA', *CYPN*, 12 October.

51. NYA, 2014, *Youth Services in England: Changes and Trends in the Provision of Services*, Leicester, NYA/Network of Regional Youth Work Units England, November; Laura McCardle, 2015, 'Councils Redeploy Youth Workers to Social Care Roles, Warns Report', 12 January.

52. Tom Crewe, 2016, 'The Strange Death of Municipal England', *London Review of Books*, Vol. 28, No. 34, 15 December, pp. 6–10.

53. Andy Hillier, 2011, 'Volunteers Unable to Fill Gaps Left by Loss of Council Youth Services, Warns Scouts Chief', *CYPN*, 10 February.

54. Neil Puffett, 2011c, 'Camden Protects Voluntary Sector Youth Service Funding', *CYPN*, 13 December; Janaki Mahadevan, 2012, 'Brighton Councillors Vote to Strengthen Ties with Voluntary Youth Organisations', *CYPN*, 25 January.

55. *CYPN*, 2010, 'Birmingham Axes Youth Grants', 9 February.
56. Paul Dale, 2011, 'Birmingham City Council Social Care Cuts Ruled Unlawful by High Court', *Birmingham Post*, 20 April.
57. Andy Hillier, 2010, 'True Scale of Youth Service Cuts Around the Corner', *CYPN*, 12 October.
58. David Wright, 2011, 'Keeping the Youth Work Flame Alive', *The Edge*, January, p. 8.
59. NCVYS, 2010, 'Comprehensive Cuts—Part 2: Taking Stock of Changes in Funding and Policies and Their Impact on Young People and the Voluntary and Community Youth Sector', NCYVS, December.
60. *Rapport*, January 2011.
61. Laura McCardle, 2014c, 'Hampshire Plans to Halve Youth Service Spend', 1 December.
62. Adam Offord, 2016, 'Council Revamps Youth Service to Target Potential Offenders', *CYPN*, 26 May.
63. Joe Lepper, 2010a, 'West Sussex Youth Services Hit by £2m of Cuts', 4 August.
64. Ross Watson, 2010b, 'Sixty Youth Service Post Under Threat in Blackpool', *CYPN*, 29 June.
65. Sue Shanks, 2017, 'The Cuts Are Taking Youth Clubs Back to Their Victorian Roots', *Guardian*, 20 March.
66. Robin Murray, 2017, 'Derelict Cabin Transformed into Youth Centre by Young Volunteers', *Wiltshire Times*, 1 March.
67. Tom Wright, 2017, 'Yatton Youth Club Handed £10,000 by Generous Stranger', *North Somerset Times*, 7 June.
68. Joe Lepper, 2017, 'Tories Propose Political Pay Cuts to Save Youth Services', *CYPN*, 21 February.
69. Joe Lepper, 2010b, 'Excessive Demands for Data Hinder Youth Work Charities', *CYPN*, 23 June.
70. Andy Hillier, 2011b, 'Select Committee Chairman Blasts Youth Sector for Lack of Evidence', *CYPN*, 26 January.
71. Joe Lepper, 2015, 'Early Intervention Chief: Youth Sector Fails to Prove Value', *CYPN*, 27 April.
72. Jon Jolly, 2011, 'Youth Sector Criticised for Lack of Evidence', 28 January, http://www.jonjolly.com/youth-sector-criticised-for-lack-of-evidence/.
73. Charlotte Goddard, 2012, 'Outcomes for Adolescents', *CYPN*, 27 November; Bethia McNeil, et al., 2012, *A Framework of Outcomes for*

*Young People*, The Young Foundation, https://youngfoundation.org/publications/framework-of-outcomes-for-young-people/.

74. Neil Puffett, 2013f, 'NCVYS Launches Youth Work Evidence Hub', *CYPN*, 10 July.

75. Cabinet Office, 2014, *Outcomes Framework: A Guide to Providers and Commissioners of Youth Services*, December

76. Neil Puffett, 2011d, 'Labour Conference 2011: Payment-by-Results "the Only Game in Town" for Early Intervention', *CYPN*, 26 September.

77. Adam Offord, 2015a, 'Government Launches £80m Payment-by-Results Fund to Tackle Social Problems', *CYPN*, 5 July.

78. Joe Lepper, 2011, 'Social Impact Bonds to Raise £40m Investment in Early Intervention', *CYPN*, 26 August; Ravi Chandiramani, 2012, 'Bang for a Buck', *CYPN*, 7 February; Gabriella Jozwiak, 2013, 'Government Urged to Underwrite Social Impact Bonds', *CYPN*, 7 May.

79. Polly Toynbee, 2011, 'Where Is Britain's Warren Buffet or Liliane Bettencourt?', *Guardian*, 26 August.

80. Gabriella Jozwiak, 2013, 'Youth Organisations Unprepared for Social Investment, Study Finds', *CYPN*, 4 April.

81. Adam Offord, 2015b, 'Prince's Trust Programme Generates £3 for Every £1 Spent', *CYPN*, 10 August.

82. HM Government, 2011, *Positive for Youth: Executive Summary*, December, p. 11.

83. GOV.UK, 2014, 'The Centre for Youth Impact Launches', Cabinet Office, 5 September, https://www.gov.uk/government/news/the-centre-for-youth-impact-launches; Adam Offord, 2015c, 'Centre for Youth Impact to Take on "National Leadership" Role', *CYPN*, 18 October.

84. Tony Taylor and Marilyn Taylor, 2013, 'Threatening Youth Work: The Illusions of Outcomes', IDYW, July, https://indefenceofyouthwork.com/tag/threatening-youth-work/; Tania de St Croix, 2017, 'Youth Work, Performativity and the New Youth Impact Agenda: Getting Paid for Numbers?' *Journal of Education Policy*, Vol. 33, No. 3, September, pp. 414–438.

85. Adam Offord, 2016, 'Major Study to Investigate Impact of Youth Work Launches', *CYPN*, 8 February; Jon Ord, et al., 2018, *The Impact of Youth Work in Europe: A Study of Five European Countries*, Helsinki, Erasmus+/Humak University of Applied Publications.

86. See for example Tania de St Croix, undated, 'Questioning the Youth Impact Agenda', CYI; Tony Taylor, 2017, 'Reassuring, but Not Measuring: Personal and Social Development', *Youth and Policy*, 27 July, http://www.youthandpolicy.org/articles/treasuring-not-measuring; Tania de St Croix, 2018, 'Youth Work Beyond the Measurement Imperative? Reflections on the Youth Investment Fund Learning Project from a Critical Friend', 7 February, http://www.youthimpact.uk/blogs/youth-work-beyond-the-measurement-imperative-reflections-on-the-youth-investment-fund-learning-project-from-a-critical-friend.

# Further Reading

Brent, Colin. 2018. 'Embracing Chaos in Youth Work'. *Youth and Policy*. September. http://www.youthandpolicy.org/articles/embracing-chaos-in-youth-work/.

Cooper, Susan. 2011. 'Reconnecting with Evaluation: The Benefits of Adopting a Participatory Approach to Assess Impact'. *Youth and Policy*. No. 107. November, pp. 56–70.

Cooper, Susan and Anu, Gretschel. 2018. 'Evaluating Youth Work in Its Contexts', in Alldred, Pam, et al. (eds), *The Sage Handbook of Youth Work Practice*. London: Sage, pp. 608–622.

Crewe, Tom. 2016. 'The Strange Death of Municipal England'. *London Review of Books*. Vol. 28, No. 34. 15 December, pp. 6–10.

Crimmins, David et al. 2004. *Reaching Socially Excluded Young People: A National Study of Street-Based Youth Work*. Leicester: NYA.

de St Croix, Tania. 2016. *Grassroots Youth Work: Policy, Passion and Resistance in Practice*. Bristol: Policy Press.

de St Croix, Tania. 2017. 'Youth Work, Performativity and the New Youth Impact Agenda: Getting Paid for Numbers?' *Journal of Education Policy*. Vol. 33, No. 3. September, pp. 414–438.

Devlin, Maurice and Anna, Gunning. 2009. *The Purpose and Outcomes of Youth Work*. Dublin: Irish Youth Work Press.

Faucher-King, Florence and Patrick, Le Galès. 2010. *The New Labour Experiment: Change and Reform Under Blair and Brown*. Stanford, CA: Stanford University Press.

Gratton, Nic. 2012. *The Shape of Youth Work in the West Midlands: A Profession at Risk or an Opportunity for Innovation?* Stoke on Trent: Staffordshire University.

Hastings, Annette et al. 2012. *Serving Deprived Communities in a Recession.* York: Joseph Rowntrees Foundation.

McNeil, Bethia et al. 2012. *A Framework of Outcomes for Young People.* The Young Foundation. https://youngfoundation.org/publications/framework-of-outcomes-for-young-people/.

Merton, Bryan et al. 2004. *An Evaluation of the Impact of Youth Work in England.* Nottingham: DfES Publications.

Ord, Jon. 2014. 'Aristotle's *Phronesis* and Youth Work: Beyond Instrumentality'. *Youth and Policy.* No. 112. April, pp. 56–73.

Ord, Jon et al. 2018. *The Impact of Youth Work in Europe: A Study of Five European Countries.* Helsinki: Erasmus+/Humak University of Applied Publications.

Spence, Jean and Devanney, Carol. 2006. *Youth Work: Voices of Practice.* Leicester: NYA.

Taylor, Tony and Marilyn, Taylor. 2013. 'Threatening Youth Work: The Illusions of Outcomes'. IDYW. July. https://indefenceofyouthwork.com/tag/threatening-youth-work/.

Unison. 2014. *The Damage: UK Youth Services—How Cuts are Removing Opportunities for Young People and Damaging Their Lives.* London: Unison.

Unison. 2016. *The Damage: A Future at Risk—Cuts in Youth Services.* London: Unison.

YMCA. 2018. *Youth and Consequences: A Report Examining Local Authority Expenditure on Youth Services in England and Wales.* May.

# 5

# The Local Youth Service Experience

## In Spite of 'Austerity'

Two surveys of 'senior youth service managers' in the spring of 2010 and 2011 suggested that, despite the ongoing budget cuts, most councils remained committed to this 'universal' provision and were resisting government pressures to concentrate only on targeted work with 'vulnerable' young people. Reflecting the continuing impact of the New Labour reforms, most by them nonetheless favoured 'integrated services' covering, for example, information, advice and guidance, teenage pregnancy and youth offending as well as 'positive activities'. Though a third of the 90 councils surveyed were considering 'alternative funding models', 75% had also at that stage kept their youth services in-house.[1]

Even as 'austerity' bit into councils' budgets, some local authorities continued to protect open access youth work provision which, according to a 2013 NCVYS report, was still being used regularly or sampled by up to 30% of the 13–19 age group, particularly 13–16 year olds.[2] In 2016, for example, Nottinghamshire was funding 31 Young People's Centres operating between 4 and 7 evenings per week, three in partnership with the voluntary sector—because, according to senior councillor,

© The Author(s) 2019                                                    **89**
B. Davies, *Austerity, Youth Policy and the Deconstruction of the Youth Service in England*, https://doi.org/10.1007/978-3-030-03886-1_5

'Every penny that the Council have spent on the Youth Service has been worth it'. Four mobile youth centres also continued to operate four evenings a week and three youth clubs one evening a week—all supported by a voluntary youth work development and support team.[3]

Despite repeated cuts to its budget, the Ealing's Youth and Connexions Service also continued to fund a range of open access facilities throughout this period. Its stated aims remained to give young people opportunities to 'gain new skills …, have a say in issues affecting them, get advice and support to prepare for the future (and) have fun and make friends'.[4]

Small amounts of money from lower tier local councils also provided some ad hoc support for youth work provision:

- In 2013, following county council cuts in 2011 of at least £4 million, eleven West Sussex parish councils came together in 'clusters' to deliver 'hyper-local youth services'—a move supported also by Horsham District Council.[5]
- In 2016 Westhoughton Town Council gave a £10,000 grant to Bolton Lads and Girls Club to set up an outpost in its area.[6]
- In 2018 Leamington Town Council provided £600 for printing a booklet of young refugees' and asylum-seekers' stories gathered by the local detached work team.[7]
- Also in 2018, Oswestry Town Council allocated an additional £5500 a year to provide two weekly two-hour youth club sessions.[8]
- Parish councils in Essex and Buckinghamshire also provided funding to employ youth workers.[9]

State funding for 'youth work' also came via more high profile initiatives—though these often turned out to be targeted rather than open access. Sadiq Khan, the newly elected Mayor of London, announced in December 2016, for example, that the water cannon bought by his predecessor Boris Johnson were to be sold and the estimated £175,000 saved was to be used over eight years to 'boost youth work numbers' for work with young gang members involved in knife crime.[10]

# And Then the Cuts

Over time, however, these better news stories proved increasingly to be exceptions to a much more negative rule.[11] Statistics attached to a 2014 House of Commons early day motion (EDM) gave a snapshot of what had happened in just one region since 2010 (Table 5.1).

A BBC report in the same year provided an equally revealing list (Table 5.2).

Enquiries carried out by 2016 Green Party Mayoral candidate Sian Berry revealed that in London alone £22 million was removed from Youth Service budgets between 2010–2011 and 2016–2017. In sixteen of the twenty-three councils which responded the average cut was £1

**Table 5.1**   Youth service budget cuts in the Yorkshire region—2010

| Authority | Cut (£) | Cut (%) |
|---|---|---|
| Doncaster | £4.591 million | 73 |
| Barnsley | £3.632 million | 65 |
| Sheffield | £7.544 million | 57 |
| Leeds | £3.763 million | 50 |
| Bradford | £3.1 million | 49 |
| Rotherham | £3.607 million | 40.6 |
| North Yorks | £2.248 million | 27 |
| Calderdale | £565,340 | 25 |
| York | £518,172 | 15 |
| Wakefield | £724,117 | 12 |
| Kirklees | £174,802 | 3.5 |

**Table 5.2**   Selection of youth service budget cuts—2010[a]

| Authority | Cut (£) (million) | Cut (%) |
|---|---|---|
| Kensington & Chelsea | £5.1 | 78 |
| Waltham Forest | £5.9 | 77 |
| Westminster | £4.5 | 74 |
| Tameside | £4.7 | 74 |
| Stoke-on-Trent | £5.3 | 71 |
| Warrington | £3 | 71 |

[a]Tom Barton and Tom Edgington, 2014, 'Youth services spending down by one-third', BBC News, 25 March, http://www.bbc.uk/news/uk-26714184

million or 36%, resulting in the closure of more than thirty youth centres, the loss of at least 12,700 places for young people and a reduction
in Youth Service jobs of on average 39%. In some council areas, funding for voluntary sector youth work had fallen by an average of 35%.
Follow-up enquiries indicated that ten of the responding councils were
predicting cuts of another £3.6 million in 2017–2018 and of another
£1.2 million by 15 councils in 2018–2019.[12]

# Beyond the Statutory Youth Service: Mutuals and Other Social Enterprises

As a direct consequence of these budget pressures local authorities
across the country closed down all or most of their directly provided
open access facilities, often claiming that some of this would be taken
over by voluntary organisations. In some areas, some staff were moved
within the local authority to other, usually more 'targeted', work defined
as 'early intervention', 'early help' or 'support for troubled families' (see
Chapter 6).

Often with the explicit aim of sustaining open access provision,
a range of new forms of organisation also emerged. 'Social enterprises',
for example—in effect 'market-oriented' versions of a voluntary organisation—'applied commercial strategies to maximize improvements in
human and environmental well-being' and, though not excluding 'profits for external shareholders',[13] often committed themselves to spending surpluses on 'good works'. With the support of Coalition ministers
and some local authorities, these were used by some redundant Youth
Service staff to re-establish themselves in practice with young people.[14]

Overlapping with the social enterprise, and again sometimes staff-
led, was the co-operative or 'mutual'. An example, like 'social action'
(see Chapter 12), of neo-liberalism's appropriation of a concept with
a long radical history, its application in this context was according to
one academic 'a concerted attack on the concept, the nature and the
existence of the "public" to the benefit of private ownership'.[15] Both
the Coalition from its earliest days and some local authorities saw the
co-operative as a vital substitute for directly provided and funded state

provision, not least because of the cover this provided for cuts to Youth Services. When suggesting in 2010 that the voluntary sector could provide up to 25% of local government work,[16] Cabinet Office minister Francis Maude claimed for example that:

> There are literally thousands of frontline employees who can see how things can be done better, but at the moment, within the existing constraints, they just can't get it done. Now this is going to change.[17]

His Office then initiated twenty two 'mutual pathfinder projects' between August 2010 and November 2011 as possible blueprints for a future range of public services across the country. At the time the training consultancy FMP was already working with fifteen client organisations interested in forming a mutual,[18] including some within the youth sector.[19]

Forming and successfully operating a mutual could, however, be challenging.[20] The Chief Executive of Capita—a FTSE-listed multi-national consultancy advertising itself as offering 'business process management and integrated professional support service solutions'[21]—warned for example that the government was relying too heavily on 'mutually owned public service start-up companies' for achieving the budget reductions it was seeking.[22] By the end of 2011 the Labour Party, too, was questioning the encouragement ministers were giving to them.[23]

Evidence also emerged from the pathfinders that 'setting up public service mutuals is not easy'.[24] With four of them failing in the first year (2011), this—particularly because of uncertainties over funding—was subsequently acknowledged by the Cabinet Office.[25] Nonetheless, by 2013 109 groups of professionals had had support from the government's Mutual Information Service[26] and the London Boroughs of Hammersmith and Fulham[27] and Chelsea and Kensington had announced the creation of their staff-led Youth Service mutuals.[28] They were followed a year later by Knowsley with a commitment to giving young people a central role in the new body's governance.[29]

By then the Cabinet Office was running a £10 million Mutuals Support Programme offering help with start-up costs and through a team of 'mutual ambassadors'.[30] By June 2014 a Mutuals Success training programme was also operating[31] which the next year was allocated £500,000 from the Delivering Differently for Young People fund[32] (see Chapter 13). Of the eight councils taking part in this programme, one (Torbay), explained that its decision to 'progress towards a mutual' by June 2014 had been prompted by the 'unprecedented budget cuts from central government'.[33] A second (Thurrock) announced in September 2015 that it, too, was to transfer its 'youth services' and their workers to a staff mutual.[34] Other authorities taking or considering this route by late 2016 and early 2017 included the London Boroughs of Lewisham,[35] Wandsworth, and Lambeth, Windsor and Maidenhead and Sunderland.[36]

In this list, too, was Devon where the Youth Service budget in 2014 had been cut by £970,000, 32 facilities had been closed and 60 posts removed. In September 2016 the Council announced that, to run the Service, it was awarding a three-year £5.15 million contract to 'an independent staff-run social enterprise', DYS Space Ltd—later described as a 'not-for-profit, public sector mutual … offering open access youth work from eight youth clubs across Devon' as well as 'targeted youth work, education and other services …' With youth work staff employed on Joint Negotiating Committee (JNC) salaries and conditions of service, in 2017—the first year since 2008 without staff redundancies—it was recruiting new workers and had taken on two apprentices and was advertising for a third.[37]

By June 2016 the Chelsea and Kensington and Knowsley mutuals were also reporting increased income and, in the case of the former, additional staff.[38] 'Monetised' gains were also suggesting that every £1 spent by the Chelsea and Hammersmith mutual on 'employability support' was generating £2.24 of 'social value' and that the 'return' of its 'serious youth violence programmes' was £3.59.[39] Six months later its chief executive was advocating that, in a situation where 'local authorities may sooner or later vacate the youth services arena altogether … investment in the sector that pays dividends (literally) proportionate to actual savings has to be explored'.[40]

The view of the Knowsley chief executive was more mixed. On the positive side, he saw the model as involving 'a lot less bureaucracy' in its decision-making processes—a view confirmed by the DYS Space experience. More problematic, however, was the specification in its four-year contract that its council income would fall by 10% a year—equating after two years to £700,000–800,000. By 2016 he was thus judging the model as 'in a way … quite flawed'.[41]

# In Search of New Money

A 2013 *CYPN* survey of Youth Service cuts[42] revealed that for nearly 80% of respondents fund-raising was by then a growing priority. Here, smaller projects with limited infrastructure capacity struggled to negotiate funders' often complex and labour-intensive bidding and evaluation procedures, especially when competing with well resourced national bodies.[43] For organisations and projects committed to providing predominantly open access youth work facilities, the increasing emphasis of even non-government funders on targeted work and payment by results contracts also increased their vulnerability.

## The Lottery…

In this environment, as a source of at least time-limited funding and often again with a 'targeting' requirement, the Lottery helped shore up some local youth provision, albeit in at least one case on a pay-ment-by-results basis.[44] Awards by the Big Lottery's 'Reaching Communities' programme, for example, included:

- In September 2011—at a time when Oxfordshire Council was planning to end financial support for twenty six youth centres[45]—£296,000 to Oxfordshire Association of Youth Clubs to employ three qualified workers to help set up twenty one 'volunteer clubs' across the county.[46]
- In May 2016, £464,709 to Young Cumbria 'to support young people with an offending history or those at risk of offending', to be focused in part on 'employability skills and building peer support' and provided through street work and drop-in sessions at schools and colleges.[47]
- Also in 2016, £283,000 to YMCA Derbyshire to work over twelve months with 'vulnerable and disadvantaged 18–30 year olds'.[48]

## … Philanthropy…

Though offering voluntary organisations another more familiar route to funding, in the new financial climate charities often made clear their reluctance to fill the gaps left by the state's withdrawal. Competition for their (again usually time-limited) awards anyway became increasingly fierce while, as Lord Salisbury, a major benefactor, admitted in 2017, philanthropic money was not being provided as a citizen's right but according to how powerful people like him 'judged other people's worthiness'.[49]

Nonetheless, these charitable bodies continued to provide sometimes substantial funding. Examples included:

- In September 2010 a £3.6 million grant from the RAF Benevolent Fund to 4 Children to employ around 80 youth workers to run a three-year 'positive activities' programme at 28 RAF bases across the country.[50]
- In September 2013 a three-year grant of £300,000 by the Clothworkers' Foundation to YMCA England for setting up 'street work projects in 'some of the most deprived areas' in England with 'young people at risk of getting involved in gangs'. One aim was to 'fill… the void left by youth work cuts' and so 'tackle the root causes of the August 2011 riots' in which young people were seen to have played a major part[51] (see Chapter 6).
- The participation in October 2013 of six London youth groups in a new 'City Pitch'—'a Dragon's Den-style bidding process' through which each could receive up to £700 for running 'community projects'. This, delivered by London Youth, was funded in part by the Santander Foundation.[52]
- In September 2015 £200,000 awarded by the Royal Masonic Trust for Girls and Boys to the Scout Association's 'Better Prepared' campaign to help meet its commitment to give every young person in the UK a chance to be involved in Scouting. In support of the Campaign's plan to open 200 new groups 'in the most deprived areas

of England and Wales', each group was to get £3200 to hire new premises, buy new equipment and train new volunteers.[53]

## … and by 'Socially Responsible' Business

In the new 'austerity' climate—though usually without explicit assessment of ethical risk or of potential reputational damage—youth sector organisations looked increasingly for both funding and in-kind support from private businesses.[54] By 2013, this was being explicitly recommended by an NYA report on a pilot project aimed at fostering links between local businesses and youth groups which had been run in collaboration with Manchester City Council and the British Chamber of Commerce.[55] While urging the sector to 'be realistic' in adopting this approach, its rationale was later affirmed by the former chief executive of UK Youth, Charlotte Hill. Her starting point was that, when (in 2010) she joined UK Youth

> … we had a huge amount of money from grants from different (government) departments. Those grants have disappeared now, so if we had carried on relying on them, I have no doubt that we would be a significantly smaller organisation if we had still been an organisation at all.

Since then, she pointed out, UK Youth had moved from being largely 'government-dependent' to generating 33% of its funding through 'corporation partners' with another 26% coming from 'sales'.[56] When Hill left UK Youth, the trustees' intention to develop these strategies seemed to be confirmed by their appointment of a new chief executive whose previous experience included running a consultancy for private equity companies and venture capitalists.[57]

Evidence on the ground had already emerged of significant business funding for some of the New Labour-promoted MyPlace centres[58] and, later, for the OnSide youth zones developed after 2010 (see Chapters 3 and 13). By the time the 2013 *CYPN* survey was carried out, groups and projects were increasingly taking this route, with over 21% saying they had secured support from the private sector.[59]

Such collaborations took a number of forms:

- In 2010, just as more young people were being trapped in a low wage/zero hours economy, Barclays Bank invited proposals from youth organisations for improving young people's ability to manage their money. The offer, taken up by NYA amongst others, was renewed in 2014,[60] by which time Barclays was being investigated by a US Senate committee for 'dubious' use of some financial products.[61]
- Two years later, as part of its wider 'Helping Britain Prosper Plan', Lloyds Banking Group funded its own three-year £3 million 'personal money management programme'. Run by UK Youth, its aim was again 'to help young people manage their money better by improving their knowledge, confidence and skills'.[62]
- UK Youth—which emerged as a market leader in this new funding environment[63]—established a partnership in 2012 with Microsoft to provide 30 local youth clubs with a mentor and a 'technology makeover' so that young people could gain 'essential life skills'. A year later the scheme—which by then had supported 2000 young people—was opened up to another 35 youth groups.[64]
- For running some NCS programmes, in 2012–2013 UK Youth and the NYA established a partnership with Serco[65]—another multi-national business with questionable ethical practices (see Chapter 4).
- In January 2017 Starbucks—a company accused of UK tax avoidance—provided continuation funding for UK Youth's Youth Action programme whose aim was to 'empower... disadvantaged young people with the confidence, skills and experience needed to feel ready for the workplace' (Through a previous partnership with Starbucks, UK Youth had 'offered over 100 grants to successful 16–25 year olds to bring their community ideas to life').[66]

From the early years of the Coalition government, voluntary sector links with 'socially responsible' businesses were also developed in a more co-ordinated way through a United Futures consortium. Part of the government's *Positive for Youth* policy strategy (see Chapter 9) and funded by the Department for Education (DfE), this brought together

Business in the Community—'a network of progressive businesses who … want to make a difference within society'—with, for example, UK Youth. By May 2012 United Futures, 'working to develop a model for brokering relationships between businesses and the youth sector', had launched pilots which included 'pairing' Plymouth YMCA with the pasty company Ginsters.[67] Regional 'speed dating' events were also planned and a 'Working with Business' guide published in 2012.

Children's minister Tim Loughton claimed early in the development of the programme that 'in a tough economic climate, bringing in charities and businesses to help develop and provide youth services is the way forward'. By June 2012, however, a report was warning that 'sustainable ways of providing support need to be identified once United Futures grant comes to an end'.[68] An evaluation report published the following March also raised more fundamental questions, identifying 'numerous barriers' to the co-operation envisaged. These included the youth sector's lack of 'a clear image'; groups' limited capacity for making themselves known to private companies; the limited staff time available on both sides of the partnerships; and a mismatch between future expectations of both youth groups and businesses. The report also warned:

> (O)ne should be careful that a focus on youth organisations' difficulties and needs does not reinforce a latent image of incompetence found amongst the businesses we interviewed.

Though the youth organisations which participated in the evaluation were hopeful that businesses would substantially increase their support for the sector, the companies interviewed were expecting no change or even a decline in the help they could offer.[69]

## Survival Without Sustainability

Beyond these top-down initiatives, over the period a range of other ad hoc efforts were made to attract new money to support youth work provision. In March 2016, for example, £1 million was allocated to Girlguiding from what was dubbed the 'tampon tax fund'—the VAT raised on sanitary products and distributed to a number of women's groups. Girlguiding used this to equip young women 'with skills for success, a safe place to develop, as well as providing them with more amazing opportunities for outdoor adventure … and to make a positive difference to their communities'.[70]

By their very nature, however, such time-limited awards, like most of the other new forms of income on which youth work providers came to rely, offered no long term security to, especially smaller, projects. When for example one youth club's Lottery money ran out, the local authority had to pledge £42,000 to keep it going—though even then for only six months.[71] As many of the grants were targeted on specific categories of young people, they were neither intended nor able to provide the week-by-week, community-based open-access facilities which local Youth Services had offered.

# Notes

1. Joe Lepper, 2011a, 'Local Authorities Fight to Keep Integrated Youth Services Universal, Research Reveals', *CYPN*, 6 September.
2. NCVYS, 2013, *Youth Report*, p. 2.
3. IDYW, 2016, 'Celebrating Nottinghamshire County Council's Continuing Youth Service Offer', 16 November, https://indefenceofyouthwork.com/2016/11/16/celebrating-nottinghamshire-county-councils-continuing-youth-service-offer/.
4. Young Ealing, 2017, 'Ealing's Youth and Connexions Service', http://www.youngealing.co.uk/about/.
5. Gabriella Jozwiak, 2013, 'Parish Councils Fill Youth Work Void', *CYPN*, 13 May.
6. Adam Offord, 2016a, 'Youth Work Roundup', *CYPN*, 4 April.
7. Warwickshire County Council, 2018, *YOU: Stories of Asylum*, http://www.warwickshire.gov.uk/lillingtonyouthcentre.
8. Neil Puffett, 2018, 'Youth Work Roundup: Funding', *CYPN*, 12 March.
9. Gabriella Jozwiak, 2013, op. cit.
10. Adam Offord, 2016b, 'Sadiq Khan Announces Plans to Boost Youth Work Numbers in London', *CYPN*, 5 December; Adam Offord,

2016c, 'Sale of Controversial Water Cannons Set to Fund Youth Projects', *CYPN*, 19 December.

11. Unison, 2014, *The Damage: UK Youth Services—How Cuts Are Removing Opportunities for Young People and Damaging Their Lives*, London, Unison, p. 5; Unison, 2016, *The Damage: A Future at Risk— Cuts in Youth Services*, London, Unison, p. 5; YMCA, 2018, Youth and Consequences: A Report Examining Local Authority Expenditure on Youth Services in England and Wales, May.

12. Sian Berry, 2017a, *The Dramatic Disappearance of Support and Facilities for Young People in London*, Green Party, January; Sian Berry, 2017b, *Youth Service Cuts in London—What Next?* Green Party, March; Sian Berry, 2018, *London's Lost Youth Services 2018*, Green Party, March.

13. Wikipedia, 2013, 'Social Enterprise', May, https://en.wikipedia.org/wiki/Social_enterprise.

14. *Rapport,* 2018, 'Space*: 1st Anniversary', Spring/Summer, p. 21.

15. John Schostak, 2010, 'Is the Proposal to Set Up Mutuals or Co-operatives in the Context of Public Sector Cuts Anything Other than Collusion with the Cuts?' unpublished, December.

16. Paul O'Brien, 2011, 'Co-ops, Mutuals and Public Services', *Guardian*, 6 September.

17. Joe Lepper, 2013a, 'Mutual Benefits', *CYPN*, 19 February.

18. Neil Puffett, 2011a, 'Staff-led Youth Services Gather Pace', *CYPN*, 13 December.

19. FMP, 2010, 'Going Mutual: A One-Day Seminar on Developing Mutual Organisations to Deliver Public Services', Autumn; FMP, 2010, 'Youth First: A New Mutual Model for Services for Young People', Autumn.

20. Paul O'Brien, 2011, op. cit.; Richard Vize, 2011, 'Guardian Roundtable: Mutual Respect', *Guardian*, 5 October.

21. Capita, 2017, 'About Us', http://www.capita.com/about-us/.

22. Simon Bowers, 2010, 'Capita Boss Highlights Problems with Government Spending Cuts Plans', *Guardian*, 22 November.

23. Randeem Ramesh, 2011, 'Where's the Mutual Trust in Opening Up Public Services?', *Guardian*, 25 October.

24. Julian Le Grand, 2011, 'Making Mutuals Sustainable Is No Easy Task', *Guardian*, 8 November.

25. Neil Puffett, 2011a, op. cit.

26. Neil Puffett, 2013a, 'Youth Services Seek Advice on Setting Up Mutuals', *CYPN*, 25 February.
27. Joe Lepper, 2013b, 'Mutual Benefits', *CYPN*, 19 February.
28. Neil Puffett, 2012a, 'Pioneering Youth Service Mutual Gets Green Light', *CYPN*, 24 July.
29. Laura McCardle, 2013a, 'Second Youth Service Mutual Gets Go Ahead', *CYPN*, 20 November; Laura McCardle, 2014a, 'Knowsley Launches Youth Service Mutual', *CYPN*, 1 April; Laura McCardle, 2014b, 'Youth Service Mutual to Be Governed by Young People', *CYPN*, 16 April.
30. Joe Lepper, 2013c, Mutual Benefits', *CYPN*, 19 February.
31. Laura McCardle, 2014c, 'Cabinet Office Supports Development of Eight Youth Mutuals', *CYPN*, 4 June.
32. Joe Lepper, 2014, 'Government Launches Funding for Alternative Models of Youth Services', *CYPN*, 21 July.
33. Laura McCardle, 2014c, op. cit.
34. Adam Offord, 2015a, 'Youth Work "Staff Mutual" Gets Councillors' Backing', *CYPN*, 24 September.
35. Adam Offord, 2016d, 'Council Launches Youth Service Mutual', *CYPN*, 26 September.
36. Adam Offord, 2016e, 'Children's Services Mutual Set to Expand to Third Local Authority', *CYPN*, 22 September; Adam Offord, 2016d, op. cit.; Gabriella Jozwiak, 2017a, 'Council Launches £5m Youth Services Mutual', *CYPN*, 6 February; Joe Lepper, 2013d, 'Mutual Benefits', *CYPN*, 19 February.
37. Gabriella Jozwiak, 2017a, op. cit.; *Rapport*, 2018, 'Space*: 1st Anniversary', Spring/Summer, p. 21.
38. Adam Offord, 2016f, 'First Youth Mutuals Prosper by Extending Reach and Expertise', *CYPN*, 21 June.
39. Adam Offord, 2016g, 'Youth Mutual "Generates £2 in Social Value for Every £1 Spent"', *CYPN*, 25 August.
40. Gabriella Jozwiak, 2017b, 'Youth Services "Face Oblivion" Unless They Pursue Social Investment', *CYPN*, 27 February.
41. Laura McCardle, 2014d, 'Mutual Appreciation', *CYPN*, 5 August; Adam Offord, 2016f, op. cit.
42. Andy Hillier, 2011a, 'Youth Groups Find Alternative Funding to Make Up for Government Spending Cuts', *CYPN*, 14 June; Neil Puffett, 2013b, 'Youth Sector on a "Knife-Edge" as Third of Organisations at Risk', *CYPN*, 16 April.

43. NCIA/Penny Waterhouse, 2014, 'Commissioning & Consortia—An Advantage or a Threat?' December, http://independentaction.net/blog/2014/12/10/commissioning-consortia-an-advantage-or-a-threat/; Neil Puffett, 2012b, 'Small Youth Charities to Bear the Brunt of Funding Cuts', *CYPN*, 13 January.

44. Adam Offord, 2015b, 'New Youth Work Funding Method to Be Trialled', *CYPN*, 2 November.

45. Alexandra Topping, 2011, 'Youth Workers in David Cameron's Oxfordshire Base Strike Over Cuts', *Guardian*, 23 August.

46. Joe Lepper, 2011b, 'Oxfordshire Receives Cash Boost for Volunteer Youth Clubs', *CYPN*, 20 September.

47. Adam Offord, 2016h, 'Youth Projects Among Beneficiaries of £49m Funding Boost', *CYPN*, 20 May.

48. Adam Offord, 2016h, op. cit.

49. Jane Dudman, 2017, 'Lord Salisbury: "This Is Why I Believe in the Welfare State: Certain Things Should Be a Right"', *Guardian*, 19 September.

50. Ross Watson, 2010, '4 Children Secures Contract to Deliver Youth Programmes at Air Force Bases', *CYPN*, 6 July.

51. Tristan Donovan, 2013a, 'YMCA Lands £300,000 for Street Youth Work', *CYPN*, 21 August; Laura McCardle, 2014e, 'Young and At-Risk Saved on the Street', *CYPN*, 9 December; Laura McCardle, 2014f, 'YMCA Detached Youth Work Project Bridges Gap Left by Youth Cuts', *CYPN*, 9 December.

52. Laura McCardle, 2013b, 'City Pitch Funds Youth-Led Community Projects', *CYPN*, 11 October.

53. Scout Association, 2015, 'Better Prepared Gains Funding from RMTGB', 29 September, http://scouts.org.uk/news/2015/09/news-better-prepared-gains-200k-support-of-funding-to-help-transform-lives/.

54. Andy Hillier, 2011a, op. cit.; Neil Puffett, 2013b, op. cit.

55. Tristan Donovan, 2013b, 'Youth Groups Should Come Together to Charm Business, Says Report', *CYPN*, 8 April.

56. Laura McCardle, 2014g, 'Stepping up for Social Action', *CYPN*, 18 February.

57. Laura McCardle, 2014h, 'UK Youth Announces New Chief Executive', *CYPN*, 18 September.

58. Laura McCardle, 2014j, 'Youth Centres to Get Support from Businesses', *CYPN*, 27 October.

59. Neil Puffett, 2013b, op. cit.
60. Jo Stephenson, 2014, 'Champions of Money Matters', *CYPN*, 8 July.
61. Dominic Rushe, 2014, 'Senators Accuse Banks Over "Dubious" Products', *Guardian*, 22 July.
62. Adam Offord, 2016j, 'Money Management Programme to Launch for Young People', *CYPN*, 16 May.
63. UK Youth, 2018, 'State of the Membership', March; Joe Lepper, 2018, 'UK Youth Sets Out Plans to Attract Investment in Sector', *CYPN*, 2 March.
64. Neil Puffett, 2012c, 'UK Youth Seals Partnership with Microsoft', *CYPN*, 9 July; Darren Hayes, 2013, 'Network of IT Hubs Set to Expand', *CYPN*, 19 September.
65. N. Puffett, 2012d, 'Serco Consortium Wins Six NCS Contracts', CYPN, 13 September.
66. UK Youth, 2017, 'Starbucks Youth Action Applications—Now Open', UK Youth website; UK Youth, 2017, 'Starbucks Youth Action', http://www.ukyouth.org/starbucks-youth-action.html.
67. Laura McCardle, 2014J, op. cit.
68. Becky Fauth and Ivana La Valle with Jennifer Gibb and Joanna Lea, 2012, *Exploring the Potential of Employers to Support Youth Services.* Business in the Community, London: National Children's Bureau/UK Youth; Neil Puffett, 2012e, 'Forms of Business Support for Youth Sector Identified', *CYPN*, 4 May; Neil Puffett, 2012f, 'Brokerage Service to Help Link Youth Work with Business', *CYPN*, 26 June; NCVYS, 2012, 'Guide to Help Youth Organisations Work with Business', *NCVYS Information Service Bulletin*, 12 October.
69. Tristan Donovan, 2013c, 'Youth Groups Struggle to Win Support from Businesses', *CYPN*, 27 March.
70. Jess Brown, 2016, 'Osborne Allocates £12m for Women and Girls Projects', *CYPN*, 17 March.
71. Adam Offord, 2016a, op. cit.

# Further Reading

Bell, Michael, et al. 2013. 'It's Business as Usual: Newcastle, Commissioning and Cuts'. *Youth and Policy*. No 110. May, pp. 88–94.
Berry, Sian. 2017a. *The Dramatic Disappearance of Support and Facilities for Young People in London*. Green Party. January.

Berry, Sian. 2017b. *Youth Service Cuts in London—What Next?* Green Party. March.

Berry, Sian. 2018. *London's Lost Youth Services 2018*. Green Party. March.

Chakelian, Anoosh. 2018. 'The False Economy of Youth Club Closures: Haringey's Struggle to Protect Services'. *New Statesman*. 31 August, pp. 13–14.

Fauth, Becky, et al. 2012. *Exploring the Potential of Employers to Support Youth Services*. Business in the Community. London: National Children's Bureau/ UK Youth.

Mason, Will. 2015. 'Austerity Youth Policy: Exploring the Distinctions Between Youth Work in Principle and Youth Work in Practice'. *Youth and Policy*. No. 114. May, pp. 55–74.

NCIA/Waterhouse, Penny. 2014. 'Commissioning & Consortia—An Advantage or a Threat?' December. http://independentaction.net/blog/2014/12/10/ commissioning-consortia-an-advantage-or-a-threat/.

Norris, Pat and Pugh, Carole. 2015. 'Local Authority Youth Work', in Bright, Graham (ed). *Youth Work: Histories, Policy, Contexts*. London: Palgrave, pp. 80–101, 236–251.

Unison. 2014. *The Damage: UK Youth Services—How Cuts Are Removing Opportunities for Young People and Damaging Their Lives*. London: Unison.

Unison. 2016. *The Damage: A Future at Risk—Cuts in Youth Services*. London: Unison.

YMCA. 2018. *Youth and Consequences: A Report Examining Local Authority Expenditure on Youth Services in England and Wales*. May.

# Part III

## Wider Youth Policy Agendas

# 6

# Remaking 'The Broken Society'

## 'From Big Government to Big Society'

### Changing the Political Philosophy

Though economic policies post-2010 clearly had the most direct and long-term consequences for services for young people, not least local authority Youth Services, other government policies shaped by its neo-liberal ideology also had significant impacts. One 'change that Britain needs' explained in uncompromising terms by the Conservative Party's 2010 General Election Manifesto was, 'from big government to Big Society'—that is

> … From the idea that the role of the state is to direct society and micro-manage public services, to the idea that the role of the state is to strengthen society and make public services serve the people who use them.[1]

Two months after he became Prime Minister, David Cameron talked of the task of reducing the budget deficit as a 'duty'. What by contrast

© The Author(s) 2019
B. Davies, *Austerity, Youth Policy and the Deconstruction of the Youth Service in England*, https://doi.org/10.1007/978-3-030-03886-1_6

excited him, he claimed, were 'things you do because it's your passion'—
such as, for him, giving individuals and communities more control
over their destinies. The Big Society schemes he was planning would,
he promised, bring about 'the biggest, most dramatic redistribution of
power from elites in Whitehall to the man and woman on the street'
with a Big Society Bank, again drawing on unclaimed bank assets,
hopefully providing start-up funding of millions of pounds. Matched
by private investment, this, Cameron claimed, would enable voluntary
and neighbourhood groups, charities and social enterprises to start running public services.

From the start, the community projects Cameron identified as
examples of the Big Society in action—a local buy-out of a rural pub,
recruiting volunteers to keep museums open[2]—suggested only modest
downwards transfers of power. It later emerged, too, that of the 5000
'community organisers' who were to be a centrepiece of the Big Society
enterprise, only 500 would be full-time paid. The three-year £15 million contract for training them, moreover, was awarded, not to Citizens
UK, a body influenced by radical thinkers such as Saul Alinsky and
Paulo Freire, but to the more conformist Locality.[3]

## Doubts and Critiques

Questions about the Big Society plans emerged quickly. In February
2011, for example, half of one poll's respondents thought it was a gim-
mick and 41% that it was a cover for cuts.[4] Also early in 2011, two-
thirds of a thousand 16–24 year olds surveyed said they didn't know
what it meant for them and 46% that they didn't trust the government
'to make the right cuts'.[5]

At a time when so many people were losing jobs and benefits and
struggling to deal with everyday pressures, many queried where all the
volunteers were to come from given that in 2009 41% of adults had
already been volunteering.[6] By September 2011, 95% of 500 voluntary sector interviewees were saying that they had seen no Big Society-
inspired increase in volunteer numbers.[7] Nor was it clear how these new
recruits could replace the skills or experience of the professionals who
were being made redundant.

Like many local community groups,[8] the Chief Executive of the Association of Chief Executives of Voluntary Organisations (ACEVO), Steve Bubb—usually cautious in his criticisms of government—also distanced himself from the Big Society label. Against the background of a 'tidal wave of growing needs and rising cuts', he called it 'more soundbite than programme for government' which was 'hitting the buffers' and causing 'a tide of cynicism'.[9]

Underpinning these criticisms were often questions about the plan's core assumptions. Could such a bottom-up movement, for example, be created top down? Might this not anyway result in existing local democratic forms of accountability being bypassed?[10,11] Were the 'communities' on which so much of the Big Society's success would depend as straightforwardly homogeneous as seemed to be assumed? Might not treating them only as geographical entities anyway overlook important collective identities defined by ethnicity, gender, disability, sexual orientation and—of particular significance for young people— age? Indeed, might not women in particular find themselves having to take on tasks previously carried out by the state.[12] In a 2016 report the Centre for Ageing Better also pointed to a class issue—that, by favouring rich areas where volunteers were most available, problems could be exacerbated in poorer areas where people had much less 'disposable time'.[13]

Serious financial challenges also emerged. With cuts in state funding for the voluntary sector estimated as early as October 2010 as between £3.2 and £5.1 billion,[14] many of the organisations on which Cameron was depending, even assuming they still existed, had reducing capacity to meet his expectations. The government's own Office for Civil Society (OCS)—replacement for Labour's Office of the Third Sector— had already cut £11 million from its funding for organisations supporting volunteering. In August 2010 Boris Johnson reduced his London Mayor's Development Fund for volunteer and community groups by £2 million.[15] In the year after the Cameron launch speech, as the number of registered charities fell by 1600,[16] reports from across the country were providing other evidence of the sector's problems in engaging in realistic ways with 'Big Society' aspirations.[17]

## From Re-Launch to …?

Enunciating slogans which resurfaced throughout the austerity years, an early Cameron response to such reservations was to tell councils:

> When it comes to trimming your budgets, don't do the easy things, which is to cut money to the voluntary bodies and organisations working in communities. Look at your core costs. Look at how you can do more for less. Look at the value for money you get from working with the voluntary sector.[18]

Though George Osborne's October spending review did earmark funds for 'Big Society' projects including recruiting community organisers, this and his previous emergency budget speech in May included only one Big Society reference.[19]

Despite the creation of an independent 'Big Society Network' to help people understand and engage with its ideas and the legislation underpinning it,[20] turning Cameron's rhetoric into action thus proved difficult. In February 2011, Liverpool—the city where he had launched the programme and one of the four 'vanguard' authorities—withdrew from the pilot. Citing funding cuts and lack of support in ironing out problems,[21] the Council's deputy leader dismissed the programme as 'the emperor's new clothes'.[22]

With opposition also building within powerful sections of the Conservative Party,[23] the 'Big Society' idea thus required periodic re-launching. In February 2011 Cameron, insisting that he would never abandon it, promised to make £200 million available for new initiatives through the Big Society Bank—albeit, it later emerged, at commercial lending rates.[24] By April 2013, the £119 million which the renamed Big Society Capital had to distribute was expected to rise to £600 million by 2018.

Commitments to the Big Society reappeared in the 2015 Conservative Party election manifesto focused on three policy areas which included the NCS and young people's 'social action'[25] (see Chapters 10–12). In December 2016 Big Society Capital announced 'a unique £10 million Crowd Match Fund' designed to give investors in charities and social enterprises a 30% tax break on their money.[26] With Theresa May's government enthusiasm apparently cooling, however, by 2017 the Big Society was being called 'a failed fantasy of an already forgotten prime minister'.[27]

## Big Society, Youth Policies and the Youth Service

Throughout the Big Society's development, overlaps with work with young people were occasionally made explicit, including with the Youth Service and youth work. Within days of the Coalition coming to power—in May 2010—NCVYS published a briefing paper on what it was intended to be and do. While welcoming its 'focus on volunteering, charitable giving and community activism', it also cautioned that 'investment in local infrastructure will be particularly important' and that collaboration between government, local statutory agencies and the voluntary and community sector would be needed 'to turn the vision … into a reality for young people and communities'.[28]

Within months, however, the problems of achieving this were demonstrated in a very direct way. In November 2010 Tim Loughton told a NCVYS conference that he had 'won the battle' for £300–£400 million of the Big Society Bank's assets to be spent on young people—only to be contradicted almost immediately by the Cabinet Office's insistence that the government could not require the Bank to prioritise particular projects.[29] The Big Society Fund did, however, occasionally come to the rescue of some 'youth work facilities'. It for example prioritised the NCS and young people's social action, both of which often presented themselves as the new way of doing youth work (see Chapters 10–12). Repeated references to the Big Society label were also made by local councils to 'gloss' their Youth Service cuts, as when in September 2011 Oxfordshire Council announced that, with the help of the county's Association of Youth Clubs, it would use £600,000 of a Big Society allocation to save nine youth centres from closure.[30]

# 'Serious About Localism'

Such 'glossing', however, took other forms, and was used also by government ministers. In December 2014, for example, when the then youth minister Rob Wilson was challenged on why he was refusing to sign a Commons EDM proposing to strengthen the Youth Service's statutory base, his response was: 'If you're serious about localism, and I am in particular, then you have to trust and respect local choices…'[31]

This reference to 'localism' specifically in relation to youth provision and the Youth Service was rare. However, Wilson's use of it to justify ministers' refusal to interfere in local policy decisions highlights another of the strategic ways in which the Cameron government sought to implement its offer of change from big government. Localism's overlap also with the Big Society volunteering agenda was made explicit in the 'Essential Guide' to the Localism Bill published in December 2014[32] and by the creation of the new body of local community organisers.[33]

Localism's core aspiration was for a more formal transfer of powers and responsibilities 'to local councils, communities and individuals'. The Bill particularly sought to empower councils to devolve more decisions to people in their neighbourhoods, including a right to challenge council policies and bid to buy local amenities such as libraries and children's centres (and therefore also, presumably, youth centres). It also created a 'community right' to build new amenities in towns and cities.

The NYA clearly saw the Bill as sufficiently relevant to youth workers to circulate a briefing on it within days of its publication. As well as outlining its key proposals, this included a range of critical reactions. Ted Cantle, author of the report on 'community cohesion' in multi-ethnic areas prompted by the 2001 'race riots' (see Chapter 2), pointed out that asking people in the name of localism '… to run libraries, parks and other facilities to build the Big Society … may be the only way they can be retained at all'. Guardian columnist Peter Hetherington doubted whether, as in the Big Society discourse, the 'local communities' referred to in a largely idealised way had the appetite, the capacity or the cash to take on the proposed degree of decentralisation. A former senior manager at the Audit Commission also commented that the whole strategy was 'a con'.[34]

As the Bill made its way through Parliament more grass roots criticisms emerged. A joint response to it by the Runnymede Trust and Race on the Agenda pointed to the potential risks of councils opting out of key equalities duties.[35] A local gypsies and travellers support group expressed concerns that delegating powers to local communities would play to divisive stereotypes and so end up discriminating against out-of-favour groups like theirs, asylum-seekers and sex workers.[36] A more top-down response came from the consultancy firm Deloitte which, in a report published in January 2011 entitled 'A little local difficulty', pointed to 'tensions between central government intent and local government readiness' and 'further uncertainty' within a 'fast-moving policy environment'.[37]

Six month later a Communities and Local Government Select Committee report called the government's plans for devolving power 'incoherent and inconsistent', labelled its definition of localism as 'extremely elastic', and concluded that support for the proposals was being undermined by differing interpretations of what it meant. The Committee also pointed out, as had others previously, that ministers were quick to abandon their 'localist' principles when it suited them— as when Eric Pickles, the minister who had guided the Act onto the statute book, instructed Liverpool City Council to reverse its cuts-driven decision to reduce household waste collections.[38]

One close observer of developments also suggested that, while 'predatory oligopolies like Serco, Capita and G4S' were taking advantage of the 'marketable' opportunities' it offered, '… most local groups remain unaware that these (community) rights exist'. In addition

> What the government calls localism … is more about local government and civil society being forced to carry the can operationally, while the private sector cherrypicks marketable public services and central government accumulates greater powers. When attempts were made to use them, what often was revealed was not cosy unity but the fractured nature of some communities.[39]

Though Localism's provisions and structures remained in place, as with the Big Society its political profile reduced significantly over the Coalition's time in power and subsequently. Nonetheless, as illustrated by Wilson's comment in late December 2014, it continued to give the government cover for cutting public spending and (see Chapter 9) for ministers' repeated hands-off response to the resultant run-down of local public services such as local authority Youth Services.

## Early Intervention...

As the budget cuts took hold, 'early intervention'—another of the Coalition's high-profile social policies—got much more substantive youth policy attention. Indeed, in many areas it was used to 're-badge' the Youth Service and move its workers into new and, for most, unfamiliar roles often with social care-type titles.[40]

As a way of preventing or at least ameliorating future problems and cutting the cost of public services,[41] New Labour had made 'intervening early' in children's lives an important priority,[42] including for example, between 2008 and 2011, through a Parenting Early Intervention Programme. Within a month of coming to power Cameron asked Labour MP Graham Allen to carry out 'a review of early intervention'—long Allen's special area of interest. In 2009 he had co-authored a paper with Cameron's future Secretary of State for Work and Pensions, Iain Duncan-Smith which had been published by the Centre for Social Justice. This had been set up by Duncan-Smith following what was described as his 'Easterhouse Epiphany'—his conversion during a visit to the struggling Glasgow housing estate to 'a radical new form of Conservatism' rooted in the belief that 'family dysfunction was the chief cause of poverty, and not the other way round'.[43]

According to the press release for their paper, Allen and Duncan-Smith 'paint(ed) an apocalyptic vision of worsening violent crime and social disorder unless radical steps are taken early in the lives of young children...'[44] Its title—*Early Intervention, good parents, great kids, better citizens*—also clearly indicated where Allen would be starting his early intervention review. 'Keeping in mind the Government's stance on public expenditure and its policy agendas of decentralisation, localism and the creation of the Big Society', his first report, published in January 2011, recommended that early intervention should act as 'a social and emotional bedrock for the current and future generations of babies, children and young people by helping them and their parents (or other main caregivers) before problems arise'. It urged the government to 'encourage the best and most rigorously proven Early Intervention programmes ... pulled together using the best methodology and science available....' It proposed, too, that the government promote an independent Early Intervention Foundation 'to motivate those in the Early Intervention sector' and raise additional long-term finance for early intervention from non-governmental sources.[45]

A second report, *Early Intervention: Smart Investment, Massive Savings*, published the following July, focussed on funding the recommended programmes. It suggested that the Treasury use its next comprehensive spending review to, over time, rebalance government spending towards early intervention and that, working closely with the Big Society Bank, an early intervention fund be created. A key premise, too, was that the outcomes of the recommended early intervention programmes could be 'monetised' by demonstrating financial savings for the national economy.[46]

The Early Intervention Foundation (EIF), eventually launched in July 2013, was funded by the DCLG and the Departments of Education, Health and Work and Pensions (DWP). As an independent charity, its remit was to assess the evidence on which interventions work and their relative value for money; to advise central government, local councils and agencies, charities and investors on what works for whom and when; and to advocate for early intervention to important decision-makers.[47]

In defining 'the varying environments in which children grow up and shape their development', the Foundation recognised that 'family income' and 'economic deprivation' were influential factors. The report also sought to extend the then predominant 'early intervention' focus on the nuclear family and the care of young children to include potentially valuable preventative interventions in adolescence—for example with teenage gangs. In addressing the actual 'intervention' issues, however,

references to 'warm and nurturing homes' and levels of parents' education continued to shape its and the wider public, political and policy
discourses.[48] Particularly at a time of major cuts in state and especially
local government spending, the risk remained, therefore, that support
for young people on their own terms would be rated a low priority and
even as an unacceptable diversion.[49]

Indications that perhaps government enthusiasm for the strategy was
waning first came with a £49 million reduction in early intervention
funding for 2013/2014 and 2014/2015. This was followed by a further cut of 8% in 2015/2016.[50] A year later the EIF itself argued that
the government and local authorities should prioritise evaluating the
approach more thoroughly because of a lack of UK-based evidence that
the programmes were working.[51]

Nonetheless, often very explicitly, the policy had significant influence on youth policies generally and especially on how many local
authorities presented their Youth Service cuts. Though this saved some
posts, staff who survived—for example, in Croydon, Oxfordshire and
Warwickshire[52]—were often moved into jobs funded out of government early intervention grants, to reappear as youth social workers
working with referred 'clients' in one-to-one or family situations.

## … into Troubled Families

To help fill some of the emerging gaps in their youth provision, a number of local authorities used funding from another Coalition initiative—
its 'troubled families' programme.[53] This was established in the
aftermath of the 2011 summer 'riots' in response, according to Pickles,
to 'the common refrain' emerging from the disturbances 'Where are the
parents? Why aren't they keeping their kids indoors? Why weren't they
with them in court?' As a result, he claimed '… the whole country got a
sudden, unwelcome insight into our problem families'.[54]

The following October, Cameron, having already 'set out an ambi-
tion of turning the lives of these families around by the end of
Parliament', announced a Troubled Families Unit to be located in the
DCLG. Pickles himself told council leaders that, though the estimated

120,000-plus families to be targeted made up less than 1% of the population, they were each year costing the economy over £8 billion and local services up to £330,000 a family. Instead of what he called 'the traditional single agency silo approach', the new programme would adopt a co-ordinated and integrated intervention. This would bring together a number of central government funding streams in what was later described as 'the first national, systematic approach to driving real change in outcomes for families with multiple problems and to change the services that worked with them'.[55] As a result, the average expenditure per family would be reduced by 2015 to £14,000.[56] In June 2013, the Treasury announced an expansion of the programme costing £200 million, to reach an additional 400,000 families in 2015/2016.[57]

Duncan Smith later revealed that he and other ministers had 'issues' with the programme, particularly its 'slightly nebulous' targets.[58] Despite a government claim of 100% success, by 2015 others, too, were raising questions about its effectiveness. The Centre for Crime and Justice Studies, for example, suggested that, against the backdrop of the cuts to services and the punishing welfare reforms, 'the reported successes … are too good to be true'.[59] The final national evaluation report published in October 2016 concluded that it was 'unable to find consistent evidence that the programme had any significant or systematic impact'.[60] The House of Commons Public Accounts Committee also dismissed the government's claimed success rate and questioned a payment-by-results procedure which, it said, encouraged 'perverse' behaviour by local authorities who rushed families through the programme.[61]

The first DCLG annual report on the second phase of the programme published in April 2017 regretted that 'public commentary on the evaluation (of the first programme) focused almost exclusively on (one) finding'—its inability 'to attribute positive outcomes … in employment, school attendance or youth crime to the … Programme *specifically*' (Emphasis in the original). It did concede, however, that 'in retrospect … measurements of impact achieved were taken too early and within too narrow time frames'. Nonetheless, its own conclusion was that, despite 'continued budgetary pressures',

… workers are being trained in 'whole family working' and are using their skills, passion and commitment to support families to aspire to and achieve a better future.

With 'services … coming together across organisational boundaries', it thus felt able to claim that 'families' lives' are changing for the better'.[62]

On the argument that youth workers' distinctive skills could be particularly helpful in working with the 'troubled' teenagers of these 'troubled' families—including in one case by offering 'anger management'[63]—some local authorities used it funding to protect some youth work posts. According to one 'integrated youth services manager' for example

A lot of families struggle to engage with the state, but by adopting a youth work approach they can stay more engaged.[64]

However, here and also in response to the other high profile policy priorities of post-2010 governments, the focus of this 'youth work approach' on informal education was increasingly replaced by individualised forms of 'child-saving'.[65]

# Notes

1. Conservative Party, 2010, *Invitation to Join the Government of Britain*, Conservative Party, April, pp. vi, vii; BBC, 2010, 'At-a-Glance: Conservative Manifesto', 13 April, http://news.bbc.co.uk/1/hi/uk_politics/election_2010/8617433.stm.
2. BBC News, 2010, 'David Cameron Launches Tories "Big Society" Plan', 19 July.
3. Madeleine Bunting, 2011, 'How Cameron Fell Out of Love with His Citizen Organisers', *Guardian*, 14 February; Kaye Wiggins, 2011, 'Locality Wins £15m Community Organisers Programme', *Third Sector*, 18 February.
4. Matt Chorley, 2011, 'Battle of the Big Society: Tories Go on the Offensive', *Independent*, 13 February.
5. Janaki Mahadevan, 2011a, 'Young People Asked to Define the Big Society', *CYPN*, 1 February.

6. Hilary Barnard, 2010, *Big Society, Cuts and Consequences: A Thinkpiece*, Cass Business School, November, p. 10.
7. Tom Traynor, 2011, 'Quick Survey Analysis', Directory of Social Change, September.
8. Peter Hetherington, 2013, 'Is this the end of Cameron's big society?' *Guardian*, 5 March.
9. Polly Toynbee, 2011, 'Big Society's a Busted Flush, But Who Will Admit It First', *Guardian*, 7 February.
10. Gabriel Chanan and Colin Miller, 2011, *The Big Society and Public Services: Complementarity or Erosion?* Paces, Winter, p. 7.
11. ADUR Voluntary Action, 2011, 'A Critical Take on Big Society', *AVA Inter Active*, February.
12. Selma James, 2010, 'The Tory "Big Society" Relies on Women Replacing Welfare', Guardian.co.uk, 21 October.
13. Dan Jones, Aideen Young, and Neil Reeder, 2016, *The Benefits of Making a Contribution to Your Community in Later Life*, Centre for Ageing Better, https://16881-presscdn-0-15-pagely.netdna-ssl.com/wp-content/uploads/2016/12/Evidence-Review-Community-Contributions.pdf; Rachel Williams, 2011, 'Big Society "Could Widen Volunteer Gap Between Town and Country"', *Guardian*, 11 February; Neil Puffett, 2011a, 'Affluent Areas Will Benefit Most from Big Society, Warns Charity Chief Executive', *CYPN*, 16 February.
14. Hilary Barnard, 2010, op. cit., p. 13.
15. Polly Toynbee, 2010, 'The "Big Society" Is a Big Fat Lie—Just Follow the Money', Guardian.co.uk, 6 August; Pippa Crerar, 2010, 'Blow for "Big Society" as £4 Million Fund Is Axed', *London Evening Standard*, 11 August.
16. James Ball, 2011, 'Charity Numbers Fall Leaving "Big Society" Pledge Under Threat', *Guardian*, 5 June.
17. Rachel Williams, 2010, 'Cuts Could Put Paid to Fledgling "Big Society" Schemes', Guardian.co.uk, 27 October.
18. Hilary Barnard, 2010, op. cit., p. 13.
19. Gabriella Jozwiak, 2010a. 'Spending Review: Government Creates £100m Fund for Voluntary and Community Organisations', *CYPN*, 20 October; Hilary Barnard, 2010, op. cit., p. 6.
20. Gabriella Jozwiak, 2010b, 'Big Society Network Appoints Founding Member Steve Moore as Its Director', *CYPN*, 3 December.
21. Gemma Spence, 2011, 'Liverpool Pulls Out of Big Society Pilot After Government Cuts "Put Community Groups at Risk"', *CYPN*, 3 February.

22. Matt Chorley, 2011, op. cit.
23. Allegra Stratton, 2011, 'Andy Coulson Takes the Rap in the Big Society Blame Game', *Guardian*, 9 February.
24. Toby Helm, 2011. 'David Cameron to Rescue "Big Society" with Extra Cash', *Guardian*, 12 February; David Cameron, 2011, 'David Cameron: Have No Doubt, the Big Society Is on Its Way', *Guardian*, 12 February; Matt Chorley, 2011, op. cit.
25. Sam Burne James, 2015 'Tories Promise to Build on Big Society in General Election Manifesto', *Third Sector*, 14 April, https://www.third-sector.co.uk/tories-promise-build-big-society-general-election-manifesto/policy-and-politics/article/1342626.
26. Big Society Capital, 2016, 'Crowdfunder, Ethex and Thin Cats to Partner Big Society Capital in New Crowd Match Fund', 7 December.
27. Poly Toynbee and David Walker, 2017, *Dismembered: How the Attack on the State Harms Us All*, Guardian Books, London, p. 3.
28. NCVYS, 2010, 'Building the Big Society: A Briefing Paper...', May, Section 4, p. 2.
29. UK Parliament, 2010, 'Youth Sector Will Benefit from Big Society Bank Says Children's Minister', 9 November; Joe Lepper, 2010a, 'Government Will Have No Power to Prioritise Youth Projects for Big Society Bank Money', *CYPN*, 10 November; Joe Lepper, 2010b, 'Mix-Up Over Big Society Bank Cash Sparks Anger', *CYPN*, 16 November.
30. Joe Lepper, 2011, 'Oxfordshire Received Cash Boost for Volunteer Youth Clubs', *CYPN*, 20 September.
31. Laura McCardle, 2014a, 'Youth Minister Rob Wilson Rejects Statutory Services Motion', *CYPN*, 4 December; Laura McCardle, 2014b, 'Rob Wilson's Commitment to Young People Questioned', *CYPN*, 5 December.
32. HM Government, 2010, *Decentralisation and Localism Bill: An Essential Guide*, December.
33. Jesse Steele, 2011, 'How Dare the Lord?' *Spinning Plates*, 25 May, https://jesssteele.wordpress.com/2011/05/25/how-dare-the-lord/.
34. NYA, 2010, 'The Localism Bill', *Insight*, Issue 15, 15 December.
35. Runnymede Trust/Race on the Agenda, 2011, 'Joint Submission to House of Commons Committee Stage of the Localism Bill', 17 February.

36. Bernard Davies, 2014, 'One Size Does Not Fit All', 16 December, http://independentaction.net/blog/2014/12/16/be-brave-be-independent/.

37. Deloitte, 2011, *A Little Local Difficulty*, January.

38. Polly Curtis, 2011, 'David Cameron's Localism Bill Is Incoherent, Say MP's', *Guardian*, 9 June.

39. Laird Ryan, 2015, 'As If People Mattered', National Coalition for Independent Action, 14 July, http://legacy.independentaction.net/wp-content/uploads/sites/8/2015/12/Localism-As-If-People-Mattered-Legacy-1.pdf.

40. Laura McCardle, 2015a, 'Councils Redeploy Youth Workers to Social Care Roles, Warns Report', *CYPN*, 12 January.

41. Early Years Commission, 2008, *Break Through Britain: The Next Generation*, September, http://www.centreforsocialjustice.org.uk/library/next-generation-report-early-years-commission-report.

42. Geoff Lindsay, Steve Strand, Mairi Ann Cullen, Stephen Cullen, Sue Band, Hilton Davis, Gavan Conlon, Jane Barlow, and Ray Evans, 2011, *Parenting Early Intervention Programme*, DFE, May, https://www.gov.uk/government/uploads/system/uploads/attachment_data/file/182715/DFE-RR121A.pdf.

43. *The Herald*, 2002, 'How Iain Duncan Smith Came to Easterhouse and Left with a New Vision for the Tory Party', 23 March; Lynsey Hanley, 2016, *Respectable: Crossing the Class Divide*, Penguin Books, p. 168.

44. Centre for Social Justice, 2008, 'Senior MPs Launch Cross-Party Bid to Avert Social Collapse', September, http://www.centreforsocialjustice.org.uk/press-releases/early-intervention-good-parents-great-kids-better-citizens.

45. GOV.UK, 2011a, *Early Intervention: The Next Steps*, January, https://www.gov.uk/government/publications/early-intervention-the-next-steps—2.

46. GOV.UK, 2011b, *Early Intervention: Smart Investment, Massive Savings*, July, https://www.gov.uk/government/publications/early-intervention-smart-investment-massive-savings.

47. GOV.UK, 2013, 'What Works Network', 28 June, https://www.gov.uk/guidance/what-works-network.

48. Early Intervention Foundation, undated, 'How Do We Know Early Intervention Works?' http://www.eif.org.uk/how-do-we-know-early-intervention-works/; Stephanie Waddell and Jonathon Toy, 2015, *Early Intervention to Prevent Gang Involvement and Youth Violence: A Practical Guide*, http://www.eif.org.uk/wp-content/uploads/2016/06/

Early-Intervention-to-Prevent-Gang-Involvement-and-Youth-Violence-A-Practical-Guide-1.pdf.

49. Mike Stein, 2011, 'The Fixation on Early Years Intervention Is Naïve', Guardian.co.uk, 11 January.
50. Gabriella Jozwiak, 2013, 'Early Intervention Funding Cut by a Further £49m', *CYPN*, 15 January; Neil Puffett, 2015, 'Early Intervention Continues to Bear the Brunt of Spending Cuts', *CYPN*, 6 July.
51. Jess Brown, 2016, 'Call for Government to Test Effectiveness of Early Intervention Work', *CYPN*, 11 July.
52. Laura McCardle, 2014c, 'Council Enlists Charities to Deliver Youth Services', *CYPN*, 9 January; Alexandra Topping, 2011, 'Youth Workers in David Cameron's Oxfordshire Base Strike Over Cuts', *Guardian*, 23 August; Neil Puffett, 2011b, 'Warwickshire to Close All But Five Youth Centres', *CYPN*, 17 June.
53. Neil Puffett, 2012, 'Youth Innovation Zones Yield Mixed Results', *CYPN*, 15 October, p. 3 (N2); Laura McCardle, 2015b, 'Councils Redeploy Youth Workers to Social Care Roles, Warns Report', *CYPN*, 12 January.
54. Eric Pickles, 2011a, 17 October, https://www.gov.uk/government/speeches/action-on-problem-families.
55. DCLG, 2016a, *The First Troubled Families Programme 2012–2015: An Overview*, October, https://www.gov.uk/government/uploads/system/uploads/attachment_data/file/560776/The_first_Troubled_Families_Programme_an_overview.pdf.
56. Eric Pickles, 2011b, 17 October, https://www.gov.uk/government/news/its-time-to-stop-leaving-problem-families-in-crisis; Lauren Higgs, 2011, 'New Government Unit to Co-ordinate Help for Troubled Families', *CYPN*, 4 October.
57. DCLG, 2016b, *National Evaluation of the Troubled Families Programme: Final Synthesis Report*, October, https://www.gov.uk/government/uploads/system/uploads/attachment_data/file/560499/Troubled_Families_Evaluation_Synthesis_Report.pdf.
58. Neil Puffett, 2018, 'Daily Roundup…Troubled Families', *CYPN*, 24 May …'.
59. Stephen Crossley, 2015, 'The Troubled Families Programme: The Perfect Social Policy?', Centre for Crime and Justice Studies, 11 November, https://www.crimeandjustice.org.uk/publications/troubled-families-programme-perfect-social-policy.

60. Neil Puffett, 2016, 'Troubled Families Programme "Has Little Impact"', *CYPN*, 18 October.
61. *Guardian*, 2016, 'Government Misled Public with 99% Success Rate Claim on Troubled Families, Say MPs', 20 December.
62. DCLG, 2017, *Supporting Disadvantaged Families: Troubled Families Programme 2015–2020: Progress so Far*, April.
63. Neil Puffett, 2012, op. cit.; Laura McCardle, 2015c, 'Councils Redeploy Youth Workers to Social Care Roles, Warns Report', *CYPN*, 12 January.
64. DCLG, 2017, *Supporting Disadvantaged Families: Troubled Families Programme 2015–2020—Progress so Far*, April, https://www.gov.uk/government/uploads/system/uploads/attachment_data/file/611991/Supporting_disadvantaged_families.pdf.
65. NYA, 2014, *Youth Services in England: Changes and Trends in Provision of Services*, NYA, November.

# Further Reading

Barnard, Hilary. 2010. *Big Society, Cuts and Consequences: A Thinkpiece*. Cass Business School. November.
Chanan, Gabriel and Miller, Colin. 2011. *The Big Society and Public Services: Complementarity or Erosion?* Paces. https://www.scribd.com/document/46256387/Big-Society-Public-Services-Press-Release.
Cooper, Charlie. 2012. 'Understanding the English "Riots" of 2011: "Mindless Criminality" or Youth "Mekin Histri" in Austerity Britain?' *Youth and Policy*. Vol. 109. September, pp. 6–26.
Crossley, Stephen. 2015. 'The Troubled Families Programme: The Perfect Social Policy?' Centre for Crime and Justice Studies. https://www.crimeandjustice.org.uk/sites/crimeandjustice.org.uk/files/The%20Troubled%20Families%20Programme%2C%20Nov%202015.pdf.
DCLG. 2016a. *The First Troubled Families Programme 2012–2015: An Overview*. October.
DCLG. 2016b. *National Evaluation of the Troubled Families Programme: Final Synthesis Report*. October.
de St Croix, Tania. 2015. 'Volunteers and Entrepreneurs? Youth Work and the Big Society', in Bright, Graham (ed), *Youth Work: Histories, Policy, Contexts*. London: Palgrave, pp. 58–79.
GOV.UK. 2011a. *Early Intervention: The Next Steps*. January.

GOV.UK. 2011b. *Early Intervention: Smart Investment, Massive Savings*. July.

Ishkanian, Armine and Szreter, Simon. 2012. *The Big Society Debate: A New Agenda for Social Welfare*. Cheltenham: Edward Elgar.

NCIA. 2014. 'How Local Is Localism? The Grassroots View'. http://legacy. independentaction.net/wp-content/uploads/sites/8/2015/12/How-Local-is-Localism-Legacy.pdf.

NCIA. 2015. 'What Now for Localism?' http://legacy.independentaction.net/ wp-content/uploads/sites/8/2015/12/What-Now-for-Localism-Legacy.pdf.

NCVYS. 2010. 'Building the Big Society: A Briefing Paper...'. May.

# 7

# Remoralising the Young

## 'Instilling Character'

One growing youth policy aspiration over the period—long a youth work preoccupation—was to develop young people's 'character'. According to a 2017 DfE report this was understood as

> ... the role that certain ... traits or attributes such as resilience, self-regulation, and emotional and social skills can play in enabling children and young people to achieve positive health, education, employment and other outcomes.[1]

In December 2014, Education Secretary Nicky Morgan outlined a 'package of measures' to provide extra funding for local authorities, voluntary, community or social enterprise organisations, or other profit or non-profit organisations for 'projects run by former armed service personnel which help turn around the lives of disadvantaged children'.[2] Most of the package's £3.5 million, however—to be increased to £6 million the following year[3]—was for 'character education' in schools.[4] Subsequently, the policy was underpinned by the findings of three evaluation and research reports: in 2015, from the University

© The Author(s) 2019
B. Davies, *Austerity, Youth Policy and the Deconstruction of the Youth Service in England*, https://doi.org/10.1007/978-3-030-03886-1_7

of Birmingham's Jubilee Centre for Character and Virtues[5]; in 2016, from Personal Development Point—a consultancy which under the strap line 'Inspire. Realise. Transform' was headed by Paul Oginsky, a 'leading thinker in youth service ... and Youth Policy Advisor to David Cameron'[6]; and in 2017, jointly from NatCen Social Research and the National Children's Bureau (NCB).[7]

In January 2016, alongside what she called 'pioneers of what excellent character education should look like', Morgan hosted the first DfE 'character symposium'. At this she expressed herself pleased that 'the debate is shifting' since 'for too long, character has been seen as "soft" and "a nice thing to do"'. Again ignoring any wider structural factors that might be limiting their achievements, she also insisted that 'character education prepares our young people for life in Britain, regardless of their background or where they grew up'. Edward Timpson, the minister 'responsible for character', also spoke at the symposium.[8]

A key element of the initiative was a 'Character Awards' scheme to 'help give schools and organisations the tools and support they need to ensure they develop well-rounded pupils to go onto to an apprenticeship, university or the world of work'.[9] The awards were particularly intended to 'support young people to develop traits that support academic attainment, are valued by employers (and) enable them to make positive contributions to British society'. Such outcomes were seen as necessary because

> ... all young people deserve opportunities to learn how to persevere and work to achieve; how to understand the importance of respect and how to show it to others; how to bounce back if faced with failure; (and) how to collaborate and build strong relationships with others at work and in their private lives.[10]

By October 2017 the think-tank Demos was also suggesting that government support was needed for 'improving the character of school pupils' in order to combat cyberbullying.[11]

In January 2014 the Chief Executive of London Youth, Rosie Ferguson, detected what she called 'emerging thinking from the Cabinet Office endors(ing) the role of youth work in the development of young people's character…'.[12] Reflecting the central place that this had long had in youth work thinking,[13] Ambition (formerly the National Association of Boys Clubs) was thus soon proactively seeking to contribute to the new government initiatives. In March 2017, it announced its participation in a 'character research workshop' which, it said, had come out of ongoing joint work with the Home Office. Focusing on the current evidence on character, its starting premises were 'that certain character traits are strongly linked with offending, for example impulsivity (lack of self-control) and lack of empathy'; and that such traits, though 'not necessarily innate', could have been affected by negative early-years experiences. The workshop was also to provide 'an opportunity to explore adolescent cognitive development and how this can affect decision making'.[14] Shortly before merging with Ambition in 2016 (see Chapter 14), UK Youth (formerly the National Association of Mixed Clubs) had also been involved an 'expert seminar' on 'character' partly sponsored by the Home Office.[15]

## Nurturing 'Wellbeing'

In a widely publicised speech in November 2010 David Cameron announced another of his 'flagship' policies—to

> …start measuring our progress as a country, not just by how our economy is growing, but by how our lives are improving; not just by our standard of living, but by our quality of life.

This, he said, would take very seriously people's immediate personal concerns such as 'going out in the evening and shopping at the weekend'.[16]

This commitment—a key measure of what his government was doing 'to create a more family-friendly country'—injected into the political discourse the concepts of 'wellbeing' and 'happiness'. According to the founder of the children's charity Whizz Kidz, the latter 'isn't really about feeling good – it's about being good': a condition which encouraged 'generosity – and caring for others'.[17] Here again, therefore, the structural inequalities constraining people's lives were treated as, at most, secondary; or, when they were considered, were formulated in such abstract and macro terms as 'getting the economy moving'.[18]

To operationalise the concept of 'wellbeing', in April 2011 the Office for National Statistics (ONS) was allocated research funding—rumoured to be £2 million—to gather data for an 'index on happiness'. Each year between 2011 and 2015 large samples of UK those over 16 were asked four 'well-being' questions:

- Overall, how satisfied are you with your life nowadays?
- Overall, to what extent do you feel the things you do in your life are worthwhile?
- Overall, how happy did you feel yesterday?
- Overall, how anxious did you feel yesterday?

Amongst the evidence that emerged was that health, relationships and employment were all factors which contributed to personal well-being. However, an acknowledgement that the circumstances of each local authority area needed to be taken in account also suggested that broader social and economic conditions might also be influential factors.[19]

By 2012, 'wellbeing' had been inserted into the title of the statutory guidance on the 2006 Education and Inspections Act, making it a specified element of the intended 'improvement' for young people and one feature of 'youth work and other services and activities'. For implementing these, local authorities were required to take the strategic lead in working with, amongst others, the Health and Wellbeing Boards which, as a key element of the Cameron-inspired National Wellbeing Programme, were established by legislation in April 2013.[20]

By then Loughton, as 'children's' minister, had made an attempt to connect the youth work field directly with the government's 'wellbeing' objectives. At an NYA-organised event at the 2011 Conservative Party Conference, he predicted that the Boards would become 'a very significant player', including for those working with young people.

There will be resources for lots of activities to combat dangerous behaviours around teenagers. At last we will be able to have a better link between health, local authorities and the voluntary sector around everything from binge drinking and mental health to sexual health and teenage pregnancy.[21]

A rather different picture emerged, however, from a paper from the independent Kings' Fund published soon after the Boards were established. Their powers, it pointed out, were limited and, in the absence of any formal statutory guidance, their role was far from clear. A danger existed, therefore, of unrealistic expectations of what they could deliver and how quickly.[22]

A £6 million programme funded by the Paul Hamlyn Trust between 2009 and 2014 and run jointly with the Mental Health Foundation did use a range of youth work approaches in four areas 'to support the mental wellbeing of young people in the UK aged 16–25'.[23] However, a paper on improving young people's health and wellbeing published by Public Health England and the Association for Young People's Health in January 2015 provided little evidence that Loughton's promise was being fulfilled. It contained just one reference to youth workers and only a very general one to the need for 'youth services', with other council services, to 'demonstrate a shared culture of values about supporting positive youth development'.[24] In this period, growing mental health problems amongst young people were identified, leaving mental health services' struggling to respond (see Chapters 1 and 18).

# The 'Prevent' Strategy—Updated

Other than being refocused in 2011 on twenty five local areas identified as at greatest risk of 'extremism', much of the 'Prevent' strategy inherited from Labour (see Chapter 2) initially remained in place under the Coalition government. Between 2007 and 2012, for example, Channel, the Home Office programme for 15–24 year olds seen as at risk of involvement in extremist activity, received 2500 referrals, of whom over 500 went through the scheme. By 2014 the number of referrals had risen by 1681 and in 2015 rose again by nearly 4000.[25]

The murder of the soldier Lee Rigby in May 2013 opened up a new national debate on 'Muslim extremism', leading to the creation of an 'extremism taskforce' chaired by David Cameron himself. Each government department was required to report on what it was doing to prevent extremism and make practical suggestions for action.[26] A Counter-Terrorism and Security Act passed two years later placed a legal duty on 'specified authorities … to have due regard to the need to prevent people from being drawn into terrorism'. The statutory guidance on the Act made it clear that schools, childcare providers, the Youth Justice Board and youth offending teams were all expected 'to assess the risk of children being drawn into terrorism, including support for extremist ideas that are part of terrorist ideology'.[27] Similar duties were placed on higher education and further education institutions. As the effects of these new policies were felt, too, by youth workers and organisations working with Muslim young people,[28] in the summer of 2016 the Home Office announced a £1.5 million 'innovations fund' to support projects seeking to prevent especially young people's 'radicalisation'. This was open to, amongst others, community and voluntary groups and out-of-school settings.[29]

As it had under New Labour, the new strategy remained controversial. It was seen as posing a threat to freedom of debate on controversial political issues as well as, by stealth, creating a 'surveillance state' implemented by professionals such as doctors, teachers and university lecturers.[30] With many Muslim and non-Muslim organisations and individuals—particularly young people—still experiencing Prevent as demonising, discriminatory and oppressive, the new legislative was also criticised for adding to Muslims' feelings of alienation and disillusion and so as counter-productive. In June 2017, one Muslim youth organisations thus refused to take Prevent money because, it said, 'young British Muslims find it very toxic'.[31]

Muslims were critical of the strategy, too, because by 2016 only 10% of referrals nationally had been for right wing extremism,[32] with the first trials for anti-Muslim statements and activities only taking place in early 2018.[33] For these communities, therefore, not only was the strategy failing to confront some very threatening organisations. Its overwhelming focus on Muslims was also seen still as encouraging attacks on them and their institutions, including mosques.

Prevent's reliance on largely 'separatist' approaches to the Muslim communities was to some extent also challenged towards the end of 2016 by a report by Louise Casey, a long-standing government adviser who had previously headed its Troubled Families Unit. This high-lighted how, in areas which had experienced the most rapid population changes, all governments—Labour, Coalition and Conservative—had failed to prioritise 'integration' and (reviving a term which by then seemed to have passed its use-by date) 'social cohesion'.

The credibility of her report was to some extent undermined, how-ever, by its again disproportionate concentration on Muslims and their communities which attracted 249 references compared with just fourteen to Polish communities and other growing immigrants groups. The report also again was seen as blaming most of the problems and tensions it documented on Muslims themselves. In acknowledging the 'clear link between the level of English spoken and the level of quali-fications attained', for example, Casey chastised Muslims for failing to improve their English—though without recording the Coalition's 50% cut of £400 million in 2011 to the adult skills budget out of which classes in English as a second language were funded.[34]

In the aftermath of Lee Rigby's murder, Labour Party leader Ed Miliband had pointed to the need for earlier intervention to pre-vent Muslim young people being 'radicalised'. He referred specifically to youth workers in Woolwich where Rigby had been killed who, he said, had identified 'the link between violent extremism and gang-re-lated activity'.[35] Other evidence indicated that 'Prevent (had) worked with large number of young people nationally, often through youth work organisations and methods'.[36] According Bradford's Youth Service manager, for example, youth workers there, working with schools and the police, had been helping young people 'develop the critical think-ing skills to empower them to make more informed choices'. The city's YMCA had also concentrated on encouraging understanding between faiths and ethnicities.[37]

Though their concerns about the effectiveness of the Prevent strategy were dismissed by the Home Office minister responsible, by early 2017 MPs, too, were calling for its overhaul, particularly by adopting less stigmatising ways of engaging with Muslim young people.[38] In the highly fraught aftermath of 'terror' attacks in London and Manchester later that year, youth workers were being identified as 'central' to implementing these approaches, with the leader of Plaid Cymru in Wales suggesting during the 2017 general election campaign that the UK was 'less safe' because there were fewer youth workers engaging with young people.[39]

However, where they did exist, such approaches continued to be overshadowed by the Prevent strategy's preoccupation with working with Muslim young people largely in isolation. Not only did this result in some white young people and their often 'deprived' communities seeing Prevent as another example of minority groups getting government money while their needs were being ignored. The programme—which in mid-2018 was given continued unqualified support by the new Home Secretary Sajid Javid[40]—also at least implicitly blamed the young people for their 'wrong' attitudes and beliefs. By contrast, youth workers working with sexually abused young people in Rotherham had a decade or more earlier started from the premise they were meeting a highly vulnerable section of the population who were being groomed by powerful and manipulating adults. For them, therefore, the workers' first tasks were assumed to be listening to the young people and then acting on what they were saying.[41]

According to a 2017 DfE-commissioned research report, even within child protection services this was still 'an uncomfortable area of practice for some staff' whose confidence was influenced by whether there was an 'internal consensus' within children's services on how to respond.[42] For identifying appropriate and helpful responses to Muslim young people touched by 'radicalising' influences, such a debate seemed barely to have begun.

## Separate Policies; Shared Ideological Drivers

At points the Prevent strategy did break with neo-liberal governments' predominately individualistic ways of defining social problems. Emphasis was put repeatedly, for example, on the importance of 'communities' and—albeit usually without acknowledging how governments' own actions might have contributed to current threats—on the influence of global events on attitudes and behaviours within them. However, attention and indeed action—especially state action—was consistently and far from accidentally diverted away from what even the government, in its language, termed the 'enormous social mobility challenge' holding back young Muslims 'from reaching their full potential at every stage of their lives'.[43]

The influence of these kinds of structural factors on the other policies outlined in this and the previous chapter was similarly limited. The focus of Cameron's notion of Britain as a 'broken' or 'sick' society, for example, offered no critique of the systemic inequalities resulting from many young people's poor educational opportunities, low wages, job insecurity and limited housing options, all often exacerbated by gender, race, disability and indeed age discrimination. For him and his government the causes lay entirely in the attitudes and actions of a failing underclass made up of individuals and their 'troubled' families or of 'radicalised' communities. All were expected to take first responsibility for both changing their current circumstances and preventing any longer-term negative 'outcomes'. Interventions, therefore, had to be 'targeted' at the deficiencies of these citizens in as 'scientific' a way as possible in order to behaviourally adjust and socially engineer them into more conforming and economically productive ways of behaving.

This was true, too, even of programmes with titles ('character building'; 'wellbeing') which suggested more optimistic perspectives, and also of those ('Big Society'; 'Localism') which seemed focused on more collective responses. As well as being 'community' based and often small scale, these, too, skirted round any possible need for wider societal change, relying ultimately on nurturing those individualistic traits defined, within narrowly set societal boundaries, as constituting 'character'.

These often at least implicitly victim-blaming assumptions shaped the neo-liberal hoops through which, in this period, local authority Youth Services and their youth work provision were also required to jump if they were to have any chance of winning central government support. The constantly reiterated need to 'balance the budget' was, from 2010 on, a bottom-line cause of their decimation. Crucial too, however, was the view amongst policy-makers—from their perspective not wholly misplaced—that a Service so unashamedly committed to enabling young people to negotiate relevant 'outcomes' as <u>they</u> defined them could not be trusted to 'deliver' neo-liberalism's taken-for-granted expectations and requirements.

Even under New Labour this gap in perspectives and expectations had been widening. As the policy priorities outlined in last two chapters took hold, in the period after the 2007–2008 financial crisis it came to seem less and less bridgeable.

# Notes

1. NatCen Social Research and NCB Research and Policy Team, 2017, *Developing Character Skills in Schools: Summary Report*, DfE/ Government Social Research, August, p. 3.
2. GOV.UK, 2014, 'Measures to Help Schools Instil Character in Pupils Announced', 8 December, https://www.gov.uk/government/ news/measures-to-help-schools-instil-character-in-pupils-announced.
3. Jess Brown, 2016, 'DfE Increases "Character" Funding to £6m', *CYPN*, 27 May.
4. GOV.UK, 2014, 'Measures to Help Schools Instil Character…', op. cit.
5. James Arthur, et al., 2015, *Character Education in UK Schools*, Jubilee Centre for Character and Virtues/University of Birmingham, February.
6. Personal Development Point website, http://www.pdpuk.com/2016/04/15/ pdp-conference-2016/.
7. NatCen Social Research and NCB Research and Policy Team, 2017, op. cit.
8. Nicky Morgan, 2016, 'Nicky Morgan Open Character Symposium at Floreat School', 21 January.
9. Laura McCardle, 2015, 'DfE to Fund School Character-Building Projects', *CYPN*, 7 January.
10. GOV.UK, 2016, 'News Story: Awards Launched for Schools Best at Instilling Character', 12 April.
11. Neil Puffett, 2017a, 'DfE Urged to Reinvigorate Character Drive to Combat Cyberbullying', *CYPN*, 2 October.

12. Rosie Ferguson, 2014, 'The 2014 Report: Youth Work', *CYPN*, 7 January.
13. See for example Basil Henriques, 1937, *Club Leadership*, London, Oxford University Press, p. 1.
14. Ambition Policy Newsletter Number 15, December 2016.
15. UK Youth, 2016, 'Character, Circumstances, Crime and Criminal Careers', http://members-events.ukyouth.org/member/detail/51/1517216400000.
16. GOV.UK, 2010, 'PM Speech on Wellbeing', 25 November, https://www.gov.uk/government/speeches/pm-speech-on-wellbeing; Cabinet Office, Department of Health, DCLG, Department for Work and Pensions, 2013, 'National Wellbeing', https://www.gov.uk/government/collections/national-wellbeing.
17. Mike Dickson, 2011, 'What Makes People Happy?', *The Big Issue*, 24 January.
18. GOV.UK, 2010, 'PM Speech on Wellbeing', op. cit.; Cabinet Office, et al., 2013, op. cit.
19. Office for National Statistics, 2016, *Statistical Bulletin: Personal Well-Being in the UK: Local Authority Update, 2015 to 2016*, https://www.ons.gov.uk/peoplepopulationandcommunity/wellbeing/bulletins/measuringnationalwellbeing/localauthorityupdate2015to2016#background-notes.
20. DfE, 2012, 'Statutory Guidance to Local Authorities on Services and Activities to Improve Young People's Well-being', DfE, June, para. 2e, 4.
21. Lauren Higgs, 2011, 'Conservative Conference 2011: Wellbeing Boards to Be a "Significant Player" in Youth Service Provision', *CYPN*, 3 October.
22. The King's Fund, 2016, 'Health and Wellbeing Boards (HWB) Explained', 22 June, https://www.kingsfund.org.uk/topics/integrated-care/health-wellbeing-boards-explained.
23. Paul Hamlyn Foundation, undated, 'Right Here: How to … Promote Mental Health Wellbeing in Youth Work Practice', http://www.phf.org.uk/reader/right-promote-mental-wellbeing-youth-work-practice/guide-needed/.
24. Public Health England/Association for Young People's Health, 2015, *Improving Young People's Health and Wellbeing*, https://www.gov.uk/government/uploads/system/uploads/attachment_data/file/399391/20150128_YP_HW_Framework_FINAL_WP__3_.pdf, pp. 5, 17, 23.

25. Gabriella Jozwiak, 2013, 'Projects to Prevent Extremism in Young People Under the Spotlight', *CYPN*, 25 June; Josh Halliday, 2016, 'Almost 4000 People Referred to UK Deradicalisation Scheme Last Year', *Guardian*, 20 March.
26. Gabriella Jozwiak, 2013, op. cit.
27. DfE, 2015, *The Prevent Duty: Departmental Advice for Schools and Child Care Providers*, DfE, June, https://www.gov.uk/government/uploads/system/uploads/attachment_data/file/439598/prevent-duty-departmental-advice-v6.pdf.
28. Paul Thomas, 2018, 'The Challenges for British Youth Workers of Government Strategies to "Prevent Terrorism"', in Alldred, Pam, et al. (eds), *The Sage Handbook of Youth Work Practice*, London, Sage, pp. 369–383.
29. Jes Brown, 2016, 'Innovation Fund Opens for Anti-radicalisation Projects', *CYPN*, 30 August.
30. CAGE, 2013, *The Prevent Strategy: A Cradle to the Grave Police State*, CAGE, https://www.scribd.com/document/207085039/The-PREVENT-Strategy-A-Cradle-to-Grave-Police-State; Ian Cobain, 2016, 'UK's Prevent Counter-Radicalisation Policy "Badly Flawed"', *Guardian*, 19 October; Karma Nabulsi, 2017, 'Don't Go to the Doctor', *London Review of Books*, Vol. 39, No. 10, 18 May, pp. 27–28.
31. Joe Lepper, 2017a, 'Muslim Youth Group Criticises "Toxic" Prevent Strategy', *CYPN*, 7 June.
32. Press Association, 2016, 'Anti-extremism Scheme Reports Rise of Far Right', *Guardian*, 27 December.
33. Lizzie Dearden, 2018, 'Jayden Fransen: Britain First's Deputy Leader to Face Trial Over "Threatening" Belfast Speech on Islam', *Independent*, 9 January.
34. Louise Casey, 2016, *The Casey Review: A Review into Opportunity and Integration*, DCLG, December, para. 6.56, https://www.gov.uk/government/uploads/system/uploads/attachment_data/file/575973/The_Casey_Review_Report.pdf; Alan Travis, 2016, 'Louise Casey's Integration Plan Behind the Times', *Guardian*, 5 December; Anushka Asthana and Peter Walker, 2016, 'Casey Review Raises Alarm Over Social Integration in the UK', *Guardian*, 5 December.
35. Gabriella Jozwiak, 2013, op. cit.
36. Paul Thomas, 2013, 'Expert View', *CYPN*, 25 June.
37. Gabriella Jozwiak, 2013, op. cit.

38. Joe Lepper, 2017b, 'MPs Call for Counter-Terrorism Overhaul to Better Engage Young People', *CYPN*, 6 February.
39. Neil Puffett, 2017b, 'Youth Work Central to Combating Terrorism, Former Chief Prosecutor Says', *CYPN*, 5 June; Neil Puffett, 2017c, 'How Youth Work Can Play a Pivotal Role in Combating Radicalisation', *CYPN*, 29 June.
40. Nina Jacobs, 2018, 'Government to Retain Controversial Prevent Anti-radicalisation Programme', *CYPN*, 4 June.
41. Alexis Jay, 2014, *Independent Inquiry into Child Sexual Exploitation in Rotherham, 1991–2013*, Rotherham Metropolitan Borough Council, August.
42. Nina Jacobs, 2017, 'Practitioners Lack Confidence in Tackling Radicalisation, Study Reveals', *CYPN*, 8 August.
43. Social Mobility Commission, 2017, 'Young Muslims in the UK Face Enormous Social Mobility Barriers', GOV.UK.

# Further Reading

Belton, Brian. 2015. 'Questioning "Muslim Youth": Categorization and Marginalization', in Bright, Graham (ed), *Youth Work: Histories, Policy, Contexts*. London: Palgrave, pp. 161–181.
Casey, L. 2016. *The Casey Review: A Review into Opportunity and Integration*. London: DCLG. December.
James, A., et al. 2015. *Character Education in UK Schools*. Jubilee Centre for Character and Virtues/University of Birmingham.
Khan, M. G. 2013. *Young Muslims, Pedagogy and Islam: Contexts and Concepts*. Bristol: Policy Press.
NatCen Social Research and the National Children's Bureau Research and Policy Team. 2017. *Developing Character Skills in Schools: Summary Report*. DfE/Government Social Research.
Public Health England/Association for Young People's Health. 2015. *Improving Young People's Health and Wellbeing*. London: Public Health England.
Thomas, Paul. 2018. 'The Challenges for British Youth Workers of Government Strategies to "Prevent Terrorism"', in Alldred, Pam, et al. (eds). *The Sage Handbook of Youth Work Practice*. London: Sage, pp. 369–383.

# 8

# Parliamentary Scrutiny

## Remit and Process

In June 2011 the Commons Education Select Committee, advised by the former NYA Chief Executive Tom Wylie,[1] reported on its inquiry into 'services for young people'.[2] The government's response in September[3] prompted a second Committee report a month later on the grounds that 'a number of our recommendations have been only partially addressed'.[4] A second government's response to this was released in January 2012.[5]

The Committee had announced its inquiry, focused on 'services beyond the school/college day for young people primarily ...aged 13-25', in October 2010, six months after the Coalition came into office. It set as its brief to examine and recommend on:

- The relationship between universal and targeted services;
- How services for young people can meet the Government priorities for volunteering, including the role of the National Citizen Service;

© The Author(s) 2019
B. Davies, *Austerity, Youth Policy and the Deconstruction of the Youth Service in England*, https://doi.org/10.1007/978-3-030-03886-1_8

- Which young people access the services, what they want from those services and their role in shaping them;
- The relative roles of the voluntary, community, statutory and private sectors…;
- The training and workforce development needs of the sector;
- The impact of public sector cuts on funding and commissioning of services, including how available resources can best be maximised, and whether payment by results is desirable and achievable;
- How local government structures and statutory frameworks impact on service provision; and
- How the value and effectiveness of services could be assessed.[6]

In highlighting a range of specific youth policy issues facing the new government, this remit started from some influential policy assumptions. One—that volunteering and in particular the NCS would have a central role in future youth provision—justified a Committee visit to Berlin 'to investigate the reasons for Germany's strong rates of youth volunteering and engagement'.[7] Another was that commissioning would in future be a main route for allocating funding, with private businesses having a significant role as 'providers'.

Over nine months the Committee interviewed five groups of 'witnesses', including Tim Loughton and the Cabinet Office Minister for Civil Society, Nick Hurd. It also received 158 written submissions and ran online 'discussion threads' to gather young people's views.[8]

## Open Access or Targeted?

In the Introduction to its first report, the Committee provided definitions of both 'the Youth Service' and of youth work,[9] in the process acknowledging that 'a core principle' of 'universal' (or, as it chose to call it, 'open access') provision was that 'young people involve themselves by choice'.[10] It recognised too, however, that the government's position was that (other than through NCS) 'public funds should be refocused on targeted interventions'[11] and that therefore there was likely to be 'a prioritisation of public funds for disadvantaged young people, and of targeted services over open access ones.'[12] In recording the fall in the proportion of the Youth Service's open access provision over the ten years to 2010 from 90% to 'about 50% to 60%', it quoted evidence from one witness that one council had already decided to close all its open access facilities.[13]

The Committee did quote witnesses, including Loughton, who—not least because of public funding cuts—favoured prioritising targeted work or ensuring that this operated in tandem with open access provision.[14] However, though often framing it as New Labour's 'positive activities', the Committee made a strong case for open access provision, drawing on young people's evidence of 'the tremendous impact' this could have. While accepting that 'when public funding is limited priority may be given to services which support the most disadvantaged', it therefore set as 'an important point of principle' that

> ... youth services should primarily be to offer positive activities and (about) enriching personal and social experiences and not solely ... seen as a mechanism to divert young people from misbehaviour. This is especially important given that 85% of young people's time is spent outside formal education...

Referring to its evidence 'that open-access services can sometimes be as effective as targeted ones in reaching those young people', it also urged local authorities when commissioning services '(to) recognise that an open-access service could be more appropriate than a targeted one for improving certain outcomes for young people'.[15] To support this, it proposed that the Government, after taking young people's views into account, '... announce publicly its intention to retain the statutory duty on local authorities to secure their access to sufficient educational and recreational leisure-time activities'.[16]

The Committee also explicitly adopted a 'contrary' view to Loughton's comment 'that spending of £350 million per year - equating to around £77 per young person aged 13 to 19 - on youth services in England equates to "large slugs of public money"'. Instead, it 'congratulate(d) the sector for its longstanding dexterity in making limited resources go a long way and for continuing to support young people despite reliance on a patchwork of different funds'.[17]

## 'Measuring Value and Impact'

Some of the Committee's other conclusions and recommendations, however were much more challenging for both open access youth work and local authority Youth Services. Having received 'a huge amount of persuasive anecdotal and personal evidence about the value that services can have for young people'—not least the 30 out of 55 young people's postings on its on-line forum which 'praised the importance of youth clubs'[18]—it had, it said, 'little doubt that good youth work can have a transformative effect on young people's lives'.[19] The Committee also accepted 'that the outcomes of individual youth work relationships can be hard to quantify and that the impact of encounters with young people may take time to become clear and be complex'. All this, therefore, made it 'hard to reject the basic tenet expounded by a range of youth service representatives and young people themselves that "you know good youth work when you see it"'.[20] Its review of a number of 'external evaluations' and 'research studies' also included a carefully balanced paragraph on the Feinstein research into young people's participation in leisure time activities which, by implication, chastised past New Labour ministers for misrepresenting its findings[21] (see Chapter 3).

However, calling the available research 'limited and somewhat outdated',[22] the Committee admitted that its investigations had been 'plagued' by difficulties in finding 'objective evidence of the impact of services'.[23] This had left it 'frustrated in (its) efforts to uncover a robust outcome measurement framework … (to) allow services to be compared in order to assess their relative impact'.[24] It was also therefore alarmed 'that the Department for Education is expecting local authorities to make spending decisions on the basis of such poor data about what services are being provided, let alone which are effective'.[25] However, according to the chair, the Committee's frustration had been fuelled, too, by the failure of the senior voluntary sector managers interviewed 'to make a better fist of the difference you make'. Though the individuals concerned defended their contributions, some in the youth work field did subsequently agree 'that the organisations chosen to represent the sector … did not make a strong enough case for the value of youth services'.[26]

Though the report acknowledged that it wanted 'to guard against inappropriate or distorting measures like simple head counting', one Committee recommendation, framed in a section title 'Identifying successful services: measuring value and impact', was for a university-led 'meta analysis of studies relating to the impact and effectiveness of youth services'.[27] More generally it concluded, too, that 'with a tight spending settlement and an increase in commissioning ... it is essential that publicly funded services are able to demonstrate what difference they make to young people'.[28]

For the kinds of open access youth work it had affirmed earlier in its report, these recommendations were likely to prove seriously constraining. In particular, in concluding that 'there is no good reason why robust but sophisticated outcome measures should not be developed', it welcomed the government's decision to commission NCVYS 'to deliver an outcomes framework for application across the sector' (see Chapter 14). It also pointed to the New Philanthropy Capital 'wellbeing index' which, it said, offered 'a good template for initial consideration'.[29]

## Finding and Funding 'Providers': From Commissioning to Payment by Results

One of the Committee's conclusions was that, though 'the Government appeared not to have a detailed view of where local authorities were making disproportionate cuts',[30] according to its own assessment these were 'being applied ... to "salami slice" youth services, where they were continuing at all', rather than on the basis of need.[31] Its evidence also showed that charities and the private sector were reluctant to fill the gaps left by this loss of statutory funding.

Nonetheless it proposed that 'services ... redouble their efforts to leverage in ... philanthropic and charitable funds and private sector investment' and that the Government and local authorities '... broker partnerships' with these alternative funders.[32] In response to a government whose 'youth' minister had told it that 'funding decisions are not made by us, they are made by local authorities',[33] the Committee also suggested that 'in setting out its strategic vision ... (the government) should indicate its expectations of the range and standards of youth services which should be available across the country'.[34] It also proposed it use its powers to direct local authorities failing to meet their statutory duty to commission adequate provision.[35]

Not only did this last recommendation assume that the local authorities cuts were unavoidable. It also took it as a given that such services, rather than being provided directly by local authorities, would be contracted out. CHYPS's evidence did at least argue for 'a mixed economy of voluntary and local authority direct delivered services'. This however was almost enthusiastically contradicted by the head of a large county Youth Service who, in giving uncritical support to the Committee's position, assured it that his local authority 'could save money without "reduc(ing) services, outputs, or the hours of youth work that are delivered on the ground"'. Similar assurances were given by NYA's Fiona Blacke[36]—followed a year later by a 'practical guide', *Involving Young People in Commissioning*,[37] which at no point asked young people to consider whether commissioning was the only funding option.

The Committee held to this stance even though it received evidence that commissioning 'would favour big providers'[38] and that 'commissioning against specific outcomes could be to the detriment of young people's overall development'.[39] However, while emphasising the need for a strong young people 'voice' in shaping services, it ultimately 'support(ed) the broad principle that local authorities should primarily become strategic commissioners rather than simply the default providers of youth services'. Quoting examples of work in progress, it also endorsed the dominant 'truths' of the time: that 'to make significant savings local authorities will need to consider radical options - for instance, converting entire youth services departments into social enterprises ... or handing management of youth centres to the voluntary sector'.[40]

When considering how youth services might be funded in this new environment, a sub-section of the report examined the pros and cons of payment by results and the related use of social impact bonds (see Chapter 4). It eventually concluded that these were not suitable for funding youth services, 'particularly open access ones'. This was supported by an associate director of the consultancy Social Finance which described itself as a 'partner with government, social sector and the financial community to find better solutions to society's most difficult problems'. On social bonds, he argued:

> If government was sufficiently convinced that numbers of heads coming through the doors of a youth centre … was indicative of future benefit to the public sector, then arguably they'd be prepared to pay it. My guess is that they would not be prepared for that.[41]

The Committee nonetheless decided that there was scope for a form of impact bond which would 'encourage social investment in a basket of outcomes for young people in a local area'. It also recommended a 'feasibility study on such a system', while adding the somewhat optimistic caveat that 'the government bear … in mind that it should be in addition to current spending on youth services, not an alternative'.[42] Here as at other points, it thus chose to ignore ministers' repeated refusal to direct or even seek to influence local authority policy-making on youth provision (see Chapter 9).

This was only one example of the Committee's search for compromises which might enable open access youth work and local authority Youth Services to survive. On the one hand, it offered positive and often principled arguments and evidence in their defence. On the other, it settled for some pragmatic responses to the anti-state/pro-private sector ideology driving government policies generally; to the deep budget cuts already decimating local Youth Services; and to ministerial scepticism about the role and practice of these Services. Subsequent events were to show, too, that its more supportive 'take' on youth work would in the long run be overridden by policy-makers' increasing reliance on commissioning, measuring outcomes and payment by results, to all of which it had to vary degrees given its endorsement.

## Debating the Report

Out of the exchanges between government and the Committee over the next six months, some areas of consensus emerged:

- Both agreed on the use of the term 'open access' rather than 'universal' services—on the not unimportant grounds that this clarified their distinction from 'targeted' provision.[43]
- Both acknowledged the weakness of 'research evidence for effective youth services', 'the need for a common outcomes framework for the sector'[44] and that 'concerns about the quality of commissioning practice persist'.[45] In making its own case on these issues, the government gave repeated support to, for example, the work of the NCVYS-led work on an appropriate 'outcomes framework'. It also highlighted the suggested establishment of a Centre for Excellence and Outcomes in Children and Young People's Services and a Centre for Analysis of Youth Transitions.[46]
- Agreement existed, too, on the need 'to retain the statutory duty on local authorities to secure young people's access to sufficient educational and recreational leisure-time activities'. The government promised '"much shorter updated guidance" to reflect its forthcoming policy statement'[47] *Positive for Youth* (see Chapter 9). In its second response it also agreed to act on an OFSTED suggestion that local authorities publish their own 'local offer of services to young people'.[48]

On a range of other issues, however, the Committee and the government differed, sometimes sharply.

## The Primary Purpose of Government Funding for Youth Services[49] and the Priority to Be Given to Open Access Provision[50]

Two of the government's starting propositions were that

> … a large majority of young people receive the opportunities and support they need from their families, friends and the wider community or from school and college.

- and that therefore

> …the primary purpose of publicly funded services for young people is to work with a minority of young people[51]

This made unreservedly explicit what was in youth policy statements usually only implicit: that little if any public money needed to be or would be available for the non-school/non-work related activities of the overwhelming majority of the age group.

By implication this position was also underlined by the government's rationale for spending on 'youth services'—to:

- make sure young people at risk of dropping out of learning or not achieving their full potential engage and attain in education or training;
- develop young people's resilience to engagement in risky behaviour; help prevent involvement in crime or substance misuse; and reduce the risk of teenage pregnancy and other poor outcomes...; and
- provide opportunities, for those who wouldn't otherwise have them, to develop the personal and social skills and qualities they need for learning, work and their transition to adulthood....[52]

These priorities were underpinned by a repeated emphasis on 'intervening early to address problematic behaviours...'[53] (see Chapter 6).

In its second report the Committee sought to distance itself from these aims. In the process it by implication reiterated its commitment to open access facilities which it justified not just for targeting labelled problematic groups but as valuable in their own right and, for many young people, on their terms. It for example noted that, 'somewhat at odds' with the government's position, its conclusion was

… that the purpose should be to "offer positive activities and enriching personal and social experiences and not solely to be seen as a mechanism to divert young people from misbehaviour".[54]

The Committee also pointed out that the government had itself agreed that

… open access services such as youth clubs and youth centres can be non-stigmatising settings in which to identify and engage young people who need more intensive or specialist support, and an important means of integrating such young people into mainstream activities.[55]

It reminded the government, too, that:

> ... a mix of open access and targeted services were the ones most appreci-
> ated by young people and their families or carers, and that specialist ser-
> vices co-located in open access settings can address concerns around the
> stigma which might otherwise be attached to accessing these services.[56]

## The Government's Role in Directing or Influencing Local Authorities' Youth Provision and Ensuring That They Meet Their Statutory Duties

In noting that 'a number of the Committee's ... recommendations go
against the principle of local flexibility', the government's first response
again insisted that 'local areas are best placed to make decisions' and
that therefore 'it will not prescribe the range or type of services that
should be provided in order to meet statutory duties'.[57] It made specific
reference to its Localism Bill then going through Parliament (see
Chapter 6) which, it said, would

> ... give voluntary and community bodies, local authority employees
> wishing to form a mutual to deliver a service, and parish councils more
> opportunities to take over running services for which local authorities are
> currently responsible.[58]

Unmoved, the Committee however recommended that

> ... *the Government set out grounds on which it will judge a local
> authority to have failed to provide sufficient services, and in what
> ways Ministers will act to secure improvement in such circumstances.
> In this context, we underline our finding that some local author-
> ity youth services have already closed altogether.*[59] (Emphasis in the
> original)

The government, however, was equally unbending. It was not aware,
it said, 'of any local authority that has ceased to commission services

for young people'—a comment which not only failed to address the point the Committee was making but, by talking broadly of 'services for young people', deliberately avoided acknowledging that some local authorities were closing or threatening to close all their open access youth facilities (see Chapter 5).

Again, too, the government insisted:

> It is a matter for councils to decide which services can be made available with little or no public funding and which need to be commissioned with public funding. It is also for them to decide whether the particular services they do decide to fund, such as youth work, are delivered directly or via funding third parties. The Government will not deem councils to be failing against their duties simply because they decide not to commission an in-house youth service.[60]

Though conceding that 'Ministers ... will act to secure improvement where there is evidence of significant or long-standing failure', the government's strategy was later even more explicitly stated as:

> Ministers want(ing) to see a decisive shift in accountability for service improvement away from central Government towards self-driven improvement by local authorities themselves, supported by the sector.[61]

## Levels of Public Funding for the Youth Service—And/Or 'Youth Services'?

Having had 'great difficulty in securing a reliable figure for public spending on youth services across the country', the Committee had estimated in its first report that for 2009–2010 this had been £350 million.[62] Again ignoring the shift of focus away from 'the Youth Service' and open access youth work, the government however insisted that:

> (This) does not represent a complete view of the spending on services for young people (which) have been pooled within the Early Intervention Grant ... as it excludes a number of additional funding streams.[63]

After the Committee had pointed out that this claim had been made without any supporting figures, the detail in the government second response again made clear that its overwhelming priority for any such public expenditure was to target at-risk groups. Though its list did find a place for 'positive activities', the provision on which local authorities were said to be spending 'significant sums' included 'information, advice and guidance; teenage pregnancy; substance misuse and discretionary support for young people'. On this basis, the government proposed a 'gross spend by local authorities on services for young people in 2009-10 of £1,104m'.[64]

Embedded therefore in these exchanges was that more fundamental debate about which facilities and services were to be considered when spending patterns were being analysed. For the Committee, it seemed, specific attention still needed to be given to local authority Youth Services whose mandate, in partnership with their voluntary sector, was to provide open access youth work. For the government, however, this no longer seemed a priority—or even an intention. Its focus was on 'youth services' or 'services for young people', many (even most) of whose work would target named categories of at-risk young people. Indeed on this the government was only reaffirming its position that all local authority spend on services for young people needed to be taken into account and not just spending on the Youth Service.

## Should a 'Common Outcomes Framework' Be Applied Nationally?

The Committee also differed from the government on the use and application of a common framework of outcomes for the youth sector. Both agreed that this was needed, with the government demonstrating its commitment to it in a very material way through its funding for the NCVYS Catalyst consortium (see Chapter 14).[65] However, in order as always to avoid 'creating any new burdens on local areas',[66] the government rejected the Committee's suggestion that such a framework should eventually be imposed on all local authorities.

# Missed Opportunities; Reinforced Policy Assumptions

The Select Committee's reports provided the last close Parliamentary scrutiny of youth services until 2018 when an All Party Group launched an enquiry into youth work.[67] By raising for public debate a range of key challenges facing the youth sector, the Committee forced the government into more public positions on its thinking and future plans. However, the determination of this potentially influential body to balance supportive defence with pragmatic accommodation of the government's ideological and policy stances resulted in an important missed opportunity for providing a principled and sustained defence of local authority Youth Services and their youth work practice.

# Notes

1. Andy Hillier, 2011, 'Tom Wyle Appointed Adviser to Education Select Committee', *CYPN*, 3 February.
2. House of Commons Education Committee (HoCEC), 2011a, *Services for Young People: Third Report of Session 2010–12, Volume 1*, London, Stationery Office, 23 June.
3. House of Commons Education Committee (HoCEC), 2011b, *Services for Young People: The Government Response*, September.
4. House of Commons Education Committee (HoCEC), 2011c, *Services for Young People: Sixth Report of Session 2010–12*, October.
5. House of Commons Education Committee (HoCEC), 2012, *Services for Young People …: Government Response to the Committee's Sixth Report of Session 2010–12*, January.
6. HoCEC, 2011a, op. cit., para. 1.
7. HoCEC, 2011a, op. cit., para. 3.
8. HoCEC, 2011a, op. cit., paras. 2, 3.
9. HoCEC, 2011a, op. cit., para. 2.
10. HoCEC, 2011a, op. cit., para. 10.
11. HoCEC, 2011a, op. cit., para. 21.
12. HoCEC, 2011a, op. cit., para. 15.

13. HoCEC, 2011a, op. cit., para. 20.
14. HoCEC, 2011a, op. cit., paras. 24, 25, 26.
15. HoCEC, 2011a, op. cit., paras. 27, 28.
16. HoCEC, 2011a, op. cit., para. 27.
17. HoCEC, 2011a, op. cit., para. 61.
18. HoCEC, 2011a, op. cit., para. 29.
19. HoCEC, 2011a, op. cit., para. 39.
20. HoCEC, 2011a, op. cit., para. 40.
21. HoCEC, 2011a, op. cit., para. 34.
22. HoCEC, 2011a, op. cit., para. 36.
23. HoCEC, 2011a, op. cit., para. 40.
24. HoCEC, 2011a, op. cit., para. 39.
25. HoCEC, 2011a, op. cit., para. 39.
26. Andy Hillier, 2011, 'Select Committee Chairman Blasts Youth Sector for Lack of Evidence', *CYPN*, 26 January; Janaki Mahadevan, 2011, 'NYA Chief Defends Youth Work Evidence Base', *CYPN*, 28 January.
27. HoCEC, 2011a, op. cit., para. 36.
28. HoCEC, 2011a, op. cit., para. 40.
29. HoCEC, 2011a, op. cit., para. 51.
30. HoCEC, 2011a, op. cit., para. 64.
31. HoCEC, 2011a, op. cit., para. 68.
32. HoCEC, 2011a, op. cit., para. 61.
33. HoCEC, 2011a, op. cit., p. 61.
34. HoCEC, 2011a, op. cit., para. 69.
35. HoCEC, 2011a, op. cit., para. 70.
36. HoCEC, 2011a, op. cit., para. 74.
37. NYA/LGA, 2012, *A Practical Guide to Commissioning Services for Young People—Part 10: Involving Young People in Commissioning*, Leicester, NYA/LGA, May.
38. HoCEC, 2011a, op. cit., para. 75.
39. HoCEC, 2011a, op. cit., para. 77.
40. HoCEC, 2011a, op. cit., para. 83.
41. Andy Hillier, 2011, 'Private Funders Cannot Rescue Youth Sector Ravaged by Cuts, MP's Told', *CYPN*, 30 March.
42. HoCEC, 2011a, op. cit., para. 91.
43. HoCEC, 2011c, para. 3.
44. HoCEC, 2011c, paras. 3, 4.
45. HoCEC, 2011c, para. 9.

46. HoCEC, 2011b, para. 4; HoCEC, 2011c, para. 4.
47. HoCEC, 2011c, para. 6; HoCEC, 2012, para. 2.
48. HoCEC, 2012, para. 2, p. 3.
49. HoCEC, 2011b, paras. 1, 2; HoCEC, 2011c, p. 3.
50. HoCEC, 2011b, p. 3.
51. HoCEC, 2011b, para. 1, p. 8.
52. HoCEC, 2011b, para. 1.
53. HoCEC, 2011b, para. 2, p. 9.
54. HoCEC, 2011c, para. 3.
55. HoCEC, 2011b, para. 3.
56. HoCEC, 2011b, para. 3.
57. HoCEC, 2011b, para. 10, p. 9.
58. HoCEC, 2011b, para. 12, p. 17.
59. HoCEC, 2011c, para. 7.
60. HoCEC, 2012, para. 2.
61. HoCEC, 2012, paras. 2, 3, January.
62. HoCEC, 2011a. para. 53.
63. HoCEC, 2011c, para. 8.
64. HoCEC, 2012, para. 3.
65. HoCEC, 2011c, para. 5.
66. HoCEC, 2012, para. 1.
67. NYA, 2018, 'APPG Enquiry into Youth Work', https://nya.org.uk/
    appg-inquiry/.

# Further Reading

House of Commons Education Committee. 2011a. *Services for Young People: Third Report of Session 2010–12, Volume 1*. London: Stationery Office. 23 June.

House of Commons Education Committee. 2011b. *Services for Young People: The Government Response*. September.

House of Commons Education Committee. 2011c. *Services for Young People: Sixth Report of Session 2010–12*. October.

House of Commons Education Committee. 2012. *Services for Young People …: Government Response to the Committee's Sixth Report of Session 2010–12*. January.

# 9

# Government Policy: How Positive for Youth?

## Youth Policy—Whose Priority?

Throughout this period, one constantly repeated central government mantra was: 'Local priorities and decisions on levels of spend on services for young people are best left to local people…'.[1] Nonetheless, a month after the Coalition came to power Loughton made clear that this freedom came with some hard-line government expectations. Speaking to an Association of Directors of Children's Services (ADCS) conference, he rejected the assumption that '… the monopoly that local authorities have on the delivery and commissioning of youth services (was) necessarily the way to go'. His aim, he said, were 'more imaginative partnerships between local authorities and the voluntary sector and others ….'.[2] In a telling neo-liberal phrase, he explained this in October 2011 as a 'mixed economy' of providers—albeit one offering fewer universal facilities—to be implemented by '… more businesses … link(ing) up with local authorities and voluntary organisations'.[3] By January 2012 he was claiming that many areas '… have actually established new smarter partnerships with the voluntary sector, social enterprise and commercial organisations', adding later: 'Frankly I do not care who the provider is… it is about the quality of the service'.[4]

© The Author(s) 2019
B. Davies, *Austerity, Youth Policy and the Deconstruction of the Youth Service in England*, https://doi.org/10.1007/978-3-030-03886-1_9

It emerged subsequently that this hands-off approach had deeper roots. Now out of office, in February 2013 Loughton—who as a minister had told a Select Committee he didn't know the extent of Youth Service cuts (see Chapter 8)—launched a very public critique of his former department and its neglect of youth policy[5] and demanded the government take a lead in highlighting good youth work.[6] This neglect was quickly traced to his former boss, Michael Gove, who, it was reported, had not visited a single youth project in his two-and-a-half years in office.[7] Moreover, in reiterating that 'youth policy is a priority for local government and not central government',[8] Gove insisted that a '"discrete" youth policy should not be a top priority for (his)department'.[9] Echoing a position which Loughton himself had taken as a minister, Gove again defined 'our role in the centre' as giving '… local authorities the freedom and flexibility to make the most effective decisions, by providing them with un-ringfenced funding and removing unnecessary bureaucracy'.[10]

By July 2013, Gove had given up responsibility for youth policies.[11] Nick Hurd, the Cabinet Office minister with the 'youth' role, reputedly brought a genuine commitment to it.[12] Like his predecessors, however, his interest was to explore '… a kind of evolution from what I think has often been the core offer, which is local authorities delivering core services to the possibility of different options'.[13] Three years later, the youth policy brief was moved again, to the Department for Culture, Media and Sport (DCMS)—prompted less, it seemed, by strategic considerations than by the desire of the then 'youth' minister, Rob Wilson, to keep the role when he moved from the Cabinet Office.[14]

Wilson claimed to be 'very disappointed' at how local authorities were treating their Youth Services, in effect accusing councillors of taking an easy cuts option.[15] However, he also made it clear he wanted 'to give young people greater engagement with our sporting and cultural heritage'[16]—still a main departmental focus when Tracey Crouch took over as DCMS's junior minister for 'sport and civil society' in 2017.[17]

# Setting the Ideological Boundaries

Within this wider political context Loughton announced his intention shortly after the 2010 general election to publish a youth policy paper. A nine months 'consultation' process started in March 2011 with a 'summit' briefed 'to identify and debate key issues faced by young people today' at which over three hundred young people and professionals met with ministers and officials from seven Government departments'. A series of 'youth consultations', a 'Young people's event' and a 'Cross-sector workshop' followed.[18]

In November 2011, a month before the release of *Positive for Youth: A new approach to cross-government policy for young people aged 13 to 19*, Loughton made clear that 'there is no big cheque attached … it is about using money better …'.[19] The paper also re-emphasised the government's wider 'localism' approach—that it was not its job to decide 'which services for young people should be funded or delivered and to what level …'[20]

Other boundaries were also set for the contributors to the twenty one 'discussion' papers supporting the consultations. Though 'personal responsibility and social justice' were identified as 'core values',[21] the agenda for converting the latter into action was restricted to 'recognising the unique and diverse needs of different young people'; 'improving opportunities and early support'; and 'reaching out to those with fewest advantages'. The wider structural inequalities which might be limiting young people's 'level of access … to financial resources'[22] were again masked in references to those 'disadvantaged because of their backgrounds' and 'vulnerable because of their personal circumstances'. Poverty, when acknowledged, was treated not as possible evidence of deeper systemic features but as just one problem alongside '…drugs, violence, problems at school or with housing'. It also appeared on a 'shared list of risk factors' which included '… early family relationship problems, … a history of problem behaviour within the family or friendship groups, poor mental health, or exposure to criminal activity.' The closest Loughton came to acknowledging the impact of the 2007 financial crisis on these 'personal circumstances' was a reference to 'the current difficult economic climate'.[23]

Though never explicitly adopting Margaret Thatcher's dismissive 'there are only individuals and families', *Positive for Youth* also steered well clear of endorsing collective 'political' responses to young people's problems. Passing references were made to 'peer relationships'[24] (particularly their increasing influence on older teenagers), 'social mixing'[25] and 'team working'.[26] The need for communities to take action on a range of issues was also, repeatedly, emphasised—though, as in other government policy pronouncements, (see Chapter 6), 'community' was usually conceived as a benevolent geographical entity whose possible internal conflicts remained unacknowledged.

Ultimately, therefore, it was again the (decontextualised) up-by-their-bootstraps 'individual' young person who was both expected and seen as able to make the necessary changes. Despite evidence by 2017 that more than a quarter of 2200 16–25 year olds interviewed didn't feel in control of their life,[27] *Positive for Youth* repeatedly insisted they must have 'vision and belief that they can succeed'; 'broaden their horizons (and) raise their aspirations'; be 'independent', 'self-regulating' and 'resilient'; and develop their 'character' and 'personal and social skills and qualities … (of) relationship-building and decision-making'.[28]

*Positive for Youth* did identify another significant driver of change for young people: 'the family'. Though—again without reference to possible wider structural constraints—this was recognised as being under pressure, an early discussion paper pointed to a 'growing body of research' showing that 'family and parent training' could result in measurable reductions in antisocial behaviour, child maltreatment, underachievement at school and mental health pressures.[29] On the grounds that 'services for young people have too often focused on the young person in isolation', Loughton thus promised to 'support parents and carers, not ignore or supplant them'.[30] Emphasising that 'parents, carers and families have prime responsibility and influence to nurture young people through to adulthood',[31] *Positive for Youth* itself set services the task of adopting '… a stronger focus on supporting whole families while respecting and nurturing young people's growing sense of independence and personal responsibility'.[32] Links were made, too, to the wider government strategies of 'early intervention' and 'troubled families'.[33]

## Passionate—About 'Targeted Intervention'

Rooted in these understandings of young people's problems, Loughton's Foreword to the paper declared: 'This Government is passionate about creating a society that is positive for youth'.[34] Extending this passion to 'supporting all young people to succeed and realise their full potential', the paper then made commitments, some set within the government's wider policy frameworks, to young people's 'wellbeing' and to '…investment in (their) capability and character'. It also promised departmental and cross-departmental interventions by all 'youth services' including schools and further education, child protection and health.[35]

The titles of some of the discussion papers—for example, 'Helping young people to success in learning and finding a job' and 'Preventing youth crime and substance misuse'—made clear intended high priority 'outcomes'. Others, assuming that 'the market' and other non-state bodies' could run services better than the state, focused on 'Business brokerage..', 'Capital infrastructure…', 'Youth enterprise', 'Commissioning services ….' and 'Growing the role of community and voluntary organisations'. One, highlighting the preoccupation with young people as individuals, focused on 'Adolescent brain development'.

The policy also advocated forms of face-to-face practice which, it argued, would contribute to the desired societal change. These included 'empowering young people … to inspect and report on local services and … help "youth proof" government policy…'; reviewing the personal, social, health and 'economic' education provided for young people; and setting up a national helpline and website to support parents of teenagers. Funding of £10 million in 2011–2013 was provided for an 'Ending Gang and Youth Violence Team' to give 'practical support to up to 30 local areas…'.[36] A 'Youth Contract worth over £1bn' was to be created for a 'promoting work experience' scheme particularly to support the 'hardest to reach' young people 'into education, training or a job with training'.[37]

Sometimes closely linked to the need for 'youth services' to 'integrate',[38] 'targeting' emerged as the core *Positive for Youth* strategy for responding to young people's individualised deficiencies. In addition to those outlined above, priority was to be given to getting post-16 year olds into the new planned apprenticeship schemes[39] and preventing teenage pregnancies and youth homelessness. One sub-section focused on 'Targeted support for parents'[40]; another on 'the role of youth work, targeted provision, and open access centres'. Commissioners of services were told, too, that '… young people with additional needs and those at risk of negative outcomes … will merit particular attention'.[41]

'Hotspots'—areas where young people's behaviour was seen as particularly in need of control and redirection—were also to be targeted, with case studies illustrating how in one authority during the 2011 'disturbances' (see Chapter 2) social media sites had been monitored to direct the police into specific areas.[42] Highlighted, too, were the Department of Health's support for hospitals which, by sharing non-confidential information with the police, were helping to concentrate gun and knife crime stop-and-search activities.[43]

# Directing Local Services—From Above

Despite *Positive for Youth's* insistence on the government's non-interventionist approach, the paper gave strong, top-down and non-negotiable messages on how services were to be identified, organised and evaluated and funded. A government priority was to support 'local funders and providers (to) put in place the right combination of evidence-based services to meet local needs, with the support of communities and business.[44] The paper then explained what these 'best local arrangements' should look like[45] and what was meant by 'local funders and providers', 'evidence-based services' and 'the support of communities and business'. 'Key principles' to be observed included:

- 'a more integrated approach' by all providers of publicly and non-publicly funded services';
- 'a stronger focus … on evidence-based early help for the most disadvantaged and vulnerable';

- 'a more contestable market for publicly funded services with a stronger focus on results';
- 'a more enterprising and innovative voluntary and community sector able to ... secure diverse sources of income'.[46]

With again emphasis on 'young people driving decisions',[47] these principles were then applied in some unchallengeable ways. 'All services should be commissioned, whether they are to be delivered in house, or by a third party'[48]; commissioners were encouraged to explore the potential of alternative funding models such as payment by results and social impact bonds[49] and quality was to be judged 'by good outcomes as well as reductions in poor outcomes'.

## 'Progressing' *Positive for Youth*

In October 2012, some ten months after *Positive for Youth* was published, Loughton again voiced his backbench criticisms of his former department and, albeit in a coded way, its implementation of the new policy. Claiming that '(I)... really had to battle against various unnamed forces ... to keep the youth role of the DfE on the agenda', he promised that when the planned *Positive for Youth* progress report appeared he would table Parliamentary questions and ask for a debate 'to keep (it) on the agenda of government'.[50] He got support from the chair of the LGA's children and young people's board who, less than a year after *Positive for Youth* appeared, talked of 'things going "very quiet" on youth services in central government'.[51]

These political manoeuvrings in the early months of 2013 may well account for the six month delay in publishing the promised progress report. When finally published in July,[52] its Foreword was signed by DfE minister Edward Timpson and the Minister for Civil Society in the Cabinet Office Nic Hurd. Reaffirming the overall aim of 'set(ting) out a vision for the long term, shifting cultural norms',[53] this restated the bottom-line premise that '*youth policy is primarily a matter for local government*'[54] (italics in the original). Somewhat contradictorily, however, as well as again making 'returning power to young people' a high expectation, it again insisted that local authorities should hand over as many as possible of their operational roles to voluntary and charitable organisations and private businesses.[55]

Though Timpson and Hurd acknowledged that 'there is no magic solution to young people's needs',[56] when the report moved from vision to practical outcomes all its messages were upbeat. Section titles thus included 'Putting young people at the heart of policy making', 'Putting young people at the heart of local delivery' and 'Increasing numbers of young people in education and work-based learning ...' Other sections talked of young people 'leading safe and healthier lives', 'remain(ing) active in their local communities' and 'generally feel(ing) a sense of well-being'. Case studies from across the country and a range of organisations also presented apparently unproblematic success stories.

This largely optimistic picture of improved young people's lives and the services supporting them contrasted sharply with accumulating evidence of their 'precarity' from more objective sources (see Chapter 1). Indeed the high levels of stress and distress which many young people were by then negotiating suggested that government youth policies still lacked the comprehensive and strategic vision and direction needed to guarantee this generation well resourced support and opportunities (see Chapter 18). In response, however, all the ministers were prepared to commit to were limited instrumental 'interventions' such as 'ensuring the right department leads on specific areas and improving the way that we co-ordinate our work ...'.[57]

# The Local Authority Youth Service: 'Unreformed' and 'Unco-operative'

In January 2010, while still shadow youth minister, Loughton reprised the familiar New Labour motif that the quality of local authority Youth Services 'leaves a lot to be desired' before posing the rhetorical question: 'Why would the world fall in if a local authority contracted out the whole youth services department?'[58] The following May, in his evidence to the Education Select Committee (see Chapter 8), he again characterised the Service as 'one of the most high profile unreformed public services' whose reliance on 'huge slugs of public money' was 'unsustainable in economically straitened times'. In that same contribution he turned into a principled non-intervention stance his admission that 'he did not know the extent' of what the Committee called 'the disproportionate cuts' to Youth Services.[59] Ignoring the impact of the overall reductions in local authority funding, by November 2011 he was also laying some blame for the sector's troubles on 'prima donnas' running voluntary organisations who, he said, were getting in the way of co-operative working.[60]

Starting from this (at best) ministerial scepticism, local authority Youth Services struggled to find a place in their own right within *Positive for Youth's* 'principles and approach'. Most commonly, the references to 'youth services' in the discussion papers came in this form—as a generic plural, in lower case. Only once, in the context of a discussion of outcomes and the relationship between 'universal' and 'targeted' provision, was reference made specifically to:

> … youth services funded by local authorities (LAs) which aim to contact and deliver outcomes for young people locally, often through distinctive youth work methodologies delivered by youth workers.

Even at this initial stage, however, those outcomes were limited to enabling young people to develop those 'personal and social skills … need(ed) for learning, work and the transition to adulthood'.[61,62]

One of the discussion papers, on support for local authorities, was also explicit about the new financial constraints facing the Service as the Revenue Support Grant out of which it had 'traditionally' been funded was 'reducing significantly over the 4 year period just started'. This warning came, too, with a recognition that:

> … central government funding for other services for young people including … open access programmes of positive activities, has been subsumed within the Early Intervention Grant. This covers much wider children's and family services and is reduced in 2011-12 compared with its predecessor budgets in 2010-11.[63]

*Positive for Youth* nonetheless told 'local leaders and commissioners' that 'a credible and viable alternative' needed to be found 'to simply scaling back existing services to fit available resources'.[64] It particularly advocated for favoured Coalition youth initiatives such as the 'MyPlace' youth centre programme (see Chapters 3 and 13), the NCS, young people's volunteering and the 'opportunities to expand the Cadet Forces' (later extended to other unformed youth organisations) (see Chapter 12).[65] The *Progress Report* later supplemented this advice by pointing to a need for 'new models of delivery for youth services' through voluntary and community organisation takeovers and by converting some into 'mutuals'.[66]

## Youth Work: From a 'Narrative' …

As a first step to converting these criticisms of local authority Youth Services into Loughton's preferred local 'offer', three months before *Positive for Youth* was published Loughton commissioned 'A narrative for youth work today'.[67] Most of the contributors to the paper were described as 'key stakeholders in the youth sector'. However, one, working for the Young Foundation, later co-authored the much-quoted *Framework of outcomes for young people*[68] while another was the CEO of Applied Quantitative Research which described itself as making 'high quality psychometric tools and assessments accessible to users of all types … to support them in making better decisions about people'.[69]

Loughton's brief for the group was 'to help policy-makers and local commissioners to better understand the impact of youth work' and help 'providers of youth work services … develop a common language to describe their role and impact'. He again stressed the need for engaging young people—especially those from 'disadvantaged and chaotic backgrounds'—in 'learning, community safety and mitigating risky behaviour' by offering 'support through their family, school and community'. As well as achieving 'immediate impact … on personal and social development', youth work would be expected to have 'important knock-on impact … on education, employability and other social outcomes'.[70]

The resultant 'Narrative' struggled to negotiate the dilemmas for youth workers embedded in these expectations. It for example acknowledged that, as one of youth work's 'values' was that 'young people opted in voluntarily', the power relationship was important within a 'range of settings including youth clubs and uniformed groups'. It also pointed out that 'the (youth work) process involves collective activity'—though cautiously (and, within the *Positive for Youth* framework, compliantly) it re-interpreted this as 'team work'. In defining the youth work 'approach' as 'holistic' and the 'capabilities' young people needed to develop as 'context specific', it again hedged its *Positive-for-Youth* bets. It for example identified 'resilience' and 'mental toughness' as important individual qualities not just for young people themselves but also for their contribution to achieving '"harder" outcomes around employment, education and health'.[71]

However, on three issues raised by the *Positive for Youth* agendas, each again with significant long-term implications for Youth Services and open access youth work, the 'Narrative' helped reinforce wider government policy assumptions. One was its taken-for-granted endorsements of commissioning as the way of identifying youth work providers. A second was its efforts to show how the 'capabilities' youth work was said to 'impart' could be converted into 'measurable' 'societal outcomes'—a stance underpinned by references to, for example, the 'need to continually strengthen evaluation practices'. Thirdly, despite its acknowledgement of young people's voluntary engagement and the need to offer a variety of open access settings, the 'Narrative' also contributed to a developing reconceptualisation of youth work as any kind of work with young people. What were termed the 'youth work approach' and 'youth work methodologies and approaches' were thus seen as 'transfer(ing)' easily to other contexts'—to be taken on by for example 'Youth health advisor', 'Youth participation (housing) worker', 'Play worker ... (0–16)', 'Youth support (social care) worker/assistant' and 'Sports leader/coach'.[72]

The 'narrative's' authors were clearly anxious to use their direct line to the minister to convince him of 'youth work's real value'. However, by leaving many of his and the wider government's pre-set boundaries unchallenged, and by reinforcing many of *Positive for Youth*'s redefinitions of the practice, they—like the Select Committee reports a year before—missed opportunities to strengthen the case for (albeit reformed) local authority Youth Services and for their educationally-focused open access practice.

## … to a Redefinition

Unsurprisingly perhaps, *Positive for Youth* 'welcome(d) and endorse(d)' the draft 'Narrative'. It particularly praised its efforts 'to set out more clearly the contribution that youth work can make within a wider system of support for young people' and for helping 'commissioners and providers … to form a common view of the role and potential of both detached and centre-based youth work'.[73] The policy document itself also gave youth work some explicit endorsements. Youth workers were identified as a source of 'inspiration and support', as helping 'to develop high aspirations'[74] and as giving 'access to opportunities for personal and social development outside the classroom'. Young people were quoted as naming them alongside teachers and religious leaders as 'trusted professionals' and as 'important influences and role models'. The youth centre was recognised as a place where young people already go to 'access … advice and support' and, with detached work, as making '… a vital contribution … particularly (to) those who don't get the support or opportunities they need from their family or community'. This included 'helping to engage them in their communities and supporting their personal and social development through informal learning'. The practice's 'strengths and experiences' were also seen as providing a model for the then still emerging NCS.[75]

*Positive for Youth's* penultimate chapter, 'Working Together to Support Young People', gave dedicated attention to 'high quality youth work'. Significantly, however, in a sub-section entitled 'The role of youth work, targeted provision, and open access youth centres', youth work's contribution was particularly justified as an 'investment in young people's capabilities and character'. This, moreover, was in effect made conditional on it providing '… an important form of early intervention for young people at risk of poor outcomes'. To further emphasise this 'targeting' rationale, evidence was referenced which was said to show that, particularly where disadvantaged young people were concentrated, '… good quality open access youth clubs that provided structured activities … can be highly effective in meeting priority needs'.[76]

On this basis, the government committed itself to 'helping policy-makers and local commissioners to better understand the impact that high quality youth work ... can have on the lives of young people'. As part of their 'local offer of services to young people', local authorities' were also advised—indeed urged—to 'work with young people and other agencies to ... consider how ... youth work, and youth workers can contribute to delivering their priorities'.[77]

In recognising the 'valued' role of youth work, including the open access version, *Positive for Youth* thus, at best, gave only limited and qualified endorsement to it as an educational practice in its own right. Supported sometimes by case studies, it was most often defined as a support for—even as an appendage to—the practices of other services: by helping schools 'spot problems early' and work with excluded school pupils; by working within 'integrated multi-disciplinary teams' 'to provide opportunities during and outside the school day'; for 'improving young people's health and wellbeing'; as a form of early intervention.[78]

These gaps and elisions not only remained in the *Positive for Youth* progress report but were located in a wider ministerial view that 'We need to stop seeing youth issues through the prism of education'.[79] The report did give brief attention to the revised statutory guidance to local authorities (discussed below), though—now reframed as for 'services and activities to improve young people's wellbeing'—this too was at best ambivalent in its support for youth work. And though again youth workers made their occasional appearance in case studies—most positively in one describing their support for a 'youth voice' initiative—more often their role was as ancillary contributor to a targeted programme. Particularly significant in the longer term, too, was the report's strongly approving commentary on the Young Foundation's 'outcomes framework', not least for 'help(ing) evidence the impact of services to social investors'.[80]

Intentionally or not, *Positive for Youth's* strategic and recurring preoccupation with targeting thus had the effect of marginalising the majority of the youth population who, the Education Select Committee had pointed out only months before, merited dedicated attention because they spent 85% of their time outside formal education. Overwhelmingly, *Positive for Youth*'s message was that, to qualify for support for her or his everyday developmental efforts, a young person must fit into one of the policy's pre-defined 'problem' or 'risk' categories'.

But what if a young person didn't fit? Or—even more testing perhaps—what if, according to the definers of such categories, they did but refused to accept the 'offer' made to them? How then was the repeatedly declared commitment to empowering them to be honoured? What if, by compelling their participation, some ended up with a (perhaps reinforced) anti-authority mind-set and so further alienated from the supportive services they needed?

Limited though it was, research on young people's perceptions and experience of youth work[81] pointed to the possibility of a different—even contrary—'outcome'. Some at least of the young people on which *Positive for Youth* was most focused were, it appeared, choosing to enter open access spaces in part because they were received there simply as (unlabelled) young people and with a focus on their developmental potential rather than their deficits. In these spaces, some also came to experience the personally tailored 'on the wing'[82] adult responses which over time they came to recognise as 'helpful' and 'supportive' in just the ways *Positive for Youth* was seeking.

By contrast—as evidenced for example by two reports in this period on how child sexual abuse in Rotherham was handled[83]—the face-to-face practice of many of the state institutions through which *Positive for Youth*'s targeted interventions would have to be made were heavily bureaucratised and had adult authority at their heart. Some of *Positive for Youth*'s bottom-line requirements were also likely to impose new limitations on how these services worked with 'challenging' young people by for example demanding that they provide 'measured' and even 'monetised' evidence of outcomes. Nor did the new policy offer guidance on how potential practice dilemmas and ambiguities stemming from some of its core expectations were to be resolved—such as the frequent tension between supporting young people's emerging 'right to have their voice heard' while helping them negotiate their changing relationship with parents or carers.[84]

# In Search of a Stronger Statutory Base for the Youth Service

Running alongside the development and implementation of the *Positive for Youth* policies were much more low key government efforts to strengthen the Youth Service's legislative base. Two months before the Coalition came to power, Ian Wright the New Labour minister responsible for '14-19 reform', had talked about the '…madness for a local authority to think of youth services (as) an easy cut' and, conditional on their contributing to the government's 'preventative' agendas, had pledged to consider strengthening its statutory base.[85]

For the Coalition, such a commitment was always constrained by its refusal to interfere in local policy-making. By Nov 2013 Nick Hurd was thus telling CHYPS: 'I'm not going to change the statutory duty',[86] while a year later his successor Rob Wilson was using the government's 'Localism' strategy to argue that the existing statutory requirements were adequate. By claiming that '… effective local youth services are already supported by the existing statutory guidance', he also ignored his own department's evidence that less than half of local authorities always were taking their legal duty into account when deciding Youth Services' budgets[87] (see Chapter 13).

Following *Positive for Youth*'s publication, in March 2012 the Local Government Information Unit (LGiU) circulated a briefing to local authorities which set out 'Government expectations for any such guidance'. After emphasising 'the removal of any sense of national prescription and a new focus on outcomes rather than inputs', this was explicit about

* a presumption against local authority (direct) delivery;
* the targeting of public funding primarily on young people at risk of poor outcomes;
* a growth in the overall role of the voluntary, community and faith sector in services and activities for young people'.[88]

Following three months of consultations, an updated version of the statutory guidance to local authorities appeared in June 2012.[89] By seeking

'... equality of access for all young people to the positive, preventative and early help they need to improve their well-being', this broadened the definition of the services covered well beyond the leisure-time 'positive activities' which had been New Labour's preoccupation. However, in explaining what the relevant services and activities 'for 16-19 year olds and for 20-24 year olds with learning difficulties' were to cover, youth work was not mentioned as one of the approved methods.[90] Moreover, by retaining the qualification that local authorities' were responsible for securing the 'local offer' only 'as far as is reasonably practicable', as budget pressures grew more and more councils in England used this as the loophole for systematically deconstructing their Youth Services.

# Notes

1. Neil Puffett, 2011, 'Government Will Not Step into Protect Youth Services, Loughton Admits', *CYPN*, 24 October.
2. Lauren Higgs, 2010a, 'Loughton Calls for Overhaul of Local Authority Youth Services', *CYPN*, 8 July.
3. Lauren Higgs, 2011, 'Conservative Conference 2011: Wellbeing Boards to Be a "Significant Player" in Youth Service Provision', *CYPN*, 3 October.
4. www.parliament.uk, 2012, 'Oral Answers to Questions—Education', 16 January, https://publications.parliament.uk/pa/cm201212/cmhansrd/cm12 0116/debtext/120116-0001.htm.
5. Gabriella Jozwiak, 2013a, 'Gove Under Fire for Disregarding Youth Policy at His Department', *CYPN*, 19 February.
6. Laura McCardle, 2014a, 'Loughton Urges Cabinet Office to Promote Good Youth Work', *CYPN*, 11 July.
7. Neil Puffett, 2013a, 'Gove "Fails to Visit any Youth Project" During Time at DfE', *CYPN*, 21 January.
8. Gabriella Jozwiak, 2013b, 'Gove: Youth Policy Not a Central Government Priority', *CYPN*, 25 January.
9. Gabriella Jozwiak, 2013c, 'Gove Letter Fails to Commit to Whitehall Youth Policy', *CYPN*, 27 February.
10. Gabriella Jozwiak, 2013a, op. cit.
11. Neil Puffett, 2013b, 'New Era for Youth Policy as Cabinet Office Move Marks Historic Shift', *CYPN*, 9 July.

12. John Freeman, 2013, 'Councils Can Be the Glue in the Minister's Youth Work Vision', *CYPN*, 17 December.
13. Laura McCardle, 2013, 'Hurd Still Unclear on Council Role in Youth Services', *CYPN*, 6 November.
14. Tony Jeffs, 2015, 'What Sort of Future?', in Stanton Naomi (ed), *Innovation in Youth Work: Thinking in Practice*, London, George Williams College, pp. 11–17.
15. Adam Offord, 2015, 'Minister "Very Disappointed" with Council Youth Service Cuts', *CYPN*, 6 July; Jess Brown, 2016, 'Councils "Take Easy Option" to Cut Youth Services, Says Youth Minister', *CYPN*, 3 August.
16. Adam Offord, 2016, 'Government Set to Publish Three-Year Youth Strategy', *CYPN*, 8 November.
17. Gabriella Jozwiak, 2017, 'Youth Brief Handed to Sports Minister', *CYPN*, 15 June.
18. HM Government, 2011, *Positive for Youth: A New Approach to Cross-Government Policy for Young People Aged 13 to 19*, https://assets.publishing.service.gov.uk/government/uploads/system/uploads/attachment_data/file/175496/DFE-00133-2011.pdf, para. 1.3.
19. Janaki Mahadevan, 2011, 'Loughton Blames "Big Personalities" for Lack of Co-operation in Youth Sector', *CYPN*, 2 November.
20. HM Government, 2011, op. cit., paras. 5.5, 5.63 Exec Sum, 10–11
21. HM Government, 2011, op. cit., para. 3.3.
22. HM Government, 2011, op. cit., paras. 2.10, 2.23, 2.25, 2.26.
23. HM Government, 2011, op. cit., Ministerial Foreword, p. 4.
24. HM Government, 2011, op. cit., paras. 2.10, 2.14, 2.20, 4.8.
25. HM Government, 2011, op. cit., paras. 3.4, 3.8, 4.72, 4.80.
26. HM Government, 2011, op. cit., paras. 4.49, 4.56, 4.60, 4.64.
27. Neil Puffett, 2017, 'One in Four Young People "Don't Feel in Control of Their Life"', *CYPN*, 6 January.
28. HM Government, 2011, op. cit., paras. 2.10, 2.23, 3.3, 4.5, 4.60, 4.61, 5.20, 5.29, 5.4.
29. DfE, 2011a, 'The Outcomes of Services for Young People and the Relationship Between Universal and Targeted Services', para. 26, https://www.gov.uk/government/publications/positive-for-youth-the-collaborative-process; GOV.UK, 2012, Policy Paper, '*Positive for Youth—The Collaborative Process*', 14 June, https://www.gov.uk/government/publications/positive-for-youth-the-collaborative-process.
30. HM Government, 2011, op. cit., p. 2.

31. HM Government, 2011, op. cit., para. 4.58.
32. HM Government, 2011, op. cit., para. 5.3.
33. HM Government, 2011, op. cit., paras. 4.23, 4.6.
34. HM Government, 2011, op. cit., p. 1.
35. HM Government, 2011, op. cit., paras. 1.1, 3.15, 4.114, 5.20.
36. HM Government, 2011, op. cit., para. 5.73.
37. Education Funding Agency, 2016, 'Youth Contract Provision: 16- and 17 Year Olds', 15 December, https://www.gov.uk/government/publications/youth-contract-16-and-17-year-olds/youth-contract-provision-16-and-17-year-olds#delivery-data-for-the-youth-contract.
38. HM Government, 2011, op. cit., para. 5.35.
39. HM Government, 2011, op. cit., paras. 4.48, 4.98, 4.134.
40. HM Government, 2011, op. cit., paras. 4.14, 5.20–5.24.
41. HM Government, 2011, op. cit., para. 5.28
42. HM Government, 2011, op. cit., para. 4.137.
43. HM Government, 2011, op. cit., para. 4.143.
44. HM Government, 2011, op. cit., p. 2.
45. HM Government, 2011, op. cit., para. 5.3.
46. HM Government, 2011, op. cit., para. 5.3.
47. HM Government, 2011, op. cit., p. 65.
48. HM Government, 2011, op. cit., para. 5.25.
49. HM Government, 2011, op. cit., paras. 5.32, 5.37.
50. Lauren Higgs, 2012, 'Youth Services in Danger at DfE, Warns Loughton', *CYPN*, 9 October.
51. Neil Puffett, 2012, 'Councils "Must Re-build" Youth Services', *CYPN*, 7 November.
52. HM Government, 2013, *Positive for Youth: Progress Since December 2011*, July, https://www.gov.uk/government/uploads/system/uploads/attachment_data/file/210383/Positive-for-Youth-progress-update.pdf.
53. HM Government, 2013, op. cit., p. 7.
54. HM Government, 2013, op. cit., p. 32.
55. HM Government, 2013, op. cit., pp. 7, 14, 22.
56. HM Government, 2013, op. cit., p. 6.
57. HM Government, 2013, op. cit., p. 6.
58. Gore, M. 2010, 'Joint Working—Minister-in-Waiting Gets Ready for Battle', *CYPN*, 12 January.
59. House of Commons Education Select Committee, 2011, *Services for Young People*, London, Stationery Office, paras. 14, 56, 64.

60. Janaki Mahadevan, 2011, op. cit.
61. DfE, 2011A, op. cit., paras. 2, 10, 21, iii, p. 7.
62. Outcomes paper, para. 21.
63. DfE, 2011B, 'Positive for Youth—Discussion Paper: Support for Local Authorities', paras. 2 (i), 2 (ii).
64. HM Government, 2011, op. cit., paras. 5.34, 5.35.
65. HM Government, 2011, op. cit., paras. 4.76–4.84.
66. HM Government, 2013, op. cit., pp. 24, 33.
67. GOV.UK, 2012, 'Positive for Youth: The Collaborative Process', 14 June, file:///C:/Users/Owner/Desktop/Documents/PolicyPapersetc/P4Y/P4YDiscPapers%20-%20GOV.UK.htm.
68. Bethia McNeil, Neil Reeder, and Julia Rich, *A Framework of Outcomes for Young People*, Young Foundation, 2012.
69. AQR International, AQR's Goals and Approach, https://www.aqr.com/who-we-are; http://aqrinternational.co.uk/what-is-aqr-international/goals.
70. DfE, 2011c, 'A Narrative for Youth Work Today', p. 8, https://assets.publishing.service.gov.uk/government/uploads/system/uploads/attachment_data/file/210380/a-narrative-for-youth-work-today.pdf.
71. DfE, 2011c, op. cit., pp. 2, 3, 4, 5.
72. DfE, 2011c, op. cit., pp. 2, 3, 4, (Table).
73. HM Government, 2011, op. cit., paras. 5.1, 5.21.
74. HM Government, 2011, op. cit., para. 2.18.
75. HM Government, 2011, op. cit., paras. 2.22, 2.14, 4.73, 4.81.
76. HM Government, 2011, op. cit., p. 69, paras. 5.20–5.24.
77. HM Government, 2011, op. cit., paras. 5.20/21/22, 5.9.
78. HM Government, 2011, op. cit., paras. 3.11, 4.42, 4.91, 4.61, 5.49.
79. HM Government, 2013, op. cit., pp. 6, 20, 19, 10, 13, 25.
80. HM Government, 2013, op. cit., pp. 6, 20, 19, 10, 13, 25.
81. DES, 1987, *Education Observed: Effective Youth Work: A Report by HM Inspectors*, Stanmore, Middlesex, DES.
82. David Crimmens, et al., 2004, *Reaching Socially Excluded Young People: A National Study of Street-Based Youth Work*, Leicester, NYA; Bryan Merton, et al., 2004, *An Evaluation of the Impact of Youth Work*, Nottingham, DfES; Jean Spence and Carol Devanney, 2006, *Youth Work: Voices of Practice*, Leicester, NYA; Maurice Devlin and Anna Gunning, 2009, *The Purposes and Outcomes of Youth Work*, Dublin, Irish Youth Work Press.

83. Jay, A. 2014, *Independent Inquiry into Child Sexual Exploitation in Rotherham 1997–2013*, Rotherham Metropolitan Council, August, http://www.rotherham.gov.uk/downloads/file/1407/independent_inquiry_cse_in_rotherham; Louise Casey, 2015, *Report of Inspection of Rotherham Metropolitan Council*, London, GOV.UK/Ministry of Housing, Communities and Local Government, February, https://www.gov.uk/government/publications/report-of-inspection-of-rotherham-metropolitan-borough-council.
84. HM Government, 2011, op. cit., para. 2.17, p. 2.
85. Lauren Higgs, 2010b, 'Cutting Youth Services Is "Madness", Says Minister', *Youth Work News*, 3 March.
86. Laura McCardle, 2013, op. cit.
87. Laura McCardle, 2014b, 'Youth Minister Rob Wilson Rejects Services Motion', *CYPN*, 4 December (X1, X2).
88. LGiU, 2012, 'Draft Statutory Guidance for Local Authorities on Services and Activities to Improve Young People's Wellbeing', 30 March, pp. 4–5, https://www.lgiu.org.uk/wp-content/uploads/2012/04/Draft-Statutory-Guidance-for-Local-Authorities-on-Services-and-Activities-to-Improve-Young-People%E2%80%99s-Wellbeing.pdf.
89. Department for Education, 2012, 'Statutory Guidance for Local Authorities on Services and Activities to Improve Young People's Well-being', June, https://www.dorsetforyou.gov.uk/media/210074/DfE-Statutory-Guidance-for-LAs-on-services-and-activities-to-improve-young-peoples-wellbeing/pdf/DfE_-_Statutory_Guidance_for_LAs_on_services_and_activities_to_improve_young_peoples_wellbeing.pdf; See also Chris Hayes, 2016, 'CSN Policy Briefing: Youth Service: The Delivering Differently for Young People (DDYP) Programme', LGiU, 10 February, p. 2.
90. Department for Education, 2012, op. cit.; Chris Hayes, 2016, 'CSN Policy Briefing: Youth Service: The Delivering Differently for Young People (DDYP) Programme', LGiU, 10 February, p. 2.

# Further Reading

Buckland, L. 2013. 'Positive for Youth: A Critique'. *The Encyclopaedia of Informal Education*. http://infed.org/mobi/positive-for-youth-a-critique/.
Davies, Bernard. 2011. 'Thinking Space: What's Positive for Youth?' *Youth and Policy*. No. 107. November, pp. 99–103.

Davies, Bernard. 2013. 'Youth Work in a Changing Policy Landscape: The View from England'. *Youth and Policy*. No. 110. May, pp. 6–32.

DfE. 2011. 'A Narrative for Youth Work Today'. https://assets.publishing. service.gov.uk/government/uploads/system/uploads/attachment_data/ file/210380/a-narrative-for-youth-work-today.pdf.

HM Government. 2011. *Positive for Youth: A New Approach to Cross-Government Policy for Young People Aged 13 to 19.*

HM Government. 2013. *Positive for Youth: Progress Since December 2011.* July.

McNeil, Bethia, et al. 2012. *A Framework of Outcomes for Young People.* Young Foundation.

Tiffany, Graeme. 2011. 'Positive for Youth: Thoughts from a Detached Youth Work Point of View'. January. https://indefenceofyouthwork. com/2012/01/15/a-detached-view-of-positive-for-youth/.

# Part IV
## Youth Policies in Action

# 10

# Towards a National Service for Youth

## From 'Community Service'...

Governments' refusal after 2010 to intervene in local authorities' deconstruction of their Youth Services contrasted sharply with their enthusiastic promotion of range of other youth initiatives. Though in some cases presented as substitutes for the lost facilities, the high pro-file ministerial support they received from the Prime Minister down, as well as the public money allocated to them, carried other implicit messages. One was that these 'failing' local facilities needed to be replaced. Another was that future practice with young people needed to meet the policy objectives as for example set out in *Positive for Youth*.

Particularly influential here was a government-wide determination to encourage more young people to volunteer for a worthy cause. Political parties as well as many voluntary youth organisations had long aspired to get the young to take on what fifty years earlier the Youth Service Development Council had called 'community service',[1] prompting even then a question of whether this was an attempt to tame the young.[2] By the 1980s, as levels of youth unemployment rose, policy-makers also

© The Author(s) 2019
B. Davies, *Austerity, Youth Policy and the Deconstruction of the Youth Service in England*, https://doi.org/10.1007/978-3-030-03886-1_10

began to consider whether such volunteering could be converted into compulsory 'national service', including perhaps 'a military option'.[3]

In 2009, these aspirations re-emerged when Gordon Brown suggested that, by requiring young people to do fifty hours of 'voluntary' work, 'community service will become a normal part of growing up in Britain'.[4] By then he and his Home Secretary David Blunkett had given strong support to the creation in 2006 of 'V'[5] (renamed 'vinpsired' in 2011). As youth policies focused increasingly on young people's deficits, the new organisation justified its two-year £23 million expenditure on providing volunteering opportunities as an 'investment' in 'help(ing) young people develop ... skills, which employers say they need'.[6]

Young people were not always convinced of volunteering's benefits. According to a 2009 report many saw their role in rural conservation projects as '"slave labour" and "grunt work"'.[7] Other evidence suggested that only just over half of the 18–34 age group believed all young people should be required to do community service[8] and that they were strongly opposed to even a 'civic' version of compulsory national service.[9] Nonetheless, as a way of 'clos(ing) the generation gap', in March 2010 Brown and his Secretary of State for Children Ed Balls announced a £6 million fund for five two-year 'pilot' programmes of 'community activity' opportunities for 14–16 year olds.[10]

# ... to 'Social Action'

With the ground thus laid, the Coalition government and its Conservative successors promoted a much more interconnected range of youth volunteering initiatives. Despite their normally negative view of the state as a public service provider, its interventions and funding were for these justified as essential. A crucial condition, however, was again that the favoured programmes would aim to induct the young into the core neo-liberal qualities of 'character', 'resilience' and 'independence' required by well adjusted and 'contributing' citizens, workers and parents.

A strategic commitment to this form of 'work with young people' was flagged up in June 2012 by David Cameron when he announced an enquiry into 'how ... Government, business, the voluntary and education sectors (can) work together to support young people to engage in social action between the ages of 10 and 20'. This was carried out by Dame Julia Cleverdon, a former Chief Executive of Business in the Community, and Amanda Jordan OBE, a co-founding director of the global management consultancy Corporate Citizenship. As their brief required, their report, published in December 2012, 'rebadged' youth volunteering as 'social action'—a concept whose origins lay in radical forms of collective campaigning. This was redefined as 'practical action in the service of others' with a vision that by 2020:

> … all sectors will have contributed to making our country a place where the majority of young people are involved in social action and are encouraged, recognised and valued for their contribution to society.[11]

## From a Gleam in Cameron's Eye…

By far the most high profile way in which the Coalition and its successors implemented this vision was through NCS—repeatedly described by both advocates and critics as a government 'flagship' initiative and by more sceptical commentators as Cameron's 'vanity project'.[12]

The Conservatives' 2010 general election manifesto included a commitment to

> … provide a programme for 16 year olds to give them a chance to develop the skills needed to be active and responsible citizens, mix with people from different backgrounds, and start getting involved in their communities.[13]

Deeply embedded in Cameron's vision of 'The Big Society' (see Chapter 6), this survived the Party's Coalition negotiations with the Liberal Democrats and, as the National Citizen Service, became the central feature of government youth policies over the following decade.

The origins of Cameron's aspiration for a youth 'citizenship' training programme can be traced back at least to a speech in August 2005 shortly after he became Conservative Party leader. In this he pointed to the 'inspiring' work of the Duke of Edinburgh Award Scheme, the Prince's Trust and also of the United States Peace Corps. Apparently seeing these as possible models, he talked of the need for a 'school leaver programme lasting a few months' which 'prepares young people for their responsibilities as adult citizens', teaching them that 'self-respect and self-esteem come from respecting others and putting their needs first'. What was required, he suggested, was a 'new national movement'—'a new national framework for youth engagement and volunteering'—which would become 'an essential part of growing up to be a British citizen, not just an add-on for a select few'.[14]

After restating his ambition the following November to establish 'a school leaver programme',[15] he told 'an incredibly positive and constructive meeting' with 'leading youth organisations' in January 2006 that he was 'struck powerfully by the enthusiasm for this idea'.[16] A commitment then followed in an August 2006 Conservative statement of aims and values to:

> Enabling the voluntary sector to create a national programme for young people to support their personal development and promote a sense of social responsibility as they move from childhood to adult life.[17]

## … via Consultation and 'Piloting'[18] …

Two months later the rhetoric was converted into a more grounded proposal for action when a new organisation, the Young Adult Trust (YAT), announced plans for a small programme to pilot the proposed initiative. As explained by Cameron at the organisation's launch, this would be

> Something like National Service. Not military. Not compulsory. But in the same spirit. Mixing up classes and backgrounds. A residential programme, so young people have real time to live together, work together, get to know each other.[19]

Before it closed down in 2008 through lack of funds,[20] YAT carried out what the Conservatives later called a 'detailed consultation' which later, it acknowledged, was influential in shaping the proposed programme.[21]

More detailed plans for this were set out in 2007 in a Conservative Party 'green paper', *It's time to inspire Britain's teenagers*. In a personally signed Foreword, Cameron talked of what had now become a 'national citizen service for the 21$^{st}$ century'. With the aim of healing 'Britain's broken society', this was required, he claimed, because, 'just as our economy needed radical treatment in the seventies and eighties, so our social fabric urgently needs repair today'. With '(youth) crime, substance abuse or addiction' listed as important indicators of 'a pressing need for change', from very early on a deficit view of young people thus again emerged as underpinning the optimistic expectations he and the programme were setting for them.

Cameron went on to define the NCS 'offer' as 'a six week rites of passage programme for every school leaver … instilling the values of self-respect and social responsibility'. This would 'challenge' participants to, amongst other things, 'push themselves, put in long hours, practise self-discipline … and demonstrate the characteristics of adulthood'. A six-week timeframe was outlined in three implementation examples – one labelled 'Military Week', one 'Three Peaks' and one 'Mini triathlon'.

The green paper also explained the role of a Policy Group, to be co-chaired by Michael Gove, Shadow Secretary of State for Children, Schools and Families, and 'entrepreneur and philanthropist' Martyn Rose. Loughton as shadow youth minister and Paul Oginsky, Cameron's 'youth policy advisor' and founder of YAT, were named as carrying the group's 'executive function'. Group members included business executives, a retired Territorial Army officer and a co-founder and Executive Director of the think tank the Centre for Social Justice.[22]

Action finally followed in March 2009 with the launch of The Challenge. Registered as a charity, this was influenced by a key inspirer of Cameron's Big Society initiative, Lord Wei, and 'led by corporate managers from companies including Poundland, McKinsey management consultancy, Rio Tinto and Deloitte'.[23] Seen as a possible pilot for the NCS, The Challenge aimed to offer 'intensive schemes' of training in leadership, management and communication skills to young people in London and Birmingham.[24] Introducing the scheme, its 'leadership director' said he was 'sure the Conservative Party will be interested to see how things go with a view to testing potential models for its National Citizen Service'.[25]

Between 2009 and 2010, 670 16 year olds participated in the programmes, described as offering 'physical, creative and civic challenges, including running their own community project'.[26]

## ... to a Movement for Cultural and Societal Change

Indicating the closeness of the personal and organisational relationships involved, Cameron made specific reference to The Challenge when he launched NCS in pilot form in Liverpool just two months after he became Prime Minister.[27] He again described young people both 'as passionate and idealistic as any generation before – perhaps more passionate'—and as often 'appear(ing) lost and feel(ing) their lives lack shape and direction'. The NCS—which, he asserted, 'will help to change that'—he defined as

> A kind of non-military national service, it's going to mix young people from different backgrounds ... to teach them what it means to be socially responsible. Above all it's going to inspire a generation of young people to appreciate what they can achieve and how they can be part of the Big Society.

Participants were to spend a minimum of 10 days and nights away from home in order 'to give them the opportunity to develop life skills and resilience and to serve their community'. Amongst its goals were to 'build ... a better understanding of others'; 'encourage team work'; 'challenge young people'; and 'celebrate success'.[28] The pilots, which were to run from June to September 2011 and recruit 'around 10,000 young people', were also expected to contribute to significant cultural changes—to a more cohesive society by mixing participants of different backgrounds; a more responsible society by supporting their transition into adulthood; and a more engaged society by enabling them to work together to create social action projects in their local communities.[29]

Following a competitive tendering process attracting 250 bids, the first contracts for summer projects for 11,000 young people and worth

£30 million were awarded to twelve organisations in November 2010. These included The Prince's Trust, vinspired and a number of locally or regionally based organisations. A national consortium led by Catch 22, described as 'a social business',[30] was awarded the second highest number of places (1515). However, awarded one third (3240) of the places and £7 million, The Challenge emerged as by far 'the lead provider', prompting some (strongly denied) accusations of cronyism.[31]

# Why a National Citizen Service?

Though usually overshadowed by the rhetoric emanating from the highest levels of government, expressions of doubt about the need for and actual form of NCS were raised from the earliest days of its development. The 2011 Commons Education Select Committee report on 'youth services', for example, noted that some of their witnesses saw NCS's introduction as 'inappropriate at a time when other youth services were being cut'. They were concerned, too, that in the longer term it 'might end up in direct competition with other youth services for funds at local authority level' (see Chapter 8).

The Committee also raised early questions about NCS's funding. At that stage, for a six week programme, the cost per participant was set at £1182—compared with only £1228, the Committee pointed out, for Germany's year-long work-based volunteering equivalent. Concluding that 'we cannot support the continued development of National Citizen Service in its current form', the report recommended that the scheme be redesigned as 'a form of accreditation for existing programmes' able to meet NCS's core expectations.[32]

After the government had made clear its disappointment at the Committee's recommendations,[33] the MPs' second report again expressed doubts about NCS's long-term funding arrangements and its likely costs and take-up by 16 year olds. The government, however, remained adamant that, though it 'does not expect to fund the full cost of delivering the programme', it had 'no plans to cease funding (it) … beyond the pilot years' and that 'modelling is being undertaken on likely future costs'.[34]

## Beyond Piloting to Roll-Out

In September 2012 a second round of contracts was announced, to run for two years with the option of a further year up to 2015. In total worth £200 million, these were to provide 30,000 places across the country on programmes run by 120 sub-contracted local projects and groups.[35] In the words of the Chief Executive of The Challenge Network (which this time won five contracts), they would help 'overcome entrenched social division and raise levels of trust in the community'.[36]

Catch 22 and vinspired were again successful bidders as were now the NYA and UK Youth. However, the lead provider, awarded six out of the nineteen regional contracts, was Serco—a multi-national for-profit corporation[37] already facing accusations of unethical practices.[38] Though additional evidence emerged of fraud and manipulation of target data,[39] Civil Society Minister Nick Hurd still felt able to claim that:

> … we are awarding contracts to organisations who have demonstrated that they have the capacity and expertise to deliver high-quality NCS programmes that appeal to young people, benefit communities and offer value for money to the tax payer.

(Serco subsequently withdrew from all subsequent bidding processes.[40]) In October 2014, The Challenge was again the lead provider for the 2015–2018 programmes with contracts for seven of the nineteen regions.[41]

NCS continued to commission the programme's delivery through regional bodies until 2018 when, initially in three regions, it contracted directly with local organisations in order to cut management costs.[42]

## NCS: The New Statutory 'Youth Service'

From its inception in 2010, the NCS had been funded entirely from state sources and overseen by ministers in the Cabinet Office. However, in 2012 it was announced that responsibility for the scheme would be passed to a social enterprise constituted as a trust which, notionally to run from 2013–2014 to 2017–2018, was formally established in February 2014.[43] Its unpaid Chair—Stephen Greene, who had already made a substantial volunteer input into its development—was co-founder and Chief Executive of RockCorps. A charity working with bands, this aimed to 'channel the power of music and celebrity towards making volunteering a part of youth lifestyle' by offering young people concert tickets in return for four hours volunteering.[44]

On taking up his post, Greene made clear that his top priority was to 'depoliticise' the scheme—that is, by no longer taking government money, ensure it could become fully independent. For managing the programme and indeed expanding its reach, 'independence' for Greene meant having a portion of NCS spending funded by such 'corporate sponsors' as the mobile phone company O2 and the supermarket chain ASDA. He also aimed to increase NCS staff from twenty five to thirty five, adding a marketing and communications team. A board of volunteer non-executive members was to be appointed[45] and later a National Youth Board of twenty young people.[46]

In January 2014, the Trust appointed as its first Chief Executive Michael Lynas, a former Cameron senior policy adviser on 'civil society, culture and philanthropy' who had helped establish NCS and was then its director of strategy.[47] He at once re-emphasised the wider social-change aspirations which Cameron had set NCS, saying that for him the priority was 'to build a movement of young people dedicated to making our country a better place, community by community'.[48] He later also endorsed Cameron's description of the scheme as 'a rite of passage'[49] by defining its role as 'to help young people make a really healthy transition to adulthood'.[50]

To carry through the Conservative Party's commitment to the scheme's further expansion—reaffirmed in its 2015 election manifesto—an otherwise deeply neo-liberal government had to suspend its scepticism about the state's role as a public service provider. In May 2016 it announced that, as part of its wider aspirations to 'build a big society', the NCS would be put on a 'permanent statutory footing'—a move which, after many years of campaigning for youth work to be made statutory, left the Chair of the newly formed Institute of Youth Work 'feeling quite hurt'.[51] To raise awareness amongst 'every eligible young person' and their parents, 'particularly those from disadvantaged backgrounds', a legal duty to promote NCS was to be placed on local authorities, secondary schools including academies, sixth-form colleges and independent schools. Discussions were also to be held with devolved administrations on extending the Bill to Scotland, Wales and Northern Ireland.[52]

The Bill to 'secure the NCS's future' was introduced into Parliament in October 2016 and received royal assent in April 2017.[53] The Trust, as well as having a Royal Charter 'to help (it) demonstrate its independence from government and party politics',[54] was also intended to provide a legislative mechanism 'with the aim of making it a national institution while preserving its independent ethos'. This would ensure that, 'with proper accountability to government and Parliament', the Trust had the administrative arrangements and resources needed to manage its increased public funding; and 'an appropriate level of government control for a body in receipt of public funds'.[55]

In January 2018 the government re-affirmed its commitment to the scheme when the then youth minister Tracey Crouch dismissed a Labour Party demand that NCS's effectiveness be evaluated against that of the 'traditional youth services'.[56] By which time—no longer Prime Minister—David Cameron had taken on the 'senior role' of unpaid 'chairman' of the Trust 'patrons'.[57]

# Notes

1. Department of Education and Science, 1965, *Service by Youth*, London, HMSO.
2. DES, 1966, *Service by Youth: Report of a Committee of the Youth Service Development Council*, London, HMSO; Bernard Davies, 1967, 'An Attempt to Tame the Young?', *New Society*, 24 August.
3. Bernard Davies, 1999, *From Thatcherism to New Labour: A History of the Youth Service in England, Volume 2, 1979–1999*, Leicester, National Youth Agency, *Volume 2, 1979–1999*, pp. 79–82.

4. Ian Kirby, 2009, 'Kid's Charity Call-Up: Brown Planning to Force 50 Hours Work on Teens', *News of the World*, 12 April.

5. Bernard Davies, 2008, *The New Labour Years: A History of the Youth Service in England, Volume 3, 1997–2007*, Leicester, National Youth Agency, pp. 123–129.

6. WM Enterprise, 2009, *Evaluation of V's Programme*, April; V, 2008, *Discovering Talent Developing Skills: The Contribution of Volunteering*, September, http://www.wearev.com/images/stories/downloads/discovering%20_talent_-_developing_skills.pdf.

7. Ross Watson, 2009, 'Young People Feel Conservation Work Is "Slave Labour"', *CYPN*, 14 August.

8. Andrew Mycock and Jonathan Tongue, 2011, 'A Big Idea for the Big Society? The Advent of National Citizen Service', *The Political Quarterly*, January–March.

9. Ross Watson, 2010, 'Compulsory National Civic Service Fails to Get Support of Young People', *CYPN*, 6 May.

10. Joe Lepper, 2010, 'Government Announces £6m Teen Volunteering Pilots', *CYPN*, 24 March.

11. Julia Cleverdon and Amanda Jordan, 2012, *In the Service of Others: A Vision for Youth Social Action by 2020*, December, https://www.gov.uk/government/uploads/system/uploads/attachment_data/file/211937/In_the_Service_of_Others_-_A_vision_for_youth_social_action_by_2020.pdf.

12. Sean Murphy, 2017, 'The National Citizen Service and the "Magic Money Tree"', *Youth and Policy*, 9 October, http://www.youthandpolicy.org/articles/ncs-money-tree/.

13. Conservative Party, 2010, *An Invitation to Join the Government of Britain: The Conservative Party Manifesto 2010*, https://www.conservatives.com/~/media/Files/Manifesto2010.

14. David Cameron, 2005a, 'Speech to the Foreign Policy Centre', 24 August, http://fpc.org.uk/fsblob/560.pdf.

15. David Cameron, 2005b, 'Cameron: Bringing Britain Together: Extracts from a Speech to the Political Studies Association', 28 November, http://conservative-speeches.sayit.mysociety.org/speech/600186.

16. Conservatives, 2007, 'It's Time to Inspire Britain's Teenagers: National Citizen Service for the 21st Century: A Six-Week Programme for Every School Leaver', p. 3, http://conservativehome.blogs.com/interviews/files/timetoinspire.pdf.

17. Conservative Party, 2006, *Built to Last: The Aims and Values of the Conservative Party*, London, George Bridges on Behalf or the Conservative Party, http://news.bbc.co.uk/1/shared/bsp/hi/pdfs/16_08_06_cameron.pdf.
18. Tania de St Croix, 2011, 'Struggles and Silences: Policy, Youth Work and the National Citizen Service', *Youth and Policy*, No. 106, May, pp. 43–59.
19. Say-it, 2006, 'David Cameron: Young Adult Trust Will Make a Constructive Difference', October, http://conservative-speeches.sayit.mysociety.org/speech/599955.
20. Tania de St Croix, 2011, op. cit., p. 47.
21. Conservatives, 2007, op. cit., pp. 1–2.
22. Conservatives, 2007, op. cit., pp. 1–2, 12–15, 7, 22.
23. Tania de St Croix, 2015, 'Volunteers and Entrepreneurs? Youth Work and the Big Society', in Bright, Graham (ed), *Youth Work: Histories, Policy and Contexts*, London, Palgrave, pp. 58–79.
24. The Shaftesbury Partnership, 2010, 'The Challenge to Be Model for Conservative' National Citizen Service', the Shaftesbury Partnership, August 2010, http://www.shaftesburypartnership.org/news/challenge-be-model-conservatives%E2%80%99-national-citizen-service; Gabriella Jozwiak, 2010, 'The Challenge Network Announced as Lead Provider of National Citizen Service', *CYPN*, 10 November.
25. Janaki Mahadevan, 2009, 'Charity to Test Concept of National Citizen Service', *CYPN*, 31 March.
26. Gabriella Jozwiak, 2010, op. cit.
27. The Shaftesbury Partnership, 2010, op. cit.
28. GOV.UK, 2010, 'PM to Launch National Citizen Service Pilots for Young People', 22 July, https://www.gov.uk/government/news/prime-minister-to-launch-national-citizen-service-pilots-for-young-people.
29. Cabinet Office, 2010, 'National Citizen Service', Press Release, 29 July.
30. Catch 22, 2018, 'A Social Business', https://www.catch-22.org.uk/?s=income.
31. Neil Puffett, 2012a, 'National Citizen Servant', *CYPN*, 15 May; Gabriella Jozwiak, 2010, op. cit.; Kaye Wiggins, 2010, 'Providers Announced for National Citizen Service Pilot Scheme', *Third Sector*, 11 November.
32. House of Commons Education Committee, 2011, *Services for Young People: Third Report of Session 2010–12, Volume 1*, London, Stationery Office, 23 June; *CYPN*, 2010, paras. 122, 123–131, p. 79.
33. House of Commons Education Committee, 2011, 'Services for Young People: The Government Response: 6th Report of Session 2010–12', London, Stationery Office, September, p. 25.

34. House of Commons Education Committee, 2011, op. cit., para. 13, p. 8.
35. Cabinet Office Press Release, 2012, 'Government Announces Organisations Selected to Deliver National Citizen Service Contracts', 13 September.
36. Neil Puffett, 2012b, 'Serco Consortium Wins Six NCS Contracts', *CYPN*, 13 September.
37. Neil Puffett, 2012b, op. cit.
38. See Corporate Watch, 2012, 'How to Beat Up Refugees, the Serco Way', 30 March, http://www.corporatewatch.org/?lid=4264.
39. Neil Puffett, 2012c, 'Concern Over Serco Involvement in NCS Bid', *CYPN*, 13 August; Neil Puffett, 2013, 'Police to Probe Serco Prisoner Contractor Fraud Claims', *CYPN*, 29 August; Felicity Lawrence, 2013a, 'Private Health Contractor's Staff Told to Cut 999 Calls to Meet Targets', *Guardian*, 23 January; Felicity Lawrence, 2013b, 'Private Contractor Fiddled Data When Reporting to NHS, Says Watchdog', *Guardian*, 7 March.
40. Laura McCardle, 2014a, 'Serco to End National Citizen Service Involvement', *CYPN*, 9 September.
41. Laura McCardle, 2014b, 'NCS Announces Future Regional Providers', *CYPN*, 3 October.
42. Tristan Donovan, 2018, 'NCS Rollout New Contracts to Boost Links with Local Groups', *CYPN*, 16 August.
43. Laura McCardle, 2014c, 'Hurd Hands NCS Over to Independent Trust', *CYPN*, 6 February.
44. Gabriella Jozwiak, 2013, 'Putting the Sparkle into Citizenship', *CYPN*, 17 September; RockCorps, 2017, 'How It All Started', http://www.rockcorps.com/?page_id=5.
45. Gabriella Jozwiak, 2013, op. cit.
46. Laura McCardle, 2014d, 'NCs Trust Appoints First Chief Executive', *CYPN*, 24 January.
47. Laura McCardle, 2014d, op. cit.
48. Laura McCardle, 2014d, op. cit.
49. Darren Hayes, 2014, 'Prime Minister Pledges "NCS for All"', *CYPN*, 2 October.
50. Laura McCardle, 2014e, 'Newfound Independence', *CYPN*, 19 August.
51. Adam Offord, 2016e, 'Youth Sector "Hurt" by Government Plans for NCS', *CYPN*, 3 June.
52. IDYW, 2016, 'Two Fingers to Youth Service as NCS Put on Statutory Footing', 18 May, https://indefenceofyouthwork.com/2016/05/18/

two-fingers-to-youth-service-as-ncs-put-on-statutory-footing/;    Alison
Sharman, 2016, 'National Citizen Service to Have Permanent Statutory
Status, Queen's Speech Says', *Civil Society News*, 18 May, https://www.
civilsociety.co.uk/news/national-citizen-service-to-have-permanent-stat-
utory-status--queen-s-speech-says.html.
53. Neil Puffett, 2017, 'NCS Achieves Statutory Status', *CYPN*, 28 April.
54. GOV.UK, 2016, 'News Story: Government Introduces National
    Citizen Service (NCS) Bill to Parliament', 12 October, https://
    www.gov.uk/government/news/government-introduces-national-
    citizen-service-ncs-bill-to-parliament.
55. www.parliament.uk, 2017, 'National Citizen Service Bill: Commons
    Remaining Stages', 15 March, http://www.parliament.uk/business/
    news/2017/january/national-citizen-service-bill-commons-committee-
    stage/.
56. Joe Lepper, 2018, 'Crouch Dismisses Calls for NCS to Be Evaluated
    Against Traditional Youth Services', *CYPN*, 26 January.
57. Adam Offord, 2016, 'Cameron Takes on Senior NCS Role', *CYPN*, 12
    October.

# Further Reading

Davies, Bernard. 2017. 'Youth Volunteering: The New Panacea?' *Youth &
    Policy*. 30 June.
de St Croix, Tania. 2011. 'Struggles and Silences: Policy, Youth Work and the
    National Citizen Service'. *Youth and Policy*. No. 106, May, pp. 43–59.
de St Croix, Tania. 2015. 'Volunteers and Entrepreneurs? Youth Work and
    the Big Society', in Bright, Graham (ed), *Youth Work: Histories, Policy and
    Contexts,* London: Palgrave, pp. 58–79.
Murphy, Sean. 2014. 'National Citizen's Service (NCS) Is Simply Cameron's
    "Vanity Project"'. *YouthThink Web Blog.* https://youththink.wordpress.
    com/2014/02/17/national-citizens-service-ncs-is-just-camerons-vanity-project/.
Mycock, Andrew and Jonathan Tongue. 2011. 'A Big Idea for the Big Society?
    The Advent of National Citizen Service'. *Political Quarterly*. Vol. 82, No. 1.
    January–March, pp. 56–66.

# 11

# Implementing a National Citizen Service

## The Programmes

Over the years of the NCS's development, headline-catching suggestions were made on what its programme might offer. In 2011 David
Cameron talked about its potential for preventing young people repeat-
ing the previous summer's riots[1] while 'leaked documents' in 2015 suggested he was planning to include fox hunting in the programme.[2] Later
that year there were proposals that it deal with young people in trouble
with the law[3] and, by Cameron's former spokesperson Andy Coulson,
that it be made compulsory and used to combat Muslim 'radicalisation'.[4] By 2017, because, it was claimed, it was 'uniquely placed to help
young people to engage with the digital economy', it was being tasked
with improving young people's employability[5]; and by the new Prime
Minister Teresa May, with offering 'mental health wellbeing support' for
coping with exam and family pressures.[6]

By then, the school summer holidays version of the programme
offered two five-day residentials focused on outdoor activities and on
giving participants 'skills in a particular area whilst discovering more
about the local community'. Two non-residential weeks followed during

© The Author(s) 2019                                                    **195**
B. Davies, *Austerity, Youth Policy and the Deconstruction of the Youth Service
in England*, https://doi.org/10.1007/978-3-030-03886-1_11

which participants met a local charity or community organisation and, as a 'team', had to 'come up with ideas for a project to make a difference'. After getting feedback, their proposal was implemented through 30 hours of 'social action'.[7] From 2012—with the minister for civil society Nick Hurd pressing for accreditation of NCS participants[8]—shorter programmes were on offer in the autumn and, from 2014, in the spring half-terms.[9]

## Staffing: Roles, Recruitment and Training

The staff structure created for the pilot programmes was described as

> … strategic, intermediate or cross-cutting. Among smaller and/or direct delivery providers, structures were flatter and did not always include separate intermediary staff (strategic staff played these roles).[10]

These arrangements provided residential and community-based roles for workers with a range of skills and qualifications, including those wanting to gain experience ranging from face-to-face practice to project management. Some job advertisements asked for front-line practitioners with 'relevant diploma and/or degree courses which can cover youth work, SEND education, residential care work, social work, challenging behaviour and behaviour analysis'. For managers, 'a strong academic record or equivalent relevant experience' was required. According to the evaluation of the pilots, however:

> All providers noted the importance of professional experience, yet not all required specific qualifications and felt personal qualities were more important; another view was that qualifications were required but that they should not be enough on their own.[11]

With many advertisements making no reference to qualifications, at the pilot stage one view of the programmes was that staff were 'largely untrained'.[12]

Given the nature of the programmes, for most staff the roles provided only short-term employment, no job security and limited prospects of career progression through NCS itself. Concerns thus emerged from the pilots about whether enough staff with appropriate experience could be recruited. By 2012 one response was to offer placements to students on youth work courses[13]—a source of face-to-face workers which anecdotal evidence suggested remained important. In an effort to attract newly qualified teachers, in 2015 NCS also partnered with Teach First which promoted a two-year employment-based teacher training programme.[14]

Staff training for the pilots focused on 'three key areas'—'NCS orientation, working with young people and practical necessities'. However, the 2012 evaluation report recommended that:

> Staffing models should aim to include clear roles and lines of responsibility, information-sharing mechanisms, suitable staff numbers and consistency of approach in working with young people.[15]

The report also identified lessons applied from the pilots—for example, that 'staff from schools or with existing youth work experience … were able to "hit the ground running" with limited supervision' while 'those new to working with young people required more support.[16] However, reinforcing the conclusion of another analysis that staff could be 'poorly supported',[17] it also concluded that providers hadn't adequately anticipated 'the level of support needed in teams where young people had specific needs or challenging behaviour'.[18]

Later evidence indicated an NCS approach to staffing which assumed two and half unpaid days of compulsory training, long working hours (often including overnight stays at residentials) and pay at low daily rates, with managers carrying heavy staff responsibilities as well as for young people.[19]

## Participants' Recruitment and Retention

A key strategic—and indeed political—goal for NCS was, year on year, to attract increasing numbers of participants. Though usually defined as 15–17 year olds, in January 2017 Cabinet Office minister Rob Wilson suggested that 'from time to time' and 'at its discretion, the trust may allow children who are 15 or 18–24 on the programme'—something confirmed by the draft legislation for the Trust's Royal Charter.[20]

Though ministers continued to promote the scheme as a major force for social change—a 'gateway to the big society'[21]—potential recruits were promised more pragmatic personal gains. These included relevance 'to the College course the young person is taking'; counting towards 'work experience or guided learning hours'; 'graduating' with 'a signed certificate from the Prime Minister'; and official recognition of the scheme 'by UCAS (the Universities and Colleges Admissions Service), leading universities and UK employers'.[22]

## Setting—and Missing—Recruitment Targets

From 2011 to 2016 recruitment to the programmes rose year on year (see Table 11.1). However the starting numbers were always, sometimes substantially, below target while, as one possible indication of how representative the recruits were of their age group, the evaluation of the 2011 pilots found that, before coming on the scheme, '80 per cent had engaged in one or more of a list of pro-social activities compared with 67% in the comparison sample'.[23]

A National Audit Office (NAO) report on the 2016 programmes revealed that of the 333,000 respondents who had expressed an initial interest, 36% actually registered and 28% (92,700) attended. Some 8.6% (8500) failed to complete.[24] In July 2018 the government admitted that a non-recoupable £9.8 million had been paid to providers for unfilled places.[25] By then the Trust was planning to sign a contract worth £75 million, excluding VAT, for a four-year marketing campaign, to include 'advertorial pieces' in *The Sun* newspaper, on television, online and through billboard advertising.[26] Intensified marketing was also implemented through repeated emails and texts to young people in the target age group using contact details provided by schools.[27]

Undeterred by repeatedly missed targets, the Cabinet Office committed itself in February 2016 to a further substantial expansion of the scheme by 2020/2021, to 360,000 places—60% of that year's projected

**Table 11.1** NCS recruitment 2011–2016

| | 2011[28] (Pilots) | 2012[29] | 2013[30] | 2014[31] | 2015[32,33] | 2016[34] |
|---|---|---|---|---|---|---|
| Places promised/ commissioned[35,36] | 10,000 | 32,000 | 41,000 | 90,000 | 120,000 | 150,000 |
| Places filled | 8500 | 26,000 | 65,000 | 76,000 | 76,000 | 92,700 |
| Shortfall (%) | 15 | 19 | 2.4 | 25.5 | 37 | 38 |

*Sources* Laura McCardle, 2014, 'NCS Saves as Little as Nine Pence for Every £1 Spent, Evaluation Finds', *CYPN*, 14 August; Gabriella Jozwiak, 2017, 'NCS Programmes May Lose Money, Research Suggests', *CYPN*, 9 March; Liam Kay, 2017, 'National Citizens Service Benefits Evaluation Published', *Third Sector*, 8 March; Daniel Cameron, et al., 2017, *National Citizens Service 2015—Evaluation: Main Report*, Ipsos Mori, March, https://www.ncsyes.co.uk/sites/default/files/ NCS%202015%20Evaluation%20Report%20FINAL.pdf

16 year olds and almost four times the 2016 estimated number of participants.[37] NAO calculated that, guided by the past annual rate of increase in participants, this could mean a shortfall in recruitment by 2020/2021 of 147,000, or over 40%.[38]

The NAO report also concluded that participation targets were being set 'without considering performance in previous years or what could be achieved'. It pointed out that 'the 2015-16 target required participant numbers to increase 90% from 2014, significantly more than the actual annual growth of 31% between 2014 and 2015.'[39] One apparent response to these criticisms, revealed in October 2017, was a plan to trial a three-week programme.[40] Another—to 'make sure as many teenagers as possible get to experience NCS'—was the appointment in July 2017 of new Trust 'patrons', including an 'entrepreneur' and a national voluntary sector chief executive.[41]

After legislation had made NCS statutory (see Chapter 10), in order to 'embed' NCS locally and increase recruitment, the DCMS's October 2017 guidance proposed that a senior council officer act as its lead contact locally with responsibility for its promotion.[42] By the end of 2017 the DfE was also suggesting that, to stimulate the recruitment drive, the NCS be one of the contributing organisations to the activities of twelve 'Opportunities Areas' set up in 2016 to increase social mobility.[43]

## Social 'Mixing'

Within the overall recruitment targets, the 'mixing' of social groups was throughout a high priority commitment.[44] Overall, the NAO report confirmed, this was being achieved, with 'a greater proportion being recruited from minority groups, such as those on free school meals, than the national population'. This conclusion was qualified, however, by evidence that, particularly in relation to ethnicity and income, 'at local authority level the mix of NCS participants has not always reflected local area characteristics'.[45]

An August 2015 report from the Cabinet Office reached some similar contradictory conclusions. In Surrey, for example, the fifth least deprived area in England, 2106 young people had joined up compared with 2060 in four 'deprived' London boroughs. Though Birmingham, the seventh most deprived local authority area in England, had attracted the most participants, many more 'deprived' areas had much lower levels of participation. One (Labour) MP thus suggested that '… NCS disproportionately benefits youngsters with assertive parents, while general cuts to youth services have disproportionately disadvantaged those in areas of deprivation'.[46]

# Impacts and Outcomes: Short-Term, 'Monetised' and Long-Term

Over its first five years (2011–2016) annual evaluations provided evidence of participants' overall satisfaction with the scheme.

<u>2012</u>: 88% said they 'would definitely recommend NCS to friends'.[47]
<u>2014</u>: 69% rated the staff as 'good'.[48]
<u>2015</u>: 'Around nine in ten rated the NCS staff that they spent time with as good'.[49]

Within the three 'broad aims' set for the scheme—'to make society more cohesive, more responsible and more engaged'—the evaluation reports also reported on four more specific 'identified impacts on young people':

- Improving teamwork, communication and leadership.
- Facilitating transition to adulthood.
- Improving social mixing—sometimes also linked to improving social cohesion.
- Encouraging community involvement.[50]

Here it sought 'to measure the impact … on young people's attitudes and behaviour; to 'estimate the (programme's) value for money; and to identify 'lessons for (its) design and delivery'.[51]

Ratings on some of these measures in the five years were negative—for example, for the 2015 programmes, on impacts on 'attitudes to mixing with people from different backgrounds' and for having developed wider social networks.[52] Overall, however, year-on-year in these key areas the evaluations claimed evidence of participants' positive views of the scheme.

Improving teamwork, communication and leadership

2012: The proportion of young people feeling confident in leading a team increased by 17 percentage points more among NCS participants than among the 2011 control group.[53]

2016: Participant gains were identified in all three areas as well as in their 'wellbeing'.[54]

Facilitating transition to adulthood

2011: 95% of participants said they had been helped to develop 'more skills for the future'.[55]

2013: 83% of participants said they felt 'better able to deal with the transition to adulthood'.[56]

Improving social mixing

2011: 85% of participant said they felt 'more positive towards people from different backgrounds'.[57]

Encouraging community involvement

2012: 60% said they felt a greater responsibility to their local community.[58]

2015: Summer and autumn 'completers' were giving 17 additional volunteering hours and Spring 'completers' 19 additional hours.[59]

The evaluations also gave high priority to 'monetising' young people's gains from the scheme. The 2011 report for example concluded that it had 'returned' up to £2 for every £1 invested in it, resulting in 'social benefits' worth up to £28 million. Its calculations were based on estimates of the value of the participants' volunteering; their 'improved leadership and communication' and their take-up of new educational opportunities, bolstered by 'increased confidence'. Included, too, were estimates of the wages participants could earn in the future and the extra £3 million in tax revenues this would generate.[60]

The 2012 evaluation, however, acknowledged that the 2011 social benefits figure of £28 million was 'overly optimistic' and needed to be 'revised down to £10–11 million'. Nonetheless, on the grounds that 'significant changes had been put in place … to encourage and support participants', the researchers put an even higher monetary value on that year's gains, calculating that, at £102 million, the 'social benefits' of the summer programme were 2.8 times greater than the £36.8 million it cost.[61]

The estimated monetary gains identified subsequently varied from year to year but generally were more modest:

2013: For every £1 spent, gains for the summer programme were estimated at between £1.39 and £6.10 and for the autumn programme at between £1.09 and £6.09.[62]

2014: With three programmes running over the year, the claimed benefit-to-cost ratios were:

- spring programme: between £0.75 and £3.11 for every £1 spent;
- summer programme: between £1.12 and £3.98 for every £1 spent;
- autumn programme: between £0.96 and £1.71 for every £1 spent.[63]

2015: Using different methodologies from previous years, estimated benefit-to-cost figures were 70p for each £1 spent on the spring programme, with only the autumn programme providing a 'social benefit return'. However, a new consultancy contracted to assess 'wellbeing impact' reported benefits of between £2.20 and £4.15 for every £1 invested.[64]

<u>2016</u>: For every pound spent, economic and volunteering benefits for the summer were estimated as worth £1.79 and for the autumn £2.21.[65]

These yearly evaluations did give indications of possible longer-term impacts. In May 2017, for example, former NCS participants were said to be 4% more likely to go to university, with higher proportions (7.62% for boys and 9.8% for girls) coming from 'poor background'.[66] However, given that the evaluations were usually carried out, at most, sixteen months after the programmes ended, the claimed impacts identified were mostly short-term.

The evaluators—for example of the 2013 programme—were themselves sometimes cautious about the sustainability of individual young people's personal gains. Though that year's report concluded that the scheme may 'potentially deliver several long-term benefits' and that 'the most robust methods' had been used for estimating these, it added that 'there is inevitably some uncertainty in the results at this stage'.[67] The following year evaluators warned that the expected impact on educational participation had 'not emerged in the manner originally anticipated',[68] with some of them for example suggesting that

> … (the) positive attitudes of the NCS participation in 2011 towards education were not reflected in the actual uptake of educational opportunities between 2011 and 2012. Thus the anticipated impact of NCS 2011 on education did not appear to materialise.[69]

Nonetheless, from its earliest conception, the NCS vision went beyond immediate personal gains for individual participants to, as Lynas put in 2014, '… helping to build a more socially cohesive, mobile and engaged country'.[70] By 2017, however, the NAO was concluding that the scheme (now moved from the Cabinet Office into the DCMS) '… has not yet established a baseline to assess longer-term performance or identified how longer-term outcomes could be tracked, which can be difficult to do'.[71] A Commons Public Accounts Select Committee report released two months later also pointed to the absence of 'the data to measure long-term outcomes or understand what works' given that the evaluations so far had only 'assess(ed) the short-term impact of NCS on a sample of participants'.[72]

# Open Cheque-Book Funding

At a time when the government's unrelenting 'austerity' message was that there was no alternative but to cut crucial public services such as the NHS, the police, adult social care and welfare benefits, these efforts to demonstrate NCS's value-for-money were seen as essential for justifying the increasing amounts of public money provided for it. With its cost already increased by 2012 to £84.2 million,[73] a total of £200 million of 'investment' in the scheme was being forecast by 2014.[74] Two years later, the announcement that the NCS was to be made statutory came with a government commitment to provide a further £1.2 billion up to 2020/21.[75] A line in one of the tables in the 2017 FAO report captured these year-on-year increases in actual, forecast and/or planned spending over these six financial years[76] (Table 11.2).

In August 2015 it also emerged that for 2016–2017 the Cabinet Office had in addition allocated the NCS Trust £4.9 million for 'marketing and communications', with a further £3.6 million promised in November.

Rising, too, year-on-year was the cost of each NCS place (Table 11.3).

The NAO's reaction to these figures in 2017 was again forthright:

> The cost per participant needs to fall by 29%, to £1,314 in 2019, for the Trust to provide 300,000 places and stay within the funding envelope made available as part of the autumn Spending Review.[77]

**Table 11.2** Actual, forecast or planned spending on NCS—2011–2016

|  | 2014–2015 (actual) | 2015–2016 (actual) | 2016–2017 (forecast) | 2017–2018 (plan) | 2018–2019 (plan) | 2019–2020 (plan) |
|---|---|---|---|---|---|---|
| Total spend | £118 million | £157 million | £187 million | £219 million | £282 million | £322 million |

**Table 11.3** Cost per NCS place—2011–2016

| Year | 2011 | ....2012 | 2014 | 2016 |
|---|---|---|---|---|
| Cost per place | £1553 | .....£1662 | £1385–£1620 | £1863 (estimated) |

# Beyond the Political Consensus

In August 2013, the response of Labour's shadow education minister to the 2012 NCS evaluation was that '… youth services have a positive impact on educational attainment, social inclusion, community cohesion and a whole range of other benefits'. The nearest he came to a critique of the scheme was to suggest that the data assessing its impact needed to be as robust as possible.[78]

The NAO report, discussed above, was in fact the first substantial challenge to the dominant positive consensus on NCS since the 2011 House of Commons Education Select Committee report (see Chapter 8). Many of the NAO criticism's re-appeared two months later in the 2017 Commons Public Accounts Select Committee report which also questioned the achievability even of the lowered recruitment target for 2020–2021 announced the previous month—down from 360,000 to 247,000. Pointing out that still this 'requires an increase in the rate of participant growth from 17,000 to 38,500 … each year', the Committee 'expected' the Trust to produce 'detailed plans to support achieving the revised participation figures within six months'.

No less forthright were its comments on the handling of the scheme's financing. It compared 'the 2016 expected cost per participant … (of) £1863 of taxpayers' money' with the '£550 to create a place in the scouts that lasts at least four years'. It, too, was critical not only of the 'around £10 million in 2016 (paid) for places that were not filled' but also of 'the Trust's relaxed attitude about non-recovery of these funds'. It questioned its 'standards of transparency'—for example over some salary increases—given that since 2014–2015 the 'expected £475 million of taxpayers' money' it had received constituted 99% of its income. Indeed, for a body with such near-total dependence on public funds, it suggested that its establishment as a trust had been allowed to happen 'without appropriate governance arrangements'. (The report was published nearly a year after the liquidation of Engage4Life which, with NCS contracts worth nearly £1 billion, had run up debts of more than £500,000 including £400,000 owed to nine local sub-contracted providers.[79])

Also unusual for such a high profile body, the Committee also queried the NCS's face-to-face practice and staffing. Was the 'dispersed delivery model involving different organisations' robust enough to assure the safety of the young people going through the programme? Did the Trust in fact have 'the skills and expertise necessary to oversee a project of this scale' given that it had 'been expanding its staff numbers rapidly since 2013, but only appointed a "Chief People Officer" in summer 2016'? The report recorded that

> The Chief Executive … told us that he has no experience running an organisation of this size but has set up a youth organisation and worked with bigger budgets than NCS as a consultant. We were unclear how these roles equated to setting up a project and implementing changes of the scale required.[80]

Calling the Select Committee report 'damning', the Labour Party's shadow 'youth minister' Steve Reed then insisted that '(t)he public need to know that every penny spent by the NCS is better spent by them than on the many other youth activities the Tories have cut'.[81] In March 2017 the Liberal Democrats' spokesperson in the Lords demanded that the NCS Bill be halted because, she argued, NCS did not meet the basic requirements for a Royal Charter. For this to be awarded, she pointed out, 'a professional body or charity needed to have a solid record of achievement and (be) financially sound'. As 'a government vanity project, delivered by a favoured organisation with a high-profile chair' and with 'a weak governance structure and a patchy performance record', NCS, she said, had failed to meet these standards.[82]

# So Again—Where Is the Youth Service; Where Is the Youth Work?

## NCS—A Replacement for Open Access Youth Work?

From time to time, both by those within NCS but also, significantly, by some within the voluntary youth sector, the scheme was explained as at least helping to sustain and even as further developing youth work and its open access facilities. In 2012, for example, some of the £900,000 NYA received from the government's Social Action Fund (matched by an additional £500,000 from the private mobile phone company O2) was to pay for youth workers in four English regions to support former NCS participants' continuing volunteering activities in their communities. The following year, while still Chief Executive of London Youth, Charlotte Hill claimed the scheme was encouraging previously 'disengaged' young people to join youth clubs.[83] By then (2012), the minister for civil society was talking of 'look(ing) for ways of linking NCS with all other youth programmes'[84] while in 2015 Rob Wilson suggested that NCS was 'complementary to, not a replacement for', local authority facilities.[85]

Youth work organisations, too, courted NCS collaboration. In 2016, UK Youth's Chief Executive suggested in an open letter to David Cameron that 'the solution to the NCS growth challenge … may lie with other players in the youth sector who have had longer to build their reach'.[86] This offer, which the NCS Trust itself seemed keen to take up,[87] was given practical expression in 2017 through 'a three-year partnership deal' aimed at 'integrating' the NCS experience into Scouting in order to 'support the growth of both organisations …'[88]

Other responses, however—such as the Labour MP's comment quoted above on the NCS's 'disproportionate benefits' for young people with assertive parents—not only cast doubt on these more optimistic 'takes' on NCS as a vehicle for open access youth work. They also saw it as potentially inflicting further damage on the Youth Service. The LGA for example argued that

> … with many local services under pressure since 2010 following substantial cuts to local government spending, it is vital that money to run NCS should not be at the expense of restoring and supporting local services for young people.[89]

One question not considered by the Public Accounts Select Committee's report was how far the NCS's £1.26 billion funding to 2020 could have helped that restoration. If, for example, the planned

NCS budget had been reduced in proportion to the 31% cut in its recruitment target announced in February 2017, the amount saved would have come close to matching the accumulated five-year cuts in local authority Youth Service budgets—some £387 million—identified by Unison's research.[90] By 2017 the Network of Regional Youth Work Units and In Defence of Youth Work (IDYW) (see Chapter 17) were thus both arguing for some if not all of the NCS budget to be refocused on year-round, community-based open access youth work provision.[91]

## NCS—Process with Task?

Beyond these top-down policy and funding questions, what also remained disputed was how far, in its face-to-face practice, the relationship within the NCS programmes between task and process was given an explicit practice focus. Given that some participants might have mental health needs[92] or even that they might use the trusting adult relationships developed to make serious personal disclosures, it was not clear how practitioners balanced, on the one hand, meeting the policy-makers' high priority goal of a 'successfully completed' community project with, on the other, responding to these young people's in-the-moment, perhaps pressing, needs and expectations. A parallel ambiguity existed over the scheme's prioritisation of participants' here-and-now concerns and the longer-term 'transition-to-adulthood' objectives it was expected to achieve.

Other significant practice questions also lacked explicit responses. How far, for example, were the apparently 'safe' forms of 'social action' being used explicitly committed to tipping balances of power in young people's favour? Rather than assuming that just bringing young people together in the same room or on the same cliff face—or in the same 'community'—would generate its own 'organic' benefits, how far did the scheme's strong emphasis on 'social mixing' allow and support staff to openly address prejudiced and oppressive behaviour as this actually occurred amongst the participants?

As Tania de St Croix pointed out as early in NCS's development as 2011, throughout its build-up and then in its early evaluations, the language in which both its aspirations and its outcomes was framed was highly simplistic. It for example seemed to take little account of the increasingly lengthy and complex transition into adulthood of the 16 year olds it was recruiting, especially in the aftermath of the 2007 financial crisis. It seemed to regard and treat the 'team work' it was advocating as 'unproblematically … a simple matter of meeting and doing things together'. Given its 'familiar old-fashioned and simplified view of youth activities' and that 'different adults (were) involved in each element of the scheme, many of them volunteers', it also seemed to have 'little notion of skilled workers building positive relationships with and between young people'.

Indeed, with those workers 'referred to as "youth leaders", a term long seen in the profession as non-egalitarian', de St Croix's conclusion was that ultimately 'the concept of youth work is absent'. Staff, she pointed out, were for example allowed little time to prepare for discussions on such complex matters as what young people had learnt about themselves and what they had learnt about adulthood, community and Britishness. A worker's role thus in effect ended up '… limited to supervising and leading rather than being based on notions of informal education and empowerment'.[93]

Far, therefore, from responding when appropriate in improvisational ways to what participants brought with them, most NCS staff were required to implement pre-planned sessions based on standardised content, timings, outcomes and evaluations. With similar constraints operating within the social action activities,[94] prima facie, the NCS's face-to-face practice thus differed substantially from the informal educational approaches of an open access youth centre or a detached youth work project.

# Notes

1. Rachel Williams, 2011, 'Will the National Citizens Service Stop Young People Rioting?' *Guardian*, 30 August, https://www.theguardian.com/society/2011/aug/30/national-citizen-service-prevent-rioting.

2. Neil Puffett, 2015, 'Tories to Include Fox Hunting in National Citizens Service', *CYPN*, 1 April.
3. Adam Offord, 2015a, 'NCS Under Consideration as "Intervention" for Young Offenders', *CYPN*, 24 November.
4. Kate McCann, 2015, 'Andy Coulson: David Cameron Must Make National Service Compulsory to Curb Extremism and Leave a Legacy', *The Telegraph*, 13 December, http://www.telegraph.co.uk/news/politics/12048386/Andy-Coulson-David-Cameron-must-make-National-Service-compulsory-to-curb-extremism-and-leave-a-legacy.html.
5. Joe Lepper, 2017a, 'NCS to Take on Careers Role', *CYPN*, 2 March.
6. Tristan Donovan, 2017a, 'Mental Health Support to Be Offered as Part of National Citizens Service', *CYPN*, 17 August.
7. Inspire, Guide, Change, 'NCS Programmes—Autumn '16, Spring '17, Summer '17', www.teamigc.co.uk/app/download/.../NCS+2016+-+2017+Programme+Dates.pdf.
8. Lauren Higgs, 2012, 'Conservative Conference: Hurd Seeks Accreditation for Youth Scheme Participations', *CYPN*, 8 October.
9. Caroline Booth, et al., 2015, *National Citizens Service 2014 Evaluation: Main Report*, Ipsos Mori, December, https://www.ipsos-mori.com/researchpublications/publications/1692/National-Citizen-Service-2013-Evaluation.aspx; Inspire, Guide, Change, 'NCS Programmes—Autumn '16, Spring '17, Summer '17', 9 April 2017, www.teamigc.co.uk/app/download/.../NCS+2016+-+2017+Programme+Dates.pdf.
10. NatCen, 2012, *Evaluation of National Citizens Service Pilots: Interim Report*, NatCen Social Research, May, para. 7.2.3, p. 61, https://www.bl.uk/collection-items/evaluation-of-national-citizen-service-pilots-interim-report.
11. NatCen, 2012, op. cit., para. 7.2.2, p. 60.
12. Tania de St Croix, 2015, 'Volunteers and Entrepreneurs? Youth Work and the Big Society', in Bright, Graham (ed), *Youth Work: Histories, Policy and Contexts*, London, Palgrave, pp. 58–79.
13. Neil Puffett, 2012a, 'Flagship NCS Scheme to Provide Placements for Youth Work Students', *CYPN*, 30 April.
14. Adam Offord, 2015b, 'Thousands of Teachers Expected to Work on National Citizens Service', *CYPN*, 7 August.
15. NatCen, 2013, *Findings from the Evaluations of the 2012 Summer and Autumn NCS Programmes*, NatCen Social Research, July, p. 15; Neil Puffett, 2012b, 'Government Hails Success of National Citizens Service Scheme', *CYPN*, 17 May; NatCen, 2012, op. cit.

16. NatCen, 2012, op. cit.; NatCen, 2013, op. cit., para. 6.3.1, p. 65.
17. Tania de St Croix, 2015, op. cit.
18. NatCen, 2012, op. cit.; NatCen, 2013, op. cit., July, para. 6.4.1, p. 66.
19. Tania de St Croix, 2017, 'Youth Work, Performativity and the New Youth Impact Agenda: Getting Paid for Numbers?', *Journal of Education Policy*, Vol. 33, No. 3, September, pp. 414–438.
20. Joe Lepper, 2017b, 'Government to Legislate to Make National Citizens Service Available for 25-Year-Olds', *CYPN*, 18 January; Neil Puffett, 2017a, 'NCS "Will Not Proactively Recruit" 18- to 25-Year Olds', *CYPN*, 30 January.
21. Rachel Williams, 2010, 'Young Volunteer Try Out Model for the National Citizens Service', Guardian.co.uk, 10 November.
22. NCS, 2017, 'It All Starts at Yes: NCS Programmes—Autumn '16, Spring '17, Summer '17'.
23. NatCen, 2012, op. cit., p. 8; Neil Puffett, 2012b, op. cit.
24. National Audit Office, 2017, *National Citizens Service*, Summary, para. 15; Figure 12, p. 34.
25. Joe Lepper, 2018, 'Youth Minister Prioritises Reducing Unfilled NCS Places', *CYPN*, 19 July.
26. Adam Offord, 2016b, 'NCS Marketing Budget Tops £8m in 2015', *CYPN*, 31 August.
27. Personal Communication.
28. Neil Puffett, 2012b, op. cit.; NatCen, 2012, op. cit.
29. Darren Hayes, 2013, 'National Citizens Service Participation Rises Three-Fold', *CYPN*, 1 August.
30. National Audit Office, 2017, *National Citizens Service*, National Audit Office, January, https://www.nao.org.uk/wp-content/uploads/2017/02/National-Citizen-Service.pdf.
31. Adam Offord, 2015c, 'National Citizens Service Take-Up Hit by Lack of Demand', *CYPN*, 7 October; Adam Offord, 2016a, 'NCS Spring and Autumn Programmes "May Lose Money"', *CYPN*, 4 January; Liam Kay, 2015, 'Report Reveals Impact of National Citizens Service Scheme', *Third Sector*, 23 December.
32. Gabriella Jozwiak, 2017, op. cit.; Liam Kay, 2017, op. cit.; Daniel Cameron, et al., 2017, op. cit.
33. Tristan Donovan, 2017b, 'NCS Evaluation Finds "Positive Short-Term Impact"', *CYPN*, 21 December.
34. Tristan Donovan, 2017b, op. cit.

35. Darren Hayes, 2013, op. cit.
36. Neil Puffett, 2012b, op. cit.; NatCen, 2012, op. cit., NatCen, 2013, op. cit., July, p. 19.
37. David Ainsworth, 2016, 'National Citizens Service to Grow to 360,000 Places a Year at Likely Costs of £470m a Year', *Civil Society News*, 22 February; National Audit Office, 2017, op. cit., 'Key Facts', para. 2.13.
38. Adam Offord, 2016a, op. cit.
39. National Audit Office, 2017, op. cit., para. 2.13, p. 34.
40. Joe Lepper, 2017c, 'NCS Programme "Could Be Shortened to Save Money"', *CYPN*, 13 October.
41. Neil Puffett, 2017b, 'NCS Appoints 18 Patrons in Effort to Boost Uptake', *CYPN*, 14 July.
42. Neil Puffett, 2017c, 'Government Calls on Councils to Take on NCS Role', *CYPN*, 25 October.
43. Naim Moukarzel, 2018, 'How Councils Are Working to Boost NCS Prospects for Young People', *CYPN*, 2 January.
44. Neil Puffett, 2012b, op. cit.; NatCen, 2012, op. cit.
45. National Audit Office, 2017, op. cit.
46. Adam Offord, 2015d, 'NCS Figures Highlight Low Uptake in Deprived Areas', *CYPN*, 11 August.
47. Darren Hayes, 2013, op. cit.; NatCen, 2013, op. cit., July.
48. Caroline Booth, et al., 2015, op. cit., p. 21.
49. David Cameron, et al., 2017, op. cit., p. 13.
50. NatCen, 2012, op. cit., Section 1.1, p. 16.
51. NatCen, 2012, op. cit., Section 2.1, p. 18.
52. Gabriella Jozwiak, 2017, op. cit.; Liam Kay, 2017, op. cit.; Daniel Cameron, et al., 2017, op. cit.
53. NatCen, 2013, op. cit., July.
54. Sally Panayiotou, et al., 2017, *National Citizens Service 2016 Evaluation*, Kantar/LSE, December, p. 27, https://www.ncsyes.co.uk/sites/default/files/NCS%202016%20EvaluationReport_FINAL.pdf.
55. Neil Puffett, 2012b, op. cit.; NatCen, 2012, op. cit.
56. Neil Puffett, 2012b, op. cit.; NatCen, 2012, op. cit.
57. Neil Puffett, 2012b, op. cit.; NatCen, 2012, op. cit.
58. Neil Puffett, 2012b, op. cit.; NatCen, 2012, op. cit.
59. David Cameron, et al., 2017, op. cit.
60. Neil Puffett, 2012b, op. cit.; NatCen, 2012, op. cit.
61. Darren Hayes, 2013, op. cit.; NatCen, 2013, op. cit.

62. Laura McCardle, 2014, op. cit.; Caroline Booth, et al., 2015, op. cit.
63. Adam Offord, 2016a, op. cit.; Liam Kay, 2015, op. cit.
64. Gabriella Jozwiak, 2017, op. cit.; Liam Kay, 2017, op. cit.; Daniel Cameron, et al., 2017, op. cit.
65. Sally Panayiotou, et al., 2107, op. cit.; Tristan Donovan, 2017c, 'NCS Evaluation Finds "Positive Short-Term Impact"', *CYPN*, 21 December.
66. Joe Lepper, 2017d, 'NCS Graduates "More Likely to Go to University", Study Claims', *CYPN*, 3 May.
67. Laura McCardle, 2014, op. cit.; Caroline Booth, et al., 2015, op. cit.
68. Adam Offord, 2016a, op. cit.; Liam Kay, 2015, op. cit.
69. Laura McCardle, 2014, op. cit.; Caroline Booth, et al., 2015, op. cit.
70. Adam Offord, 2016a, op. cit.
71. National Audit Office, 2017, op. cit., 'Summary'.
72. Public Accounts Committee, 2017, *National Citizens Service Enquiry*, Conclusion 1, https://www.parliament.uk/business/committees/committees-a-z/commons-select/public-accounts-committee/inquiries/parliament-2015/national-citizen-service-16-17/.
73. Adam Offord, 2016a, op. cit.; Liam Kay, 2015, op. cit.
74. Neil Puffett, 2012b, op. cit.; NatCen, 2012, op. cit.
75. Neil Puffett, 2016, 'Queen's Speech: £1.2bn Set Aside for NCS Expansion', *CYPN*, 18 May; Adam Offord, 2016a, op. cit.; Liam Kay, 2015, op. cit.
76. National Audit Office, 2017, op. cit., Figure 8, p. 26.
77. National Audit Office, 2017, op. cit., 'Summary', p. 10, para. 23.
78. Darren Hayes, 2013, op. cit.
79. Neil Puffett, 2017d, 'Exclusive: Major National Citizens Service Provider Goes Bust', *CYPN*, 13 March.
80. Public Accounts Committee, 2017, op. cit., 'Conclusions 2, 8, 5, 6, 7, 3, 8'.
81. Neil Puffett, 2017e, 'Labour Pushes for Action on NCS "Failings"', *CYPN*, 14 March.
82. Andy Hillier, 2017, 'Lib Dems Call for Halt in National Citizens Service Bill', *Third Sector*, 4 April; Elizabeth (Baroness) Barker, 2017, 'National Citizens Service Is Simply a Vanity Project', *Third Sector*, 4 April.
83. Gabriella Jozwiak, 2013, 'Conservative Conference: NCS "Widens Reach of Youth Services"', *CYPN*, 2 October.
84. Lauren Higgs, 2012, op. cit.

85. Adam Offord, 2015e, 'Minister "Very Disappointed" with Council Youth Service Cuts', *CYPN*, 6 July.
86. Adam Offord, 2016c, 'Youth Sector Could Help Tackle NCS "Growth Challenge"', *CYPN*, 8 June.
87. Adam Offord, 2016d, 'Bid to Get Grassroots Organisations Involved with NCS', *CYPN*, 13 July.
88. Neil Puffett, 2017f, 'National Citizens Service and Scouts Strike Partnership Deal', *CYPN*, 21 July.
89. Adam Offord, 2016e, 'NCS Investment Prompts Youth Services Warning', *CYPN*, 19 May.
90. See Unison, 2014, *The Damage: UK Youth Services—How Cuts Are Removing Opportunities for Young People and Damaging Their Lives*, London, Unison; Unison, 2016, *The Damage: A Future at Risk—Cuts in Youth Services*, London, Unison; Hannah Richardson, 2016, 'Youth Services Heading Towards Collapse, Says Union', BBC, 12 August, file:///C:/Users/Owner/Desktop/Documents/Writing/Book4/Research/Damage2'BBCRpt.htm.
91. Tristan Donovan, 2017c, 'Youth Work Network Calls for Redistribution of NCS Cash', *CYPN*, 8 August; Neil Puffett, 2017f, 'Call for NCS Budget to Be Diverted to Youth Work', *CYPN*, 9 October.
92. Tristan Donovan, 2017a, op. cit.
93. Tania de St Croix, 2011, 'Struggles and Silences: Policy, Youth Work and the National Citizens Service', *Youth and Policy*, No. 106, May, pp. 50–53.
94. Tania de St Croix, 2017, op. cit.

# Further Reading

Booth, Caroline, et al. 2015. *National Citizen Service 2014 Evaluation: Main Report*. Ipsos Mori.
Cameron, Daniel, et al. 2017. *National Citizen Service 2015—Evaluation: Main Report*. Ipsos Mori. March.
de St Croix, Tania. 2015. 'Volunteers and Entrepreneurs? Youth Work and the Big Society', in Bright, Graham (ed), *Youth Work: Histories, Policy and Contexts*. London: Palgrave, pp. 58–79.

de St Croix, Tania. 2017. 'Time to Say Goodbye to the National Citizen Service?' *Youth and Policy*. June 2017. http://www.youthandpolicy.org/articles/time-to-say-goodbye-ncs/.

Mills, Sarah and Waite, Catherine. 2017. 'Brands of Youth Citizenship and the Politics of Scale: National Citizen Service in the United Kingdom'. *Political Geography*. Vol 56. January, pp. 66–76.

NatCen. 2012. *Evaluation of National Citizen Service Pilots: Interim Report*. NatCen Social Research. May.

National Audit Office. 2017. *National Citizen Service*. National Audit Office. January.

Panayiotou, Sally, et al. 2017. *National Citizen Service 2016 Evaluation*. Kantar/LSE. December.

House of Commons Public Accounts Committee. 2017. *National Citizen Service Enquiry*.

# 12

# Youth Volunteering—The New Panacea

Though, for all governments after 2010, NCS remained central to their approved forms of youth volunteering, two other routes attracted strong state support including significant amounts of public funding. One was through the uniformed youth organisations—both those with long youth work histories such as the Scouts, Girlguiding and the Boys and Girls' Brigades and also cadet forces linked to the armed services. The other was Step Up To Serve—a new body set up in 2013 with the specific task of opening up volunteering opportunities for young people.

## Youth Work in Uniform

### Developing Independently: Two Brief Case Studies

Between 2007 and 2012—that is well before any new government 'expansion' money came on stream—Scouting's 'young leaders' programme for 14–18 year olds grew by 70%.[1] Activity programmes were overhauled and new badges introduced for, for example, computer skills, disability awareness, understanding global issues and involvement

© The Author(s) 2019
B. Davies, *Austerity, Youth Policy and the Deconstruction of the Youth Service in England*, https://doi.org/10.1007/978-3-030-03886-1_12

in 'community-based projects such as food banks'.[2] By 2013 it had set up 834 units in 'deprived areas'[3] and in 2014, as part of a four-year strategy for ensuring young people had a greater say in the organisation, appointed the first 'youth champion' to its national leadership team.[4]

Its membership also changed. By 2015 young women accounted for nearly 71% of new recruits, a year later a quarter of the membership was female[5] and by 2017 its waiting list was at an all-time high of 51,000.[6] During 2016, 350 young people with physical and learning difficulties joined 27 special Scout units in the South East, the Midlands and the East of England.[7]

Girlguiding UK's membership was also growing—by 8000 in 2011[8] and again in 2012.[9] According to its research reported in 2013, its members most valued meeting in single sex groups—'a unique, safe, non-judgemental space where girls can ... speak out without fear of being judged or laughed at'[10] and where they were helped to address the 'role model deficit' affecting girls and young women.[11] The organisation also sought to reclaim some of social action's more radical origins by replacing the traditional bake sales' with 'more advocacy and campaigning work' (for example on gender equality)[12] and by gathering 500,000-plus signatures for a petition to end *The Sun's* Page Three girls feature.[13] Its annual 'Girls' Attitudes Survey' in 2015 gave early warning of young women's growing mental health problems[14] while in 2017 (as the Scouts had done in 2014) membership was opened to transgender young people.[15]

## State Support—Not to Be Refused

Despite these examples of independent action—and despite the strings attached—in a tightening financial climate uniformed organisations remained open to government offers of funding. From 2012 onwards this invariably came with the requirement that it be used to target young people from what in 2017 the Minister for Civil Society called 'the most deprived and undeserved (sic) parts of the country'.[16] Much of this money was channelled through the Youth United Foundation (YUF), set up after a meeting 'over tea' between Prince Charles and Rod Jarman who at the time was a deputy assistant commissioner of the Metropolitan Police and later became YUF's first Chief Executive.[17]

A distinctive achievement of YUF was to bring together the 'traditional' uniformed youth work bodies with the police and armed services' cadet forces. For some of the former this required a significant and, in some cases, not wholly comfortable shift of position as, with varying emphases, they had previously distanced themselves from militaristic connections. In 1937, when world tensions were running high, the Ninth International Scout conference had for example insisted that 'any steps to ... militarisation ... should be entirely avoided in our programmes'.[18] In 2006, the Boys' Brigade said it was planning '... to soften its militaristic image' and 'replace military exercises with leisure activities such as football and computer games'.[19] In his promotion of YUF, however, Prince Charles glossed over these distinctions when, in a matter-of-fact way, he talked of 'my own experiences ... in my school cadet unit'.[20]

With the Army, Sea, Air and Combined cadet forces already getting an estimated £179 million from the Ministry of Defence,[21] over the five years from 2012–2013 the YUF organisations received additional public money eventually totalling at least £70 million. To this, in January 2012, the Mayor of London Boris Johnson added £1.3 million, awarded to ten YUF organisations for recruiting more adults and young people and creating new groups. In the next three years thirty eight were set up attracting some 8000 young people, two thirds in 'areas of high deprivation'. Johnson's explicit rationale, shared by central government, was that:

> Uniformed groups ... help equip (young people) with the skills they need to succeed in life... By instilling self-reliance, discipline and a sense of competition, young people can aspire to a better future.[22]

A month later, Communities Secretary Eric Pickles 'unexpectedly' announced a £10 million grant to 'uniformed youth work' to be channelled through YUF. Over the following two and a half years this was to be used to recruit 2700 new volunteers for 400 new groups and an extra 10,000 young people in, again, 'deprived areas ... where historically there have been limited opportunities'. This prompted a somewhat guarded response from the senior policy officer of Volunteering England who questioned both the lack of consultation and, as 'a lot of money (was) being pulled out of the sector', whether this award would 'have the most impact'. The head of a volunteering consultancy also doubted the wisdom of this amount of funding going to the chosen organisations 'if it is going to be spent ... doing what they've always done'.[23]

Nonetheless, by August 2012 significant progress was being reported. Thirty two group leaders had been recruited to run a new police cadet unit in Haringey, a St. Johns Ambulance group in Birmingham and six fire cadet units in Manchester. A hundred and twenty five of the available 199 places for young people had been filled with, according to Jarman, 'the poorest areas' being targeted first.[24] By the following March, he was forecasting that 'progress is ahead of schedule' with fifty-two new groups expected to be operating by the end of the month.[25]

This, however, was just the first expression of government enthusiasm for this form of youth work. Using some of the £150 million fines imposed on banks for fraudulently manipulating interest rates, the government's 2014 budget provided funding for a new 'Uniformed Youth Social Action Fund' (UYSAF)[26]—described by Pickles as 'the best £10m I've ever spent'.[27] With the aim of creating 15,000 new places for young people, fourteen uniformed groups, again including both youth work organisations and cadet units, were in October awarded first round grants. A second bidding round in February 2015 allocated another £1.45 million to five uniformed organisations.[28]

By July that year YUF was reporting that 80% of the promised places had already been created. These included units formed or planned by the Jewish Lads' Brigade; by the Boys' Brigade in rural areas where there were transport difficulties; by the Woodcraft Folk, specifically 'for recent immigrants'; and, jointly by the Scouts and the charity Scope, for disabled young people.[29] By the November YUF figures indicated that since 2012 a total of 1005 'new uniformed youth work units' had been established across the UK attracting over 12,700 young people and over 3400 adult volunteers.[30] Three months later these figures were revised upwards to 20,000 new places for young people—5000 above the government target for the UYSAF scheme.[31] Though by 2016 YUF's Chief Executive felt the need to acknowledge 'We're not saying uniformed youth work is the only thing that is good for young people', she added that '... given that there are so many … opportunities for young people (that) are declining we are really excited we can play our part.'[32]

An important government aim for this support was to increase the number of cadet units in state schools. In June 2014 £1 million was set aside for a Cadet Bursary Scheme to create 100 new groups for 10–20 year olds[33]—a modest sum compared to the £50 million announced in the budget for increasing to 500 the cadet units in state schools. This was welcomed by the Chief Executive of the Sea Cadets as 'evidence of the value investing in young people brings … so that they can weather the challenges they face as young adults'. NYA's deputy Chief Executive was less convinced, however, calling the decision 'a real missed opportunity not to have invested some of (the money) in good quality youth work which delivers "character" and a whole lot more besides for young people'.[34] By then, too, concerns were being voiced about the risks of recruiting 16- and 17-year olds into the armed services.[35]

Nonetheless, as YUF's total spend reached £4.1 million for 2015–2016,[36] Defence Secretary Michael Fallon remained upbeat, reporting to the 2016 Conservative Party conference that 25 of 150 of the new units were due to open in the following twelve months. One of these—located in a Birmingham school investigated for fundamentalist Muslim influences on its management and teaching—was greeted by the head as 'undoubtedly' helpful for achieving the school's vision.[37] By February 2017 another 24 schools had been identified as locations for cadet units.[38]

## 'Impacts'

In July 2015 researchers reported that over 80% of the participants in a Uniformed Youth Social Action Fund (UYSAF) scheme had 'a 'strong feeling' of wanting to make a difference to their communities; that 70% felt more involved; and that three-quarters were volunteering once a month. In response, YUF's Chief Executive commented that '…joining a uniformed group and being part of volunteering … has massive benefits on character and social action'.[39] An Ipsos MORI evaluation of phase one of the 2016 UYSAF programme also identified in 'beneficiaries' high levels of satisfaction with the 'social action' activities—particularly when they had direct contact with young people. These included community gardening, visits to a local care home and 'campaigning activities' relating to 'Remembrance Day activities, such as parading'. These contacts were also found to be likely to motivate others to become volunteers.[40] Prince Charles again registered his support for these schemes in January 2017 at a Buckingham Palace event for 300 guests at which he presented YUF awards for 'dedication', 'impact' and 'team work'—including one to a group whose litter picking campaign had collected 78 kg of rubbish.[41]

The phase two Ipsos MORI report, which focused more on the impact on the organisations themselves and on their practice, also concluded that they 'can be accessible and appealing to a wide spectrum of young people including those from ethnic minority groups and disabled children'. The evaluation's five case study groups talked, too, of their 'capacity to engage with children and young people considered "hard to reach"'. A four-year study published in late October 2017 also concluded that 'excluded children who joined the cadets were more likely to have improved attendance and behaviour on their return to school'.[42]

Though the Ipsos MORI report cautioned that 'recruiting volunteers was challenging' and that—in part because the funding was short-term—'securing the sustainability of the pilots (had) taken priority over social action',[43] some more fundamental questions remained unanswered—indeed usually unasked. Such as—at least for the long-established youth work organisations—how far had they compromised their stance as non- and even anti-militaristic by their association with youth groups integral to the armed services and often funded by the Ministry of Defence? And, with wider significance: how far had they compromised their independence as critical civil society bodies by taking funding tied to non-negotiable government policy priorities?

# Stepping Up to Serve

Six months after the Cleverdon–Jordan report on youth volunteering appeared in June 2013 (see Chapter 10), the Minister for Civil Society, Nic Hurd, launched a 'campaign' which embedded the new 'cool' title of social action even more firmly in the youth policy discourse. With immediate public endorsement from Prince Charles' and the Chair of the British Youth Council (BYC), this was underpinned by a new Youth Social Action Fund of, initially, £5 million to encourage 10–20 to year olds to take on 'local activities such as restoring a community property or organising a charity event'.[44]

Later that year, Hurd announced two further funding allocations: £2 million for charities supporting projects helping 'vulnerable young people'[45] and £6 million for a two-year Youth Social Action Journey Fund for charities, social enterprises and businesses to help 10–20 year olds' social action projects. In making the second announcement, a Cabinet Office spokesperson again hinted at the possibility of compulsion by suggesting that the UK should move beyond the 29% of 16–24 year olds who were volunteering to a policy, closer to Canada's,[46] which would require young people to complete an agreed number of volunteering hours before they could graduate from school.[47]

With the definition of social action extended to include 'getting involved to change others, communities or society for the better', the campaign was consolidated the following month in a new body, Step Up To Serve. Again launched by Prince Charles, its Cabinet Office remit was

> … for adults across the UK to sign up and volunteer to help double the level of participation of young people in helping others.

They were asked, too, to 'pledge a personal #iwill commitment and share it on Twitter'.[48] Three months after it was established, in February 2014, the new body allocated £11 million to 41 voluntary and community organisations, including UK Youth, NCVYS and the NYA '… to make sure that young people develop the skills, values and confidence they need as they move into adulthood'. As in previous announcements, NCS was identified as having a 'central' role.[49]

Funding for youth volunteering also continued to come from other sources, including again from the Mayor of London. In June 2014 for example he launched two schemes to 'enhance (young people's) CVs and equip them with the skills required for employment'.[50] A year later the Youth Social Action Fund was allocated a further £1 million as part of the government's commitments 'to build a truly compassionate society'—and to 'tackle the challenges facing disadvantaged young people and help embed social action in their lives'.[51] In partnership with Sport England, vinspired offered grants of up to £500 in April 2016 for projects to run 'sports social action' programmes.[52] Sport England created a 'Potential Fund' of £3 million the following December to support additional volunteering opportunities for young people,[53] while in August 2017 the Virgin Money Foundation announced that, with £1.7 million from the Big Lottery Fund, it was to offer grants of between £10,000 and £60,000 for up to two years to support volunteering by 10–12 year olds in the North East.[54]

It was Step Up To Serve, however, which increasingly became the high profile 'face' of youth volunteering—in 2017, for example, awarding £1 million to a charity set up by the Co-op Foundation to fund projects to 'inspire young people to take practical action to tackle loneliness'.[55] Established youth work organisations such as the NYA and UK Youth gave the new organisation a speedy and uncritical welcome while[56] Howard Williamson, Professor of European Youth Policy at Cardiff University and an experienced part-time youth worker, in dismissing as 'adult cynics' those 'complaining that such measures have displaced "proper" youth work activity', called 'the proposed "decade of social action"… an idea whose time has finally come'. Though regretting as 'unfortunate' that Charlotte Hill, Step Up To Serve's first Chief Executive, had formed an alliance with the 'aggressive' tax-avoiding Starbucks chain while at UK Youth, he nonetheless expressed himself 'absolutely delighted' at the appointment of someone '… untrammelled by youth work's history and its sometimes precious adherence to principles whose time has possibly gone'.[57] Hill herself remained unapologetic that what she called Step Up To Serve's 'collaborative campaign' was about 'raising the profile, not just of young people and their families, but also of business'.[58]

At the end of 2014 an Ipsos Mori study for Step Up To Serve—by then aiming to raise young people's participation to 4.5 million—reported that three million 10–20 year olds were involved in volunteering projects—40% of the age group.[59] Its October 2016 report also concluded, however, that:

> Overall rates of participation in social action among 10-12 year olds in the UK has been stable over the three years of (its) survey series: in 2016 42% had taken part in meaningful social action.[60]

Activities defined as 'designed to benefit their local communities' included fundraising (in which 40% of those surveyed had participated); working with a local charity (35%) and 'helping someone who needs support in their community' (25%). The young people identified the benefits for themselves as 'the enjoyment of helping others' (71%), 'having fun' (46%) and 'supporting a cause they believe in' (34%), with 21% feeling they had been helped to develop a range of skills.[61]

In April 2016 the National Council for Voluntary Organisations (NCVO) provided a more nuanced analysis of young people's responses. These suggested that between 2010–2011 and 2014–2015 the proportion of 16–25 year olds claiming to have volunteered once a month had gone up from 23 to 35%. Forty seven percent said they had volunteered once in 2014–2015—up from 38% in 2010–2011. NCVO was cautious about these findings, however, in part because the response rate was lower in 2014–2015 but also because of doubts about linking the increased numbers with the 'much effort' put into promoting volunteering to young people.[62]

More open to debate was the make up—particularly the class make-up—of the participants. The 2017 Step Up To Serve evaluation concluded that, though 58% of young people had taken part in some form of social action in the previous year, of which 39% was 'meaningful', 'there continues to be a gap in meaningful … participation between the most and least affluent young people (51% vs. 32%)'. The report also noted a 'slight decline' in the latter's involvement since 2016.[63]

Nonetheless, by the end of 2016, Rob Wilson was again proposing that more young people be given the chance to volunteer full-time—that is, for more than sixteen hours a week for at least six months.[64] How this could be achieved was part of the brief of a 'major' independent review of young people's involvement in social action projects set up in the December, again with Labour Party support. This was to be chaired by Steve Holliday, former Chief Executive of National Grid who had worked with City Gear, 'a youth and education charity supported by the utilities firm that offers full-time voluntary roles to young people in schools through a model originated in the United States'.[65]

Even while the review was in progress a City Gear-commissioned report by Pro Bono Economics—a consultancy 'helping charities understand and improve their impact and value'—concluded that 'a national full-time volunteering programme ... could boost the UK economy by up to £199m a year'.[66] When the Holliday report appeared in January 2018, however, its conclusions and recommendations were much more cautious. It was confident that 'forms of social action over an extended period have been shown to play a critical role in developing a young person's life chances, improving prospects and wellbeing'. It also acknowledged, however, that 'young people from the poorest backgrounds tend to be the least likely to access structured social action opportunities'. Though accepting that full-time social action 'plays a central role in achieving ... greater social mobility and social inclusion for young people', it therefore concluded that 'more evidence is needed before the government could instigate a major drive to increase social action programmes that are over 16 hours a week for 6 months or more'.[67] It also stopped short of proposing a change in the law to get more young people to volunteer full-time.[68]

In its response, though rejecting the review's proposal that NCS act as 'broker and quality assurance body' for young people's full-time social action, the government indicated that this was to be considered at a future cross-departmental meeting.[69] With a House of Lords Select Committee then taking evidence on 'Citizenship and Civic Engagement',[70] youth volunteering nonetheless continued to receive the uncritical endorsement from the leaders of both the Conservative and Labour Party.[71]

# Youth Volunteering—Limits and Dilemmas

## Volunteering—Why; and in Whose Interests?

Underpinning the on-going top-down policy 'push' for youth volunteering was a taken-for-granted political and voluntary sector consensus that this was 'a good thing'. Rationales for it emphasised the gains both for 'beneficiaries' and for the young people themselves. This got further support from evidence from the 2017 Ipsos Mori evaluation that young people who had volunteered reported 'higher life satisfaction' than those who had not and that 81% who had participated 'believe it will help then get a job in the future'.[72] Inducting the young into 'doing good' would also for them, it was suggested, become an on-going, even life-long, commitment and so have wider impacts on British society.

These assumptions, however, were run through with dilemmas which were rarely if ever debated either within the overall policy discourse or with young people. The, mostly implicit, definitions of 'social action', for example, and of the 'good' it sought to achieve remained largely within politically 'safe' parameters, with only for example some Girlguiding UK campaigns coming close to challenging status quo aims and practices. The unspoken rule to which these were largely exceptions, however, was that the 'doing good' into which young people would be inducted would be the outcome of worthy but conforming endeavours such as marching on Remembrance Day and collecting litter in a local neighbourhood.

## Volunteering—Beyond the Individual to the Collective

Closely linked to these constraining perceptions of volunteering were ones defining how it would be done. Much of the activity within the government programmes was carried out in groups or 'teams' and/or through formal organisational processes. Within the flurry of 'official' programmes and projects, however, these face-to-face processes were rarely presented or analysed as actual or potential forms of collective organising. Such shared 'volunteering' responses seemed to have had a particular relevance for a generation whose 'transitions' to improved futures were increasingly being squeezed by zero hours contracts, poverty-level minimum wages and the huge costs of going to university (see Chapters 1 and 18).

These limitations on how volunteering was conceived within these programmes were largely intrinsic to their key starting points. Most often, for example, the initial volunteering appeal, heavily weighted towards what she or he would gain personally from the experience, was made to the young person as an individual. High on the motivating agendas of the programmes, therefore, were offers of an added line on a CV, the promise of a reference and even perhaps a personal contact to help ease access into a job. In 2018 vinspired implicitly added a material dimension to these draws by introducing an 'Inspire card' offering young volunteers discounts in shops and for events.[73]

## Volunteering: Structured or Improvised?

Fundamental, too, to the government's interventions and those of its sponsored organisations was their commodification, bureaucratising and even in some ways professionalising of the volunteering experience. Because in effect the sponsors were recruiting young people into and requiring them to commit to unpaid 'work' roles, many of the schemes required complex management structures, marketing campaigns and (given that it was often minors to be recruited) regulatory and over-sight procedures. Sympathetic as it was to the whole social action enterprise, even the Holliday review acknowledged that such routes were not only unattractive to 'young people from the poorest background' but provided too few ways for young people to help design and deliver programmes.[74]

The formalised structures and processes of NCS or Step Up To Serve were therefore unlikely to create opportunities for young people to encounter that expression of volunteering, also with a long history, which addresses self- and/or collectively identified 'causes'. Or to open up or support the often spontaneous responses which can emerge out of the here-and-now exchanges of friend with friend, neighbour with neighbour, work colleague with work colleague—or just citizen with citizen. The 'projects' offered to young people would thus be unlikely to generate the relevant 'standing-start' understanding and skills these kinds of responses require or even perhaps the motivation for giving time without any expected pay-back other than the intrinsic satisfactions of participating and (perhaps) experiencing some success in advancing an adopted cause.

## Youth Volunteering—As Youth Work?

One final set of relevant questions concerns the implications of this national volunteering strategy for state-funded Youth Services, including the local voluntary youth organisations they had been supporting, and for their distinctive youth work practice. At a time of an unrelenting government insistence on 'austerity', from a Youth Service perspective the new programmes—particularly the NCS—absorbed disproportionate amounts of state resources. Had even a small proportion of these been used more flexibly, they could have kept open locally based open access facilities most evenings throughout the year and even at weekends as well as funding some locally generated residential programmes and events.

Secondly, though the uniformed organisations such as Scouting, Girlguiding and the various Brigades were deeply embedded in a youth work tradition, it is not clear how far some of the other new volunteering programmes offered <u>youth work</u> as their core practice. For example:

- How far were young people engaging on a genuinely voluntary basis given that nearly 75% of the participants surveyed in 2015 mentioned their school or college as their route into volunteering? (30% mentioned 'their families', 24% friends and only 18% 'structured programmes'.)[75]
- How far were the programmes' educational interventions built from and on the interests and concerns of the young people who actually participated?
- How consciously prepared were the programmes for the tensions considered specifically in Chapter 11 in relation to NCS but liable

to occur in all such outward-looking youth programmes? Between, for example, fulfilling the commitment to the task while remaining responsive to relationship-building process; and between meeting the beneficiaries' expectations while remaining responsive to the sometimes pressing personal needs of the young people taking part?[76]

As one NCS-focused research project concluded, where a high priority is that participants gain 'transitional' skills and attitudes to adulthood, 'the infrastructure is liable to frame the young people as *becomings*, rather than *beings*'.[77] Within the parameters they have set themselves, such schemes—indeed the whole volunteering strategy—are therefore always at risk of giving low priority to such key defining features of open access youth work as a responsiveness, at their pace and as they define it, to the here-and-now of the young person who actually engages.

## Notes

1. Neil Puffett, 2012a, 'Scout Leaders Top 10,000 for First Time', *CYPN*, 19 April.
2. Darren Hayes and Adam Offord, 2015, 'Daily Round Up 27 April: Scouts …', *CYPN*, 27 April.
3. Neil Puffett, 2018, 'Scouts to Expand to Further 500 Deprived Areas and Trial Early Years Provision', *CYPN*, 21 May.
4. Joe Lepper, 2014, 'Scouts Appoint Youth Champion', *CYPN*, 21 October.
5. Adam Offord, 2016a, 'Youth Work Round Up: Scout Numbers …', *CYPN*, 18 April.
6. Joe Lepper, 2017a, 'Scouts Waiting List Reaches Record High of 51,000', *CYPN*, 11 April.
7. Adam Offord, 2016b, 'Youth Work Roundup: … Scout Units', *CYPN*, 4 April.
8. Neil Puffett, 2012b, 'Girlguiding UK Experiences a Membership Surge', *CYPN*, 27 February.
9. Gabriella Jozwiak, 2013a, 'Girlguiding Growth Shows Girls' Interest in Youth Activities', *CYPN*, 9 August.

10. Gabriella Jozwiak, 2013a, op. cit.
11. Matthew Little, 2012, 'Girlguiding UK Unveils Drive to Tackle "Role Models Deficit"', *CYPN*, 17 August.
12. Tristan Donovan, 2013, 'Girls Guides to Tackle Inequality in Social Action Campaign', *CYPN*, 8 March; Jess Brown and Adam Offord, 2016, 'Daily Roundup...', *CYPN*, 16 August.
13. Neil Puffett, 2013a, 'Daily Roundup: Girl Guide Campaign ...', *CYPN*, 9 April.
14. Adam Offord, 2015a, 'Girlguiding Study Highlights Mental Health Pressures', *CYPN*, 24 August.
15. Gabriella Jozwiak, 2017, 'Transgender Children to Be Allowed to Join Guides', *CYPN*, 23 January.
16. YUF, 2017, *Impact Report 2015–16*, Pears Foundation/YUF Foundation, p. 2.
17. Neil Puffett, 2013b, 'United by Uniform', *CYPN*, 5 March.
18. John S. Wilson, 1959, *Scouting Round the World*, London, Blandford Press, pp. 100–101.
19. Marc Horne, 2006, 'Boys' Brigade Tries to Shake Off Military Image', *Sunday Times*, 12 February, http://www.thesundaytimes.co.uk/sto/news/uk_news/article204847.ece.
20. YUF, undated, 'Our Founder and Patron: His Royal Highness The Prince of Wales', http://www.youthunited.org.uk/about-us/our-founder-and-patron.
21. House of Commons Library via Private Email, 6 June 2018.
22. Joe Lepper, 2012a, 'Uniformed Groups Win Funding to Expand Services Across the Capital', *CYPN*, 19 January.
23. Neil Puffett, 2012c, 'Hunt Begins for Youth Group Volunteers', *CYPN*, 21 February; Kaye Wiggins, 2012, 'Government Gives £10m to Youth Groups', *Third Sector*, 2 February.
24. Joe Lepper, 2012b, 'Uniformed Youth Work Scheme Launches in London, Birmingham and Manchester', *CYPN*, 29 August.
25. Neil Puffett, 2013b, op. cit.
26. Laura McCardle, 2014a, 'Osborne Unveils First Youth Groups to Get Social Action Funding', *CYPN*, 26 August.
27. Adam Offord and Neil Puffett, 2014, 'Daily Round Up ... Youth Work...', *CYPN*, 12 December.
28. Sam Burne James, 2015, 'Five Charities Received Total of £1.45m from Uniformed Youth Social Action Fund', *Third Sector*, 5 February.

29. Adam Offord, 2015b, 'Uniformed Youth Groups on Course to Create 15,000 More Places', *CYPN*, 13 July.
30. Adam Offord, 2015c, 'Youth Work Roundup: Uniformed Youth Work…', *CYPN*, 2 November.
31. Adam Offord, 2016c, 'Additional 20,000 Uniformed Youth Group Places Created', *CYPN*, 12 February.
32. Adam Offord, 2016c, op. cit.
33. Laura McCardle, 2014b, 'Bank Fines Fund 100 Cadet Units in Schools', *CYPN*, 19 June.
34. Adam Offord, 2015d, 'Budget 2015: Osborne Announces Drive to Create More Cadet Units in Schools', *CYPN*, 8 July.
35. Amelia Hill, 2016, 'Under-18s in Army "Face Greater Injury, Death and Mental Health Risks"', 18 October, https://www.theguardian.com/uk-news/2016/oct/18/under-18s-in-army-face-greater-injury-death-and-mental-health-risks; Adam Offord, 2016d, 'Green Party Calls for Halt to Cadet Unit Expansion', *CYPN*, 19 October.
36. YUF Foundation, 2017, op. cit., p. 18.
37. Adam Offord, 2016e, 'Tory Party Conference: Fallon Announces New Cadet Units', *CYPN*, 5 October.
38. Neil Puffett, 2017, 'Government Announces 24 New Cadet Units', *CYPN*, 13 February.
39. Adam Offord, 2015e, 'Researchers Highlight Benefits of Uniformed Youth Work Projects', *CYPN*, 20 July.
40. Ilana Tyler-Rubinstein, et al., 2016a, *Evaluation of the Uniformed Youth Social Action Fund 1: Final Report*, London, Ipsos Mori, October.
41. YUF, 2017, 'HRH the Prince of Wales Joins Uniformed Youth Groups at Buckingham Palace to Celebrate Newly Formed Units Across the Country', January 2017, http://www.youthunited.org.uk/news/latest/post/167-hrh-the-prince-of-wales-joins-uniformed-youth-groups-at-buckingham-palace-to-celebrate-newly-formed-units-across-the-country.
42. Joe Lepper, 2017b, 'Cadet Units "Help Improve Behaviour of Excluded Children"', *CYPN*, 4 October.
43. Ilana Tyler-Rubinstein, et al., 2016b, *Evaluation of the Uniformed Youth Social Action Fund 2: Final Report*, London, Ipsos Mori, October.
44. Gabriella Jozwiak, 2013b, 'Campaign Urges Young People to Drive Social Action', *CYPN*, 28 June.
45. Laura McCardle, 2013a, 'New £2m Fund for Charities Supporting Social Action Projects', *CYPN*, 23 October.

46. Laura McCardle, 2013b, 'Government Injects £6m to Support Youth Volunteering', *CYPN*, 28 October.
47. Laura McCardle, 2014c, 'Stepping Up for Social Action', *CYPN*, 18 February.
48. GOV.UK, 2013, 'Step Up to Serve: Making It Easier for Young People to Help Others', https://www.gov.uk/government/news/step-up-to-serve-making-it-easier-for-young-people-to-help-others.
49. Laura McCardle, 2014d, 'Charities Win £11m to Boost Social Action', *CYPN*, 20 February; GOV.UK, 2014, '£11 Million Funding to Boost Opportunities for Young People', 19 February, file:///C:/Users/Owner/Desktop/Documents/PolicyPapersetc/NCS'SocAc/YthSocAcJourneyFundGOV.UK.htm.
50. Laura McCardle, 2014e, 'London Mayor Launches Youth Volunteering Schemes', *CYPN*, 3 June.
51. Jess Brown, 2015, 'Government Invests £1m in Social Action', *CYPN*, 14 July.
52. Adam Offord, 2016f, 'Youth Sports Social Action Programme Launches', *CYPN*, 21 April.
53. Joe Lepper, 2016, 'Sport England Launches £3m Youth Volunteering Fund', *CYPN*, 5 December.
54. Tristan Donovan, 2017a, 'Youth Social Action Initiative Worth £1.7m Launches', *CYPN*, 21 August.
55. Joe Lepper, 2017c, 'Step Up to Serve Hands £1m to Anti-loneliness Project', *CYPN*, 18 May.
56. Laura McCardle, 2013c, 'New £2m Fund for Charities Supporting Social Action Projects', *CYPN*, 23 October.
57. Howard Williamson, 2014, 'Can "Decade of Social Action" Win Over Young People?', *CYPN*, 4 February.
58. Laura McCardle, 2014f, 'Stepping Up for Social Action', *CYPN*, 18 February.
59. Julia Pye, et al., 2014, *Youth Social Action in the UK—2014: A Face-to-Face Survey of 10–20 Year Olds in the UK*, Ipso Public Affairs, November, https://ems.ipsos-mori.com/Assets/Docs/Publications/sri-ecf-youth-social-action-in-the-uk-2014.pdf.
60. Julia Pye and Olivia Michelmore, 2016, *National Social Action Survey 2016*, Ipsos Mori, February.
61. Laura McCardle, 2014g, 'Young Volunteers Top Three Million', *CYPN*, 24 November.

62. Adam Offord, 2016g, 'Youth Volunteering on the Rise', *CYPN*, 12 April.
63. Ipsos Mori, 2018, *National Youth Social Action Survey 2017*, Department for Digital, Culture, Media and Sport, April.
64. Adam Offord, 2016h, 'Minister Wants "Full-Time Volunteering" for Young People', *CYPN*, 15 December.
65. Joe Lepper, 2017d, 'Youth Minister Appoints Head of Volunteering Review', *CYPN*, 14 March.
66. Tristan Donovan, 2017b, 'Ministers Urged to Back Full-Time Youth Volunteering Programme', *CYPN*, 16 November.
67. Steve Holliday, 2018, *Independent Review of Full Time Social Action*, DCMS, January, pp. 1, 2.
68. Tristan Donovan, 2018, 'Youth Social Action Review Stops Short of Calling for Law Change', *CYPN*, 6 February.
69. Joe Lepper, 2018a, 'Government Rules Out Full-Time Social Action Role for NCS', *CYPN*, 25 July.
70. www.parliament.co, 'Lords Select Committee: Citizenship and Civic Engagement—Publications', http://www.parliament.uk/business/committees/committees-a-z/lords-select/citizenship-civic-engagement/publications/.
71. Step Up to Serve, 2017, 'Leaders Renew Cross-Party Support for #iwill', Newsletter, 2010 November.
72. Ipsos Mori, 2018, op. cit.
73. Joe Lepper, 2018b, 'Young People to Get Rewards for Social Action in £1m Initiative', *CYPN*, 11 May.
74. Steve Holliday, 2018, op. cit., p. 1.
75. Adam Offord, 2015f, 'Social Action "More Popular Among Affluent Young People"', *CYPN*, 25 November; Adam Offord, 2016i, 'Socio-economic Gap in Youth Social Action Participation Narrows', 29 November.
76. See for example Bernard Davies, 1967, 'An Attempt to Tame the Young?', *New Society*, 24 August.
77. Sarah Mills and Catherine Waite, 2017, 'Brands of Youth Citizenship and the Politics of Scale: National Citizens Service in the United Kingdom', *Political Geography*, Vol. 56, January, pp. 66–76.

# Further Reading

Holliday, Steve. 2018. *Independent Review of Full Time Social Action*. DCMS. January.

Ipsos Mori. 2018. *National Youth Social Action Survey 2017*. DCMS. April.

Mills, Sarah and Catherine Waite. 2017. 'Brands of Youth Citizenship and the Politics of Scale: National Citizen Service in the United Kingdom'. *Political Geography*. Vol. 56. January, pp. 66–76.

Pye, Julia, et al. 2014. *Youth Social Action in the UK—2014: A Face-to-Face Survey of 10–20 Year Olds in the UK*. Ipso Public Affairs. November.

Pye, Julia and Olivia Michelmore. 2016. *National Social Action Survey 2016*. Ipsos Mori. February.

Roberts, Jonathan. 2015. 'Uniformed Youth Work', in Bright, Graham (ed). *Youth Work: Histories, Policy, Contexts*. London: Palgrave, pp. 125–144.

Tyler-Rubinstein, Ilana, et al. 2016a. *Evaluation of the Uniformed Youth Social Action Fund 1: Final Report*. London: Ipsos Mori. October.

Tyler-Rubinstein, Ilana, et al. 2016b. *Evaluation of the Uniformed Youth Social Action Fund 2: Final Report*. London: Ipsos Mori. October.

YUF Foundation. 2017. *Impact Report 2015–16*. Pears Foundation/YUF Foundation.

# 13

## Plugging 'Youth Services' Gaps

As local authorities cut or closed their Youth Services, governments after 2010 announced a series of time-limited and relatively low-cost youth programmes with familiar neo-liberal aims to be achieved through familiar neo-liberal structures. To nurture the individual traits needed for success in a competitive economy and target those in danger of 'failing' because of 'character weaknesses', the 'deliverers', it was assumed, would not normally be the state, local or central, but charities, for-profit businesses or 'social enterprises' often run as 'mutuals'. Increasingly they were expected to adopt 'metrics' forms of evaluation sometimes embedded in payment-by-results and 'social investment' business plans.

Though within these parameters, the new initiatives offered little encouragement to locally-based year-round youth work provision, some did welcome youth workers' 'special skills' and 'informal methods'.

### From MyPlace...

One of these gap-filling initiatives was inherited from New Labour: the provision of a high quality youth building in every constituency through the 'Myplace' programme (see Chapter 3). By the time

© The Author(s) 2019
B. Davies, *Austerity, Youth Policy and the Deconstruction of the Youth Service in England*, https://doi.org/10.1007/978-3-030-03886-1_13

the evaluation report was published in 2011,[1] the new government's 'austerity' policies were raising doubts about its completion. Though Tim Loughton later called the model a 'win-win situation'—'... good for young people, the town, business, motivation and recruitment'[2]— the programme was put on hold for six months in 2010 and seven of the 70 approved projects withdrew.[3]

When the programme was revived in December 2010, the government initially provided £134 million to complete fifty seven of the buildings and then, in April 2012, another £141 million.[4] £200,000 was also allocated for the centres to share best practice. Commitment to the programme was reaffirmed in *Positive for Youth* (see Chapter 9) which talked of '... developing a national approach to exploiting the potential of these centres to be hubs for transforming local services led by communities and local businesses'.[5] By April 2012, 35 centres were operating with the rest scheduled to open within twelve months.[6]

Despite the government's substantial capital investment, the evaluation report concluded that 'in the absence of adequate or secure funding, the full potential of the Myplace programme will not be reached'—not least because, as one interviewee commented: 'We have the building now, but we still need to fund the work we do'. The Salmon Centre in Bermondsey, for example, after getting £1.1 million Myplace money to extend its premises, then had to introduce a 'slimmed down' structure. Other centres filled their revenue gaps by applying for an alcohol licence to attract corporate conference clients and commercial music promoters, by hiring out rooms and halls for meetings and by seeking long-term tenants.[7] In June 2013 the DfE allocated £1.3 million to a consortium of 13 voluntary youth organisations, including Ambition and UK Youth, to encourage school classes and individual pupils to make (free) use of the arts and sports facilities, drop-in sessions and longer projects at 15 of the centres'.[8] Ambition also received an additional £27,000 in Nov 2014 to provide six-months 'strategic support' to the 63 Myplace centres then operating, to be focussed on quality assurance, 'youth service networks' and fundraising.[9]

One of the programme's pioneers, Jeremy Glover, regarded these forms of resourcing as threatening to divert the centres from their core 'mission':

When the kids have to leave at 7pm so that you can make money in the evening, that is not what the vision was. It was to have facilities for young people that rival adult facilities.[10]

Nonetheless, though the centres were encouraged to re-examine their business plans with a view to 'diversifying their funding streams', Loughton denied any risk of young people losing out. The Coalition's more strategic responses also remained firmly in line with its wider youth policy priorities such as its expectation that a local authority's lead role in a centre's management would be shared with or transferred to local business or community groups. For Loughton, too, Myplace was to be

… a place … where NCS providers can recruit young people, as a hub where social action projects can take place and in some places NCS providers may be headquartered.[11]

# … to OnSide 'Youth Zones'

## Finding the Funding

Central government funding for the MyPlace programme—both capital and revenue—ended in March 2013.[12] By then a charity established in 2008—OnSide—was working to a similar agenda, albeit with a very different financial strategy. Its goal 'within the next generation' was to create 100 'youth zones',[13] described as '21st century youth clubs',[14] with firm plans for 20 to be operating by 2020[15] Like the Myplace centres, a key inspiration was the ambitious redevelopment of Bolton Lads and Girls Club, a 'traditional' voluntary sector youth club whose history went back to 1890. In 2002, with funding from the National Lottery, it opened a 'state-of-the-art' purpose-built town centre facility offering both 'universal' and 'targeted' services. Charging fifty pence a session and aiming to be fully accessible to a wide range of young people, attendances quickly rose from 400 to 3000 a week.[16] Endorsed in 2012 by a prime ministerial visit,[17] it came to act as the model for what quickly became a national initiative.

For securing at least half of each new centre's £6 million capital costs and a predicted £1 million running costs, private sponsorship and trust funding were crucial.[18] Examples included:

- Pledges in 2015 for the Sunderland OnSide development of £1 million by the Queen's Trust, £850,000 by the Virgin Money Foundation and £500,000 by a local philanthropist.[19]
- A £1.5 million donation in January 2016 to the OnSide organisation from the 'FTSE-listed electrical retail giant' AO.com.[20]
- Funding promises in 2016 to develop the Wigan youth zone by 'local businessmen, professional footballers playing for Wigan Athletic Football Club and the Premier League'.[21]
- Adding to £1 million of trust money, a £1 million donation in 2016 by the Chair of Wigan Onside to the Chorley Onside development[22] whose staffing plans by 2017 assumed 50 full-time workers and 100 volunteers.[23]

Philanthropic giving was however never going to be sufficient to build the centres or keep them running. Over the decade, therefore, local authorities across the country agreed to commit substantial sums to the programme.

- In 2014 Lancashire County Council provided £5 million—80% of the total—to the construction costs of the Preston OnSide centre and £900,000 for the Chorley centre. (The latter also received £1.2 million from Chorley Borough Council.)[24] Two years later Lancashire was reported to be planning cuts of £2 million to its Youth Service budget.[25]
- Lewisham Borough Council agreed in 2014 to fund a percentage of the £6 million construction costs of the south Bermondsey centre.[26] By 2016 it was proposing to cut its Youth Service budget from £3.3 million to under £1 million and replace all its full-time workers with part-timers.[27]
- After merging its early intervention and youth services in 2014 in order to save £760,000,[28] Croydon Borough Council in 2017 donated the site for a youth zone, invested £3.25 million in the building costs and provided £300,000 for running costs.[29]

- After cutting £5.3 million (71%) from its Youth Service budget in 2014,[30] Stoke City Council agreed three years later to contribute £2.5 million to the construction costs of a youth zone and, for the three financial years from 2018 to 2019, to provide £4.7 million towards its running costs.[31]
- Wolverhampton City Council, which had cut its 2014–2015 youth services' budget by £1.75 million, made 140 staff redundant and retained only eight youth worker posts,[32] contributed £3 million in 2016 for developing and running an OnSide centre.[33]

With financial backing from other local authorities across the country, by January 2018 the programme was a quarter of the way to meeting its target of 100 centres.[34]

## Role and Impacts

An evaluation of the Manchester, Oldham and Wigan youth zones published in May 2015[35] recorded high levels of satisfaction amongst young people on, for example, improved relations with their families, staying out of trouble, getting better marks at school, understanding the risks of smoking, alcohol and drugs and 'feeling more self-confident'. 'Stakeholders' also identified gains such as reduced crime and anti-social behaviour in their areas, fewer NEETs, support for 'troubled families' and 'improved social cohesion'. Other evidence later that year showed that the number of disabled young people attending the centres had risen since 2013 from 587 to over 2000.[36]

Emphasising that 'measuring social impact has become increasingly important in recent years', the OnSide evaluation also concluded that the centres were realising £2 of 'social value' for every £1 spent with on average a return of £6.66 on each £1 invested by local authorities.[37] It thus predicted 'significant cost savings in the future for local authorities and public agencies in the areas served ….'

In seeking to answer the question 'Why are the Zones successful?', the report—like much of OnSide's own PR materials—pointed to 'the state of the art facilities' as one of a range of factors identified as important by 'key partners'. Others included 'the universal and targeted support provided' and 'the expertise and dedication of the staff and volunteers'. 'Based on the evidence gathered' the evaluators also prepared an 'advocacy document' which had been used '… to demonstrate to the highest levels of government the potential public sector savings that could be generated through investment in the Youth Zone Model'.[38,39]

## Youth Zones—New Centres for Youth Work?

Though expressing reservations about its model becoming an alternative to local Youth Service facilities, as early as 2014 the OnSide Chief Executive was suggesting that the MyPlace centres—which by then were attracting 7,000 young people a week—were 'operat(ing) in harmony with existing provision'. The chair of the LGA's children and young people board went further, claiming that some councils were using the OnSide developments 'as a way of maintaining youth services despite huge reductions in funding'.

Others, however were less convinced. In 2014, CHYPS' Chief Executive, while acknowledging the youth zones' success in bringing in external funding and calling them 'a useful addition to the overall offer in communities', stressed that 'they are still reliant on local authority core funding to support them'. The head of policy at the NYA remained cautious about their ability to deliver locally the 'universal' provision that young people needed.[40] The following year, the chair of Unite's community and youth work section accused OnSide of 'exploiting' the funding cuts in the youth sector 'by promoting itself as an alternative youth service provider'. A year later one of the union's national officers called their creation in some areas 'a death sentence' for universal publicly funded youth services. He also suggested that OnSide was 'effectively privatising youth services in the areas they are operating in, since local authorities will have little or no direction in the provision…'[41]

Not only did OnSide dismiss these criticisms as 'a lack of understanding' of what the organisation was doing.[42] In a report published in February 2017 its Chief Executive argued that its youth zones were developing as credible replacements for what the lost Youth Services had provided.[43] The evaluation of the Manchester, Oldham and Wigan centres quoted above offered some support for this claim by pointing to their ability 'to engage young people, listen and respond to their needs'.[44] while the Wolverhampton centre appointed a 'youth work manager' with over ten years experience in the youth work sector.[45] Some six months later, however, after signing up half its yearly membership target of 1500 members in just two weeks, the latter's public focus was largely on its twenty nightly activities which included 'rock climbing, football, gym sessions, art, boxing (and) employability sessions'.

## Youth Innovation Zones

Strongly influenced by its wider 'localism' agenda, an early example of the Coalition's more direct efforts to fill the gaps left by Youth Service cuts were its four pilot 'youth innovation zones', announced in December 2011. Within a three months timeframe and with funding of just £40,000, these were to 'develop new, creative approaches to youth services across the country'. Presented as implementing commitments of the *Positive for Youth* policy, they could been seen as Loughton's effort to fulfil his promise to challenge 'the monopoly that local authorities have on delivery and commissioning' and so reform a service whose quality 'leaves a lot to be desired'.

As one of the examples of such innovation, Knowsley proposed to operate through two models of delivery very different from its previous Youth Services provision. One—'Youth Lite'—envisaged opening 'centres of learning' and other dedicated youth facilities across the borough as an integral part of the school day. The other—'Youth Deep'— would provide a free school for 14–19 year olds seen as unsuitable for 'universal' provision offering intensive and targeted support from staff recruited from industry, education and the voluntary sector as well as the 'traditional youth services'. The council's lead member for leisure, culture and community (not education) described the plan as 'great news for the borough's young people', not least because it would build on its £5 million MyPlace youth facility.[46]

Though in April 2012 £500,000 was allocated for another ten innovation zones, the project leader for one of the organisations overseeing the programme was by then expressing doubts about the applicability of its lessons to other local authorities. Even though the phase two schemes were to run for a full year, he especially questioned 'the short space of time' allowed for the pilots given that the 'learning points' from the schemes 'highlight particular issues, rather than ways of dealing with them'. What was emerging, he said, was that, as 'some of the work involved is fairly complicated and "game-changing" for the nature of youth work', 'we would expect it to take several years'.[47]

Three months after the Youth Innovation Zones programme ended in March 2013, the Cabinet Office's progress report on implementing *Positive for Youth* talked of the 'radical new system-wide approaches' which it had 'tested'. Alongside the efforts highlighted to give young people a greater say in how services were being developed, emphasis was again often put on targeting problematic sections of an area's youth population and commissioning voluntary and private organisations to take over services from local authorities.[48]

The retrospective view from the field, however, was often less upbeat. Disappointment was expressed that the programme had not had more time to produce genuinely transferable lessons. The Chief Executive of CHYPS labelled the on-going activity 'legacy work' and doubted whether any of the schemes 'will continue to operate in the same way'. Others linked their scepticism about the claims being made for the programme to the 'new challenges' posed for local authorities by the Localism Act's devolution of powers.[49]

Amidst all the positive PR, the day-to-day financial realities facing local authorities were again never confronted openly by ministers promoting the programme. This gap was thrown into sharp relief in Norfolk, one of the second phase participating authorities. In the year the council was cutting its Youth Service budget from £4 million to £900,000, its £50,000 grant was, within twelve months, supposed to enable it both to 'innovate' a radical new approach to its provision and generate 'good practice examples' for other councils to follow.[50]

# Delivering Differently for Young People

In January 2014 the government posed a 'Delivering Differently Challenge' to all council services in order, it said, to 'help to improve public services through using new structures such as mutuals and voluntary organisations'.[51] The following July the Cabinet Office, together with the DCLG, the LGA and the Society of Local Authority Chief Executives, released one of only two 'prospectuses' for the initiative—for a Delivering Differently for Young People (DDYP) programme.[52]

The 'youth' prospectus's opening sentence came as close as any government statement to acknowledging the damage being inflicted on local youth provision when it declared that 'the Cabinet Office is aware of the challenges facing many local authorities and their services for young people' and that (unspecified) 'policy and funding changes' had prompted councils to rethink how they were meeting their statutory duty. As a result, the prospectus asserted, they were now 'embracing new, innovative ways of delivering high quality services that respond to local need and remain focussed on the well-being of young people'. To support these moves, the proposed DDYP programme would

> … support ten successful local authorities with up to £50,000 (each) of bespoke technical, legal and consultancy support to look at the full range of alternative delivery models that lie between in-house delivery and traditional outsourcing …

Completing an 'appraisal' stage of the work and developing an implementation plan were to take twenty weeks.

Though the programme was described as 'agnostic' about possible 'alternative delivery models', four examples were outlined with strong echoes of the government's wider Big Society and privatisation agendas:

- 'Spin outs, including Public Service Mutuals';
- '… working with local communities to empower them to delivery services';
- 'Public/Private Partnerships'; and

- 'Commissioning out to VCSE organisations' (a government-inspired acronym which embedded social enterprises within the 'voluntary and community' sector).

Participating councils were also expected to share their learning across their authority and, via the Cabinet Office, with other authorities.

A further round of £200,000 DDYP funding was announced in September 2015, though with the allocation to each of the five new authorities now reduced to £40,000. A new rider had also been added to the prospectus which all but made explicit youth work's collapse within current youth policy-making into any form of work with young people:

> These services and activities (for young people) are now referred to using terms that range from a traditional 'youth service' to 'early intervention', 'positive activities', and 'access and engagement'.[53]

Successful applicants were also required to demonstrate commitments to partnership working, 'giving young people a voice', making them an 'integrated offer' and focusing on 'outcomes and impact measurement'.[54]

Six months later—in February 2016—the LGiU's Children's Services Network (CSN) produced a DDYP 'policy briefing'. This acknowledged that, given 'the discretionary nature of funding for youth work and the wider financial pressures faced by local authorities', 'significant changes and reductions to youth services across the country over recent years' had resulted in 'spending reductions of nearly £500m since 2010'. It also pointed to evidence from the Cabinet Office's own 2014 survey (which Rob Wilson had chosen to ignore—see Chapter 4) that 'less than half of local authorities always take into account their (statutory) duty ... when making decisions about youth service funding'. It noted, too, that councils' growing priority was 'outreach and targeted youth work with disadvantaged groups of young people'.[55]

While accepting that 'Youth services' were '...still recognised in law as being educational as well as recreational', its emphasis nonetheless was on their delivering 'wider outcomes'. These again included participation in employment and education, reducing substance misuse and teenage pregnancy, reducing offending and anti-social behaviour, and improving community cohesion.[56] In identifying the models used, the CSN paper gave specific attention to the Kensington and Chelsea and Knowsley mutuals which the original DDYP prospectuses had judged 'successful' (see Chapter 5). It noted, however, that only two of the first ten authorities funded had adopted this model with the majority favouring 'service transformation by commissioning out and/or integrating existing services'.

The briefing also referenced NYA reports which had raised two, as yet unanswered, questions from within the youth sector: '… about the long-term viability of mutuals in a competitive business environment … (and) the impact on the local voluntary sector with mutuals likely to attract preferential funding'. While accepting that the DDYP programme provided local authorities with an incentive to find their own solution, it also concluded that DDYP 'is not the answer to an uncertain future and diminishing resources for youth work'.[57]

However, given that most of the seventeen authorities which received DDYP funding had in this period planned or implemented often substantial cuts to their Youth Services' budgets, the CSN paper ignored some key wider resourcing issues—particularly, in comparison to their previous Youth Service budgets, the low levels of start-up funding available to the participating authorities to invest in new structures.

## Youth Engagement Fund

More on the fringes of traditional Youth Service activity but significant as an indicator of where the Coalition government's youth policy priorities lay was the £16 million Youth Engagement Fund, announced in July 2014. The money was provided by the DWP which, building on its experience of a wider Innovation Fund, collaborated with the Cabinet Office and the Ministry of Justice to prevent 'long term, damaging effects on young people's lives and future prospects'. Others concerns included the 'significant drain on the public purse' resulting from so many young people being 'NEET'—at that stage estimated at 925,000—and the 'strong links between poor educational achievement and offending'. Key goals for the programme were thus to provide 'positive education and employment outcomes … that support disadvantaged young people between the ages of 14 and 17', with gang members, teenage parents, refugees and homeless young people getting special attention.[58]

The Fund's launch Prospectus made clear to potential bidders that 'Social investment and, in particular, social impact bonds, are a way … (of) enabling socially-minded investors to fund the provision of a service delivered by a social enterprise or charity …' Payment by results procedures would therefore need to be agreed with 'investors funding innovative initiatives to prevent young people from becoming NEET'—all on the understanding that 'Government will only pay if the initiatives are successful and lead to positive outcomes'. Alongside more qualitative methods, the programme's evaluation would therefore use:

> …a range of metrics regarding the effectiveness of the programme, including comparing the outcomes of programme beneficiaries against a comparison group using a quasi-experimental approach.[59]

By October 2014 among the thirty nine 'social investment partnerships' selected to bid were Essex Boys and Girls Clubs—'working with voluntary youth clubs to support young people to realise their potential'; Sheffield Futures—the successor organisation to Sheffield Youth Service; and the Prince's Trust.[60]

# Youth Investment Fund

With a new Prime Minister in place, in September 2016 yet another new 'youth' initiative was announced—a Youth Investment Fund, again intended 'to support schemes in targeted disadvantaged communities across England'. In words attributed to Theresa May herself, this '… will help young people go as far as their talents can take them' because, she added, 'I want Britain to be the greatest meritocracy of the world'.

The £80 million programme—funded jointly by the government and the BLF—was intended to '… open up opportunities for young people to get involved in their communities…, to support their personal development, build character and help them succeed in the future'. The money—open to bids from local voluntary youth groups—was described as a way of implementing 'the Prime Minister's commitment to building a country that works for all through creating opportunity and developing individual potential'. Examples offered of potential 'winning youth projects' included '… clubs offering activities from football to basketball, arts and drama courses, enterprise training or volunteering opportunities such as … supporting charities and awareness campaigns such as Guide Dog Week'. An 'explicit objective', too, was 'to strengthen the evidence base on the impact of non-formal learning for young people'.[61]

Only half of the money up to 2020—the BLF's contribution—was specifically for these new initiatives. As the BLF was also to provide half of the remaining £40 million up to 2020 as 'continued support for Step Up To Serve's successful #iwill youth social action campaign', the Government's own contribution was thus just £20 million. Wilson made it clear, too, that he was looking 'to attract even more investment from … local organisations, businesses and philanthropists'.[62]

## Gesture Policies—Continued

Though often funded jointly with charitable trusts, governments throughout the period introduced a number of other time-limited youth programmes. For example a Life Chances Fund launched in July 2016 with funding which eventually totalled £81 million in May 2018 awarded £40,000 to Barking and Dagenham Council for one-to-one coaching for NEET young people.[63] In March 2018, three government departments jointly with the BLF provided £90 million from dormant bank accounts for programmes whose aims included 'demonstrating (young people's) value to the economy'.[64] The following month the Home office announced it was contributing £11 million from Early Intervention Fund to support the government's 'serious violence strategy'.[65]

In the context of the five-year cumulative fall of over £700 million in spending on local authority Youth Services in England,[66] the government's own figures, released in July 2018, nonetheless confirmed how marginal these programme were within its overall youth policies. Most telling was the release of figures in August 2018 which revealed that, of the £668 million spent on 'youth services' between 2014–2015 and 2017–2018, 90%—£634 million—had gone to the NCS.[67]

# Notes

1. Jean Spence and Mark K. Smith, 2011, *Myplace Evaluation—Final Report*, Department for Education, April.
2. Charlotte Goddard, 2012, 'Places to Be', *CYPN*, 1 May.
3. Richard Waite, 2011, 'Cuts Threaten Success of £270m Myplace Youth Centres', *Architects Journal*, 9 September.
4. Charlotte Goddard, 2012, op. cit.
5. HM Government, 2011, *Positive for Youth: A New Approach to Cross-Government Policy for Young People Aged 13–19*, December.
6. Charlotte Goddard, 2012, op. cit.
7. Charlotte Goddard, 2012, op. cit.
8. Gabriella Jozwiak, 2013a, 'Myplace Centres Open Doors to Schools', *CYPN*, 26 June.
9. Laura McCardle, 2014a, 'Youth Charity to Support Myplace Network', *CYPN*, 27 November.
10. Neil Puffett, 2012a, 'Youth Centre Game Changer', *CYPN*, 12 June.
11. Charlotte Goddard, 2012, op. cit.
12. GOV.UK, 2014, 'Myplace Programme Information', https://www.gov.uk/government/publications/Myplace-programme/Myplace-programme-information.
13. Gabriella Jozwiak, 2014, 'Youth Charity Unveils Plans for £6m Youth Zone', *CYPN*, 30 March.
14. Adam Offord, 2016a, 'Charity Targets Construction of 100 Youth Zones', *CYPN*, 7 July.
15. Adam Offord, 2015a, 'Plans for £6m Youth Zone Unveiled', *CYPN*, 1 December.
16. Laura McCardle, 2014b, 'Popularity of Youth Zones Prompts Ambitious Plans for Expansion', *CYPN*, 21 January.

17. Wikipedia, 'Bolton Lads and Girls Club', https://en.wikipedia.org/wiki/Bolton_Lads_and_Girls_Club#History.
18. *Chester Chronicle*, 2014, '£6m "Youth Zone" Plan for City Centre Site', 20 February; Laura McCardle, 2014c, 'Onside Reveals Plans for £6m Preston Youth Zone', *CYPN*, 29 October; Neil Puffett, 2017a, '£6m Youth Zone Given Go-ahead', *CYPN*, 4 January.
19. Adam Offord, 2015a, op. cit.
20. OnSide, 2016a, 'AO.COM Boss Gifts £1.5 million to Young People', 27 January.
21. Adam Offord, 2016b, 'OnSide Makes Case for Expanding State-of-the-Art Youth Centres', *CYPN*, 19 July.
22. OnSide, 2016b, 'Martin Ainscough Donates £1m to Chorley's Young People', 7 June; Laura McCardle, 2014c, op. cit.
23. Gabriella Jozwiak, 2017a, 'Construction Begins on £4.8m Youth Zone', *CYPN*, 16 January.
24. Laura McCardle, 2014c, op. cit.
25. Adam Offord, 2016c, 'Youth Services Cut by £387m in Six Years', *CYPN*, 12 August.
26. Laura McCardle, 2014c, op. cit.
27. Tony Taylor, 2016, 'Southwark Plans 73 per cent Cut to Youth & Play: Youth Council Ignored', IDYW, 22 January, https://indefenceofyouthwork.com/2016/01/22/southwark-plans-73-cut-to-youth-play-youth-council-ignored/.
28. Laura McCardle, 2014d, 'Council Enlists Charities to Deliver Youth Services', *CYPN*, 9 January.
29. Gabriella Jozwiak, 2017b, 'Plans for £6m Youth Zone in London Unveiled', *CYPN*, 10 April.
30. Tom Barton and Tom Edgington, 2014, 'Youth Services Spending Down by One-Third', *BBC News*, 25 March, http://www.bbc.uk/news/uk-26714184.
31. Neil Puffett, 2017b, 'Council Sets Aside £7m for New Youth Zone', *CYPN*, 6 March.
32. Tony Taylor, 2014, 'Cuts Watch: Policy Update on Local Authority Cuts to Youth Services', IDYW, 29 December, https://indefenceofyouthwork.com/2014/12/29/cuts-watch-policy-update-on-local-authority-cuts-to-youth-services/.
33. *Wolverhampton Express and Star*, 2016, 'Wolverhampton's the Way Youth Zone Attracts 1500 in Two Weeks', 5 February.

34. Neil Puffett, 2017c, 'Planners Approve £6m Youth Zone in London', *CYPN*, 28 July; Nina Jacobs, 2017, 'London Youth Zone Gets Planning Go-ahead', *CYPN*, 7 September; Sophie Eminson, 2017, 'London Youth Zone Gets Go-ahead', *CYPN*, 21 September; Joe Lepper, 2018a, 'Charity in Talks to Establish 12 More Youth Zones', *CYPN*, 19 January; Neil Puffett, 2018a, 'OnSide Announces Plans for Further Youth Zone in London', *CYPN*, 20 March.

35. Amion Consulting, 2015, *Defining the Impact of OnSide Youth Zones: Final Report*, May, http://www.socialvalueuk.org/app/uploads/2016/03/OnSide-Defining-the-Impact-of-a-Youth-Zone-Final-with-exec-summary-M....pdf.

36. Adam Offord, 2015b, 'Massive Increase in Disabled Young People Using Youth Zones', *CYPN*, 16 November.

37. Adam Offord, 2015c, 'Youth Zones "Worth £2 for Every £1 Invested"', *CYPN*, 20 May.

38. Amion Consulting, 2017, 'Client: OnSide Youth Zones', http://www.amion.co.uk/case-studies/defining-the-impact-of-the-youth-zone-model/.

39. Amion Consulting, 2017, op. cit.

40. Laura McCardle, 2014e, 'Popularity of Youth Zones Prompts Ambitious Plans for Expansion', *CYPN*, 21 January.

41. Adam Offord, 2016d, 'OnSide Makes Case for Expanding State-of-the-Art Youth Centres', *CYPN*, 19 July.

42. Adam Offord, 2016d, op. cit.

43. Kathryn Morley, 2017, 'Lack of Investment in Youth Services Is Failing Future Generations', *Guardian*, 24 November; Kathryn Morley, 2017, 'The Way Forward for Youth Provision: Local Authority Decision Makers' Views on the Future of Universal Provision', Onside, November.

44. Amion Consulting, 2017, op. cit.

45. Rebecca Baron, 2015, 'The Way Appoints New Staff', www.thewayyouthzone.org/vacancies/.

46. DfE, 2011, 'Press Release: Government Sets Out Strategy for Being Positive for Youth', 19 December, https://www.gov.uk/government/news/government-sets-out-strategy-to-be-positive-for-youth; Neil Puffett, 2011, 'Councils Begin to Develop Youth Innovation Zones', *CYPN*, 20 December.

47. Neil Puffett, 2012b, 'Youth Innovation Zones Yield Mixed Results', *CYPN*, 15 October.

48. HM Government, 2013, *Positive for Youth: Progress Since December 2011*, p. 22, https://www.gov.uk/government/uploads/system/uploads/attachment_data/file/210383/Positive-for-Youth-progress-update.pdf.

49. Gabriella Jozwiak, 2013b, 'Youth Leaders Question Future of Youth Innovation Zones', *CYPN*, 22 July.

50. Gabriella Jozwiak, 2013b, op. cit.

51. GOV.UK, 2014, 'Delivering Differently Programmes', 10 January/14 July, https://www.gov.uk/government/collections/delivering-differently-programme-for-local-authorities.

52. Cabinet Office, 2014, *Delivering Differently for Young People*, Cabinet Office, July, https://www.gov.uk/government/publications/delivering-differently-for-young-people-programme-prospectus.

53. Cabinet Office, 2015, *Delivering Differently for Young People*, Cabinet Office, September, https://www.gov.uk/government/publications/delivering-differently-for-young-people-programme-prospectus-and-form.

54. Chris Hayes, 2016, 'CSN Policy Briefing: Youth Service: The Delivering Differently for Young People (DDYP) Programme', LGiU, 10 February, p. 2.

55. Chris Hayes, 2016, op. cit., p. 2.

56. Chris Hayes, 2016, op. cit., p. 1.

57. Chris Hayes, 2016, op. cit., pp. 8–9.

58. HM Government, 2014, 'Youth Engagement Fund: Prospectus', May, https://www.gov.uk/government/publications/youth-engagement-fund-prospectus.

59. Ecorys, 2014, 'Ecorys to Evaluate Youth Engagement Fund Social Impact Bond Programme', https://uk.ecorys.com/news/ecorys-evaluate-youth-engagement-fund-social-impact-bond-programme.

60. HM Government, 2014, op. cit.

61. Adam Offord, 2016e, 'Guide to Youth Investment Fund', *CYPN*, 17 September; Tania de St. Croix, 2018, 'Youth Work Beyond the Measurement Imperative? Reflections on the Youth Investment Fund Learning Project from a Critical Friend', Centre for Youth Impact, 7 March, https://www.civilsociety.co.uk/news/dcms-awards-40m-to-86-youth-organisations.html.

62. GOV.UK, 2016, 'Government Delivers £80m Boost to Help Give Young People the Best Start in Life', 11 September, https://www.gov.uk/government/news/government-delivers-80-million-boost-to-help-give-young-people-the-best-start-in-life; Andy Ricketts, 2016,

'Government to Back Youth Social Action Projects with £80m', *Third Sector*, 12 September.

63. Neil Puffett, 2018b, 'Council Receives £19m Government Funding for Youth Projects', *CYPN*, 8 May.

64. Joe Lepper, 2018b, 'Young People to be Central to Design of £90m Youth Programme', *CYPN*, 20 March.

65. Neil Puffett, 2018c, 'Serious Violence Strategy: Youth Projects to Get £11m', *CYPN*, 9 April.

66. Darren Hayes, 2018, 'Charity Calls for "Drastic Action" to Protect Youth Services', *CYPN*, 4 May.

67. Nina Jacobs, 2018, 'LGA: Give NCS Cash to Councils to Fund Year-Round Youth Work', *CYPN*, 2 August 2018.

# Further Reading

Amion Consulting. 2015. *Defining the Impact of OnSide Youth Zones: Final Report*. May. http://www.socialvalueuk.org/app/uploads/2016/03/OnSide-Defining-the-Impact-of-a-Youth-Zone-Final-with-exec-summary-M....pdf.

Cabinet Office. 2014. *Delivering Differently for Young People*. July. https://www.gov.uk/government/publications/delivering-differently-for-young-people-programme-prospectus.

Cabinet Office. 2015. *Delivering Differently for Young People*. September. https://www.gov.uk/government/publications/delivering-differently-for-young-people-programme-prospectus-and-form.

Davies, Bernard. 2013. 'Youth Work in a Changing Policy Landscape: The View From England'. *Youth and Policy*. No. 110. May, pp. 6–33.

de St. Croix, Tania. 2018. 'Youth Work Beyond the Measurement Imperative? Reflections on the Youth Investment Fund Learning Project from a Critical Friend'. Centre for Youth Impact. 7 March. https://www.civilsociety.co.uk/news/dcms-awards-40m-to-86-youth-organisations.html.

Ronicle, James, et al. 2014. *Social Investment Bonds: The State of Play*. Escorts. November.

Spence, Jean and Smith, Mark K. 2011. *Myplace Evaluation—Final Report*. Department for Education. April.

# 14

# Beyond the State: How 'Voluntary' Is the Voluntary Youth Sector?

## 'Austerity' in Action

Cuts to state funding for the voluntary youth sector began even before 'austerity' took its toll. In February 2010, for example, Birmingham Council announced that it would stop grant-aid totalling nearly £800,000 for some 400 youth organisations.[1] By the following January Birmingham Youth Action Network, whose approximately 100 affiliated organisations provided volunteering opportunities for young people, announced that, as it would run out of money by September, it would have to close.[2] When two months later the city's St Paul's Community Trust—quoted by David Cameron as a Big Society inspiration—lost a third of its council funding, it decided it could no longer run the only youth work facilities in the area it served and made its six youth work staff redundant.[3]

Though in 2012 fewer than a quarter of voluntary organisations were getting state funding,[4] by then survival had become a dominant preoccupation for much of the sector. Four months into the Coalition government, a NCVYS survey had revealed that in the previous year the income of nearly 70% of the 135 respondents had reduced—for most

© The Author(s) 2019
B. Davies, *Austerity, Youth Policy and the Deconstruction of the Youth Service in England*, https://doi.org/10.1007/978-3-030-03886-1_14

by over 20% and for 10% by half. Over 75% of those not yet facing reductions were cutting projects, with 20% considering actual closure. 'Hundreds' of employees were being made redundant and whole programmes ended, including many aimed at the very groups—'NEETs', young people at risk of offending—repeatedly identified as government priorities.[5]

Most of the cuts could be traced to the Treasury's much reduced financial support for local councils including a £311 million reduction in the area-based grants programme. A number of other government funding streams were also scaled down or—for example the Youth Capital and Youth Opportunities Funds—ended altogether. Often 'with little notice', already commissioned projects also lost their funding.[6]

Councils in poorer areas—some raising as little as 10–18% of their income from council tax—were hit particularly hard.[7] Lambeth, which anticipated a £65 million reduction in its overall budget up to April 2014, announced that from January 2011 it would cut funding for voluntary organisations supporting young people by up to 35%. Greenwich Council warned that it might have to take 50% or more out of its voluntary sector budget.[8]

In June 2011 a *CYPN*-UK Youth survey of eighteen associations and clubs serving almost 300,000 young people revealed that 67% of respondents said that they or their member organisations had been affected by cuts. Seventy six percent said that affiliated groups had lost youth workers, reduce opening hours or closed projects.[9] When Warwickshire Association of Youth Clubs, for example, predicted in February 2011 that both its budget and its staffing would by April have been reduced by half,[10] the Council agreed a £180,000 'transition fund grant' to help fill the £500,000 gap in its operational budget.[11]

Over the next five years these financial pressures intensified. According to *CYPN*'s 2013 survey of 110 professionals, in 'the hostile climate for youth work' 'one in three organisations that provide services to young people face closure within the next 12 months'. (Ninety four percent of respondents judged the Big Society as 'not having a positive effect on youth services', with one dismissing it as simply meaning '… more volunteers available to replace staff'.[12]) Two years later an annual survey of charities' accounts found that, though the income the responding organisations received from individuals had gone up by £26.4 million, government money for those working with children and young people had fallen by £175.2 million.[13]

Local examples of the impacts included:

- Following a cut in its income in 2010 of £200,000 (40%), Sheffield Children and Young People Empowerment Project's decision to scale back its work with disabled and LGBT young people.[14]
- Also in 2010, the loss of 25% of its funding by the Devon-based Wings South West—described as working in 'one of the most deprived rural regions in the UK'.[15]
- The closure in 2011 of Calderdale Gay and Lesbian Youth.[16]

## Government Funding—And Its Limits

Despite the extent and depth of these cuts, over half of the respondents to the 2011 *CYPN* survey reported they were still making plans to meet ministers' and councils' expectations that they would fill emerging gaps in services.[17] That year, at an ADCS conference, Loughton again made clear that this remained central to government strategy when he talked of 'a new approach to delivering services to young people in partnership with the voluntary sector'—a proposal immediately endorsed by CHYPS's Chief Executive.[18]

In 2011, a government gesture to help the sector implement the policy came in the form of, initially, a two-year, £60 million a year DfE grant scheme 'to support vital children's services while providers identify alternative finance'. In its first year, as well as £1.49 million allocated to NCVYS, £4.5 million went to one organisation, Kids Company,[19] which collapsed three years later.[20] By 2016 more than £200 million had been distributed through the scheme to voluntary and community groups working with children and young people, including UK Youth.[21]

In September 2011 the DCLG also issued a 'Best Value Statutory Guidance' paper urging councils not to cut their local voluntary organisations disproportionately.[22] When it emerged in November 2012 at a conference partly sponsored by UK Youth and NCVYS that the advice was being widely ignored, the junior minister present, after pleading ignorance, promised to 'to look into the issue'. In line with the government's wider Localism policies (see Chapter 6), he nonetheless still insisted that funding for local authority youth services would not be ring-fenced.[23]

As the cuts continued—by 2015, voluntary organisations' income from government for work with children and young people had fallen by £152.6 million[24]—a range of pragmatic responses were being adopted. According to its 'director of operations', for example, the newly (and 'more relevantly') rebadged Ambition[25] was by then 'looking to provide more support and training for (volunteers) where they are taking the place of qualified youth workers'.[26] More broadly, 62% of respondents to the 2013 *CYPN* survey were reducing their staffing and nearly a third their opening hours and programmes. Over 40% had closed projects while over a third had increased or would be introducing charges for young people. Others were providing services for other organisations[27] while over 65%—at least in one case prompted by their local council[28]—were sharing information and facilities.

## From Collaboration and Alliances …

Under these financial pressures, the sector increasingly opened itself up to often radical forms of realignment and restructuring. A 2015 Partnership for Young London report, for example, recommended greater collaboration in the form of what were called 'lobbying alliances' specifically aimed of getting a better government deal for the sector. Benefits of such an approach were listed as promoting a 'collective voice'; splitting 'the capacity burden' by 'encouraging team-working'; extending 'reach'; and getting 'increased authenticity' by 'sharing data and analysis.. (to) add evidential weight and clout to each other's arguments and initiatives'.[29]

Some such moves in the 'children and youth' field had by then already occurred. As far back as November 2011, NCVYS and the NCB had agreed 'a strategic alliance in an effort to reduce duplication in the sector'.[30] A 'Creative Collisions' initiative sponsored by the Wellcome

Trust was launched at a conference in November 2013 backed by ten 'partners' including UK Youth, London Youth, NCVYS, NYA, vin-spired and the NCS. With the overall aim of 'catalys(ing) change for young people', a launch conference attracted 'over 700 youth sector pro-fessionals, journalists and young delegates'. Two further conferences, in November 2014 and in May 2017 also had wide sector support with attendances of 500–600, including in 2017 200–250 free places for 16–25 year olds.[31]

In October 2015 NCVYS, UK Youth and Ambition launched a 'Youth Sector Collaboration Consultation'—a way of working which two years earlier Ambition's chief executive had described as 'her mantra'.[32] As funding cuts gathered pace, Anna Smee, the UK Youth's Chief Executive, talked of 'a clear need for leadership' in order to 'transform the sector' by creating more innovative ways of working. In a policy climate which continued to place competition between organisations at the core of its funding procedures and within a policy framework primarily focused on individualised achievement, the advantages of 'collective impact' also suddenly attracted renewed approval.[33]

The first planned consultations—six events held in London, Manchester and Windsor in late 2015[34]—were followed by a two-day by-invitation event, 'Changing the Trajectory – Charting a New Course for Youth Services'. This was attended by government and local authority representatives, academics, funders, the Director of the CYI and, with the BYC and the National Union of Students (NUS) pro-viding the youth 'voice', by thirty 'leading figures' from national and some local voluntary youth organisations. Organisations not invited included the somewhat maverick Woodcraft Folk, the newly formed IYW, the youth work trade unions including Unite's campaigning arm ChooseYouth and IDYW (see Chapter 17). Practitioners also had lim-ited representation.[35]

Based on the feedback from these events, in January 2016 the three sponsoring organisations circulated 'for discussion' a 'Youth Sector Briefing' on the consultations' findings and proposed actions.[36] They also announced the launch of a 'collective impact project'—described more generally as

... an innovative and structured approach to making collaboration work across government, business, philanthropy, non-profit organisations and citizens to achieve significant and lasting social change.[37]

Its seven objectives included developing 'cross sector alliances to support agreed outcomes', a 'youth offer' based on 'a shared vision for young people' and the identification of 'key players'—specifically NCVYS, UK Youth and Ambition—to provide the sector leadership. Highlighted, too, were commitments to create new business models 'to keep the sector sustainable' and develop measures to demonstrate youth work's positive impact for young people, with the newly established CYI identified as playing a key role.[38] As Anna Smee made clear, the collaboration which the lead bodies had in mind—and which they were to develop further through a 'joint Chairs Taskforce'[39]—was 'not just within the youth sector but also (with) the private sector, government and other charitable bodies'.[40]

Another product of these events was the proposal in 2016 to adopt a 'framework to map the sector and explain its impact', described as a 'Social Development Journey'. This was to be used particularly 'to identify where and how to strengthen the pipeline for NCS (sic) and apprenticeships to achieve Government targets'.[41] With UK Youth as the lead body, the premise underpinning the framework was to 'use non-formal learning approaches to complement (and in some cases replace) formal academic learning to provide truly rounded education for young people'. The 'four key enablers' shaping the framework were to be 'social engagement', 'social learning', 'social action' and 'social leadership'. The upward arched and arrowed trajectory of the journey envisaged that many young people

... will begin with their Social Engagement in their local youth groups at an early age and progress through the four stages as they get older, culminating in them finding a productive role for themselves as young adults. Other young people may engage one or two of these steps to address skills gaps or to improve specific capabilities...[42]

## ... to Mergers

In November 2012, at a conference partly organised by NCVYS and UK Youth, the sector was urged by a senior DfE official to consider mergers as a way of responding to the growing expectation that it would 'do more with less'.[43] By 2016, with the explicit intention of consolidating the number of organisations within it, one aim of the proposed 'collective impact project' was thus to form a taskforce to identify opportunities not just for partnerships but for mergers[44]—a first step in what turned out to be a fundamental restructuring of the sector, particularly at national level.

An indication of this direction of travel emerged early with the merger in January 2011 of The Prince's Trust with Fairbridge,[45] an organisation with a long history of working with young people. By then UK Youth and what became Ambition had also had merger discussions which had stalled because of disagreement on 'the structure of a single organisation'. After telling its members two years later that she was 'keeping an open mind on how far these discussions might lead',[46] by July 2013 Ambition's Chief Executive was reporting that 'there were other, better options for us'.[47] One of these was, with NCVYS, her efforts to increase sector collaboration.[48]

By mid-2016, in order to save money, UK Youth was in 'preliminary' discussions with the NYA about merging their 'back office' functions.[49] However, it was Ambition which led the way down the merger route. In what turned out to be a resignation issue for one principal youth officer,[50] in April 2015[51] it joined up with CHYPS, a move justified on the grounds that pooling resources would '... ensure services remained of a high standard despite funding cuts'.[52] Much more significant in the longer-term was the announcement in early 2016 that it was in merger talks with NCVYS, of which it and its predecessor organisations had long been an influential member. The plan to merge, first revealed in January 2016 as part of the launch of the collaborative 'collective impact project', was confirmed the following March[53] 'exactly 80 years and one week after (NCVYS's) beginning'.[54,55]

Under the merger Ambition took responsibility for 'the membership service, sector representation and related functions of NCVYS' and for its 'much-valued policy information service and other key work programmes'. NCVYS's Award Network for promoting and sharing good practice across youth services was transferred to UK Youth together with its safeguarding resources and services, its partnership with the Muslim Council of Britain and a collaborative project with the CYI.[56]

This, however, turned out to be just a stage in the sector's wider restructuring-by-merger. In August 2017 UK Youth and Ambition 'rubber-stamped' a deal which initially made Ambition a subsidiary of UK Youth and which, after consultations, would by April 2018 lead to a unified membership offer. Anna Smee explained the move on the grounds of increased credibility 'as one leading organisation … works across non-uniformed and, to some extent, uniformed organisations'. She justified it, too, on financial grounds, with the 'cash-rich' UK Youth welcoming the buildings which Ambition would bring to the new body.[57]

Though some at the time welcomed the UK Youth-Ambition merger, many grassroots groups were sceptical. In response in part to how Ambition was already operating, a new organisation, the National Association of Boys and Girls Clubs, was created. By 2018 this was reaching 100,000 young people via 1000 affiliated clubs operating 'in the most deprived areas'.[58]

## Drifting 'Missions'

As with all such developments, these funding and structural changes did not occur in an ideological vacuum. Shifts in the values and aims of the sector overall and of individual organisations had begun under New Labour which, it was argued subsequently, had invented the term 'voluntary sector' in order to draw its constituent bodies into delivering state policies.[59] Rebadged 'the Third Sector', it was thereby located as a 'partner' of the state and private sectors, though without acknowledgement even by the organisations themselves of the embedded imbalances of power within these relationships.

From 2010 on, as funding insecurities increased, ministers' growing expectation—again, too, shared by many in the sector itself though not always by the wider public[60]—was that to gain access to any state funding still on offer organisations needed to take on government aims and approved forms of 'delivery'. Over time this resulted in a sometimes radical reformulation of the distinctive values which had historically shaped 'voluntary' activity and to which most organisations continued to claim commitment.[61] One such premise under threat was that, in the words of a Carnegie Trust report, they had 'never (been) ... just providers of services' but 'thrive... best when ... not afraid to make trouble'.[62] By acting as critical friend to government, such 'trouble' could mean going beyond muted expressions of 'reservations' or 'concerns' to openly campaigning against government proposals. More positively, this older 'mission' had also involved proactively pressing for facilities when the organisations' own engagement with their communities revealed significant gaps in provision.

Tensions in the sector's relations with government did emerge. During 2013, for example, its pressure for increased public spending led some ministers' and MPs' to label the organisations involved 'fake charities'.[63] As a response to the 2014 Lobbying Act which limited voluntary organisations' campaigning in the run up to elections,[64] over 100 charities signed a letter to the Minister for Civil Society asking for an overhaul of legislation which, Girlguiding's Chief Executive said, was silencing their voices.[65]

More often, however, the sector found itself acting, sometimes willingly, as Trojan horses for government policies. High profile national organisations such as Barnardo's and Catch 22, for example, used their bidding expertise to win contracts in geographical and practice areas where they had little if any previous track record, in the process sometimes squeezing out long-established local youth work projects.[66]

These external manifestations of the changed nature of the sector were mirrored in how organisations operated internally. To gain credibility in the new funding environment, many re-redefined themselves as 'businesses' with plans explicitly focused on securing greater 'market share'. For achieving this they increasingly adopted managerialist forms of top-down decision-making and evaluation procedures, with some reconceptualising their services as 'products' and users as 'customers' or 'consumers'.[67] These 'marketising' shifts could also result in paid specialist and trained staff being replaced by volunteers with roles in effect formalised as unpaid employees.[68]

# Government Policies: From Reservations and 'Concerns'...

This 'mission drift' was neither instant nor without contradictory pulls. Initially some organisations took positions which, though usually falling short of challenging the dominant ideology of the time, indicated genuine concern about the wider conditions affecting young people's lives and emerging government responses. A report published by Clubs for Young People in 2009 (later Ambition) mounted a strong defence of the open access club work to which it had long been committed. It saw the government as having 'still some way to go before the value of clubs is fully understood' and criticised public sector commissioners for being 'too narrowly focused on some specific "problem" group such as … NEETs'.[69]

A month after the Coalition came to power, NCVYS, NYA and CHYPS formed a Youth Work Expert Group, joined also by Unite and BYC, though by then its concern was less threats to the nature of the practice than that 'we don't want youth work to be seen as a soft target (for cuts)'.[70] In those early Coalition months NCVYS also produced its cautionary report on the impact already of cuts—which, it noted, the 'Big Society' agenda was not taking into account.[71] On the back of the government's unwillingness to fulfil 'the existing commitment to young people as priority of (Big Society Bank) funds', two months later NCVYS proposed a 'Big Society Blueprint Programme' to focus on groups such as BME and rural young people and young women.[72] By 2017 a new report from London Youth was more broadly highlighting that 'poverty and inequality are worse here (in London) than anywhere else in the UK' and urging the government and the Mayor of London to give young people more attention.[73]

Though a main reservation was that his inaction might 'jeopardise the success of ... the National Citizen Service',[74] the revelations about Michael Gove's disinterest in youth policy in 2013 (see Chapter 9) also prompted 'huge concerns' within the sector. NCVYS joined twenty six other voluntary youth organisations to accuse him of 'marginalising' young people and, with the 2011 riots as its reference point, of 'risk(ing) social unrest'. When writing to congratulate David Cameron on his re-election as Prime Minister in May 2015, NCVYS and eleven other voluntary organisations put a more positive spin on these concerns by arguing specifically for 'education in non formal settings' and for 'a comprehensive youth support offer'—albeit now justified in government-speak as 'building the character and skills of young people'.[75]

Other key political moments were used to go public on these issues. In the run up to the 2016 EU referendum, UK Youth worked with Bite the Ballot and Hope Not Hate to encourage 18–25 year olds to join local debates.[76] During the general election campaign twelve months later, fifty 'youth leaders' including the chief executives of UK Youth, BYC and Girlguiding asked all the political parties to make firm pledges to the younger generation most affected by the Brexit negotiations in order to 'restore young people's confidence in democracy'.[77] Some, together with the Scout Association, the NYA and Ambition, as well as urging the parties to provide 'a universally accessible high quality youth service', pointed out that 'social mobility is an issue which has been growing since the 1990s' and asked for young people to be given better access to housing, work and educational opportunities.[78] In the aftermath of the 2017 election's indecisive outcome, a number of organisations including UK Youth, Ambition, the BYC, the NYA and the IYW as well as the CYI responded to the government's promise of a new youth policy paper by meeting with the LGA 'to explore a future vision for youth services'. Discussions included whether local authorities should play 'a co-ordinating role or (be) ... part of the service delivery'.[79]

Some organisations also encouraged young people to look critically at issues affecting them and, exceptionally, to respond by taking collective action. As we saw in Chapter 12, it was in this period that Girlguiding encouraged its members to come together to highlight the mental health problems facing young women.[80] At a fringe meeting of the 2014 Conservative Party conference, albeit on the somewhat narrow grounds that it helped build 'soft skills' such as resilience and confidence, its chief executive again made the case for informal education.[81] The Young Women's Trust—formerly the YWCA—also regularly published material and campaigned on issues affecting young women.[82] More broadly in March 2014 the YMCA, drawing on its own research findings, gave voice to criticisms of the welfare system as this was experienced by young people living in sheltered accommodation[83] and in 2018 published its findings on the cuts to youth work provision.[84]

Perhaps explaining why it was not on the invitation list for the 'Changing the Trajectory' consultation event discussed above, it was however the Woodcraft Folk which most explicitly asserted a critical independence from government and its policies. In 2010 for example it announced that it would

> … enthusiastically support action taken by young people to protest against government cuts to education. This includes walkouts and non-violent direct action.[85]

A year later its members were urged to avoid doing anything to 'undermine legal and legitimate industrial action by crossing any picket line'.[86] It also sought to launch campaigns in support of asylum-seekers and refugees and against the UK Border Agency's restrictive visa policies.[87]

## … to Engagement and Delivery

Such open anti-government campaigns, even ones using limited forms of collective action such as petitioning, remained the exception however. This was true even when policies were having seriously damaging consequences for the organisations' members such as the abolition of the Education Maintenance Allowance EMA in 2010 and the proposal in 2014 to end 18–12 year olds' right to housing benefit. Few were forthright in confronting—even often it seemed noticing—the free-market ideologies which, beyond the destruction of local authority Youth Services, were increasingly leaving young people in insecure and low paid jobs and with fewer welfare benefits. Open stances by the sector's organisational 'leaders' against the Coalition's policies and their demands and their underlying rationale became even rarer as, in highly strategic ways, many positioned themselves to exploit as a progressive opportunity the government's determination to substitute the voluntary sector for the state.

Indeed rather than opposition, or even reservations, what marked many of these responses was a growing willingness—often in taken-for-granted ways—to go beyond just endorsing to proactively promoting and implementing government initiatives. Within a month of helping to put together the NCVYS 'Expert' alliance, CHYPS qualified its condemnation of the Youth Service cuts by endorsing Tim Loughton's demand that 'councils … be more imaginative in a tough economic climate'.[88] An NYA young people's 'Practical Guide' on commissioning services published in 2012 at no point asked its users even to consider whether commissioning was the only or best way of providing the facilities they wanted.[89] Acceptance of the on-going recasting of youth work as any kind work with young people was evident, too, in the advice given to government by UK Youth's Chief Executive in 2016: that it use youth workers to help implement its proposed 'extended day' in some secondary schools.[90]

Perhaps the most explicit indicator of the sector's direction of travel, however, was the acceptance between 2011 and 2013 of £2.6 million of DoE funding by NCVYS—'the independent voice of the voluntary youth sector'. This was to be used to co-ordinate and contribute to the 'Catalyst' consortium whose members—NYA, the Young Foundation and Social Enterprise UK—had all in their different ways registered their support for the 'reform' of public services generally and for a voluntary sector committed to market-oriented values and approaches. Their overall brief was to '… establish a social finance retailer that can pilot and then promote a youth sector specific social investment approach based on evidence of impact'. To achieve this 'a vigorous and responsive' sector was to be created, 'freed from dependency on grant-based funding and better equipped to operate within a payment-by-results environment'. More specific aims included '… strengthening the youth sector market, equipping the sector to work in partnership with Government and coordinating a skills development strategy for the youth sector's workforce'.[91]

By January 2012 Catalyst was announcing an 'intensive' nine-month 'Replication in Action Programme' to 'encourage ... growth amongst Youth organisations/enterprises through developing appropriate business models for replication'. Via 'a series of workshops, master classes and expert coaching', these organisations were to be supported to

• make an informed assessment on whether or not franchising/licensing is the most appropriate model for growing their organisations, and if this is the case,
• develop a pilot franchise or licence package.[92]

Over this period NCVYS embedded itself in other ways in the dominant policy discourses of the period. Its immediate reaction to the 2011 'youth riots', for example, was to propose a divisive 'Not in my name' campaign[93] which not only publicly distanced it from any young person who had been involved. It also, before any reliable evidence was available on who these young people were or why they had participated, at least implicitly endorsed hostile 'youth' stereotypes shaping government and media reactions. In this period, too, NCVYS established a partnership with Respublica, a think tank committed to promoting 'a vibrant democracy and market economy' and 'a future (in which) the benefits of capital, trade and entrepreneurship are open to all' whose founder and director, Philip Blond, was described as 'a driving force behind the Big Society agenda'.[94] This led eighteen months later to the two organisations setting up a twelve-month 'Commission on Youth' as a response to 'one of the worst waves of civil unrest in a generation'.[95] The following year, it appointed Tim Loughton as its 'ambassador'[96]—the minister who had described the £350 million a year spent on youth services in England as "large slugs of public money" (see Chapter 8).

Even as it had been voicing criticism of Michael Gove's indifference to youth policies, NCVYS had also publicly identified itself as his Department's 'strategic partner for young people'.[97] Once the Cabinet Office took over responsibility for youth policies, however, NCVYS, together with for example NYA, still felt able to put a positive spin on the change [98]—as did UK Youth three years later, in 2016, when the responsibility moved again to the DCMS.[99]

After taking over as the collective voice of the sector, Ambition, in acknowledging that 'great challenges' remained, did concede that 'education would seem to be a more natural home'—though significantly on the grounds that the DfE 'includes character, wellbeing, life skills employability …'. Nonetheless—though without explaining how this would help the survival of the open access youth work to which its predecessor bodies had been so committed—it declared itself encouraged by the fact that 'at the … DCMS the Sports Strategy recognised the vital role of local authorities and voluntary sector partners'.[100]

Indeed over the following twelve months and beyond, even as economic pressures on young people intensified, Ambition re-emphasised its focus on changing them one-by-one—for example via joint development work with the Home Office on what was labelled 'preventing youth crime: the associated aspects of character and potential interventions'.[101] Through webinars focused on the 'development of mental toughness and a positive mindset', it collaborated, too, with a consultancy, AQR International, whose remit was 'to make high quality psychometric tools and assessments accessible to users of all types'.[102]

In taking up these positions, Ambition was not alone. Under the UK Youth banner, though with NCVYS and Ambition's name attached, the first section of the Briefing on the findings of their Youth Sector Collaboration Consultation announced that 'Government and the youth sector are united in their aim to improve outcomes for young people'. After restating the promised results of the consultations for the sector itself, endorsement followed for such government-sponsored 'outcomes' as 'increase(d) NCS participation'; '50% of all 10 to 20 year olds to be engaged in social action by 2020'; and the wider sharing and creation of 'character related materials for every school in the country'. Again absent from the paper was any reference to the closure of hundreds of youth work facilities or to how the loss of the EMA and mental health facilities or the threat to their housing benefit was contributing to young people's 'improved outcomes'.

# In Defence of the Voluntary Youth Sector

In August 2017 UK Youth's newly appointed interim Chief Executive made clear that the organisation's work continued to be embedded in 'a strong vision, innovative new programmes and a clear strategic plan', including commitments to young people's 'access (to) equal opportunities regardless of background or circumstance' and to 'a chance to reach their potential'.[103] Nonetheless, for achieving these aims, she reiterated that the organisation's priorities remained 'forging new corporate partnerships' and 'improving impact measurement'.

Similar positions had already had passionate expression in January 2016 by UK Youth's Director of Partnerships and Policy, Matt Lent. This came in a blog response to an IDYW posting which had labelled organisations like UK Youth 'unprincipled pragmatists'. Some of Lent's starting points were the 'severe cuts' to youth provision, a central government which was failing to offer direction or guidance and the need still for 'a universal, open access youth service to support young people'. Lent's case for this, however, was not primarily educational but a concern that without such provision

> … particularly (for) those most vulnerable, it will only be a matter of time before we see an increase in criminal activity, a rise in drug use, more STIs, teenage pregnancies, alcohol related anti-social behaviour, and even more youth unemployment and under-employment.

Lent, in embracing the label of pragmatist, went on to list recent voluntary sector developments as evidence, not just of progress, but also of principled action. He pointed to the sector-wide consultation on priorities; to the mergers, particularly of NCVYS and Ambition; and to UK Youth's own vision of a Social Development Journey for young people. In support, he outlined a wide range of grassroots projects UK Youth had initiated such as the 'dozens' of IT Hubs in youth clubs and the 'hundreds of disaffected and impoverished young people' engaged in its Big Music Project. Lent was also explicit about his determination to 'call the government to account when I think they are wrong', including to 'make plain my disapproval of stringent and short-sighted cuts'.

However, his powerful defence of the stance of his organisation and of the sector generally also captured a crucial element of their over-arching 'political' strategy: their willingness ultimately to embrace the government-imposed policy regimes of the day:

*I will sit down, I will talk, I will collaborate, I will seek common ground and I will compromise when needed, because that is how I can ensure we protect and create the very best open access **and** targeted intervention opportunities for young people.* (Emphasis in the original)[104]

# Notes

1. Ross Watson, 2010a, 'Birmingham Axes Youth Grants', *CYPN*, 9 February.
2. Youth Action Network, 2010, 'Headline Results from YAN Members' Survey 2010', YAN, 14 December; Andy Hillier, 2011a, 'Youth Action Network to Close After Losing Funding', *CYPN*, 21 January.
3. Joe Lepper, 2011, 'Trust That Inspired Big Society to Lose Its Youth Services', *CYPN*, 11 March.
4. Colin Rochester, 2013, *Rediscovering Voluntary Action: The Beat of a Different Drum*, Basingstoke, Palgrave Macmillan, p. 83.
5. NCVYS, 2010, *Comprehensive Cuts: Report on Funding Changes in the Voluntary and Community Youth Sector*, October.
6. Amanda Fitzgerald, et al., 2013, *Hard Times, New Directions: The Impact of the Local Government Cuts in London*, Interim Report, LSE, http://sticerd.lse.ac.uk/dps/case/spcc/wp07.pdf; + http://eprints.lse.ac.uk/58048/.
7. Amanda Fitzgerald, et al., 2013, op. cit.
8. NCVYS, 2010, op. cit.
9. Andy Hillier, 2011b, 'Youth Groups Find Alternative Funding to Make Up for Government Spending Cuts', *CYPN*, 14 June.
10. *Leamington Spa Courier*, 2011, 'Youth Charity Faces Funding Strains', 11 February.
11. Jamie Smith, 2011, 'Youth Organisation Gets £180,000 Boost', *Leamington Spa Courier*, 8 April.

12. Neil Puffett, 2013a, 'Youth Sector on a "Knife-Edge" as Third of Organisations at Risk', *CYPN*, 16 April.
13. Jess Brown, 2015, op. cit.
14. NCVYS, 2010, op. cit.
15. NCVYS, 2010, op. cit.
16. Neil Puffett, 2012a, 'Small Youth Charities to Bear the Brunt of Funding Cuts', *CYPN*, 13 January.
17. Janaki Mahadevan, 2012, 'Brighton Councillors Vote to Strengthen Ties with Voluntary Youth Organisations', *CYPN*, 25 January; Andy Hillier, 2011b, op. cit.
18. Ross Watson, 2010b, 'Youth Service Chiefs Back Plans for Shake-Up', *CYPN*, 13 July.
19. Neil Puffett, 2011, '£60m of Community Grants Unveiled', *CYPN*, 25 February; Neil Puffett, 2016a, 'DfE Set to Axe £200m Grant Scheme for Children's Charities', *CYPN*, 12 February.
20. Neil Puffett, 2011, op. cit.
21. Neil Puffett, 2016a, op. cit.
22. DCLG, 2011, 'Best Value Statutory Guidance', September, para. 5, https://assets.publishing.service.gov.uk/government/uploads/system/uploads/attachment_data/file/5945/1976926.pdf.
23. Neil Puffett, 2012b, 'Minister to Investigate "Unfair" Cuts to Voluntary Sector Youth Services', *CYPN*, 29 November.
24. Jess Brown, 2015, 'Funding for Children's Charities Cut by £150m', *CYPN*, 8 June.
25. Neil Puffett, 2012c, 'Clubs for Young People Changes Its Name to Ambition', *CYPN*, 4 July.
26. Neil Puffett, 2012d, 'Training Pledge for Volunteer Youth Workers', *CYPN*, 7 November.
27. Andy Hillier, 2011b, op. cit.; Neil Puffett, 2013, op. cit.
28. Ross Watson, 2010c, 'Bolton Creates Information-Sharing Forum for Youth Service Providers', *CYPN*, 14 May.
29. Joe Lepper, 2015, 'Call for Youth Group Collaboration to Increase Influence', *CYPN*, 17 April; Alex Munn, 2015, *Who Stands for Youth? A Call for Better Collaboration to Influence Youth Policy in London*, Partnership for London, April.
30. Gabriella Jozwiak, 2010, 'NCB and NCVYS Form an Alliance to Improve the Efficiency of Their Work', *CYPN*, 10 November.

31. Creative Collisions, 2014, 'Creative Collisions', https://creativecollisions.wordpress.com/.
32. Gabriella Jozwiak, 2013a, 'Partnerships Plotter', *CYPN*, 9 July.
33. CYI, 2016, 'Exploring the Potential of Collective Impact in the Youth Sector ...', 1 March, http://www.youthimpact.uk/news--events/exploring-the-potential-of-collective-impact-in-the-youth-sector-a-framing-paper-from-npc-and-the-centre-for-youth-impact.
34. Adam Offord, 2015a, 'Call for Greater Youth Sector Collaboration', *CYPN*, 23 October.
35. Tony Taylor, 2015, 'How Pluralist and Representative Is the NCVYS/AMBITION/UK YOUTH Consultation?', IDYW, 14 December, https://indefenceofyouthwork.com/2015/12/.
36. UK Youth, 2016a, 'Youth Sector Briefing: Consultation Findings and Proposed Actions—For Discussion', 19 January.
37. Collaboration for Impact, 2017, 'The Collective Impact Framework', http://www.collaborationforimpact.com/collective-impact/.
38. Darren Hayes, 2016, 'Youth Bodies Unveil Plans for Sector Collaboration', *CYPN*, 21 January.
39. UK Youth, 2016a, op. cit.
40. Darren Hayes, 2016, op. cit.
41. UK Youth, 2016a, op. cit., p. 3.
42. UK Youth, 2016b, 'Our Approach'.
43. Neil Puffett, 2012e, 'Youth Organisation Mergers Vital in the Face of Dwindling Budgets, DfE Official Says', *CYPN*, 30 November.
44. Darren Hayes, 2016, op. cit.
45. Neil Puffett, 2012e, op. cit.
46. Andy Hillier, 2010, 'Youth Work Bodies Merger Back On', *CYPN*, 20 July.
47. Gabriella Jozwiak, 2013a, op. cit.
48. Adam Offord, 2015b, 'Call for Greater Youth Service Collaboration', *CYPN*, 23 October.
49. Adam Offord, 2016a, 'NYA and UK Youth in Talks Over Sharing Back Office Functions', *CYPN*, 3 August.
50. Laura McCardle, 2014a, 'Youth Service Boss Quits Chyps Over Merger Plans', *CYPN*, 29 October.
51. Neil Puffett, 2015, 'Ambitions and Chyps Confirm Merger', *CYPN*, 26 February.

52. Laura McCardle, 2014b, 'Ambition Boss: Chyps Merger "Will Improve Youth Service Quality"', *CYPN*, 5 November.
53. Darren Hayes, 2016, op. cit.
54. Adam Offord, 2016b, 'Ambition and NCVYS Confirm Merger', *CYPN*, 11 March; Ambition, 2016, 'Ambition to Continue the Membership Services and Policy Work of NCVYS', http://ambitionuk.org/news/338796/Ambition-to-continue-the-membership-services-and-policy-work-of-NCVYS.htm.
55. Ambition, 2016, op. cit.
56. Liam Kay, 2016, 'Chief Executive Susanna Rauprich Among Redundancies as Youth Charity Closes', *Third Sector*, 31 March; Neil Puffett, 2016b, 'YUK Youth to Take on NCVYS Functions', *CYPN*, 31 March.
57. Tristan Donovan, 2017, 'Major Youth Work Charities Announce Merger', *CYPN*, 22 September.
58. National Association of Boys and Girls Clubs, 2018, 'Who We Are', http://www.nabgc.org.uk/who-we-are/.
59. Colin Rochester, 2013, op. cit.
60. Darren Hayes, 2014, 'Public Sceptical of Charities' Role in Delivering Services', *CYPN*, 6 March.
61. NCIA, 2015, 'NCIA Inquiry into the Future of Voluntary Services: Fight or Fright—Voluntary Services in 2015: A Summary and Discussion of the Inquiry Findings', January, http://www.independentaction.net/wp-content/uploads/sites/8/2015/02/NCIA-Inquiry-summary-report-final.pdf.
62. Tony Taylor, 2012a, 'Driven to Market: Youth Work's Sheepish Response', IDYW, 7 March, https://indefenceofyouthwork.com/2012/03/07/driven-to-market-youth-works-sheepish-response/; Lauren Higgs, 2012, 'Are Children's Charities Too Afraid Now to "Bite the Hand That Feeds?"', *CYPN*, 8 January.
63. Barings Foundation, 2013, *Independence Under Threat: The Voluntary Sector in 2013*, Barings Foundation, p. 9, http://www.independencepanel.org.uk/wp-content/uploads/2013/01/Independence-Under-Threat_The-Voluntary-Sector-in-2013_WebVersion12.pdf.
64. Patrick Butler, 2016, 'Charities Told: Don't Lobby Us, Unless We Like What You Say', *Guardian Society*, 9 February.

65. George Greenwood, 2017, 'Girl Guides Among Charities to Urge Lobbying Rethink', BBC, 30 August, http://www.bbc.co.uk/news/uk-politics-41083318.
66. Michael Bell, 2012, 'From Co-operation to Competition and Fragmentation', NCIA, 22 November 2012, http://www.independentaction.net/2012/11/22/from-co-operation-to-competition-and-fragmentation/; Bernard Davies, 2013, 'Youth Work in a Changing Policy Landscape: The View from England', *Youth and Policy*, May, pp. 6–32.
67. Colin Rochester, 2013, op. cit., p. 85.
68. Colin Rochester, 2013, op. cit., Chapter 4.
69. Clubs for Young People, 2009, *Somewhere to Belong: A Blueprint for 21st Century Youth Clubs*, London, Clubs for Young People, pp. 8–9.
70. Ross Watson, 2010, 'Youth Sector Unites to Defend Work', *CYPN*, 8 June.
71. NCVYS, 2010, op. cit.; Andy Hillier, 2011b, op. cit.
72. Lauren Higgs, 2010, 'NCVYS Appeals for Organisations to Trial Big Society Vision', *CYPN*, 12 August.
73. London Youth, 2017, *Young People's Capital of the World? Understanding and Responding to Young Londoners*, London Youth in partnership with UBS and Centre for London, March; Joe Lepper, 2017a, 'Charity Calls for Sadiq Khan to Take Action on Youth Services', *CYPN*, 17 March.
74. Neil Puffett, 2013b, 'Sector Raises "Huge Concerns" Over Government Approach to Youth Policy', *CYPN*, 28 January.
75. NCVYS, 2015, 'Letter to the Prime Minister', 28 May; Adam Offord, 2015c, 'Sector urges Cameron to Improve Youth Services Offer', *CYPN*, 1 June.
76. Anna Smee, 2016, 'Should I Stay or Should I Go? Young People Debate the EU and Brexit', *Guardian*, 31 May.
77. Joe Lepper, 2017b, 'Youth Leaders Demand Election Commitments for Young People', *CYPN*, 25 April.
78. Joe Lepper, 2017c, 'Youth Organisations Call for Election Pledges on Social Mobility', *CYPN*, 2 May.
79. News from Ambition, 2017, 'Local Government Association—Vision for Youth Services Roundtable', 24 August.
80. Adam Offord, 2015d, 'Girlguiding Study Highlights Mental Health Pressures', *CYPN*, 24 August.
81. Laura McCardle, 2014c, 'Conservative Party Conference: Call for Youth Sector to Promote Informal Education', *CYPN*, 30 September.

82. Young Women's Trust, 2013, *Young Women: The Real Story*, http://www.youngwomenstrust.org/assets/0000/0002/YWT_Report.pdf.

83. Laura McCardle, 2014d, 'Welfare System Is Failing Young People, Warns YMCA Chief', *CYPN*, 6 March.

84. YMCA, 2018, *Youth & Consequences: A Report Examining Local Authority Expenditure on Youth Services in England and Wales*, May.

85. IDYW, 2010, 'Woodcraft Folk Stand Up to Be Counted!', http://www.indefenceofyouthwork.org.uk/wordpress/?p=894, posted 26 November 2010.

86. IDYW, 2011, 'The Right to Strike: Woodcraft Folk', http://www.indefenceofyouthwork.org.uk/wordpress/?p=1719, posted 29 November 2011.

87. Woodcraft Folk, 2013, 'Woodcraft Folk Campaign Hub', at http://woodcraft.org.uk/campaigns.

88. Ross Watson, 2010d, 'Youth Service Chiefs Back Plans for Shake-Up', *CYPN*, 13 July.

89. NYA, 2012, *A Practical Guide to Commissioning Services for Young People—Part 10: Involving Young People in Commissioning*, NYA/LGA, May.

90. Adam Offord, 2016c, 'Call for Youth Work to Support Extended School Day Plans', *CYPN*, 18 March.

91. Neil Puffett, 2012f, 'Catalyst Group Bids to Be Source of Strength for Youth Sector', *CYPN*, 10 July; Ross Watson, 2010d, op. cit.; NCVYS, 2012, 'Catalyst Consortium—FAQs', at http://www.ncvys.org.uk/UserFiles/Catalyst%20FAQs%202_1.pdf, posted 14 February 2012; NCVYS, 2013, 'About the Catalyst Programme', at http://www.ncvys.org.uk/Catalyst.html; The Young Foundation, undated, 'Catalyst', https://youngfoundation.org/projects/catalyst/; Neil Puffett, 2012f, op. cit.

92. Tony Taylor, 2012b, 'Replication in Action: WHAT?', IDYW, 13 January, https://indefenceofyouthwork.com/2012/01/13/replication-in-action-programme-what/.

93. NCVYS, 2011, 'Not in My Name', https://www.facebook.com/media/set/?set=a.192570047474496.51394.143181745746660.

94. P. Hennessy, 2010, 'Minister Backs Plan for Massive State Sell Off of Assets', *The Daily Telegraph*, 13 November.

95. NCVYS, 2012, 'Respublica and NCVYS Launching Commission on Youth', https://www.ncvys.org.uk/blogs.php?act=view_topic&id=261;

Respublica, 2012, 'Respublica/NCVYS Commission on Youth Launches Video Interviews with Key Public Figures', http://www. respublica.org.uk/item/ResPublica-NCVYS-Commission-on-Youth-launches-video-interviews-with-key-public-figures.

96. Gabriella Jozwiak, 2013b, 'Loughton Become Ambition Ambassador', *CYPN*, 2 August.

97. Gabriella Jozwiak, 2013c, 'Voluntary Sector Consortium Becomes DfE Strategic Partner', *CYPN*, 24 May.

98. Neil Puffett, 2013c, 'Sector Reacts to Youth Policy Shift', *CYPN*, 3 July.

99. Offord, Adam, 2016, 'Youth Policy Set to Move to Department for Culture, Media and Sport', *CYPN*, 19 July.

100. Barry Williams, 2016, 'Youth Policy—From the Cabinet Office to DCMS, a Commentary from Ambition', 3 August, http://ambition-nuk.org/news/view/129.

101. Ambition, 2017, 'Preventing Youth Crime: The Associated Aspects of Character and Potential Interventions', *Ambition News*, February.

102. Ambition News, 2017, 'Webinar: Mental Toughness: Its Importance for Youth Organisations', 3 March.

103. Neil Puffett, 2017, 'UK Youth Announces Appointment of Interim Chief Executive', *CYPN*, 24 August.

104. Matt Lent, 2016, 'The Youth Sector Needs Pragmatists', The UK Youth blog, 26 January, https://medium.com/@MattSL/the-power-of-pragmatism-954511bc83f0.

## Further Reading

Barings Foundation. 2013. *Independence Under Threat: The Voluntary Sector in 2013*. Barings Foundation. http://www.independencepanel.org.uk/wp-content/uploads/2013/01/Independence-Under-Threat_The-Voluntary-Sector-in-2013_WebVersion12.pdf.

Buchroth, Ilona, and Marc Husband. 2015. 'Youth Work in the Voluntary Sector', in Bright, Graham (ed), *Youth Work: Histories, Policy, Contexts*. London: Palgrave, pp. 102–124.

Clubs for Young People. 2009. *Somewhere to Belong: A Blueprint for 21st Century Youth Clubs*. London: Clubs for Young People.

Davies, Bernard. 2014. 'Independence at Risk: The State, the Market and the Voluntary Youth Sector'. *Youth and Policy*. No. 112. April, pp. 111–122.

Lent, Matt. 2016. 'The Youth Sector Needs Pragmatists'. UK Youth blog. 26 January. https://medium.com/@MattSL/the-power-of-pragmatism-954511bc83f0.

Munn, Alex. 2015. *Who Stands for Youth? A Call for Better Collaboration to Influence Youth Policy in London.* Partnership for London.

NCIA, 2015, 'Fight or Fight': Inquiry into the Future of Voluntary Services'. http://independentaction.net/publications-resources/voluntary-services-inquiry/.

NCVYS. 2010. *Comprehensive Cuts: Report on Funding Changes in the Voluntary and Community Youth Sector.* October.

NCVYS. 2013. 'About the Catalyst Programme'. http://www.ncvys.org.uk/Catalyst.html.

Rochester, Colin. 2013. *Rediscovering Voluntary Action: The Beat of a Different Drum.* Basingstoke: Palgrave Macmillan.

Wylie, Tom. 2009. 'Youth Work and the Voluntary Sector', in Wood, Jason and Jean, Hine (eds), *Work with Young People*. London: Sage, pp. 202–212.

# Part V
## Training and Qualifying for Work with Young People

# 15

# 'Modernising' Vocational Qualifications

## New Labour Vocationalism: The Rise—And Rise—Of the NVQ

### From 'Competence' to 'Competences'

In the decade after 1997, training for the staff implementing youth policies was increasingly shaped by New Labour's overall aspiration that UK workers develop the 'hard' (technical) and 'soft' (attitudinal) skills needed to compete in an increasingly globalised market. The result by 2007 was significant shifts in the power balances between training providers, trainers and employers in 'children and young people' training programmes generally and within youth work training in particular.

Albeit unintentionally, some of the ground for these developments within youth work had been laid as far back as 1984 by *Starting from Strengths*—a report from a panel briefed 'to promote the continuing development of training'[1] for the part-time and voluntary workers. This was the 'workforce' which provided (and continued to provide) most of the face-to-face practice with young people, estimated by OFSTED

© The Author(s) 2019
B. Davies, *Austerity, Youth Policy and the Deconstruction of the Youth Service in England*, https://doi.org/10.1007/978-3-030-03886-1_15

in 1998 as comprising 'upwards of 50,000 adults, drawn from a rich social, ethnic and educational background...'[2]

One of *Starting from Strengths'* main recommendations was that trainees' should be assessed on their 'competence' as evidenced in a 'portfolio' of their practice experience and related activities. This appeared just as a National Council for Vocational Qualifications (NCVQ) was being created which, from 1986 and with strong backing from the Confederation of British Industry, was briefed to 'rationalise an incoherent and confusing pattern of vocational qualifications'.[3] It did this by designing and approving a range of work-based National Vocational Qualifications (NVQs) at the heart of which was a notion of 'competences'—the knowledge, skills and understanding required by workers 'to carry out a specific role or job at a particular level'—also often to be evidenced in a portfolio.[4]

As a debate developed within youth work on the meaning of and relationship between *Starting from Strengths'* largely worker-focused conception of 'competence' and the NVQs' much more functional and employer-defined notion of 'competences'[5] the body then endorsing its qualifications, the Council for Education and Training of Youth and Community Workers (CETYCW) 'stood aside' from NVQs in part, it was suggested, to avoid putting at risk its control over its own qualifications.[6]

## Privatising Routes to Qualification

An NYA publication on the implications of NVQs for the Youth Service noted in 1993, however, that within the voluntary sector 'accrediting competence through NVQ frameworks (was) ... seen by some ... as a way to increase recognition of their services and the quality of their training'.[7] Five years later, OFSTED reported that already many national voluntary youth organisations 'provide their own specialist programmes' for training part-time youth workers.[8] These developments, however, prompted concerns 'that initiatives by (private) awarding bodies and independent consultants ... may shape youth work qualifications and training for the future'[9]—a shift exemplified early by the London Borough of Chelsea and Kensington. Its

starting propositions were that the majority of youth worker training programmes '… did not take into account Accreditation of Prior
Learning/Achievement … and the move in training towards demonstrating competence rather than just knowledge'. It therefore set out in
the early 1990s '… to define youth work in competence terms as a first
step towards developing a training scheme…', to be achieved through
'a development process, known as functional analysis'.[10] By 1993 'The
Learning Business' had designed materials for the Borough's own
'Personal Competencies Workbook' to be used 'as a tool for personal
development' for part-time youth workers leading to awards by the City
and Guilds London Institute.[11]

As local authorities and voluntary organisations in England became
less directly involved in providing these routes to qualification,[12] private companies increasingly provided approved qualifications at NVQ
Levels 2 and 3 for which workers themselves often paid several hundred pounds. Training, rather than being undertaken and experienced
as a collective exercise, thus became a commodity sold to individuals 'as
self-development or career progression'—described by Unite in 2010 as
'a range of sub-standard off the shelf modules that can be purchased and
used…'[13] By 2017, fewer employers anyway were employing trained
part-time workers on agreed JNC salaries, conditions or qualifications.[14]

## Signing Up to NVQs

As a number of practices 'develop(ed) standards of competence in areas
applicable to youth and community work', the NYA became concerned
that staying outside the NVQ structures 'risk(ed) becoming marginalised and eventually, by default, incorporated by others'.[15] As, increasingly, the accepted vocational qualification became the NVQ gained
by demonstrating competencies through portfolio-building, a 1998
CETYCW-commissioned report gave explicit youth and community
work endorsement to validating learning from experience.[16] However,
with 'the majority of training courses … endorsed by the NYA … set at
Level 3', that same year OFSTED found 'little evidence that work contained within portfolios corresponded to this level'.[17]

The following year, a 'PAULO' consortium of eight youth work, community work and adult education bodies made the case to the DfEE for 'a national training organisation for the community-based, and non-formal education-and-development sector' in which the consortium organisations would be key partners. One of the project's aims was to 'help employers and employees in our sector to meet their training and education needs ...'; another, to 'ensure that paid and unpaid staff in all occupational roles have the knowledge, understanding, skills and desire to perform effectively, and that the supply of skilled staff meets the demand from employers'. Though the paper acknowledged that the sector was 'renowned for its ability to focus on ... people, relationships and processes...', its resort to the marketised language of 'added-value' and 'rigorous cost-benefit considerations'[18] represented an early intrusion of the 'outcomes' agenda which later came so to dominate youth policy and provision overall (see Chapter 4).

By then, the youth work sector had begun to adopt the new qualifications structures and their underlying assumptions. Developed since 1996 via a series of consultations and reports, 'national occupational standards' set out what the sector expected of 'competent' youth workers and provided a 'skills framework' for accrediting 'national awarding bodies', including private companies. By 2007, the Community and Youth Workers' Union (CYWU) was strongly endorsing the recently revised version of the standards as incorporating 'the true nature of youth work and the voluntary relationship with young people'.[19]

Youth work's integration into the new national training structures was taken further in March 2002 at a conference at Warwick University on 'Ensuring a High Quality Workforce'. This set up a 'Workforce Development Implementation Group' led by the NYA whose report, published in the summer of 2003 and submitted to the government, urged the creation of more pathways into youth work. These, it recommended, should include modern apprenticeships allowing progression to a foundation degree; more modern foundation degrees—conceived as 'a two-year full-time employment led programme developed by educational institutions in collaboration with local employers'[20]—and an

NVQ Level 4 route to 'full professional status' for 'locally qualified' workers.[21]

In response to emerging youth work sector concerns, a senior DES official later that year offered assurances that the 'foundation degrees' then being developed as an employment-based route to graduate status were intended only as a 'tool to support the development of a qualified workforce'. Nonetheless, concerns were expressed about 'the possibility of employer-led Foundation Degrees gradually replacing the current Dip HEs and BA degrees in community and youth work ...'.[22]

In 2005 approval was also given in England for a national framework for youth work apprenticeships incorporating the new national occupational standards. These were to provide young people aged 16 and above with core skills and work-based training leading to a Level 3 NVQ qualification.[23] The ministerial launch in November 2009 of a 'Young People's Workforce Reform Programme' also included proposals for funding 'advanced' apprenticeships for new and existing youth workers and youth justice and advice and information workers.[24]

## Qualifying for Youth Work: External Pressures and Internal Debates

Throughout these developments, sometimes sharply critical debates continued within youth work, many from the 1990s still concentrating on the increasing resort to assessing the 'competences' central to NVQs. In 1995, for example, when two Northern Ireland trainers talked of 'a growing interest amongst youth work training agencies in the development of a competency-based approach', colleagues in England pointed to the risks posed by 'the current pressures to locate all youth and community work qualifications within a "competence" – and in particular NVQ – framework'.[25]

By 2004 Jean Spence, an experienced youth work university tutor, was describing this framework as 'undermin(ing) the very skills, knowledge and understanding which make youth work so much in demand'. She specifically highlighted

... the recent drive by employers towards accepting NVQ Level 2 as an entrance qualification, NVQ Level 4 as the equivalent of a professional qualification, and the current initiatives involving Foundation Degrees ...[26]

Applying the NVQ framework to part time youth workers was also seen as 'superseding' the regional accreditation and monitoring panels (RAMPs). Since the 1990s[27] these had worked across England with their own NVQ 'level descriptor statements'[28] to produce comprehensive guidelines for, regionally and nationally, endorsing part-time and voluntary workers' qualifying training.[29] Though, according to Spence, the panels' standards could be 'variable',[30] a 1998 OFSTED concluded that where they worked well, 'they ... contributed to raising the quality of training submissions.'[31]

On the premise that the new 'employer-led initiatives ... are not adequate for the holistic competence required of educational youth work', Spence's broader—and prescient—conclusion was that by the early 2000s

To recruit unqualified young staff, and to use NVQ Level 2 as a starting point for training is to begin the process of 'capturing' what is designed to become an uncritical workforce trained entirely within a self-serving, employer-led system of qualification. Such a workforce will be hierarchically organised and micro managed...[32]

Expressing similar criticisms, the Chair of CYWU's Education and Training Committee restated the union's commitment to campaigning 'against the de-professionalisation of the sector by the downgrading of the qualifications threshold for paid youth work to NVQ2'.[33] Two years later, in March 2006, the union had apparently come to regard even this as over-optimistic given that by then most JNC recognised part time workers and their locally endorsed qualifications had been placed on Level 1 'without attention to the responsibilities they actually carried'.[34]

Within the youth work sector, Foundation Degrees also proved controversial. Exemplifying how youth work was being '... pushed ... inexorably away from professional autonomy towards client status', Spence for example judged their 'developing role' as

... simply add(ing) to the conviction that government and employers are ... determined to train workers in a set of functional skills which will enable organisations to more efficiently meet government "targets" ... primarily concerned with facilitating the access of young people to the labour market.

Spence also saw them as helping to replace youth work's previous use of a '... self-identified notion of competence which involved workers in the process of reflecting upon and seeking to develop their generic skill... (with) ... employer defined ideas about competences, which implied the workers being capable of carrying out a range of organisational tasks.'[35]

Spence's critique did not go unchallenged. Three Open University tutors shared her commitment to 'professional activity' and the training this required. Nonetheless, through their involvement in 'the complex, political and discursive processes through which Foundation Degrees are currently being produced', they had concluded that these were 'in some respects ... helpful to educators with an interest in bridging the traditional divide between theory and practice, education and training, liberalism and vocationalism'. Indeed as '... the workplace as a site for learning open(ed) up new possibilities for supporting knowledgeable practice', they saw it as 'premature' to dismiss Foundation Degrees as potentially undermining commitment to 'critical, thinking and principled professional workers'.[36]

## Training and Qualifying for 'Integrated Services'

Beyond these internal debates, external developments were, often radically, helping to reshape youth work's qualification routes—particularly New Labour proposals for reforming local 'children and young people' services (see Chapter 2). With 'integration' the overarching aim, these sought to develop 'a common platform of skills and training to secure and promote inter-professional working ... across the youth sector'.[37] Faced with the prospect of '"Every Child Matters" just around the corner', in 2004 CYWU talked explicitly about campaigning against the potential consequences of these changes for youth work's 'professional' and also 'pre-professional' training and qualification routes.[38]

In these debates, a key area of uncertainty and contention was which of the new government-approved validating bodies would have the final say in recognising youth work qualifications. As far back as the late 1980s CETYCW had resisted joining a consortium of social work, local government and the health service organisations on the grounds that this would compromise the 'educational roots' of its own qualifications. The DES in effect later endorsed this decision by having youth and community work withdrawn from a list of occupations covered by the 'lead body' overseeing qualifications for 'sport and recreation'. It would rather, it said, 'await the setting up of an education lead body'— a proposed development also eventually supported within the youth work sector itself.[39] By 1998 OFSTED was thus concluding that 'the accreditation of (youth work) training programmes, by a variety of awarding bodies, has done little to ensure consistency'.[40]

It was not until 2005 that LifeLong Learning UK (LLUK) was 'selected by the UK youth sector as the sector skills council best able to represent its collective interests'.[41] Two years later CYWU referred to it as 'supportive of the professional role of youth work'[42] and in May 2010 as 'endorsing a definition of youth work which the union could accept focused on young people's personal, social and educational development'.[43] By then, however, another body—the Children's Workforce Development Council (CWDC)—was overseeing areas affecting youth work training. Set up in 2005, its overall brief was to 'support employers in developing a skilled and effective workforce working with children, young people and families'. Its more specific aims included 'help(ing) the children and young people's workforce ... be the influential voice of employers and the workforce'.[44]

Ambiguities about the role of LLUK and CWDC continued throughout the New Labour period. In 2007 for example, CYWU admitted that it was

... struggling to make inroads into to Children's Workforce Development Council and LifeLong Learning UK, who continue to work towards a single qualification framework for all people working with Children and

Young People. This is clearly threatening our current professional qualification structures and we will continue to challenge the tick-box mentality of technician training through NVQs.[45]

By 2011, ChooseYouth—the campaigning group brought together by CYWU to resist the cuts to local Youth Services (see Chapter 17)—was expressing concerns that youth work could fall under the remit of the body responsible for 'Skills for Care and Development'.[46] A UK Youth survey in 2011 also identified a 'risk of losing UK wide co-ordination and active engagement of the youth work sector in how it should be represented in the future for Sector Skills Activity'.[47]

Some of the proposals of the CWDC's '2020 Children and Young People's Workforce Strategy' paper published in 2008 had given substance to these concerns,[48] indicating for example an intention to create a 'youth professional status' for senior practitioners and above, based on graduate-level skills in integrated working.[49] Though CYWU/Unite dismissed this as both 'naïve and counter-productive' and as 'a costly exercise to melt down professional specialisms',[50] it was nonetheless approved by 57% of respondents to a three-month consultation. On the premise that specialist skills development would still be ensured, more than 90% also supported the introduction of a 'skills development framework' within a model of integrated services.[51] With local authority youth services already being absorbed into Children's Trusts (see Chapter 2), one concern was that by 2010 youth and community work training would have become just one route or specialism within a wider qualification.

CWDC also updated guidance on the skills needed to work with children and produced a set of 'Youth Professional Standards' for 'the youth sector' covering, for example, 'shared values' and 'applying specialisms in an integrated workforce'. Alongside other new qualifications, it launched a foundation degree in 'Working Together For Young People' and provided funding for developing 'young people's workforces' in 150 local authorities.[52]

Its own research, however, published in January 2010 had recognised that its still-evolving models of integrated working remained 'very variable', with 'the private sector not seem(ing) to be included to any great extent'. More also needed to be done, it said, to integrate the voluntary sector—'a large part of the workforce'—into the delivery of young people's services.[53] The Council thus announced in March that, with £3.8 million funding, NCVYS was to run a 'Progress' scheme which, in partnership with George Williams College and the YMCA, would provide training for 25,000 voluntary sector youth workers. Delivered 'in bite-size chunks' by 'third sector providers', this would focus on five areas of practice including 'safeguarding', 'health and safety' and 'equality and diversity'. To enable the scheme to continue beyond 2011, up to 360 people were also to be trained to run the courses. Though not offering all the accredited qualifications NCVYS had proposed, the scheme, launched in September 2010, gave workers credits towards Level 2 and, it was hoped eventually, Level 3 NVQs.[54]

# Beyond Quangos: 'Workforce Development' Under the Coalition

By 2003 the multi-agency Workforce Development Implementation Group (see above) was reporting that, with too few resources being invested in in-service training, many of these part-timers were untrained.[55] Figures from a 2008 NYA survey quoted by the 2011 Commons Education Select Committee on youth services (see Chapter 8) showed that some local authorities were providing no in-service training for youth work staff and that the spend was 'less than half of the JNC recommended level'. (Grounded evidence of this attrition came in 2016 with the closure of Learning South West, a regional youth work unit providing part-time Level 2 and 3 qualifying courses.[56]) By then, too, most workers (full- and part-time) were unlikely to be offered on-the-job training or time with colleagues for 'building confidence, broadening knowledge, and reflecting on practice'.[57]

By 2010 CWDC research was also concluding that 'youth workers are experiencing restructuring in training with the introduction of the integrated qualifications framework, youth work occupational standards and the introduction (in 2010) of a degree-level profession'.[58] Within days of the change of government these uncertainties increased when, to allow ministers to 'consider how they will take forward their priorities', the DfE called a 'moratorium' on the work of all 'arm's length bodies'. This 'pause' eventually turned into a 'bonfire of the quangos'—the closure of 192 public bodies—which included, in 2011, LLUK and, in March 2012, CWDC.[59,60]

To fill the resultant gaps, the government announced that 'leadership' of the relevant work programmes would be taken over either by the DfE itself and a new Teaching Agency or by a Children's Improvement Board.[61] However, the Select Committee report noted in June 2011 that, in line with the DfE's overall approach to 'children and young people' policies, the government would not be taking a view on workforce qualifications, development or regulations. Instead, it said, ministers regarded 'the development and recruitment of both professionals and volunteers (as) best addressed by the professionals themselves and their employers'.[62] As 'youth services' provision after 2010 was increasingly commissioned out on often short-term contracts, it however became increasingly unclear who these 'employers' were or, in a neo-liberal world, what responsibility (if any) they would accept for training a marginal workforce like part-time youth workers.

An indication of where these developments were leading did emerge in September 2011 in a proposal by the UK Commission for Employment and Skills—a 'publicly funded, industry-led but non-departmental' body which until 2017 advised government on skills and employment policy. This envisaged separating the youth work sector from the other professions in the community learning and development field and transferring it to the Sector Skills Council for Care and Development. Unite reacted to this suggestion by predicting that this meant

> … responsibility for the National Occupational Standards for Youth Work, apprenticeships and qualifications being vested in an organisation which does not have either the empowerment of young people, or education as its core purpose.[63,64]

The *Positive for Youth* discussion paper dealing with 'workforce development' (see Chapter 9) was explicit that, after the closure of the structures set up under Labour, 'greater clarity is needed … (on) where the roles and responsibilities now fall for securing and supporting work-force development'. For the Coalition, however, 'the more centralised approach ... taken by the previous Government ... is not now sustainable'. Though, albeit in coded language, it also acknowledged '... reductions in many local authorities' funding for universally available positive activities', the discussion paper's bottom line remained that '... the main responsibility for youth workforce development must lie with employers, and they must expect to meet the costs'.[65] The DfE again stated this position in its first response to the Education Select Committee report in September 2011 which, while accepting that many employers regarded a youth work degree as providing 'essential evidence of an individual's skill and professionalism', also concluded that '... a range of qualifications and training pathways are required'.[66]

The *Positive for Youth* paper itself acknowledged that 'recent reductions in spending by local authorities have reduced demand for skilled workers' and that this had created 'a risk that key skills ... are lost from organisations as staffing levels reduced'. It however continued to deny any role for government in ensuring their development, again insisting that 'employers ... work together to deliver national support for workforce development'. In the light of responses to the discussion paper, it did however suggest that, as well as developing 'a framework of competences and quality assured training for volunteers', employers' future priorities:

> ... could include developing a national professional development framework for youth workers and other professionals with quality assured training in personal and social development for those who are not youth work qualified.[67]

## Consolidating Youth Work Routes to Training and Qualification

By 2010 the CWDC report was describing a 'youth work workforce' which included 'youth workers, youth support workers and information, advice and guidance workers', comprising 77,000 paid staff (two thirds full-time) and 532,000 volunteers. Of those working in paid 'non-professional' youth work roles—that is, youth support workers—47% had a qualification equivalent to NVQ Level 4 or higher (including 32% who were graduates), 21% had a Level 3 qualification and 16% were qualified at Level 2. Forty nine percent were female and, in a population where 89% identified as 'white', 8% of 'youth leaders/managers' were from 'BME' backgrounds.[68,69]

In a context in which 'requirements for initial qualification and professional status as a youth worker have increased in recent years', the Education Select Committee also talked of 'two qualification levels for youth work'—'the lower "Youth and Community Support Worker" range and the "Professional Youth Worker" range'. To be qualified as a support worker, its report pointed out, 'individuals need to hold a Level 2 Certificate or Level 3 Diploma in Youth Work Practice'. From 2010, when the DipHE lost recognition as a 'professional' qualification, the routes to this, usually endorsed for five years by the NYA's Education and Training Sub-committee (ETS) and recognised by the JNC (see also Chapter 16), were:

- A three-year BA course or its part-time equivalent, then available at some 40 English higher education (HE) institutions.
- A one-year full-time post-graduate certificate or diploma.
- An MA or MSc 'usually involving one calendar year of full-time study or the equivalent'.[70]

Though also validated and mostly run directly by HE institutions, a number of the BA courses were by then being delivered by other organisations, including faith bodies such as the Nazarene Theological College in Manchester and the Oasis College of Education in London.[71]

By 2010, however, new (and overlapping) routes to qualification were opening up. Located within the NVQ frameworks (and much favoured by governments), of significance within youth work were:

- Modern apprenticeships: First introduced by the Conservative government in 1993–1995 and offering an NVQ Level 3 qualification, apprentices were taken on as waged employees. Between 1997 and 2010, reviews, reports and eventually legislation attempted to improve take-up and completion rates and, for example, sought to identify an 'optimal skills mix' which would contribute to economic growth, productivity and social justice. In 2018, under the general title of 'social care', apprenticeships in 'young people's services' were being advertised on the government website.[72]

- Foundation degrees: Prefigured by a number of proposals dating back at least to 1994, piloted in 2000 and formally launched in 2001,[73] these provided routes into specific professions, with work experience likely to count as more relevant for entry than formal qualifications. Initially the government was said to be anticipating they would eventually make up 80% of future HE expansion. However, after an initial surge, overall enrolments fell after 2009 and Foundation Degree Forward, a quango for promoting them, was wound up in 2011.[74] Nonetheless the degrees remained an element of the vocational training landscape, including within youth work.

- Degree apprenticeships: Funded by a Degree Apprenticeship Development Fund, these were described as '... bringing together the best of higher and vocational training'. They were seen as making possible 'university study and the invaluable on-the-job training typical of an Apprenticeship, without having to cover the cost of tuition'.[75] By late-2017 one ETS response to these developments was to circulate for consultation three sets of standards for 'Trailblazer' youth work apprenticeships. Rooted largely in employer-focused functional conceptions of practice, two were to be offered at Levels 2 and 3 and one as a professional qualification at degree-equivalent Level 6.

# In Search of Clarification

During the New Labour period and increasingly after 2010, the push by policy-makers for these alternative routes to vocational qualifications put pressure on youth work's own long-established qualification arrangements, including those leading to what was called 'professional' recognition (see Chapter 16). As boundaries between qualification routes became increasingly blurred, the 2011 Select Committee recommended that 'it would be timely to review the knowledge and skills likely to be needed by youth workers over the next decade and the range of initial training and qualifications which would help to secure these'.[76]

With this as the context, the youth work tutors' organisation, the Training Agencies Group (TAG) (which in 2010 added 'Professional Association of Lecturers in Youth and Community Work' to its title) concluded from a 2012 survey of its members that youth work's training and qualifying structures and procedures were 'not designed for (such) periods of rapid flux'.[77] Two years later, TAG, with CHYPS, again suggested that 'the traditional structures around youth work training are breaking down'. This prompted one course tutor to comment that 'perhaps we need to change the name, become something else, with all the principles and ethos that youth work has—'youth work' is never going to get us where we want to be'.[78]

By then the 'well-trodden career route' from member to 'senior member' in a youth project via a voluntary and/or part time paid role and a local part time qualification to a 'professional' qualification and a full-time post[79] had turned into 'a sometimes-bewildering maze...'[80] For potential youth workers, as the training sector diversified, a clear route to qualification had also become harder to identify. This was happening particularly, the CHYPS' Chief Executive suggested, 'as local authorities look to commission more youth work to external providers (so that) the requirements on which qualifications are needed may become less rigid'. He continued to insist that 'the need for such qualifications will remain ... (I)f you are commissioning good quality youth work you look for them to employ qualified staff'. Nonetheless, speaking as the leader of the collective voice of youth work management in England, he concluded:

> I don't think you can say it needs to be this or that particular qualification or course.[81]

By 2013, with fewer youth workers already employed under JNC conditions, he again highlighted a need for 'vigour and urgency' if the sector was 'to preserve youth work standards and values'.[82]

Insofar as those managing 'youth services' were displaying these qualities, by early 2018 they were being focused less on prioritising youth work's traditional liberal educational principles and practices than on recasting training routes so that they fitted better with employer-led conceptions of vocationalism. By then, too, these given starting points were increasingly intruding into the higher education routes to 'professional' qualifications examined in the next chapter.

# Notes

1. Steve Bolger and Duncan Scott, 1986, *Starting from Strengths*, Leicester, NYB.
2. OFSTED, 1998, *The Training of Part-time Youth Workers*, OFSTED, November, p. 1.
3. Bernard Davies and Mary Durkin, 1991, '"Skill", "Competence" and "Competences" in Youth and Community Work', *Youth and Policy*, No. 34, September, pp. 1–11.
4. Jenny Hand, 1993, *NVQs and Their Implications for the Youth Service*, NYA, May, pp. 11–12.
5. Bernard Davies, 2008, *From Thatcherism to New Labour: A History of the Youth Service in England—Volume 2, 1979–1999*, Leicester, Youth Work Press, pp. 69–70; Tania de St Croix, n.d., 'Whatever Happened to Part-Time Youth Worker Training?', unpublished, p. 9.
6. Jenny Hand, 1993, op. cit., p. 20.
7. Jenny Hand, 1993, op. cit., p. 24.
8. OFSTED, 1998, op. cit., p. 1.
9. Jenny Hand, 1993, op. cit., p. 26.
10. Royal Borough of Kensington and Chelsea, n.d., *Introduction to "Open Learning Materials for Youth Work"*, The Learning Business Limited, p. 3.
11. Royal Borough of Kensington and Chelsea, 1993, *Personal Competencies Workbook*, Royal Borough of Kensington and Chelsea, p. 5.
12. Bernard Davies, 2008, *The New Labour Years: A History of the Youth Service in England—Volume 3, 1997–2007*, Leicester, Youth Work Press, pp. 160–161, 161–162; Andy Driver, 2007, 'Youth Work National Occupational Standards Revision—Your Chance to Contribute to the Consultation', *Rapport*, January, p. 15; Emily Rogers, 2005, 'Workforce

Development: Council Authorizes Youth Work Apprenticeships', *CYPN*, 5 October; Tania de St Croix, n.d., op. cit., p. 11.

13. *Rapport*, 2010, 'Education and Training Issues', May, pp. 27–28.

14. Tania de St Croix, n.d., op. cit., pp. 11, 12.

15. Jenny Hand, 1993, op. cit., pp. 26, 27.

16. Pete Bainbridge, 1988, *Taking the Experience Route: Report on the Feasibility Study on Validating Learning from Experience*, CETYCW, January.

17. OFSTED, 1998, op. cit., p. 2.

18. PAULO, 1999, *A Revised Submission to the DfEE*, PAULO, February 1999, pp. 3, 27.

19. CYPW, undated, 'The Professional and National Occupational Standards for Youth Work', http://www.cywu.org.uk/index.php?id=8&type_id=24&category_id=18&article_id=444; *Rapport*, 2007, 'Voluntary Relationship Enshrined in the Occupational Standards', August, p. 22.

20. Tony Jeffs and Jean Spence, 2008, 'Farewell to All That? The Uncertain Future of Youth and Community Work Education', *Youth and Policy*, No. 97/98, Autumn/Winter, p. 135.

21. *CYPN*, 2003, 'The National Youth Bureau: Call for Better Training Opportunities', *CYPN*, 6 August.

22. Jean Spence, 2004, 'The Threat to Youth Work from Employer Led Initiatives', *Rapport*, January, p. 7.

23. Emily Rogers, 2005, 'Workforce Development: Council Authorizes Youth Work Apprenticeships', *CYPN*, 5 October; *Rapport*, 2007, op. cit., p. 22.

24. CWDC, 2009, 'Press releases', 2 November.

25. Robin McRoberts and Ruth Leitch, 1995, 'The Development of a Competence-Based Approach to Training Part-Time Youth Work'. *Youth and Policy*, No. 51, Winter, pp. 21–34; Bernard Davies and Rod Norton, 1996, 'Where Are Competence-Based Approaches Leading Us: A Critical Response to McRoberts and Leitch?', *Youth and Policy*, No. 53, Summer, pp. 44–52.

26. Jean Spence, 2004, op. cit., pp. 6–7.

27. Bernard Davies, 2008, op. cit., pp. 155, 160–161; OFSTED, 1998, op. cit., p. 5.

28. OFSTED, 1998, op. cit., p. 20.

29. CETCYW, 1990, Guidelines for the National Endorsement and Regional Accreditation and Moderation of Qualifying Training for

Part-Time and Volunteer Youth and Community Workers, Council for Education and Training of Youth and Community Workers, November.

30. Jean Spence, 2004, op. cit., p. 6.

31. OFSTED, 1998, op. cit., p. 3.

32. Jean Spence, 2004, op. cit., pp. 6–7.

33. Ian Richards, 2004, 'Report of the Chair of Education and Training Committee', *Rapport*, March, pp. 16–17.

34. Andy Driver, 2006, 'Workforce Reform and Remodelling: Is This the Emperor's New Clothes?', *Rapport*, January, p. 9.

35. Jean Spence, 2004, op. cit., pp. 6–7.

36. Roger Harrison, et al., 2004, 'Supporting Knowledgeable Practice Through Foundation Degrees', *Rapport*, March, pp. 10–11.

37. DES, 2011, *Positive for Youth: Discussion Paper—The Development of Young People's Workforce*, DES, June, para. 6.

38. Ian Richards, 2004, op. cit., pp. 16–17.

39. Jenny Hand, 1993, op. cit., pp. 20–21, 26.

40. OFSTED, 1998, op. cit., p. 3.

41. Charmaine Simpson, 2011, 'Sector Skills Council (SSC) and Youth Work/Community Learning and Development Survey', UK Youth, 15 August.

42. Andy Driver, 2007, op. cit., p. 15.

43. *Rapport*, 2010, op. cit., pp. 27–28.

44. CWDC, 2012, 'Annual Report and Accounts: Year Ended 32 March 2012', CWDC, June.

45. Ian Richards, 2007, 'Chair of Education and Training Committee—Report to National Conference 2007', *Rapport*, April, p. 19.

46. Tony Taylor, 2011, 'Youth Work=Care and Development!', IDYW, 11 July.

47. UK Youth, 2011, 'Sector Skills Council (SSC) and Youth Work/Community Learning and Development Survey', 15 August.

48. DfE, 2008, '2020 Children and Young People's Workforce Strategy', December, http://webarchive.nationalarchives.gov.uk/20130102211421/, https://www.education.gov.uk/publications/standard/_arc_SOP/Page10/DCSF-01052-2008.

49. Saba Salman, 2010, 'How to Become a Qualified Youth Worker', *Society Guardian*, 17 February.

50. Janaki Mahadevan, 2009a, 'Union Labels Common Skills Plan for Youth Professionals as "Naïve"', *CYPN*, 23 July; *Rapport*, 2009, 'Youth Professional Developments Criticised', August, p. 21.

51. Janaki Mahadevan, 2009b, 'New Step on Career Ladder for Youth Workers', *CYPN*, 25 August.
52. Ross Watson, 2010a, 'Cash Boost for Youth Sector Training', *CYPN*, 23 March; Joe Lepper, 2010, 'CWDC Updates Guidance on Skills for Working with Children', 24 March; CWDC, 2010a, 'Youth Professional Standards', August; Charlotte Goddard, 2012a, 'Workforce Disintegration?' *CYPN*, 20 March.
53. CWDC, 2010b, *A Picture Worth Millions: The State of the Young People's Workforce*, Leeds, January, p. 14.
54. Ross Watson, 2010b, 'Training Boost for Voluntary Sector Youth Workers', *CYPN*, 16 March; Janaki Mahadevan, 2010, 'Voluntary Youth Sector Received £3.8m for Workforce Training', *CYPN*, 23 August.
55. *CYPN*, 2003, op. cit.
56. BBC News, 2016, 'Learning South West Closes in Taunton Due to Lack of Funding', 12 April, https://www.bbc.co.uk/news/uk-england-somerset-36018143.
57. House of Commons Education Select Committee, 2011a, Services for Young People: Third Report of Session 2010–12, Volume 1, London, Stationery Office, June, para. 104; Tania de St Croix, n.d., op. cit., pp. 13–15.
58. CWDC, 2010b, op. cit., p. 14.
59. Lauren Higgs, 2010, 'Government Puts Work of Children's Sector Bodies on Hold', *CYPN*, 17 May; *Guardian*, 2012, 'Bonfire of the Quangos: The Victims', 22 August; CWDC, 2012, 'CWDC Future', 2 February, http://webarchive.nationalarchives.gov.uk/20120202142150/, http://www.cwdcouncil.org.uk/information/cwdc-future.
60. Tony Taylor, 2011, op. cit.
61. Lauren Higgs, 2010, op. cit.; *Guardian*, 2012, op. cit.; CWDC, 2012, op. cit.
62. House of Commons Education Select Committee, 2011a, op. cit., para. 97.
63. UKES, n.d., 'UK Commission for Employment and Skills', https://www.google.co.uk/search?q=UK+Commission+for+Employment+and+Skills&rlz=1C1NHXL_enGB772GB772&oq=UK+Commission+for+Employment+and+Skills&aqs=chrome..69i57j0l5.649j0j4&sourceid=chrome&ie=UTF-8.
64. *Rapport*, 2011, 'Occupational Standards Under Threat', September, p. 28.

65. DfE, 2011, '*Positive for Youth*: Discussion Paper—The Development of the Young People's Workforce', DfE, June, paras. 8, 12, 14.
66. House of Commons Education Committee, 2011b, *Services for Young People: Government the Response—Sixth Report of Session 2010–12*, Volume 1, London, Stationery Office, September, para. 18.
67. HM Government, 2011, *Positive for Youth: A New Approach to Cross-Government Policy for Young People Aged 13 to 19*, HM Government, December, paras. 5.40–5.42.
68. House of Commons Education Committee, 2011a, op. cit., paras. 93–94.
69. CWDC, 2010, op. cit., pp. 8, 10, 11, 12.
70. House of Commons Education Committee, 2011b, op. cit., para. 95; Tony Jeffs and Jean Spence, 2008, op. cit., p. 135.
71. NYA, 2017, 'Qualifications Recognised by the JNC as Conferring Professionally Qualified Status', December, http://www.nya.org. uk/wp-content/uploads/2016/04/MASTER-validation-Database-December-2017-v1.pdf; Lauren Higgs, 2010, op. cit.
72. GOV.UK, 2018, 'Social Care Apprenticeships', 23 February, https:// www.gov.uk/guidance/social-care-apprenticeships.
73. Tony Jeffs and Jean Spence, 2008, op. cit., p. 135.
74. Jo Trelfa and Dan Richmond, 2008, 'Getting the Balance Right: Training and Education Within NVQ and HE Routes to Youth Work', *Youth and Policy*, No. 97/98, Autumn/Winter, p. 120; Bernard Davies, 2008, op. cit., pp. 160–161, 159–160.
75. University of Warwick, 2017, 'New Degree Apprenticeships Starting in 2018', *CommUnity*, Autumn, p. 3; Get My First Job, n.d., 'Degree Apprenticeships', at https://www.getmyfirstjob.co.uk/Apprenticeships/ DegreeApprenticeships.aspx.
76. Tania de St Croix, n.d., op. cit., p. 12; House of Commons Education Committee, 2011a, op. cit., para. 78.
77. Charlotte Goddard, 2012b, 'Courses Adapt to Frontline Demands', *CYPN*, 10 July.
78. Charlotte Goddard, 2014, 'Youth Work—Jobs and Training Trends', *CYPN*, 24 June.
79. Jean Spence, 2017, 'Qualifying Courses and the Assault on English Youth Work Practice', unpublished draft, p. 2.
80. Charlotte Goddard, 2012b, op. cit.

81. Charlotte Goddard, 2012b, op. cit.
82. Charlotte Goddard, 2013, 'Youth Work Courses Continue to Evolve', *CYPN*, 25 June.

# Further Reading

Bolger, Steve and Scott, Duncan. 1986. *Starting from Strengths*. Leicester: NYB.

Davies, Bernard and Durkin, Mary. 1991.'"Skill", "Competence" and "Competences" in Youth and Community Work'. *Youth and Policy*. No. 34. September, pp. 1–11.

Davies, Bernard and Norton, Rod. 1996. 'Where Are Competence-Based Approaches Leading Us: A Critical Response to McRoberts and Leitch?' *Youth and Policy*. No. 53. Summer, pp. 44–52.

DES. 2011. *Positive for Youth: Discussion Paper—The Development of Young People's Workforce*. DES. June.

Jeffs, Tony and Spence, Jean. 2008. 'Farewell to All That? The Uncertain Future of Youth and Community Work Education'. *Youth and Policy*. No. 97/98. Autumn/Winter, pp. 135–166.

Jones, Helen M. F. 'Youth Work in England: A Profession with a Future?', in Alldred, Pam, et al. (eds), *The Sage Handbook of Youth Work Practice*. London: Sage, pp. 98–112.

McRoberts, Robin and Leitch, Ruth. 1995. 'The Development of a Competence-Based Approach to Training Part-Time Youth Work'. *Youth and Policy*. No. 51. Winter, pp. 21–34.

Spence, Jean. 2004. 'The Threat to Youth Work from Employer Led Initiatives'. *Rapport*. January, pp. 6–7.

Trelfa, Jo and Richmond, Dan. 2008. 'Getting the Balance Right: Training and Education Within NVQ and HE Routes to Youth Work'. *Youth and Policy*. No. 97/98. Autumn/Winter, pp. 119–134.

# 16

# Higher Education Routes in Transition

## Higher Education in a Neo-liberal World

The shifts in successive governments' policies for vocational training, outlined in the last chapter, generated tensions between NVQs and youth work's professional qualifications.[1] This also proved challenging for the higher education (HE) institutions running youth work courses.[2] At that stage, most of these were located in the 'new' universities which had converted from polytechnics in 1992. Some course, however, had long been offered by 'elite' 'Russell Group' institutions which by the 2000s were under pressure from reduced funding and government-imposed criteria for assessing 'excellence'. As a result, they increasingly prioritised research over teaching and aimed to recruit what one youth work course tutor later called 'A/B students'—which, he added, 'our students are very deliberately not…'

As a significant marker of these priorities, in 2001 Birmingham University first closed the seventy-year old full-time youth work courses it had taken over from Westhill College[3] and then in January 2007 announced the closure of the part-time course. This, it argued, was necessary because the course '… was not supported by internationally

© The Author(s) 2019                                                                303
B. Davies, *Austerity, Youth Policy and the Deconstruction of the Youth Service in England*, https://doi.org/10.1007/978-3-030-03886-1_16

competitive research, did not fit with the university's "strategic frame-work" and was not financially viable'.[4] Or, as CYWU's National Youth Work Convenor put it, 'with the University striving to move to a position of "academic excellence", it did not want to be running courses which did not demand high A level grades as an entry require-ment—or that were not bringing in enough funding'.[5] By 2008–2009 these business-driven imperatives had also contributed to the closure or suspension—sometimes despite student opposition[6]—of courses at Southampton,[7] Durham and Reading universities[8] and in 2013 at Manchester.[9]

By then, growing pressures for a better 'fit' within the new HE envi-ronment were also having impacts on course content. As part of a wider exercise 'to set out expectations about standards of degrees in a range of subject areas', institutions offering youth work courses worked with TAG to develop youth and community work 'subject benchmarks'.[10] First published in 2009 by the Quality Assurance Agency for Higher Education (QAA), these were subsequently revised—for example in 2017 '(to) acknowledge the increasing emphasis on reflective practice'.[11]

Despite growing pressure to become 'market-responsive', universities continued to offer some defence of the courses' commitment to content which was both personally educational and critical. They recognised that the 'debates prevalent in this subject signal a coherent but contested field of teaching and learning in higher education'—debates for example on 'the roles of the state, the market and the third sector in relation to the field of practice' and on 'whether professionalism is an essential part of practice or whether it is most characteristically a form of activism or volunteering'. The document also re-emphasised that 'the practice … is a value-rich activity' within which 'the development of trusting inter-personal relationships … requires a high degree of autonomy, responsi-bility and ethical conduct.'[12]

Course tutors' reception of the benchmarks was however mixed. While the course leader at Birmingham Newman University welcomed them as 'valuable work … to ensure that academically this area is rec-ognised',[13] for course tutors at Durham University they represented 'compartmentalised outcome-directed instruction (which) runs coun-ter to the very principles of good teaching'. They thus saw them as part of 'all the paraphernalia of modern education focus(ed) on measurable outcomes, on itemised "endings", on transferring competencies and on learning how to internalise and regurgitate the pre-packaged information'.[14]

## Surviving—and Adapting—In 'Difficult Economic Times'

Even before 'austerity' took hold, what in 2009 the APYCO Chief Executive called 'difficult economic times' were also having their impact. For some years before 2010, for example, none of Ruskin College's youth work students were local authority-sponsored while on the Bradford College course between 2007 and 2010 the number of sponsored students fell from 17 to 2 (out of 30 recruited).[15]

A changing demand for youth workers was indicated, too, by trends in local services' recruitment and retention. A national enquiry carried out by Bracknell Forest Youth Service in 2001 had revealed that, based on returns from 47 out of 152 local Youth Services, 94% identified recruitment as a problem, with low pay thought to be one contributory factor. Men and workers from ethnic minorities and with particular skills and experience were particularly hard to recruit, with 40% of respondents concerned about attracting staff of 'the right calibre' (62% also highlighted retention problems[16]). Evidence gathered by the NYA-led multi-agency Workforce Development Implementation Group, including from OFSTED reports, also concluded that '… many youth services are experiencing significant recruitment difficulties'.[17]

By 2005 the situation had reversed, with the annual turnover of professional local authority youth and community workers having fallen to only 13.1%.[18] Figures in the Commons Education Select Committee report (see Chapter 8) also showed that, compared to 20% in 2001, by 2009 retaining qualified youth workers was a problem for only 3% of authorities.[19] Even before the Coalition's cuts to local authority Youth Services, two experienced youth work trainers were thus suggesting that the best hope was that '… a rump (of courses) of sufficient size will survive'.[20]

# HE Routes to Youth Work Qualification: From Expansion to Contraction

## Courses Numbers

Between 2007 and 2010 the number of youth work degree courses offered by HE institutions rose from 16 to 38.[21] By 2012, 40 colleges or universities in England were offering 68 JNC-recognised courses— one more than the previous year. However, despite a small increase in 2014–2015, by the time NYA released its provisional returns in June 2018 only 28 HE institutions were offering 39 validated courses— 5 fewer than the previous November.[22]

By 2014–2015, course closures had spread beyond Russell group institutions to Liverpool John Moores and Chichester universities.[23] The University of East London, though retaining its postgraduate course, also planned to close its two undergraduate courses by 2014. In March 2017 Manchester Metropolitan University announced that it would replace the JNC-accredited course it had been offering for forty years with a three-year 'non-professionally' accredited course. Its explanation—'a slump in job prospects for youth workers due to the effects of austerity in public sector spending'—was challenged by TAG's national officer on the grounds that 'graduates from youth and community work courses go into jobs more easily because they get transferable skills…'.[24]

In the tightening economic climate, the cost of running youth work courses also became an issue for HE institutions. Not only did many still use labour-intensive individual tutorial and small group teaching methods. Extra resources were likely to be needed, too, for assessing field work and for supporting the (in 2008) 54% of students recruited through 'non-traditional' routes and the 17.5% registered disabled.[25]

Some institutions responded to these pressures in new, if pragmatic, ways. In 2010 Leeds Metropolitan University introduced a foundation degree focused on working with young people and young people's services to run alongside its accredited BA and postgraduate degree courses.[26] The following year an unnamed university talked of offering an 'accelerated degree' in youth work for practitioners with significant prior experience, to be completed in two years full time or three years part-time.[27] Jointly, the NYA and Leeds Beckett University launched a new part-time Youth Work and Community Development course in 2015 to enable practitioners '...to transfer experience and practice in youth work into a professional degree level qualification while working in a youth work related field'.[28]

## Student Targets and Intakes

As the number of courses increased, in the four years from 2008, student recruitment onto JNC-recognised courses in HE institutions in England also grew:

- In May 2008 the number recruited was recorded as approximately 1500 students.[29]
- By 2010 this had risen to 3350—41% on Dip HE courses, 27% on BA Honours degree courses and 13% on foundation degrees.[30,31]
- In 2011–2012 intake again went up, by 31%.[32]

By then, however, with a TAG survey predicting fewer students in 2012 than in 2011, tutors' confidence in reaching their recruitment targets was falling.[33] For the first time in 2011–2012, the numbers recruited fell below 1000, to 951—94% of course targets, with a third of courses failing to reach 90%.[34] By August 2013 it was being reported that 'several institutions had not been able to recruit a viable course...'[35] NYA returns for 2014–2015 showed an increase in student numbers over the previous twelve months, from 701 to 793,[36] allowing NYA's Chief Executive to suggest that 'the sector (was) ... evolving, rather than simply shrinking'.[37] However since 2008 student numbers overall had by then fallen by 13.1% and fell again by 2016–2017 to 517—down by 27.9% on the previous year. Though in 2015–2016 all the recognised HE courses recruited and overall met 97% of their targets, only 14 of the 51 programmes monitored actually reached or exceeded them.[38] Despite a reduction in recruitment targets from 1398 to 824 between

2007 and 2013, the level of missed targets over those years rose to 12%.[39]

Over this period, too, the composition of the student body changed significantly. Between 2005–2006 and 2006–2007 the proportion of male students fell from over 40 to 35%—a development which, perhaps because it came with an increase in non-white students from 29 to 31%,[40] Unite described as an 'equality record (which) is very good'.[41] By 2014–2015, 75% of students were women—up 10% on the previous year.[42]

Particularly significant, too, was the change in the ages of students recruited. In 2008–2009, the number aged 24 and under rose, with a corresponding fall in those in the 25–34 age group.[43] The 2012 TAG survey of course staff revealed that applicants were by then even younger and had less youth work experience,[44] prompting one course leader to comment in 2013: 'We have one of the youngest years we have ever had … - the oldest is 23'.[45] Though students' average age had gone up slightly by 2014–2015, 30% were now under 21 and only 21% aged 21–24.[46] By 2016–2017, their average age had continued to fall with many more in their 20s.[47]

The sector's weakening tradition of 'growing' its workers, often starting as a member in a local facility, had some particularly sharp impacts on the courses. With fewer mature applicants available, 'the typical youth work student (became) increasingly difficult to distinguish from the typical university student—more (were) fresh from school with a bundle of A-levels'.[48] As a result it became necessary to rethink widely used participative teaching methods which assumed students had substantial past and current practice experience.

## Student Funding

Also impacting significantly on student recruitment from the early 2000s[49] were both 'anxieties about fees'[50] and the replacement of grants with loans. As we saw earlier—and as CHYPS' Chief Executive pointed out in 2012—as local authorities cut their budgets they stopped funding youth work students, including voluntary sector staff.[51] Older applicants looked increasingly to part time in-service accreditation routes which allowed them to earn while studying[52,53]—though by 2012 they, too, were being put off by perceptions of poorer employment prospects. Though a cap on the level of student debt was introduced, a further disincentive was the introduction of 'full study costs' for university courses in 2013.[54]

One response to these concerns was the launch by NYA in collaboration with the mobile company O2 of a Youth Work Foundation offering ten £2000 scholarships and up to 100 bursaries of £100 for 'disadvantaged students'. With £40,000 available, this opened for applications in September 2014.[55]

## Students' Employment Prospects

Course recruitment and content were also affected by growing uncertainties in the youth work job market. Some senior Youth Service managers had long had doubts about the relevance of the HE courses' curricula to what from their perspective youth workers needed to know and do. In 2004 one course tutor pointed to '… the antagonism of many employers towards professional education within Higher Education … (and its) ideals of person-centred education based on a concern for equality and justice'[56]—a view echoed by a Unite member in 2008 who talked of '… employers (who) grumble about the skill-set delivered (by the courses)…'[57]

Previously—for example in 2004—Unite's starting position had been that '… our skills are in greater demand'.[58] A continuing need for routes to qualification was also seemingly demonstrated by a 2007 NYA finding that 'only 79 per cent of fulltime workers are qualified' and that 'these workers support over 17,000 Youth support workers'— only 52 per cent of whom were qualified'.[59] By 2013–2014, however, the proportion of students going into voluntary sector jobs in the previous twelve months had increased from 26 to 33%[60] so that by 2015 the sector was employing 44% of all youth workers.[61] By contrast only 16% of 2014 course graduates went into statutory sector posts although, significantly, an additional 5% were working in 'integrated youth support teams'.[62] Recruitment into the statutory Youth Service had fallen again by 2014–2015, from the overall 17.5% in 2013–2014 to 8.8%[63]—even though the proportion of youth workers employed across all council services had risen since 2011 from 19 to 22%. By 2016–2017, only 3% of course graduates went into jobs with council youth services[64] while, where youth work roles were being advertised, they were increasingly for lower paid support posts.[65]

With growing significance for the courses and what they taught, by 2012 a senior NYA manager thus concluded:

> Increasingly youth workers are not employed either as a 'youth worker' or to a 'youth service' but the skills and experience of youth workers are still highly sought after by employers in the statutory, voluntary and community, and private sectors'

To this, also in 2012, the CHYPS Chief Executive added: 'There is a split between … youth work and qualifications and where practitioners practice their youth work'—a situation which had, he said, accelerated in the previous two years.[66] The following year, NYA's Fiona Blacke noted that 'students are more likely to find work with a local enterprise, in hospitals, in schools and in youth offending'.[67]

By then Unite's recognition that youth work comprised 'a blend of universal and targeted services'[68] was being underpinned by assumptions that youth workers' practice, focused on individuals' 'risks', would increasingly be about 'prevention'. This was explained by the Chief Executive of the Dorset Youth Association in wholly positive terms:

> If you work with a child independently of the family then you are going to bring about a certain amount of change. But if you work with the whole family you have a much better chance of providing long-term change.

A senior Ambition manager also took it as a given by 2017 that youth workers

> … (were) being used by other council departments and voluntary services, in areas such as social care, early help for families, housing, community safety, youth offending and in education.[69]

## What Will We—What Should We—Teach?

These often radical shifts in youth workers' post-qualification roles forced courses into some fundamental rethinking of their curricula. In 2004 Jean Spence had suggested that, because HE institutions' youth work programmes 'maintain a level of independence from employers, they have been able to encourage a critical perspective upon policy and organisational practice…' Even then, however—that is, before the business ethos had become fully embedded in HE thinking—she saw this approach as 'a threat to employers and government', leading to '…pressures within HE itself to adopt increasingly functional approaches to education …'.[70] By 2008 she and her colleague Tony Jeffs were pointing specifically to the 'modularisation' of courses as resembling 'the division of labour in industry' which, by increasing 'specialisation and productivity', enabled universities to accommodate more students.[71]

The new subject benchmarks were, according to Unite, by 2008 having only '…varying degrees of success' in protecting this traditional youth work curriculum.[72] NYA's 'workforce development officer' also implicitly acknowledged that pressures within HE were leading to 'a growth in the breadth of curriculum and placements as integrated services develop to meet the needs of the new agenda'.[73] Two years later, a private email from a principal youth officer was blunt in its advice to the head of the local university's youth work programme. A 'main consideration' for courses, the officer insisted, had to be that

> … professional youth work training … quickly adapt to the changing context of youth work, particularly for those wishing to practice (sic) in the statutory sector or within highly targeted programmes. Key workforce development considerations from the frontline focus on equipping a growing number of workers with case management skills, training in CAMHS approaches, working with YP on risk taking behaviours.[74]

Emerging curriculum dilemmas such as these were highlighted again by the 2012 TAG survey of course staff. Employers' pressure for workers to have skills in outdoor pursuits, was, for example, reducing time for the specialist modules focused on the new 'child saving' roles. They were also limiting the honing of 'generic youth work skills such as the ability to engage young people with a programme of self-development'.[75]

To help balance these pressures, the YMCA George Williams College, though still prioritising 'relationship skills' in its JNC-recognised courses, sought to develop these for use in settings with children and families as well as young people.[76] Others, while seeking still to 'incorporate the pure ideals of youth work, like empowerment...' and insisting they were 'always anchor(ed) ... in the values of youth work', adapted their syllabuses to the new 'entrepreneurial' environment. 'Nimble footed and scan(ning) the horizon to spot change', by 2013 the University of Derby was offering modules on resourcing services and independent funding packages, on social enterprises and on working with children, carers and families.[77] By 2017, its course, renamed 'Working with Young People and Families and Communities', was providing 'inter-professional learning opportunities' and placements in agencies usually only available to social work, education or health course students.[78] Another course introduced programme streams focused on work with vulnerable young people in hospitals and youth offending teams and on 'informal learning posts in schools'; a third highlighted fundraising and management as 'key elements in youth work courses'.[79]

Indeed, with fewer experienced staff to supervise newly qualified workers, courses were also assuming that their students would from day one take on demanding management responsibilities.[80] One senior lecturer emphasised the need for students to learn 'how to communicate in a professional forum, to articulate what they are doing' and to be 'competent in fundraising and tendering'. In addition to launching an undergraduate degree in Social Pedagogy—'one of the new metamorphoses of youth work'—in 2012 George Williams College introduced a postgraduate degree in 'Reflective Leadership and Management' and, through a Centre for Reflective Leadership, offered MA-level short courses.[81]

In May 2017, UK Youth's Matt Lent offered strong voluntary sector support for these developments

… the youth worker is having rapidly to adapt to the required skillsets broadening beyond recognition. In order to survive, (they) now need to be fundraisers, business managers, marketing experts, lobbyists, impact assessors, data analysts, recruiters, HR managers, event planners, safeguarding officers – the list goes on. In the face of mere survival it would be easy to relegate the very particular niche skills youth workers need to do their actual job – supporting young people – so these became less important.[82]

## Placements

After a rise in the total number of placements in 2011–2012, there were steady reductions in both the average number per course—for example, between 2014–2015 and 2015–2016, from 36 into 25—and in the average number of supervisors (from 31 to 26).[83] In the Yorkshire and Humber region one response was to consider setting up 'accredited placements centres' 'where students can engage with a range of placement experiences under the auspices of a single organisation or body'.[84]

The nature of the student's placement experience also changed in this period. As far back as the academic years 2005–2006 and 2006–2007, the NYA's annual monitoring had revealed that courses were using fewer placements in traditional youth work settings and relying more on integrated youth support services. By August 2013, according to TAG's ETS representative, as budget cuts hastened that trend:

> Many employers have lost large numbers of experienced staff, and many lack the capacity to offer full-time or substantive placements, or provide appropriate levels of professional supervision.[85]

Fewer placement settings were thus available for students to practise as open access youth workers—a gap exacerbated by the fact that youth work courses often did not pay placement agencies. (In 2011 social work agencies were receiving £18 a day for each student supervised; charities £28 a day.)[86]

By 2012–2013 the NCS was emerging as a significant alternative source of placements (see Chapter 11). The De Montfort University course, for example, agreed that five second year students of the twenty five employed by the NYA on its summer NCS programme in 2012 would have their experience formally recognised as a course placement.[87] However, not only did the shortness of the NCS programme pose a problem for courses. According to the head of another course, in 2013 some of its students had that summer been the most qualified youth work staff employed on the programme.[88]

NYA continued to expect courses to ensure 'the student's experiences in placements are used to bring theory together with practice, based on the environment practitioners are working in'. Nonetheless, by 2012 one course tutor was quoting an employer's view that '... youth work graduates were less able to say how an education in generic youth work would enable them to work in a casework-load or early intervention-based agency'.[89]

# JNC Under Pressure

For a Joint Negotiating Committee heavily reliant on routes to accredited qualifications recognised by both employers and workers, the changes to the HE courses posed sometimes divisive challenges. As early as 2006 Unite noted that '(some) employers ... (had) abandoned JNC and sought to harmonise terms and condition onto inappropriate NJC conditions...'—that is, those for local authority staff generally.[90] By 2012 this had become an '... onslaught on JNC Terms and Conditions and (ETS's) validation of training ...'[91]

Three years later, in September 2015, JNC employers took the formal decision '... to seek the views of authorities on the issue of separate national collective bargaining arrangements' for the workforce in England and Wales. With evidence from the LGA that 'the number of employees covered by the JNC has fallen ... (by) about 45% between 2008 and 2013', the employers argued that there was 'no case' for retaining separate negotiating machinery.[92] On the contrary, a 'clear consensus' had emerged

> ... for both the assimilation of these employees onto local government services terms and conditions and for the National Employers to move away from separate collective bargaining arrangements ... through JNC.

Without setting a timescale for the process, employers had therefore agreed

> … to pursue and support the assimilation of Youth and Community staff to (local government) terms and conditions and withdrawal from national bargaining through the JNC.[93]

The main unions involved—Unite, Unison, the NUT and the University and College Union—rejected the move as a threat not just youth workers' terms and conditions but also to their 'professional standing'[94] and called on their members to lobby the employers to save the JNC.[95] By September 2016 the union campaign had succeeded to the extent that a new pay deal for local authority youth workers to run to 2018 had been agreed which not only preserved JNC terms and conditions but removed the employers' immediate threat to withdraw from JNC.[96]

In response to what it called '… (this) attempt by the Local Government Association … to remove the (youth workers') national collectively bargaining agreement', Unite commissioned research on JNC's future, carried out in the summer of 2017. Ninety eight percent of the 126 respondents (66 practitioners, 48 young people, 12 HE academics) 'shared evidence of … posts increasingly being advertised with a requirement for a lower level qualification (level 3 not a JNC recognised degree)'. The majority of the practitioner respondents (79%) 'had (also) experienced changes to their terms and conditions with the majority moving away from the JNC'—changes which one explained as 'mirror(ing) the change from open access work to carrying out targeted work only'. One senior youth work manager was explicit 'that they didn't want JNC qualified workers, as they are "trouble"'—nor indeed older and more experienced workers who, the respondent said, came with 'baggage'.[97]

The Unite research also revealed that 'the majority (of academics) … felt that without JNC recognition their course would change and possibly merge with other child and youth focused courses'. Indeed, some institutions were more specific, stressing that by then anyway

… their courses were led by the demands of employers and that the loss of JNC would mean that they would tailor teaching to the skills and knowledge required for the provision/services that no longer use JNC terms and conditions.

For other academic respondents, however, '… the JNC benchmark meant that they could deliver a professional course that provided quality, recognition and status'.[98] A 2017 paper co-authored by a current course tutor also claimed that the institutions running youth work courses

… have held steadfastly to a curriculum inspired by the radicalisation of social-democratic ideology through the 1970s and 1980s… (T)he focus remains firmly on informal learning, on conversation and dialogue, on identity groups and on power relations…[99]

The emerging realities on the ground, however, suggested that beyond 2018 the application—indeed, the relevance—of JNC would continue to pose the youth work field with a complex and contradictory set of dilemmas.

## Towards a New Strategy for Professional Training …

By 2017, Jean Spence was again drawing challenging conclusion on the future of HE routes to youth work qualifications. 'The disparities between the circumstances of the field and the demands of the universities are', she suggested, 'becoming too great'. In her view, 'the connections between the realities of the practice field and the principles upon which youth work education … has developed, could hardly be under greater stress than at present…' Yet for her

Without an articulated and continuously rearticulated interrelated body of ideas, values, principles, ethics, politics and methods, youth work would simply fall apart in contemporary circumstances. There would be no further requirement for the qualification.[100]

In response to these pressures both from above and below, after consulting with its membership in March 2017, TAG went in search of some more strategic responses. The following July it made a formal request to the English ETS to set up a working group to 'review the framework and support for HE courses offering qualifications in youth and community work … with a view to implementation of outcomes for the 2018–2019 academic year'.[101] Two months later it committed itself '… to continue to work with sector colleagues in securing progress with professional endorsement by ensuring that validation processes for professional courses are streamlined, sustainable and fit for purpose'. Included in these future discussions would be an update on progress on a proposed degree apprenticeship in youth and community work and on what it called 'wider HE provisions'.[102]

By the end of 2017 the NYA—now with a new 'Managing Director' in post—had confirmed that it would be appointing a full-time staff member to support the English ETS and its validation of courses.[103] An ETS working group was also focusing on 'any revisions/replacement of National Occupational Standards that are no longer being supported or funded by Government in England' and on the proposed 'Trailblazer' apprenticeships. A circulation for comment followed on the proposed standards ('knowledge, skills and behaviours (KSBs))' which in effect constituted NVQ-type 'competences' to be used for assessment within the apprenticeships.[104]

The ETS had by then (in July 2017) postponed until Spring 2019 both the renewal, due in 2018, of the bodies which awarded qualifications at Level 2 and 3 and, to 'a later date', its consideration of extending professional validation to NVQ Levels 4 and 5.[105] TAG made clear its disappointment at the '…delay to the review of professional validating processes', including its concern that

> … work on the Apprenticeship Trailblazer, and the development of a "career ladder" for youth work at Levels 4 and 5, appeared to be taking priority over professional qualifications… It is now urgent that work begins on revising professional validating processes with a view to implementation for the 2018-19 academic year'.[106]

More strategic responses were also being demanded by Unite which at the November 2016 annual conference of its Community, Youth and Playworkers section (CYPW) passed a resolution noting that 'opportunities for youth workers to undertake formal professional qualifications are shrinking' and 'the closure of youth work programmes by universities and other providers'. Students, it suggested, were 'further dissuaded from taking JNC … qualifications due to the system of loans and the virtual disappearance of grants, let alone the lack of job prospects in the sector'. Given these scenarios, the conference questioned 'whether the current structure of qualifications meets the needs of youth workers and the profession'.[107]

ETS's responses was, in December 2017, to announce a 'working group' to review the Professional Qualification Guidelines and implement revisions for the 2018–2019 academic year.[108] To support this process TAG ran eight seminars in the first half of 2018 'to foster greater levels of collaboration between higher education institutions and practice agencies in the profiling of challenges and opportunities facing youth and community work policy and practice across the UK'.[109] The consultations' initial outcomes were presented to the English ETS on in July, to be finalised for September 2018. The new guidance was to be used for all validations and revalidations stating in the academic year 2018–2019.[110]

# Notes

1. Jenny Hand, 1993, *NVQs and Their Implications for the Youth Service*, NYA, May, p. 25.
2. Tony Jeffs and Jean Spence, 2008, 'Farewell to All That? The Uncertain Future of Youth and Community Work Education', *Youth and Policy*, No. 97/98, Autumn/Winter, p. 160.
3. Wikipedia, 'Selly Oak Colleges: Final Years of the Federation', https://en.wikipedia.org/wiki/Selly_Oak_Colleges.
4. *Young People Now*, 2007, 'Birmingham to Axe Youth Work Course', 24–30 January, p. 2.
5. Andy Driver, 2007, 'Westhill College Youth Work Course to Close', *Rapport*, January, pp. 5–3.

6.  IDYW, 2009, 'Youth Work—Students Hit Back Over Axed Course', 2 April.
7.  Janaki Mahadevan, 2009, 'Universities Drop Youth Work Training Courses', *CYPN*, 19 March.
8.  P. J. White, 2011, 'Youth Work Courses Feel the Squeeze', *CYPN*, 13 June.
9.  Rapport, 2013, 'The Changing Landscape of Higher Education: Challenges and Opportunities for Youth and Community Work Education', August, pp. 8–9.
10. QAA, undated, 'The UK Quality Code for Higher Education: Subject Benchmark Statements', http://www.qaa.ac.uk/en/AssuringStandardsAndQuality/Pages/Subject-benchmark-statements.aspx.
11. QAA, 2017, 'Subject Benchmark Statement: Youth and Community Work', February, p. 4, http://www.qaa.ac.uk/en/Publications/Documents/SBS-Youth-and-Community-Work-17.pdf.
12. QAA, 2017, paras. 2.2, 2.5, 2.10.
13. Ian Richards, 2008, 'Annual Education and Training Committee Report', *Rapport*, May, pp. 18–20.
14. John Holmes, 'Youth and Community Work Qualifying Courses—Living with the Tensions?' *Youth and Policy*, No. 97/98, Autumn/Winter, p. 11; Tony Jeffs and Jean Spence, 2008, op. cit., pp. 11, 144.
15. Ian Richards, 2008, op. cit., pp. 18–20.
16. Anneli Connold, 2001, *The Recruitment and Retention of Part Time Youth Work Staff: The National Picture*, Bracknell Forest Borough Council, August, Exec Sum.
17. *CYPN*, 2003, 'National Youth Agency: Call for Better Training Opportunities', *CYPN*, 6 August.
18. CWDC, 2010, *A Picture Worth Millions: The State of the Young People's Workforce*, Leeds, January, p. 12.
19. House of Commons Education Committee, 2011, *Services for Young People: Third Report of Session 2010–12*, Vol. 1, London, Stationery Office, June, paras. 93–94.
20. Tony Jeffs and Jean Spence, 2008, op. cit., p. 161.
21. Derren Hayes, 2017a, 'Youth Work Student Numbers Plunge by 28 per cent', *CYPN*, 4 May.
22. Derren Hayes, 2017a, op. cit.; Tristan Donovan, 2018, 'Further Drop in Youth Work Courses, Figures Show', *CYPN*, 14 June.

23. P. J. White, 2011, op. cit.
24. Derren Hayes, 2017b, 'Evolution of Youth Work Courses', *CYPN*, 4 May; Joe Lepper, 2017a, 'University Axes Youth Work Course Due to Slump in Job Prospects', *CYPN*, 31 March.
25. Ian Richards, 2008, op. cit., pp. 18–20; Charlotte Goddard, 2013, 'Youth Work Courses Continue to Evolve', *CYPN*, 25 June.
26. Saba Salman, 2010, 'How to Become a Qualified Youth Worker', *Society Guardian*, 17 February.
27. *Rapport*, 2013, op. cit., pp. 8–9.
28. NYA, 2015, 'New Part-Time Youth Work Degree Launches in Leicester and Leeds', 18 August.
29. Ian Richards, 2008, op. cit., pp. 18–20.
30. CWDC, 2010, op. cit., p. 13.
31. P. J. White, 2011, op. cit.
32. Charlotte Goddard, 2012, 'Courses Adapt to Frontline Demands', *CYPN*, 10 July.
33. Charlotte Goddard, 2012, op. cit.
34. Charlotte Goddard, 2013, op. cit.
35. *Rapport*, 2013, op. cit., pp. 8–9.
36. Adam Offord, 2016a, 'Rise in Students on Youth Work Courses', *CYPN*, 20 June.
37. Charlotte Goddard, 2014, 'Youth Work—Jobs and Training Trends', *CYPN*, 24 June.
38. Derren Hayes, 2017b, op. cit.; Joe Lepper, 2017b, 'Who Are the New Youth Workers?', *CYPN*, 31 May; Joe Lepper, 2017c, 'Youth Work Student Numbers Fall to Record Low', *CYPN*, 14 August; Derren Hayes, 2017a, op. cit.
39. Charlotte Goddard, 2014, op. cit.
40. Charlotte Goddard, 2009, 'Decline in Male Youth Workers', *CYPN*, 19 January; Ian Richards, 2008, op. cit., pp. 18–20.
41. Ian Richards, 2008, op. cit., pp. 18–20.
42. Adam Offord, 2016a, op. cit.
43. *CYPN*, 2009, 'Concern Over Youth Work Training Supervisors' Qualifications', 24 August.
44. Charlotte Goddard, 2012, op. cit.
45. Charlotte Goddard, 2013, op. cit.
46. Adam Offord, 2016a, op. cit.
47. Derren Hayes, 2017b, op. cit.; Joe Lepper, 2017b, op. cit.; Joe Lepper, 2017c, op. cit.

48. Charlotte Goddard, 2013, op. cit.
49. Charlotte Goddard, 2013, op. cit.
50. Tom Lloyd, 'Training: Youth Work Courses Feel Effect of Rise in University Tuition Fees', *CYPN*, 4 May; *Rapport*, 2013, op. cit., pp. 8–9.
51. Charlotte Goddard, 2012, op. cit.
52. John Holmes, 2008, op. cit., p. 8; Tony Jeffs and Jean Spence, 2008, op. cit., p. 150; IDYW, 2009, op. cit., 2 April; Neil Puffett, 2012, 'University of Manchester to Ditch Youth Work Degree', *CYPN*, 1 October; Charlotte Goddard, 2013, op. cit.
53. Jean Spence, 2004, 'The Threat to Youth Work from Employer Led Initiatives', *Rapport*, January, pp. 6–7.
54. *Rapport*, 2013, op. cit., pp. 8–9.
55. Joe Lepper, 2013, 'Youth Work Foundation to Help Disadvantaged Students Gain Qualifications', *CYPN*, 31 October; Laura McCardle, 2014, 'Youth Work Bursary Scheme Opens for Applications', *CYPN*, 2 September.
56. Jean Spence, 2004, op. cit., pp. 6–7.
57. Ian Richards, 2008, op. cit., pp. 18–20.
58. Ian Richards, 2004, 'Report of the Chair of Education and Training Committee', *Rapport*, May, p. 16; Jean Spence, 2004, op. cit., pp. 6–7.
59. Ian Richards, 2008, op. cit., May, pp. 18–20.
60. Charlotte Goddard, 2014, op. cit.
61. Derren Hayes, 2017b, op. cit.
62. Charlotte Goddard, 2014, op. cit.
63. Joe Lepper, 2017b, op. cit.
64. Joe Lepper, 2017b, op. cit.; Joe Lepper, 2017c, op. cit.
65. Joe Lepper, 2017a, op. cit.; Joe Lepper, 2017c, op. cit.
66. Charlotte Goddard, 2012, op. cit.
67. Charlotte Goddard, 2014, op. cit.
68. Charlotte Goddard, 2014, op. cit.
69. Joe Lepper, 2017b, op. cit.; Joe Lepper, 2017c, op. cit.
70. Jean Spence, 2004, op. cit., p. 6–7.
71. Tony Jeffs and Jean Spence, 2008, op. cit., pp. 142–144.
72. Ian Richards, 2008, op. cit., pp. 18–20.
73. Charlotte Goddard, 2009, op. cit.
74. Private Communication, November 2011.
75. Charlotte Goddard, 2012, op. cit.

76. Joe Lepper, 2017a, op. cit.
77. Gabriella Jozwiak, 2013, 'Fundraising Skills Added to Youth Work Degree Syllabus', *CYPN*, 20 May.
78. University of Derby, 2017, 'Letter to the Editor: Youth Work Courses Still Championed in Derby', *CYPN*, 4 May.
79. Charlotte Goddard, 2013, op. cit.
80. Charlotte Goddard, 2013, op. cit.
81. *Rapport*, 2013, op. cit., pp. 8–9; Charlotte Goddard, 2014, op. cit.
82. Joe Lepper, 2017b, op. cit.; Joe Lepper, 2017c, op. cit.
83. Joe Lepper, 2017c, op. cit.
84. *Rapport*, 2013, op. cit., pp. 8–9.
85. *Rapport*, 2013, op. cit., pp. 8–9.
86. P. J. White, 2011, op. cit.; Charlotte Goddard, 2013, op. cit.
87. NYA, 2012, 'News: NYA Pilots Intensive Practice Placement with De Montfort University', 27 April.
88. Charlotte Goddard, 2013, op. cit.
89. Charlotte Goddard, 2012, op. cit.
90. Andy Driver, 2006, 'Workforce Reform and Remodelling: Is This the Emperor's New Clothes?', *Rapport*, January, p. 9.
91. Ian Richards, 2012, 'All Change on the Learning Front', *Rapport*, February, pp. 20–21.
92. Adam Offord, 2016b, 'Unions Slam Employers' Plans to Scrap Youth Work Pay Settlement', *CYPN*3, 1 February.
93. Letter from Simon Pannell, 2015, 'JNC Youth and Community Workers—National Collectively Bargaining', JNC for Youth and Community Workers (Employers Side), 7 December.
94. Adam Offord, 2016b, op. cit.
95. Adam Offord, 2016c, 'Unions Urge Youth Workers to Fight Pay and Condition Changes', *CYPN*, 26 February; Joe Lepper, 2017b, op. cit.; Joe Lepper, 2017c, op. cit.
96. Adam Offord, 2016d, 'Employers Make Pay Rise Offer to Council Youth Workers', *CYPN*, 17 June; Adam Offord, 2016e, 'JNC Saved After Youth Workers Accept Pay Settlement', *CYPN*, 21 September.
97. Unite, 2017, *Youth Work: Professionals Valued*, Unite, pp. 6, 22.
98. Unite, 2017, op. cit., p. 28.
99. Pauline Grace and Tony Taylor, 2017, 'Influential Theories and Concepts in UK Youth Work—What's Going on in England?', in Shild, Hanjo, et al. (eds), *Thinking Seriously About Youth Work;*

*and How to Prepare People to Do It*, Council of Europe/European Commission, p. 152.

100. Jean Spence, 2017, 'Qualifying Courses and the Assault on English Youth Work Practice', unpublished draft, pp. 2, 3, 8.

101. TAG Email Newsletter, 2017a, 'Consultation Report and Recommended Actions', 30 June.

102. TAG Email Newsletter, 2017b, 'Association Representatives to Consult with the NYA and English ETS This Month', 3 November.

103. TAG Email Newsletter, 2017c, 'English Education, Training and Standards (ETS) Committee Report', 4 December, p. 1.

104. TAG Email Newsletter, 2017d, 'Proposed Apprenticeship Standards for Youth Work', 12 December.

105. Pauline Grace, 2017, Personal Communication, 20 July.

106. TAG Email Newsletter, 2017c, op. cit., p. 2.

107. Unite/CYPW, 2017, 'Resolution 01/16: Challenging Training and Qualifications …', 'Conference Report 2016', Unite, November, p. 1.

108. Tag Email Newsletter, 2017e, 'HE Validation Review Working Group to Convene on 10th January, 2018', 22 December.

109. TAG:PALYCW Members Bulletin, 2018a, Issue No. 15, 2017–2018, 11 April.

110. TAG:PALYCW Members Bulletin, 2018b, Issue No. 22, 2017–2018, 27 July.

# Further Reading

Grace, Pauline and Taylor, Tony. 2017. 'Influential Theories and Concepts in UK Youth Work—What's Going on in England?', in Shild, Hanjo, et al (eds), *Thinking Seriously About Youth Work; and How to Prepare People to Do It*. Council of Europe/European Commission, pp. 149–160.

Holmes, John. 'Youth and Community Work Qualifying Courses—Living with the Tensions?', *Youth and Policy*. No. 97/98. Autumn/Winter, pp. 5–11.

Jeffs, Tony and Spence, Jean. 2008. 'Farewell to All That? The Uncertain Future of Youth and Community Work Education'. *Youth and Policy*. No. 97/98. Autumn/Winter, pp. 135–166.

Jones, Helen M. F. 2018. 'Youth Work in England: A Profession with a Future?', in Alldred, Pam, et al. (eds), *The Sage Handbook of Youth Work Practice*. London: Sage, pp. 98–112.

*Rapport.* 2013. 'The Changing Landscape of Higher Education: Challenges and Opportunities for Youth and Community Work Education'. August, pp. 8–9.

Sercombe, Howard. 2010. *Youth Work Ethics.* London: Sage.

Spence, Jean. 2004. 'The Threat to Youth Work from Employer Led Initiatives'. *Rapport.* January, pp. 6–7.

# Part VI

## Beyond Deconstruction

# 17

# Defending the Youth Service: Defending Youth Work

## Resistance in a Hostile Environment

Though dominant, the youth policies of this period did not go unchallenged. Oppositional responses emerged, some with greater impact, some more sustained than others. Largely hidden from public view, individual workers' 'gamed' managerial systems imposed on them from above.[1] Others—for example, a senior academic at Nottingham Trent University and an experienced youth worker made redundant by Bradford Youth Service—went public in their criticisms of the cuts to services.[2] A variety of organisations, too, opposed both the government's hands-off stance on the Youth Service and its wider youth policies. They included the London Play and Youth Work Campaign,[3] a D2N2 Youth Work Alliance—'a forum of professional Youth and Community Workers' in the East Midlands,[4] the Network of Regional Youth Work Units,[5] and the Rio Ferdinand Foundation set up by former England football captain.[6]

© The Author(s) 2019
B. Davies, *Austerity, Youth Policy and the Deconstruction of the Youth Service in England*, https://doi.org/10.1007/978-3-030-03886-1_17

# Young People as Activists: Five Case Studies

Prompted usually by what was happening to them and their friends, young people emerged in some areas as leading defenders of Youth Service facilities. Occasionally they spoke with a national voice as when, two weeks after the 2017 General Election, UK Youth Voice presented the Prime Minister with a manifesto which demanded that youth services be made a priority public service.[7] Both the BYC and the UK Youth Parliament also took up important 'youth' issues such as lowering the voting age to 16.[8]

More commonly, however, young people's activism against the cuts was expressed in local campaigns—as the case studies below illustrate.

## Warwickshire: 2010–2011[9]

In a letter to her local paper in November 2010, 16 year old Becky Williams warned that the threatened closure of her local youth centre 'would impact on the whole community'. A campaign followed aimed also a keeping a second nearby youth centre open which gathered a 16,000-signature petition and was backed by the local (Conservative) MP and the chairperson of the county association of youth clubs.

In making her case Becky repeated one of the standard arguments in defence of Youth Services—that 'anti-social behaviour will go up in the area as young people will have nothing else to do'. However, she also highlighted the positives of 'what our centre means to us'. These included 'confidential help … for a variety of different reasons'; 'be(ing) able to talk to youth workers about things that we may not be able to talk to our parents or carers about'; 'educational activities …including rock climbing, kayaking and babysitting courses … (and) computers'; and 'pool tables and a table tennis table … comfortable sofas and a quiet room'. Becky was also reported to have told the District Youth Committee that 'our youth centres are the centre of our lives'—that the centre 'is not just a case of a few ping pong tables and somewhere for young people to go on a few nights a week, there is a massive amount of work done (there)'.

Despite the efforts of Becky, her friends, local youth workers and other sympathisers, open access sessions at her centre were reduced and much of the workers' time reassigned to targeted work. More widely, the Council, declaring all but five open youth centres in the County 'surplus to requirements', sought to transfer responsibility for some of them to 'the community'. Nonetheless, after surviving further threats, Becky's youth centre was still open in mid-2018 and detached work continued in the wider area, including with newly arrived asylum-seekers.[10]

## Oxfordshire, 2010–2011[11]

In December 2010, twelve year old Nicky Wishart was taken out of his English class at school to be interviewed by anti-terrorist police. This was done in the presence of his year head but without his mother's knowledge. The police warned Nicky that if he went ahead with the picket he was organising outside David Cameron's constituency offices he would be held responsible for any disorder that resulted and, as the organiser, could be arrested. As Cameron had armed protection, there was also an implication, reports suggested, that worse might happen. (The police later apologised to Nicky and his family.)

Nicky attended the picket which he had helped organise—part of a wider Oxfordshire anti-cuts campaign—to protest against the proposed cuts to the Youth Service budget, initially reported as £4.2 million. (A demonstration and march involving 80 people also took place in Banbury.) Nicky later took his 'they say cut-back, we say fight back' chant to a national anti-cuts rally. He was also a first signatory to a letter to Cameron signed by 2000 young people from across the country, including 50 from Cameron's and Chancellor George Osborne's constituencies.

The youth workers involved successfully challenged a Council ruling preventing them giving support to the young people organising the campaign.[12] The 2011–2012 budget cut was also cut by half, so that 13 youth centres continued to be council-funded and nine others shared a £300,000 Council 'Big Society Fund' grant. (Bids to the Fund totalled £1.2 million.) However as part of a strategy for creating 'hubs', the Youth Service was merged with a range of 'young people and families' services into an 'Early Intervention Service'.

## North Somerset, 2012–2014[13]

North Somerset Council announced in February 2012 that it would reduce its Youth Service budget over the following four years by 71%—from £1.1 million to £300,000. This, it was predicted, would mean closing six 'youth groups'. It also said it would 'look at how services could be delivered in a different way rather than simply cutting them'. It talked particularly of adopting 'a model suggested by the government for providing local services using local people…'

After protests and some consultations, the cuts were delayed until April 2014 and £100,000 added to the proposed Youth Service budget. Nonetheless, in April 2012, 21 year old Aaron Hunt launched a legal challenge to the planned cuts on the grounds that they had been agreed without adequate consultation and, by failing to take into account disability, sexual orientation or race, had breached the 2010 Equality Act. Aaron, who had ADHD and learning difficulties, described his local centre as like being 'part of a family'.

After the High Court ruled in July 2012 that the Council had not acted unlawfully, Aaron took his case to the Court of Appeal which in November 2013 overturned the High Court decision. The Council, it decided, had not only failed to consider the needs of users protected by the Equality Act or to consult properly with young people. According to Aaron's lawyer, it referred, too, to the Council's statutory duties under Section 507b of the 1996 Education Act. However, as the cuts had by then been implemented, the court decided it would be 'inappropriate' to ask for the decision to be reconsidered.

After Unite highlighted the case as a warning to other authorities, some were subsequently reported to have 'appear(ed) to have heeded the … ruling by thinking more creatively about how to engage young people over proposed changes'.

## Devon, 2014[14]

In February 2014 Devon County Council proposed a £1 million cut in its £3.7 million Youth Service budget and a refocusing of resources on 'early help and prevention services'. Over 50% of its full-time equivalent posts would be lost and 24 of its 32 youth centres closed.

In response 17 year old Kelly Spurway first organised a protest gig and then a demonstration in Barnstaple 'for all the young people who didn't know how to make their voices heard'. She also took part in a consultation at the youth club where she volunteered, stressing to Devon's 'strategic director (people)' that 'targeted work … is great for those people who need it but for others there's going to be nothing whatsoever'.

By the summer of 2016 the Devon County Council had set in motion a process for tendering out its Youth Service, including eight youth centres, resulting by the end of the year in a staff-run social enterprise (see Chapter 5).

## Brighton and Hove, 2016–2017[15]

In November 2016 Brighton and Hove Council announced it was to cut its Youth Service budget by 80%—from £1 million to £200,000—including ending all funding support for the voluntary and community sector. This prompted a campaign of opposition which, led by young people, brought together youth groups, charities and youth workers. In January 2017 'hundreds marched through the streets of Brighton in protest' and a petition which eventually attracted 'around 2000 signatures' was discussed at a Council meeting early in the February. After the Labour Party lead on the Children, Young People and Skills Committee resigned, calling the cuts 'short-sighted', these were reduced to 15%.

Some of the anecdotal evidence coming out of these campaigns (for example from Brighton) suggested that some councillors gained new insights into how youth workers worked with young people and encouraged their collective as well as individual development.

Few of the campaigns, however, could claim to have saved Services or even significantly reduced the proposed cuts. These 'failures' not only had consequences for thousands of young people which were direct and personal. They may also have reinforced pre-existing doubts about democratic processes and institutions which, personally and repeatedly, they experienced as unresponsive to their demands—a potentially significant 'failure', too, for a practice which defines itself in part as seeking to tip balances of power in young people's favour.

## Political Defence—Within Limits

Sometimes interwoven with this grassroots campaigning, resistance to the Youth Service's deconstruction also found organised national expression. Some occurred within and through Parliament as when, as early as November 2010, Labour MP Julie Hilling—a former youth worker—talked at a Westminster Hall debate of the 'fallacy' 'that the voluntary sector can pick up the pieces left by a shattered local authority service'.[16]

Over the period, however, the opposition parties rarely spoke with a united or concerted voice on these issues. The Labour Party itself shifted position a number of times—for example by downgrading a pledge made in 2011 to make Youth Services statutory to, within twelve months, a promise merely to 'review ... services for young people', including considering how to locate youth clubs in school buildings.[17] A later commitment to ensuring a 'statutory' Youth Service then failed to appear in its May 2015 general election manifesto[18]—only to reappear in February 2018[19] backed by a proposal to consult on implementing a statutory service.[20] This commitment was eventually given a somewhat harder edge in June by a Labour MP's Ten Minute Rule Bill calling on the government to 'promote and secure youth services' and by a consultation initiated in July 2018 on 'Building a Statutory Youth Service'.[21]

Even while their party was helping to implement the Coalition's 'austerity' policies, some Liberal Democrats were advocating that local authorities be made legally responsible for providing a minimum level of provision for young people. The former chair of its Youth Policy Working Group, Linda Jack, insisted in February 2012 that the 'government must back youth work rhetoric with investment'. Three years later she talked, too, about 'the vanity project that is NCS' and endorsed the CYWU/Unite 'ChooseYouth' campaign (discussed below).[22]

The Green Party gave some of the most consistent support to local Youth Services, particularly in London where their Mayoral Candidate produced revealing research reports on the impact of the cuts.[23]

## Campaigning Through the Unions

Young people's efforts to defend Youth Service facilities, described above, were often part of wider trade union campaigns organised by Unison and CYWU (which merged in 2006 into what later became Unite). The former, for example, helped organise the protests which eventually led to Aaron Hunt's legal action against North Somerset Council.[24]

As workers were increasingly threatened with redundancy, union responses went beyond defending members' conditions of service—as for example against a pay cut in Coventry[25]—to trying to defend posts. CYWU/Unite took strike action in Oxfordshire in 2009 against a £2.3 million Youth Service cut,[26] continued to work to rule even after that proposal was withdrawn and, in August 2010, voted for one-day strikes when some 80 youth worker jobs were threatened.[27] In 2014 and again in 2016 Unison also published widely quoted research into how budget cuts were affecting Youth Services nationally.[28]

Faced with these growing threats, during the 2010–2011 Parliamentary session, backed by an 'E-petition', the union prompted Labour MPs to table early day motions proposing a stronger statutory base for local authority Youth Services. It later also pressed ministers on the 'illegality' of local authorities' cuts to these Services[29] and, to support its campaigns, in 2013, published *The Future of Youth Work*. Calling NCS 'poor value for money', this, in familiar New Labour language, argued for year-round 'positive activities for young people provided by a universal youth service'.[30] In 2015 the union challenged Cheshire County Council's investment of £3 million in the Warrington OnSide development (see Chapter 13) as 'the thin edge of the privatisation wedge'[31]; and in 2017 urged that the Chancellor's Autumn Statement 'financially reboot' youth services in the UK.[32]

## 'Choose Youth'…

Over the period CYWU/Unite's responses to the cuts were increasingly interwoven with the 'ChooseYouth' campaign it launched in February 2011. This brought together some thirty organisations including the NYA, UK Youth, the British Youth Council, the Woodcraft Folk and TAG and newer groupings such as Step Up To Serve and the Institute for Youth Work. Other unions—Unison, the National Union of Students (NUS) and the General Federation of Trade Unions—also joined as did the Liberal Democrat Friends of the Youth Service and IDYW.[33]

As well as voluntary and paid workers the campaign's launch rally in Solihull attracted over a 1000 young people from across the UK, some of whom spoke passionately in defence of their local youth work facilities.[34] Following a 'youth bloc' participation in March in a TUC rally in London against the broader assault on public services, ChooseYouth events were organised during 2011 and 2012 in Newcastle, the South West, the West Midlands and two in London—one to co-incide with a House of Lords debate on the Youth Service.[35] A first ChooseYouth 'Manifesto' was published in July 2011 setting out youth work's benefits (including its 'cost effectiveness') and demanding increased state investment in youth work facilities.[36]

The draft of a more substantial Manifesto was debated at ChooseYouth's first AGM in February 2013 which, in an attempt to influence Labour Party policy, was sent to over 600 Labour councillors, with a Parliamentary launch also being considered.[37] It however raised one issue—the need for a professional 'licence to practice'—which, though crucial for CYWU/Unite, was divisive within the broader youth work field including amongst ChooseYouth participants (see below).

With winning Labour Party support still a high campaign priority, the failure of its 2014 pre-manifesto policy paper to mention the Youth Service prompted ChooseYouth to call on Party's activists to press for an amendment. This proposed that

It should be the responsibility of the Secretary of State for Education to promote, secure and provide… a sufficient Youth Service whose primary purpose shall be the personal and social development of young people.[38]

A Protect Services' petition, first sent to the Party leader Ed Miliband in July 2013,[39] had by March 2015 attracted over 6500 signatures.[40] This was followed by a Labour MP's EDM tabled in November 2014, which—attracting 112 signatures within a month[41]—proposed 'universal youth services' with ringfenced funding from central government and that responsibility for youth policy be returned to the DfE.[42] Even after Labour's Election defeat in May 2015, efforts to keep the Youth Service on the political agenda continued—by, for example, circulating a new Youth Service Bill to all 650 MPs.[43]

An 'open forum' a year later on 'Youth Work and Youth Services: Our Shared Future' particularly sought to encourage discussion with alliance members on what more could be done jointly 'to protect and enhance essential services for young people through youth work'. However, the paper written for the event by ChooseYouth Chair Doug Nichols[44] started from ideological propositions which were not necessarily shared by all participants. For example, he compared the 'democratic work' processes which had been prevalent under social democratic social policies with the 'undemocratic work' imposed by the 'neo-liberal political economy'. However, in seeking to attract whatever state funding might be available, some voluntary sector 'allies' were by then looking for more conciliatory and co-operative relationships with government and so were more accepting of these neo-liberal propositions (see Chapter 14). This stance could therefore place some significant limits on collaborative action through ChooseYouth.

Given the depth and extent of the cuts to the services and the loss of so many experienced practitioners, a campaign 're-launch' at the September 2017 AGM was anyway seen as necessary.[45] A Roundtable event in Parliament in April 2018 brought together MPs, including the Labour Party's Youth Service spokesperson Cat Smith, with young people and youth workers, feeding into renewed pressure for a Youth Service Bill.[46]

# In Defence of Youth Work[1]

A much looser grouping eventually taking the title In Defence of Youth Work emerged out of the circulation of an Open Letter in February 2009 whose opening paragraph made explicit the writers' bottom-line political concerns and priorities. Youth work—a practice which, the Letter asserted, had long claimed to be on young people's side—was close to abandoning 'this distinctive commitment'. Shaped by 'the dire legacy of these neo-liberal years', it was increasingly working instead to 'the State's terms' and so 'sid(ing) with the State's agenda'. Though tracing these developments back to the 1980s, the initiative's timing was explained by the events of 2007, during which 'in the space of only a few months … (c)apitalism (was) revealed yet again as a system of crisis'.

The Letter's drafters particularly distanced themselves from 'the so-called "new managerialism"' demanding 'predictable and prescribed outcomes' and 'the micro-management of problematic and often demonised youth' whose ultimate goal was '… a generation stamped with the State's seal of approval'. These pressures were seen as transforming youth work into 'an agency of behavioural modification' which was in sharp conflict with the Letter's commitment to 'a democratic and emancipatory Youth Work'. This was captured in seven defining 'cornerstones' of which the first was '… the freedom for young people to enter into and withdraw from Youth Work as they so wish'.

In making the case for a new grouping, the Letter drew attention to campaigns of 'organised, dissident resistance' by detached youth workers and the youth work unions; in adult education and social work; and within the voluntary sector generally. While stressing that, 'in doing so, you are not agreeing to some party line', those who 'sympathise with and support the position set out in this Open Letter' were asked to 'sign up to its intent'.

The Letter's reception was by no means wholly positive. According to CHYPS' Chief Executive: 'The argument needs to … be more explicit about the outcomes of youth work intervention'. She claimed, too (though without offering supportive evidence) that by getting young people

[1]Declaration of interest: the author was a signatory to the original IDYW Open letter and was an active member of its Steering Group throughout the time this book was being written.

appointed to 'senior positions' youth work had 'impacted hugely on institutions across the country.' Michael Bracey, a 'local authority youth support manager' and later Chair of the NYA Trustees, questioned whether youth work was more at risk than it had been in the previous 30 years.[47]

Responses to IDYW's early events, however, suggested that its message had struck a chord. After conferences in London and Newcastle in May and June 2009 attracted 50 and 90 participants, 150 attended its first annual conference in Manchester in February 2010. Increasingly over the years social media proved crucial for involving this wider audience. By 2017 the IDYW website, set up in March 2009, was getting over 24,000 visits and nearly 49,000 views from some 160 countries. Its blog was viewed in 2015 nearly 53,500 times; 'conversations' were encouraged and extended by the website co-ordinator's tweets; and its Facebook page, opened in July 2009, had over 3600 members by May 2018.[48]

As the cuts took hold, IDYW moved beyond its initial defence of the practice to include a defence of the open access facilities providing it. Critical attention was given, too, to wider government policies such as NCS, the 2011 *Positive for Youth* paper and to the dominant 'outcomes' and 'measurement' agendas. Under the by-line 'Engaging critically', it also took up a range of proactive stances. Four months into the Coalition, a seminar in Manchester was reflecting on 'the implications for our work of the new political settlement'.[49] Its 2011 annual conference, with inputs from CYWU/Unite and Unison, considered 'Strategies for Resistance'; and, in 2017, 'Youth work: Education or Prevention?' Other conferences and seminars—national, regional and local—opened up debates on the 'outcomes agenda', 'Youth work and radical education', 'Ethics and politics' and 'The state, the market and the voluntary youth sector'. 'Practitioner workshops' were also organised on for example 'The ethics of banning' and 'Space in youth work'.

Critical scrutiny was also given to 'traditional' voluntary sector organisations such as NCVYS and UK Youth and newer ones such as the CYI, particularly for their possible accommodation with government policies. IDYW sought to engage with them in public debate, on occasions contributing to their events or inviting them to make inputs to its own conferences and seminars. Led by members of its Steering Group, it also contributed to significant youth work developments in Europe and beyond.

One of the most sustained IDYW initiatives was a 'From the Grassroots' project created initially to provide qualitative evidence of youth work's impacts on young people's lives. Over its first two years this gathered 'stories' of workers' and young people's first-hand experience of youth work practice. Twelve, contextualised and analysed, were published in an illustrated booklet, *This Is Youth Work: Stories from Practice*,[50] funded by Unison and Unite and launched in Parliament in October 2011. This provided a prompt for some 40 story-telling workshops, some run outside the UK and one for a visiting Japanese group, which over three years attracted up to 1000 paid and voluntary practitioner, managers, students and tutors. By sharing and analysing examples of their practice, the workshops encouraged participants to clarify both what made this distinctively youth work and their identity as youth workers. The workshop materials were published in January 2015 as an on-line resource[51] which within a year had been visited over 240 times by over 1400 people, including again by many from outside the UK.

Following the Labour Party 2017 general election gains and its promise to restore funding for public services, IDYW circulated a draft paper, 'Is the Tide Turning?', which was debated by over 200 people at eleven workshops across the country. Additional feedback from its 2018 annual conference—on for example how to persuade 'the progressive wing of British politics' to commit to restoring state-funding for open access youth work facilities—contributed to a paper, 'Reviving Youth Work and Reimaging a Youth Service',[52] which was fed into new national debates then emerging.[53]

With limited resources constraining its role as a campaigning body, in 2016 IDYW relabelled itself 'a forum' for encouraging debate on current issues and developments.[54] Questions and doubts about its role and style continued to be raised, however, including within IDYW itself—for example, about its overtly 'political' positions and the language in which these were sometimes expressed. Moreover, given the disappearance across the country of open access youth work practice as defined in its original Open Letter, its effectiveness in fulfilling its founding 'mission' was clearly also open to question.

Nonetheless, some of the responses to its 'Is the Tide Turning?' challenge suggested that, at the very least, it had helped keep alive and indeed reaffirm commitments to that practice and to occupational identities defined by it amongst practitioners and managers who by then were often working in very different settings.

# An Institute for Youth Work

In realising an aspiration which had a long pre-history, the establishment in this period of new body—the Institute for Youth Work— eventually also provided a focus for some (albeit more conventional) resistance to the dominant youth policies. That pre-history went to back at least the 1970s when the Ministry of Education's closure of its register of qualified youth workers raised concerns that, because 'youth worker' was not a 'protected' title, it could be adopted by what were later called 'dubious individuals'[55] and 'bogus people'.[56]

In 2003, in response both to problems of recruiting trained workers and to criticisms of the existing training structures, the Workforce Development Implementation Group had recommended that a General Youth Work Council be created to oversee professional recognition and ethical conduct[57]—a proposal to which CYWU eventually gave its approval.[58] With a junior minister's support, three years later CWDC also suggested that 'this might be the right time to look at a licence to practise'[59] while in 2009 the NYA investigated the feasibility of 'a Voluntary Registration scheme for youth workers'.[60]

Doubts remained, however. In 2012, for example, CYWU/Unite was again seeking assurance that what was by then being called an 'institute' 'should not be a … way of wriggling out of regulation of the workforce'.[61] Based on responses to a consultation the previous autumn, the NYA in 2012 also concluded that there was '… a desire for a much bigger structure than simply a register' while adding the significant caveat that this '… should be available to the whole workforce, not solely those with a JNC recognised qualification'.[62]

Two years later the Catalyst consortium, tasked with 'coordinating a skills development strategy for the youth sector's workforce'[63] (see

Chapter 14), initiated development work for an 'independent body governed and owned by its membership'.[64] With a response rate which CYWU judged 'low',[65] the 2011 NYA consultation—seen as a key part of Stage 1 of the IYW development process—had indicated that 92% of the 231 respondents[66] agreed that creating an Institute 'led by youth workers' would be a 'positive development', with 80% seeing its primary function as 'to provide a voice for youth work and influence policy'. However only 49% thought that an institute should hold a register of youth workers and only 40% that it should introduce a 'licence to practise'.[67]

In itself, the term 'professional' has long been critiqued for being far from the objective or neutral concept often implied by its advocates.[68] Its use has come frequently with at least implicit assumptions about the nature of the power relationship not just between worker and 'client' but also between different practices. For youth workers in Rotherham working with sexually abused young, the latter was starkly evidenced over many years by the dismissive responses to them as 'unprofessional' by local social workers, police and their managers.[69]

As perhaps as a grounded illustration of how such power imbalances might operate, many in the voluntary youth sector remained concerned about the often matter-of-fact link of the IYW proposals with demands for paid workers to be recognised as 'professional'. This, for them, carried a risk that an Institute could result in the progressive devaluation of the contribution of volunteers and of those without 'a piece of paper'. NCVYS's starting point was thus a need for 'inclusivity and the avoidance of exclusivity'—that 'a membership system based on categories of youth work practitioner' would 'not only (be) too difficult to build consensus around but would also construct artificial notions of quality and professionalism within the workforce'.[70] CYWU/Unite, on the other hand, was by 2013 explicit that the emerging proposals were not 'delivering on things like a revocable licence to practice'.[71] This, it insisted, had to be part of the IYW's brief, not least because 'appropriate safeguards' would be needed to ensure that membership was not used 'to conceal poor youth work practice or worse' or 'in the future offer an alternative, less rigorous route to qualification which could undermine (youth workers') professional status'.[72]

Even at this stage other ambiguities (at best) were discernible—especially about how the practice of 'youth work' was being understood. Though both quoted the 2008 the National Occupational Standards' definition of youth work's purpose, neither the NYA paper reporting on the 2011 consultation[73] nor a September 2012 letter from the ETS chair[74] had anything to say about the process or methods of the practice used for achieving this. And though the former described youth work as 'distinctive and different to other professions working with young people', when this distinctiveness and difference were left undefined they were explained only as 'informal learning and support for young people'. In its own submission to the Stage 2 consultations, NCVYS also in effect accepted youth work's mutation into any form of 'work with young people', arguing that the Institute should be for '… individuals working or volunteering … with young people'.[75] Attached still to many of these statements, too, apparently as an assumed feature of the practice, was the qualifier 'professional'.[76]

With a view to presenting 'a business case' for an Institute, attempts were also made to clarify the range of operational arrangement needed to establish this 'as an independent organisation'.[77] An ETS chair's letter to 'sector-leading organisations' in 2012 seeking to clarify their support thus set out the 'short-term/immediate tasks to be completed'. These included producing a 'framework for ethical, effective practice', a 'code of conduct', and 'longer term/up for debate' issues such as the 'regulatory role to protect membership', 'voluntary register' and 'debate a licence to practise'.[78]

Further consultations in the summer of 2012 had revealed that 61% of those responding said they would join an Institute. With DfE funding for the IYW start-up phase in England about to end in the October,[79] the NYA indicated that, if the consultations showed an Institute 'is necessary' and 'what the sector wants', it would fund its actual establishment.[80] Debates on its nature and role continued into 2013, focusing for example—sometimes sharply—on the 'Framework for ethical practice' which members would be required to accept and which was eventually issued, again after consultation, in March.[81]

The Institute was finally launched in September 2013 and a Council elected from its membership in December 2014. As NYA ran out of funds to support it, the Institute set out plans in April 2015[82] to become fully independent, achieving charitable status in December 2017.[83] In its first three months it attracted 300 members to 'levels' of membership defined as volunteers, students, 'members' working with young people without a formal qualification and 'certified' qualified youth workers.[84] Twenty nine 'organisational supporters', each paying a £1000 fee, also signed up early.[85]

For one experienced youth work academic this low take-up indicated an 'identity crisis' resulting from the fact that, though 'there is plenty of youth work going on… it's not generally under a youth service'.[86] However, by September 2014 membership had reached 700[87] and by May 2017 around 2000. According to IYW chair Adam Muirhead, the growth had been helped by closer links forged with employers and universities and with organisational supporters bringing in their employees. The new body also raised its profile on social media, organised events including an annual conference and, in February 2018, published a five-year strategic plan setting out its short-, medium- and long-term goals.[88]

The issues of registration and a licence to practise, however, remained contentious. Though policy-makers were seen as unlikely to legislate to make a youth work licence mandatory,[89] in February 2014 a CYPN survey revealed that nearly 95% of the 323 respondents (215 working in the public sector, 94 in the voluntary sector) regarded youth work as a profession, with the proportion in favour of a register having risen to 60%.[90] Over two years later, in August 2016, the IYW Chair was nonetheless still acknowledging 'a lot of split opinions' on the issue including whether a register should be 'self-imposed' or 'government proposed'. He also identified another 'tricky point' with strong echoes of past debates: the risk of the new body '… being exclusive or marginalising volunteers in the workforce'.[91] What thus eventually emerged for testing before the end of 2018, stopping short of a licence to practice, was a voluntary register of the qualifications held by individual workers—paid and volunteer, qualified and unqualified.[92]

Though wider recognition of the Institute within the youth (work) field remained uneven,[93] by 2018 it had begun to fulfil some early hopes that it would provide an additional independent national arena for defending youth work provision. When, for example, in November 2017, the government announced that it would not be developing a new 'dedicated youth policy',[94] it sent an 'open letter' to the minister pointing out that IYW members had regarded such a statement as 'a useful and appropriate measure to revitalise a sector that has suffered in the extreme from the austerity programme in recent years...' It asked her, too, to make clear 'the value of young people and youth work to yourself and your department'.[95] Separately, it stated that it would 'welcome consideration being given to the range of cross-sector work with young people that happens outside what has become quite a narrow field of funding support for NCS'.[96] By January 2018 it was also giving public support to an 'enforced and improved statutory footing for youth work'.[97]

# Notes

1. Tania de St Croix, 2016, *Grassroots Youth Work; Policy, Passion and Resistance in Practice*, Bristol, Policy Press, pp. 179, 182–189.
2. Laura McCardle, 2014a, 'Expert Challenges Youth Workforce's Commitment to Protecting Services', *CYPN*, 4 April; Laura McCardle, 2014b, 'Campaigners Seek Statutory Status for Youth Services', *CYPN*, 29 August.
3. Joe Lepper, 2015a, 'Campaigners Vow to Mobilise Against Youth Work and Play Cuts', *CYPN*, 26 May.
4. Tony Taylor, 2016a, 'Renewing Collective Purpose: The D2N2 Youth Work Alliance', IDYW, 17 November, https://indefenceofyouthwork. com/2016/11/17/renewing-collective-purpose-the-d2n2-youth-work-alliance/.
5. Partnership for Young London, 2017, 'A 3-Year Strategy for Young People', 17 July, http://www.partnershipforyounglondon.org.uk/uncategorized/3-year-strategy-for-young-people/; Tristan Donovan, 2017, 'Youth Work Network Calls for Redistribution of NCS Cash', *CYPN*, 8 August.
6. ITV News, 2016, 'Rio Ferdinand Kicks off Campaign to Stop Youth Services Cuts', 4 April, http://www.itv.com/news/2016-04-04/rio-ferdinand-kicks-off-campaign-to-stop-youth-services-cuts/.

7. Tony Taylor, 2017a, 'UK Youth Voice Write to a Prime Minister, Who Can't or Won't Deliver', IDYW, 22 June, https://indefenceofyouthwork.com/2017/06/22/uk-youthvoice-write-to-a-prime-minister-who-cant-and-wont-deliver/.

8. BYC, 2017, 'Our Voice, Our Journey, 2016/17', p. 8, https://www.byc.org.uk/wp-content/uploads/2017/09/British-Youth-Council-Annual-Review-2017.pdf; UK Youth Parliament, 2018, 'UK Youth Parliament Highlight Concerns with Current Youth Voting Age', 4 May, http://www.ukyouthparliament.org.uk/2018/news/uk-youth-parliament-highlight-concerns-current-voting-age/.

9. Becky Williams, 2010, 'Please Don't Close Down Our Centre' (letter), *Leamington Spa Courier*, 12 November; Oliver Williams, 2011a, 'Youngsters Hope Big Speech Will Help Save Youth Clubs', *Leamington Spa Courier*, 14 January; Oliver Williams, 2011b, 'Campaign to Save Youth Clubs Finds Backing at Council's HQ', *Leamington Spa Courier*, 21 January; Neil Puffett, 2011, 'Warwickshire to Close All But Five Youth Centres', *CYPN*, 17 June; Warwickshire County Council, 2011, 'Facing the Challenge: The Future for Youth Services', Warwickshire County Council, October.

10. Warwickshire County Council, 2018, *Youth: Stories of Asylum*, Warwickshire, Lillington Youth Centre.

11. Shiv Malik, 2010, 'Schoolboy Warned by Police Over Picket Plan at David Cameron's Office', *Guardian*, 10 December; Right to Work, 2011, 'Protesting in Cameron's Back Yard', 9 January; Janaki Mahadevan, 2011a, 'Young People Write to Cameron in Defence of Youth Services', *CYPN*, 17 January; Tom Jennings, 2011, 'Teenagers Deliver Verdict on Youth Service Cuts', *Oxford Mail*, 8 April; Joe Lepper, 2011, 'Oxfordshire Blasted Over Youth Centre Closure', *CYPN*, 28 April; *CYPN*, 2011, 'The Shape of Youth Services to Come', *CYPN*, 17 May; BBC News, 2011a, 'Oxfordshire Youth Clubs in "Big Society" Cash Award', 13 July; BBC News, 2011b, 'Oxfordshire Youth Workers Strike Over Jobs', 23 August; Tony Taylor, 2010a, 'Resistance in Banbury', IDYW, 25 August, https://indefenceofyouthwork.com/2011/08/25/resistance-in-banbury/.

12. Tony Taylor, 2011a, 'Bravo! Young People Force an Embarrassing U-Turn!', IDYW, 2 February, https://indefenceofyouthwork.com/2011/02/02/bravo-young-people-force-an-embarrassing-u-turn/.

13. BBC News, 2012a, 'North Somerset Council Youth Services' Closure Planned', 22 February; Neil Puffett, 2012a, 'Rethink on Some Youth

Services Leads to £100,000 Boost', *CYPN*, 27 April; Neil Puffett, 2012b, 'Young Person Launches Legal Challenge Against Youth Cuts', *CYPN*, 25 April; Neil Puffett, 2012c, 'Legal Challenge Over Youth Club Gets Underway', *CYPN*, 13 June; BBC News, 2012b, 'North Somerset Youth Service Cuts Challenge Dismissed', 18 July; Laura McCardle, 2013a, 'North Somerset Youth Funding Cuts Unlawful, Rule Judges', *CYPN*, 8 November; Laura McCardle, 2014c, 'Landmark Case Fails to Quell Thirst of Councils to Cut Youth Services', *CYPN*, 29 April.

14. Laura McCardle, 2014d, 'Devon Considers Early Intervention-Focused Youth Service', *CYPN*, 3 February; Elliot Anderton, 2014, 'Young People Protest Youth Service Cuts in Barnstaple', *North Devon Gazette*, 9 April; Laura McCardle, 2014e, 'More Than Half of Devon Youth Service Jobs at Risk', *CYPN*, 5 June; Adam Offord, 2016a, 'Entire Council Youth Service Put Out to Tender', *CYPN*, 23 June; Adam Offord, 2016b, 'Staff-Run Social Enterprise Set to Take on Council Youth Service', *CYPN*, 15 September.

15. Tony Taylor, 2016b, 'Brighton Campaign Strategy Unfolds', IDYW, 12 December; Tony Taylor, 2017b, 'Brighton Battles on as Politicians Resign', IDYW, 11 January; Ben Glazebrook, 2017, 'Budget Cuts That Will Put Youth Work at Risk', *Brighton and Hove Independent*, 16 January; Tony Taylor, 2017c, 'Brighton and Hove Youth Services Survive—Blog from Preventing Inequality', IDYW, 7 March; Jessica Hubbard, 2017, 'Cuts to Youth Services Reversed: Campaigners Rejoice', *The Badger*, 7 March.

16. Tony Taylor, 2010b, 'Westminster Hall Debate on the Future of the Youth Service', IDYW, 24 November, https://indefenceofyouthwork. com/2010/11/24/westminster-hall-debate-on-the-future-of-youth-work/; Joe Lepper, 2010, 'MPs Speak Out Against Youth Service Cuts', *CYPN*, 24 November.

17. Neil Puffett, 2012d, 'Labour to Explore Putting Youth Clubs in Schools', *CYPN*, 25 May.

18. Adam Offord, 2015, 'Labour Ditches Statutory Youth Services Pledge', *CYPN*, 14 April.

19. Joe Lepper, 2018, 'Labour Makes Statutory Youth Service Pledge', *CYPN*, 25 February.

20. Neil Puffett, 2018, 'Labour to Consult on Creation of a Statutory Youth Service', *CYPN*, 23 April.

21. Nina Jacobs, 2018a, 'Labour MP Makes Legislative Bid for Statutory Youth Services', *CYPN*, 8 June; Labour Party, 2018, 'Building a Statutory Youth Service', https://www.policyforum.labour.org.uk/commissions/education/youth-services.

22. Linda Jack, 2012, 'Government Must Back Youth Work Rhetoric with Investment', *CYPN*, 15 February; Linda Jack, 2015, 'Let's Work Together for Young People', *CYPN*, 29 May; Adam Offord, 2015, op. cit.

23. Sian Berry, 2017, *Youth Service Cuts in London—What Next?* Green Party, March; Sian Berry, 2018, 'London's Lost Youth Services 2018', Green Party, March.

24. BBC News, 2012a, op. cit.

25. Tony Taylor, 2016c, 'Fight for the JNC—CYWU (Unite)', 14 January, IDYW, https://indefenceofyouthwork.com/2016/01/14/fight-for-the-jnc-cywu-unite/; Duncan Gibbons, 2011, 'Youth Workers to Strike Over Coventry City Council Pay Cuts', *Coventry Live*, 3 February, https://www.coventrytelegraph.net/news/coventry-news/youth-workers-strike-over-coventry-3067963.

26. Ross Watson, 2009, 'Oxfordshire Youth Workers to Strike After Cuts Revealed', *CYPN*, 15 December.

27. Tony Taylor, 2010c, 'Support the Youth Workers Strike', Oxford, August 23, IDYW, 18 August, https://indefenceofyouthwork.com/2011/08/18/support-the-youth-workers-strike-oxford-august-23/; Alexandra Topping, 2011, 'Youth Workers in David Cameron's Oxfordshire Base Strike Over Cuts', *Guardian*, 23 August.

28. Unison, 2014, *The Damage: UK Youth Services—How Cuts Are Removing Opportunities for Young People and Damaging Their Lives*, London, Unison; Unison, 2016, *The Damage: A Future at Risk—Cuts in Youth Services*, London, Unison.

29. Tony Taylor, 2010d, 'Early Day Motion on Youth Work and the Youth Service', IDYW, 19 November, https://indefenceofyouthwork.com/2010/11/19/early-day-motion-on-youth-work-and-the-youth-service/; Tony Taylor, 2011b, 'Early Day Motion 1013 and E-Petition', IDYW, 30 October, https://indefenceofyouthwork.com/2011/10/30/early-day-motion-1013-and-e-petition/; Gabriella Jozwiak, 2010, 'Politicians to Fight "Illegal" Cuts', *CYPN*, 30 November.

30. Unite, 2013, *The Future of Youth Work*, Unite, p. 3, https://b.3cdn.net/unitevol/f9b7f490fdc5efe8c4_2rm6b3l63.pdf.

31. Joe Lepper, 2015b, 'Union Calls for Rethink on Warrington Youth Zone Plans', *CYPN*, 12 February.
32. Neil Puffett, 2017a, 'Call for Philip Hammond to Act on Youth Services', *CYPN*, 18 November.
33. ChooseYouth, 2017, Meeting Minutes, 9 September.
34. CYPW, 2011, 'Campaigns: ChooseYouth', https://www.cywu.org.uk/index.php?id=8&type_id=12&category_id=149; ChooseYouth, 2011, 'ChooseYouth London Rally: Ticket Information', 16 July.
35. Janaki Mahadevan, 2011b, 'Government Challenged to Intervene in Councils That Neglect Youth Services', *CYPN*, 26 October.
36. ChooseYouth, 2017, 'Events', https://www.ChooseYouth.org/events/choose-youth-events/; Tony Taylor, 2011c, 'ChooseYouth Manifesto', IDYW, 2 August, https://indefenceofyouthwork.com/2011/08/02/choose-youth-manifesto/; Tony Taylor, 2011d, 'ChooseYouth in Newcastle…', IDYW, 9 April, https://indefenceofyouthwork.com/2011/04/09/choose-youth-in-newcastle-april-18/.
37. Taylor, 2013a, 'ChooseYouth: Moving Forward with Both Manifesto and Open Debate', IDYW, 15 February, https://indefenceofyouthwork.com/2013/02/15/choose-youth-moving-forward-with-both-manifesto-and-open-debate/.
38. Tony Taylor, 2014, 'ChooseYouth Questions Labour's Silence Re Youth Work…', IDYW, 4 April, https://indefenceofyouthwork.com/2014/04/04/choose-youth-questions-labours-silence-re-youth-work-meanwhile-in-scotland/.
39. Tony Taylor, 2013b, 'ChooseYouth Launch Petition to "Protect Services for Young People"', IDYW, 15 July, https://indefenceofyouthwork.com/2013/07/15/choose-youth-launch-petition-to-protect-services-for-young-people/.
40. Tony Taylor, 2015a, 'ChooseYouth Urges Labour to Go Statutory in Its Manifesto', IDYW, 31 March, https://indefenceofyouthwork.com/2015/03/31/choose-youth-urges-labour-to-go-statutory-in-its-manifesto-idyw-to-explore-what-statutory-might-mean/.
41. Laura McCardle, 2014f, 'Parliamentary Motion Calls for Statutory Youth Services', *CYPN*, 10 November.
42. www.parliament.uk, 2014, 'Early Day Motion 488: Youth Services', tabled 6 November, https://www.parliament.uk/edm/2014-15/488.
43. Joe Lepper, 2015c, 'Youth Sector Demands Legislation to Protect Services', *CYPN*, 15 May.

44. Tony Taylor, 2016d, 'ChooseYouth Call for Unity: Our Shared Future', IDYW, 8 February, https://indefenceofyouthwork.com/2016/02/08/ChooseYouth-call-for-unity-our-shared-future/; Tony Taylor, 2016e, 'Youth Work and Youth Services: Our Shared Future: Doug Nichols Ponders', IDYW, 4 April, https://indefenceofyouthwork.com/2016/04/04/youth-work-and-youth-services-our-shared-future-doug-nicholls-ponders/#more-9067.

45. Tony Taylor, 2017d, 'ChooseYouth AGM and Re-launch Meeting September 2017', IDYW, 7 August, https://indefenceofyouthwork.com/2017/08/07/ChooseYouth-agm-and-re-launch-meeting-september-2017/.

46. Doug Nicholls, 2018, 'Winning a Statutory Youth Service', *Youth and Policy*, 2 May, http://www.youthandpolicy.org/articles/winning-a-statutory-youth-service/.

47. Tony Taylor, 2009, 'Senior Managers Deliver Their Judgement', IDYW, 24 April, https://indefenceofyouthwork.com/2009/04/24/senior-managers-deliver-their-judgement/; Michael Bracey, 2009, 'In Defiance of a Youth Work Revolt', *CYPN*, 10 June.

48. Tony Taylor, 2013c, 'A Brief History of Our Campaign Thus Far!', IDYW, 21 January, https://indefenceofyouthwork.com/2013/01/21/a-brief-history-of-our-campaign-thus-far/; Tony Taylor, 2018, 'The Future of in Defence of Youth Work—Steering Group Discussion', June 15, IDYW, https://indefenceofyouthwork.com/2018/06/.

49. https://indefenceofyouthwork.com/2010/07/13/youth-work-under-the-condems/.

50. IDYW, 2011, *This Is Youth Work: Stories from Practice*, https://indefenceofyouthwork.com/the-stories-project/.

51. IDYW, *Story-Telling in Youth Work*, https://indefenceofyouthwork.com/the-stories-project/story-telling-in-youth-work/.

52. Nina Jacobs, 2018b, 'Close NCS to Fund Local Youth Work, Say Campaigners', *CYPN*, 1 May.

53. IDYW, 2018a, 'Reviving Youth Work and Reimaging a Youth Service: IDYW Starting Points', IDYW, 27 April, https://indefenceofyouthwork.com/2018/04/27/17512/.

54. Tony Taylor, 2016f, 'In Defence of Youth Work: Less a Campaign, More a Forum for Critical Debate?', https://indefenceofyouthwork.com/2016/07/13/in-defence-of-youth-work-less-a-campaign-more-a-forum-of-critical-debate/.

55. Tom Wiley, 2012, 'An Institute for Youth Work?', *Youth and Policy*, 118, March, p. 88.
56. Tracey Quinn, 2015, 'Institute for Youth Work or Flogging a Dead Horse?', *Rapport*, April, p. 5.
57. *Children and Young People Now*, 2003, 'The National Youth Agency: Call for Better Training Opportunities', 6 August.
58. *Rapport*, 2005, 'Towards Quality, Respected, Qualified Professions', July, pp. 14–15.
59. *Children and Young People Now*, 2003, op. cit.; Bernard Davies, 2008, *The New Labour Years, A History of the Youth Service in England—Volume 3, 1997–2007*, Leicester, Youth Work Press, p. 168.
60. NYA, 2012a, 'The Institute for Youth Work: Gap Analysis and Impact Assessment', March.
61. Ian Richards, 2012, 'All Change on the Learning Front', *Rapport*, February, pp. 20–21.
62. NYA, 2012a, op. cit.
63. NCVYS, 2012a, 'Catalyst Consortium—FAQs', at http://www.ncvys.org.uk/UserFiles/Catalyst%20FAQs%202_1.pdf, posted 14 February 2012; NCVYS, 2013, 'About the Catalyst Programme', at http://www.ncvys.org.uk/Catalyst.html; The Young Foundation, undated, 'Catalyst', https://youngfoundation.org/projects/catalyst/; Neil Puffett, 2012e, 'Catalyst Group Bids to Be Source of Strength for Youth Sector', *CYPN*, 10 July.
64. Laura McCardle, 2014g, 'Academics Urge Institute to Refine Purpose and Broaden Horizons', *CYPN*, 30 September; NYA flyer, 2011, 'An the Institute for Youth Work?'; 'The Institute for Youth Work—Consultation', 2011, https://www.surveymonkey.com/r/HNTHTKK?sm=HVPXniG1%2b4QiXxUfIJvlEQ%3d%3d.
65. Ian Richards, 2012, op. cit., pp. 20–21.
66. NYA, 2012a, op. cit.
67. Neil Puffett, 2012f, 'Sector Gives Backing to an Institute for Youth Work', *CYPN*, 1 March; Neil Puffett, 2012g, 'NYA Considers Funding Institute for Youth Work', *CYPN*, 22 October.
68. See for example Wilding Paul, 1982, *Professional Power and Social Welfare*, London, Routledge and Kegan Paul.
69. Alexis Jay, 2014, *Independent Inquiry into Child Sexual Exploitation in Rotherham, 1991–2013*, Rotherham Metropolitan Borough Council, August.

70. NCVYS, 2012b, 'An Institute for Youth Work—Second Phase Consultation Response to the National Youth Agency: A Response from the National Council for Voluntary Youth Services (NCVYS)', July, paras. 8, 13.
71. Charlotte Goddard, 2013, 'Youth Work Courses Continue to Evolve', *CYPN*, 25 June.
72. Unite/CYWU, 2013, 'Institute for Youth Work', *Rapport*, August, p. 3.
73. NYA, 2012a, op. cit.
74. Mike Counsell, 2012, 'In Defence of Youth Work's View on the Institute for Youth Work', Letter dated 31 September, www.nya.org.uk/exploring-an-institute-for-youth-work.
75. NCVYS, 2012b, op. cit., paras. 6, 8.
76. Support and Challenge Group Paper, 2011, 'An the Institute for Youth Work?', November.
77. 'The Institute for Youth Work—Consultation', 2011, https://www.surveymonkey.com/r/HNTHTKK?sm=HVPXniG1%2b4QiXxUflJvlEQ%3d%3d.
78. Mike Counsell, 2012, op. cit.
79. Amanda Frearn, 2012/2013, 'An Institute for Youth Work?' (Slides), p. 5.
80. Neil Puffett, 2012g, op. cit.
81. NYA, 2012b, 'Institute for Youth Work: A Framework for Ethical Practice—Draft for Consultation', December; NYA, 2013, 'Institute for Youth Work: A Framework for Ethical Practice', March; Tony Taylor, 2013d, 'A Framework for Ethics: Useful or Ornamental?', 25 April, IDYW, https://indefenceofyouthwork.com/2013/04/25/a-framework-of-ethics-useful-or-ornamental/; Howard Sercombe, 2013, 'Critique of the Draft Statement of Principles for the Institute for Youth Work', April; Neil Puffett, 2013, 'Youth Work Institute to Launch in Autumn', *CYPN*, 26 April; Laura McCardle, 2013b, 'Institute for Youth Work Goes Live', *CYPN*, 26 September.
82. IYW, 2017a, 'Our History', https://iyw.org.uk/our-history/.
83. IYW, 2017b, 'IYW Achieves Charitable Status', Email, 20 December; IYW Chair's Email, 12 January 2018.
84. Laura McCardle, 2013b, op. cit.
85. Neil Puffett, 2013, op. cit.; Laura McCardle, 2013b, op. cit.; Laura McCardle, 2014g, op. cit.

86. Laura McCardle, 2013c, 'Youth Work "Identity Crisis" Behind Low Take-Up of Institute Membership', *CYPN*, 6 December.
87. Laura McCardle, 2014g, op. cit.
88. IYW, 2018, 'The IYW Launch Their 5 Year Strategic Plan', IYW, 6 February, https://iyw.org.uk/the-iyw-launch-their-5-year-strategic-plan/.
89. Neil Puffett, 2012g, op. cit.
90. Laura McCardle, 2014h, 'Youth Workers Face Up to Identity Crisis Amid Public Perceptions', *CYPN*, 4 February.
91. Adam Offord, 2016c, 'Institute for Youth Work to Explore Viability of a Youth Work Register', *CYPN*, 11 August.
92. Derren Hayes, 2018, 'Youth Worker Register "Close to LAUNCH"', *CYPN*, 6 August.
93. Tony Taylor, 2017e, 'LGA/NYA Conference: Proposing a Vision from Above—Or a Failure of the Imagination?', IDYW, 5 December, https://indefenceofyouthwork.com/2017/12/05/lga-nya-conference-proposing-a-vision-from-above-a-failure-of-the-imagination/://indefenceofyouthwork.com/2016/01/25/youth-sector-briefing-a-curious-case-of-consensus/.
94. Neil Puffett, 2017b, 'Government Ditches Youth Policy Statement', *CYPN*, 17 November.
95. IYW, 2017c, 'Ref: "Civil Society Strategy" Ministerial Statement, dated 16 November 2017', 20 November, https://indefenceofyouthwork.files.wordpress.com/2017/11/tracey-crouch-mp-open-letter-20-11-17.pdf; Darren Hayes, 2017, 'Institute for Youth Work "Seeks Assurances" Over Government's Commitment to Young People', *CYPN*, 20 November.
96. Partnership for Young London, 2017, op. cit.; Tristan Donovan, 2017, op. cit.
97. Nina Jacobs, 2018c, 'Institute for Youth Work to Push for Statutory Youth Services', *CYPN*, 22 January; Adam Muirhead, 2018, 'Is New Legislation Needed?', *CYPN*, 27 February.

# Further Reading

de St Croix, Tania. 2016. *Grassroots Youth Work; Policy, Passion and Resistance in Practice*. Bristol: Policy Press.

IDYW. 2011. *This Is Youth Work: Stories from Practice*. https://indefenceofyouthwork.com/the-stories-project/.

Nicholls, Doug. 2018. 'Winning a Statutory Youth Service'. *Youth and Policy*. 2 May. http://www.youthandpolicy.org/articles/winning-a-statutory-youth-service/.

Ord, Jon. 2016. *Youth Work Process, Product and Practice: Creating an Authentic Curriculum in Work with Young People*. Abingdon: Routledge, pp. 133–144.

Partnership for Young London. 2017. 'A 3-Year Strategy for Young People'. 17 July. http://www.partnershipforyounglondon.org.uk/uncategorized/3-year-strategy-for-young-people/.

Taylor, Tony. 2013. 'A Brief History of Our Campaign Thus Far!' IDYW. 21 January. https://indefenceofyouthwork.com/2013/01/21/a-brief-history-of-our-campaign-thus-far/.

Unite. 2013. *The Future of Youth Work*. Unite. https://b.3cdn.net/unitevol/f9b7f490fdc5efe8c4_2rm6b3l63.pdf.

Wiley, Tom. 2012. 'An Institute for Youth Work?' *Youth and Policy*. No. 108. March, pp. 88–91.

# 18

# What Future for Youth Policies?
# What Future for the Youth Service?

## Austerity and Its Consequences

Successive governments' assault on the welfare state after 2010 had impacts well beyond youth policies. Over the period, libraries, leisure centres and their swimming pools, local museums and galleries, police stations and a range of other public amenities were closed or had their opening hours reduced and/or were handed over to 'the community'.[1]

Nearly ten years after the publication of his book on the 2007–2008 banking crisis,[2] John Lanchester reflected on how this wider deconstruction of state provision had affected 'younger people's' view of the capitalist society in which they were growing up. This, he said, was a society:

> … formed by austerity, increasing inequality, the impunity and imperviousness of finance and big technology companies, and the widespread spectacle of increasing corporate profits and a rocketing stock market combined with declining real pay and the huge growth in the new phenomenon of in-work poverty…

The result: a 'fundamental breach of what used to be the social contract…'[3]

© The Author(s) 2019
B. Davies, *Austerity, Youth Policy and the Deconstruction of the Youth Service in England*, https://doi.org/10.1007/978-3-030-03886-1_18

As was outlined in Chapter 1, the young people of this new youth precariat were sometimes masked by official reports' as 'children'.[4] Nonetheless, across the country, across classes and across genders, ethnicities, (dis)abilities and sexual orientations, the consequences were experienced in very direct ways by many in their teens and often, too, in their twenties.

For example:

*Poverty*: In March 2018 the government's own figures showed that the number of children living in relative poverty had risen for the third year running to its highest level since 2007–2008.[5] By September a new measure of poverty had put that figure at 4.5 million, with more than half trapped in that situation for years.[6]

*Homelessness*: According to an April 2018 Homeless Link report, more than a quarter of young people accessing homelessness services in the previous twelve months had been aged 16 or 17.[7]

*Mental Health*:

- Between 2012–2013 and 2016–2017 the number of young people referred to the NHS's Child and Adolescent Mental Health Services (CAMHS) rose by 56%. The number attending A&E departments in England with psychiatric problems doubled to 22,000 a year between 2010–2012 and 2015–2016.[8]
- A 2018 ONS research report revealed that 10% of the 16–24 age group interviewed were found to be 'always or often' lonely—the highest proportion of any age group. According to 82% of youth workers surveyed by UK Youth that year loneliness was 'a big issue for young people'.[9]
- Young people in 2018 wrote and talked publicly about '… panic attacks, crying, nosebleeds, sleepless nights, hair loss and outbreaks of acne' as they prepared for and took the new GCSE and A level exams.[10]

*The gender divide*: A Children's Society survey of 11,000 14 year olds published in August 2018 revealed that nearly a quarter of the girls had self-harmed in a year compared with under one in ten boys.[11]

*The ethnic divide*: In April 2018 the Ministry of Justice's own figures revealed that, at a time when 13% of the population belonged to a black, Asian, mixed or other ethnic group, over 48% of under-18s then in custody were classed as BAME.[12]

# Youth Policy—'A Silent Catastrophe'

## 'Gesture' Policies—Again

At a time when 95% of government money for youth services (£634 million) was going to the NCS,[13] most of its responses to the pressures facing young people still amounted to little more than 'gestures' of the kinds discussed in Chapters 13 and 14. For example:

- In September 2016 Teresa May launched a £40 million Youth Investment Fund to develop youth facilities including youth clubs in 'disadvantaged communities across England'. An additional £40 million was provided for Step Up to Serve's #iwill youth social action campaign (see Chapter 12).[14]
- As part of a wider 'serious violence strategy', in April 2018 Home Secretary Amber Rudd announced a new £11 million 'Early Intervention Youth Fund' to help community projects steer young people away from crime.[15] The following month Sadiq Khan allocated £1.15 million to 34 local projects specifically for tackling knife crime in London.[16]
- In May 2018 the second funding round of an £80 million Life Chances Fund awarded over £19 million to Sheffield City Council to 'transform the way public services are delivered in Sheffield'. Its more specific aims included tackling mental health and wellbeing issues, homelessness and youth unemployment.[17]
- A government Green Paper published in December 2017, backed by £300 million of extra funding, promised improvements to children's mental health services which included designated senior mental health leads in every school and college and new mental health support teams linked to groups of education settings.[18]

- A £90 million government initiative announced in January 2018, to be paid for with money from dormant bank and building society accounts, aimed at helping young people into employment.[19]
- In June 2018 'youth minister' Tracey Crouch announced that young people were to be made central to the broader 'loneliness strategy' launched by the government six months earlier.[20] This was supported by a £1 million two-year DfE programme to trial mental health assessments for children coming into care[21]; and by £2 million from a wider Building Connections Fund, half of which came from the Co-op Foundation.[22]

The government made a similar (and familiar) 'gesture' response focused specifically on youth work provision (see Chapter 12) in September 2018 adding £5 million to the funding it had been giving to uniformed youth organisations since 2012. This was to be used to create 5500 new places in 'deprived' communities and reduce waiting lists by recruiting more volunteers. In the same month a £1.85 million fund was launched by a 'Foundation for Social Investment' to help 'youth services' charities and social enterprises 'develop or grow their enterprise activity and income'.[23]

Some of the responses to these policies were highly critical. Within a week of its launch, for example, the serious violence strategy was dismissed by the President of ADCS as ineffective, not least because, as cuts to youth services had left young people with 'nowhere to go', it was '...providing little for local authorities to develop local responses'.[24] A Labour Party shadow minister also pointed out that £5 million for uniformed youth organisations was 'just a tiny fraction of the vast amount … cut from youth services'—cuts which since 2010 totalled £387 million and had resulted in the closure of over 600 youth centres.[25]

## Where Is the Youth Strategy?

By then, with references to the 2011 *Positive for Youth* paper notable only by their absence (see Chapter 9), some in the 'children and youth' sector, including the ADCS, were concluding that youth policy had been 'cast adrift' since responsibility for it had been moved from the

DfE to the DCMS.[26] By September 2017, CYWU/Unite was calling for a youth affairs minister to be appointed at Cabinet level to co-ordinate youth policies[27] while in June 2018 an All Party Parliamentary Group (APPG) on a Fit and Healthy Childhood recommended a new 'department for children' led by a secretary of state.[28]

Months before concern had also been expressed that the government was 'dragging its heels' over the new youth strategy promised at an Ambition conference in November 2016. This was intended to 'highlight the opportunities that come out of the move to the DCMS, and how we can give young people greater engagement with our sporting and cultural heritage'.[29] Despite reaffirming the commitment immediately after the 2017 General Election,[30] by October the most Tracey Crouch was promising, however, was that 'any announcement ... will be made in due course'.[31] When this eventually came the following month the proposal for a stand-alone youth policy had been dropped in favour of a 'civil society' policy statement within which both youth work and social action would have a place.[32]

Though not a direct response to this decision, an LGA strategy paper published three weeks later urged that youth services should 'ideally operate within a framework established by a clear and ambitious national vision for young people'. This, it said, was not then happening as 'neither youth services nor young people are listed in the department's priorities or in the minister's role on the departmental website...'[33]

Within the fragmented and often narrowly departmentalised policies encouraged by this strategic vacuum, the government played down the impact of eight years of austerity on core public services. By 2018 some £16 billion had been stripped out of local authority budgets in England[34] and the average increases in real per-capita health spending had fallen from 5.4% a year between 1996–1997 and 2009–2010 to just 0.6% per year from then to 2015–2016.[35] Huge gaps thus existed in services which in the past had been young people's first ports of call for both developmental and preventative interventions.

*The toll of austerity—on schools ...*

The (now devolved) budgets of perhaps the key such provision, schools, were by 2018 stretched to and indeed often beyond their capacity for carrying out even their core curricular functions. A joint inquiry by the Health and Education Select Committees reported in May 2017 that their mental health support for young people was often 'the first thing to go', with 80% of the primary school heads surveyed saying that lack of money was preventing them from providing counsellors.[36] A secondary school head also pointed to cuts in pastoral care resulting from the squeeze on school budgets.[37]

A second joint Select Committee report in May 2018 concluded that pressures on the teaching force meant that schools and colleges would struggle to appoint the mental health leads proposed by the government.[38] In the same month, an NSPCC Freedom of Information request to NHS Trusts in England revealed that since 2014–2015 schools had made nearly 124,000 referrals to Child and Adolescent Mental Health Service (CAMHS) of which 31% had been refused treatment because they failed to meet the required criteria.[39]

*… council children's services …*

The cumulative impacts of austerity on local authority services were for young people often even more immediate and direct—as indicated earlier, for example, by how many councils were turning away those who were homeless. Here, 'children's services' particularly felt the effects. By January 2018, the LGA was warning that, with these services now putting the main financial pressure on councils, an estimated £2 billion funding gap needed to be filled if children were not to be left at risk. Challenged on this situation by the Education Select Committee, children's minister Nadhim Zahawi conceded two months later that his department was working with the Department of Housing, Communities and Local Government 'to look at funding properly'. More rhetorically, he talked, too, of the advantages of identifying families needing 'early intervention' before a baby was born and of 'the need to make a bigger difference' by 'get(ting) smarter, sometimes sharing data in government'.[40]

However, the reality of his claim that funding for children's services had increased in real-terms was tested two months later when it emerged that, though between 2015–2016 and 2016–2017 total spending on children and young people's services had risen from £9.14 billion to £9.18 billion (0.0044%), the number of referrals to 'children's social care' over that year had gone up by 3.97% to over 646,000.[41] Figures from the ONS showed that councils were budgeting to spend £542 million more (6.8%) on children's services in 2018–2019 than they had in 2017–2018—a faster rate of increase than for any of their services including adult social care.[42] By September, Somerset's response to these pressures was to propose that, in addition to cutting its spending on young carers by £242,000, its 'early help service' budget would be reduced by £1.68 million by 2019–2020 by cutting staffing levels and increasing caseloads.[43]

On the basis of the findings of a research report it had commissioned, the LGA, backed later by the ADCS, had already dismissed as 'misguided and shortsighted' the broader DfE view that there was no evidence that increased spending made services more effective. According to the report, the main drivers of the cost of children's services were largely out of councils' control, with deprivation accounting for 31% of the variation in their spending and emerging as the single biggest factor.[44]

Edward Timpson—children's minister for five years in the previous government—was also by 2018 describing as 'tough' the economic circumstances in which children's services departments were operating and insisted that 'those holding the purse strings ... be mindful of when that line (of adequate funding) has been crossed.'[45] Launching an all-party report, his predecessor Tim Loughton, too, talked of a crisis in child protection which—though without acknowledging he had been a member the government which had imposed the policy—he blamed on the 'woeful underfunding' of local authorities.[46] In response to the ADCS president's comment that there was 'no fat left to trim', a DfE senior official, while accepting that the overall 'difficult fiscal position', nonetheless warned that the 2019 Treasury Spending Review was unlikely to come up with 'a lot more money' for children's services.[47]

*... mental health services*

CAMHS—another public service often crucial for young people experiencing serious problems—was by 2018 also facing major policy and budgetary pressures. Over a year after a vice president of the British Medical Association (BMA) had labelled 2016 'the worst year in NHS history',[48] an assistant director of Barnardo's, Britain's largest children's charity, was still talking about educational psychologists

*… pulling their hair out—they haven't got the resources. They can't respond as fast as they need to.*[49]

In a report published in June 2018 the Association of Child Psychotherapists described this situation as a 'silent catastrophe'[50] while a second joint report of the Health and Social Care and Education Select Committees concluded that the government's December 2017 Green Paper on mental health services for young people 'lack(ed) ambition and will provide no help to the majority of children who desperately need it'.[51]

*… and the criminal justice system*

When in 2017 the MP David Lammy started his 'review into the over-representation of …(BME) individuals in the criminal justice system', he assumed, he said, that many of the causes and solutions would be traced to wider structural problems such as poverty. By the time he reported, however, his conclusion was that there was 'a significant problem in the … system itself' with 'the treatment of BAME young people showing that this problem is getting worse'.[52]

# Youth Services

*From deconstruction …*

When set alongside the under-funding of such core services, the deconstruction of local authority youth work provision was largely treated by policy-makers as a minor sacrifice—necessary for channelling some extra funding to higher priorities. Its plight only began to attract political attention when new moral panics about 'youth' emerged, some focused on their mental health problems but, with much more urgency, others on their involvement in knife crime. As a result youth work was presented as needed largely as a 'preventative intervention' into 'risky' lives of a small minority of the age group. Little account was taken, therefore, of the evidence that in 2013 up to 35%—between 800,000 and one million 10–15 year olds—had by choice been engaging at least one day a week in an open access youth work facility offering informal educational opportunities as well as more personal support where needed.[53]

*... to reconstruction?*
With the 2017 British social attitudes survey revealing immediately after the 2017 General Election that public support for austerity was 'collapsing',[54] cracks began to appear in the monolithic hold of neo-liberal thinking on youth policy-making. Despite the deep Brexit uncertainties constraining many of its domestic policies, the government thus made gesture responses to this changing public mood. Though seen at the time as falling well short of what by then was needed,[55] it for example committed to sending an extra £20 billion a year on NHS by 2023.[56]

Initially these shifts in priorities did not extend to offering any new protection to what remained of local authority Youth Services. As far back as December 2014 youth minister Rob Wilson had restated the government's refusal to make them more reliably 'statutory'.[57] In January 2018, Crouch dismissed a Labour Party demand that NCS's effectiveness be evaluated against that of 'traditional youth services'[58] even though it emerged later in the year that the scheme had reached only 12% of the eligible age group in the previous three years.[59]

Pressure to strengthen the Youth Service's statutory base continued to build, however. In the run-up up to the 2017 General Election the YMCA proposed that all local authorities be required to have a youth services strategy.[60] When six months later the government reneged on its commitment to produce its own youth policy strategy, the IYW pressed it to be more proactive in protecting the Service.[61] The following May ADCS, UK Youth and London Youth, using the opportunity offered by the first Parliamentary scrutiny of the sector since 2011—an APPG on Youth Affairs—all advocated revived state-funding for youth work provision. By mid-2018, too, the NYA was urging that consultations on the government's proposed 'civil society strategy' be used to argue for a 'youth covenant' setting out a cross-departmental commitment to young people, to include a role for them in political decisions and investment in youth provision.[62]

Over the following months, the policy environment shifted sufficiently to take on some of these demands. Though still strongly influenced by increasing rates of knife crime, in July 2018 the Labour Party committed itself if elected to make local authority Youth Services statutory and, to oversee and resource them across England, to establish a national body with dedicated and guaranteed funding. Its consultation paper on these proposals also included a draft charter which set out an entitlement for all young people to 'inclusive, open access youth services'.[63]

Though much more cautiously, the government's position was also changed by commitments made in its Civil Society Strategy, published in August 2018. Consideration of the Youth Service within this was framed by a recognition that 'despite the pressures on public sector finances new thinking has emerged, supporting innovation, new partnerships, and collaboration spanning public, private, and civil society partners.' As evidence of these claimed advances, the paper pointed to 'Local Young People's Foundations' which had brought together 'charity, local government, business, and the independent youth sector'; mutuals; and the Onside Youth Zone programme. While accepting 'the priority that local authorities must place on … child protection', it also acknowledged 'the transformational impact that youth services and trained youth workers can have, especially for young people facing multiple barriers or disadvantage'. As 'much has happened to change the way these services are provided' since the guidance on local authorities' statutory duty was last revised in 2012, it thus proposed a review to 'provide greater clarity of government's expectations, including the value added by good youth work.' It also made a commitment to improving the quality of youth work's data and evidence base.[64]

By the autumn of 2018, therefore, both the main political parties were, to different degrees, changing their positions on local authority Youth Services. These, however—operating largely still in a policy vacuum—remained under increasing budgetary pressures as was evidenced by the Somerset proposals, outlined above, which included plans to cut the Youth Service budget by another £239,000.[65] (In 2011–2012 Somerset had announced plans to cut its Youth Service budget by 75% within three years and to stop funding for 18 youth groups.[66])

However, though commitments to providing new and more secure state funding were vital, the Services' virtual disappearance across

England in the previous decade somewhat paradoxically posed a broader challenge—one which other over-bureaucratised public services were facing, particularly in how they related to their users. This was to use the austerity-enforced gaps and empty spaces as opportunities to, in fundamental ways, re-imagine the form of the state and also non-state structures through which open access youth work might be provided.

If for example the 'fit' between state structures and open access youth work was to be made more comfortable than it often had been in the past within many local authority Youth Services, such re-imagining would need to engage with some difficult bottom-line questions. As a minimum these included:

- How could decision-making structures and procedures be developed which gave greater access both to young people and to practitioners (paid and voluntary), including how to prioritise and allocate funding?
- What kinds of management structures were needed and possible, through to some senior levels, which were designed and could remain responsive to what is distinctive about open access youth work and to workers' face-to-face experience of implementing it?
- What buildings could and should be provided which, as well as offering 'state-of-the-art' facilities, were located and designed to tap into young people's peer group, community and cultural loyalties and which, both immediately but also over time, could be used flexibly?
- How could locally-based training and supervision for youth workers and workers' forums be re-established which, often focused on on-going practice, were designed to be personally and collectively as well as occupationally and organisationally developmental?
- What evaluation processes could be developed and applied, reliant less on 'measuring' short-term, purportedly 'hard' outcomes, which worked with and through person-centred qualitative methodologies more congruent with the practice?

Any would-be provider—state or non-state—seeking in late-2018 to operate on those principles would almost certainly find themselves confronting powerful state and non-state policy-makers whose thinking and practice were still deeply and often uncritically embedded within neo-liberal ideas. To have any prospect of breaking through these barriers such 'innovators' would first need to draw systematically on the critiques of those ideas which were only just surfacing and of the austerity policies these had generated. They would then also need both to take advantage of and add to the recently re-emerging awareness of the need for a more active and indeed proactive state role—local and national. Only then would it be likely that openings might be created for conceiving and implementing youth policies which took seriously young people's self-defined needs and their expectations of provision for their non-school non-work time, and which were proactively supportive of open access youth work as a contributing practice to that provision.

Given the history of the previous decade, by late-2018 these remained challenging tasks offering few if any guarantees of success.

# Notes

1. Peter S. Goodman, 2018, 'Britain's Big Freeze: In Britain, Austerity Is Changing Everything', *New York Times*, 28 May.
2. John Lanchester, 2010, *Whoops! Why Everyone Owes Everyone and No One Can Pay*, London, Penguin Books.
3. John Lanchester, 2018, 'After the Fall', *London Review of Books*, Vol. 40, No. 13, 5 July.
4. House of Commons Briefing Paper 7096, 2018, *Poverty in the UK: Statistics*, published 23 April, p. 11.
5. Tristan Donovan, 2018a, 'Child Poverty Hits Highest Level in Decade', *CYPN*, 22 March.
6. Patrick Butler, 2018, 'New Study Finds 4.5 Million UK Children Living in Poverty', *Guardian*, 17 September.
7. Joe Lepper, 2018a, 'Youth Homelessness Rise Linked to Welfare Reforms, Report Finds', *CYPN*, 16 April.
8. Denis Campbell, 2018, 'NHS Unit on the Frontline in a Child Mental Health Crisis', *Guardian*, 3 July.
9. Sean Coughlin, 2018, 'Loneliness More Likely to Affect Young People', BBC, 10 April, https://www.bbc.co.uk/news/education-43711606; Tristan Donovan, 2018b, 'Loneliness a Big Issue Among Young People, Say Youth Workers', *CYPN*, 10 August.

10. Sally Weale and Matthew Holmes, 2018, '"Panic Attacks and Crying": How the New GCSEs Affected Pupils', *Guardian*, 22 June.
11. Sarah Marsh and Amanda Boateng, 2018, 'Quarter of UK Girls Self-Harm at 14, "Deeply Worrying" Survey Reveals', *Guardian*, 29 August.
12. Neil Puffett, 2018a, 'Surge in Proportion of Black, Asian and Ethnic Minority Children in Custody', *CYPN*, 8 June.
13. Neil Puffett, 2018b, 'NCS Found to Account for 95 per cent of Government Youth Service Spend', *CYPN*, 22 June.
14. GOV.UK, 2016, 'Government Delivers £80 million Boost to Help Give Young People the Best Start in Life', https://www.gov.uk/government/news/government-delivers-80-million-boost-to-help-give-young-people-the-best-start-in-life; Neil Puffett, 2017a, 'Government Announces Beneficiaries of £40m Youth Fund', *CYPN*, 5 September.
15. Neil Puffett, 2018c, 'Serious Violence Strategy: Youth Projects to Get £11m', *CYPN*, 9 April; Neil Puffett, 2018d, 'Youth Leaders Appointed to Government's Serious Violence Taskforce', *CYPN*, 25 April.
16. Tristan Donovan, 2018c, 'Sadiq Khan Announces Funding for Youth Projects to Tackle Knife Crime', *CYPN*, 11 May.
17. Government Outcomes Lab, 2018, 'Life Chances Fund: Latest News', https://golab.bsg.ox.ac.uk/basics/outcomes-funds/life-chances-fund-latest-news/; Neil Puffett, 2018e, 'Council Received £19m Government Funding for Youth Project', *CYPN*, 8 May.
18. Joe Lepper, 2018b, 'MPs Criticise "Unambitious" Children's Mental Health Green Paper', *CYPN*, 9 May.
19. Neil Puffett, 2018f, 'Government Announces £90m for Youth Employment Initiatives', *CYPN*, 4 January.
20. Neil Puffett, 2018g, 'Young People "Central to Government Loneliness Strategy"', *CYPN*, 22 June.
21. Neil Puffett, 2018h, 'DfE Announces £1m Funding for Mental Health Check Pilots', *CYPN*, 14 June.
22. Joe Lepper, 2018c, 'Fund Launches to Tackle Youth Loneliness', *CYPN*, 15 August.
23. Gabriella Jozwiak, 2018, 'Uniformed Youth Groups to Expand with £5m Funding Boost', *CYPN*, 10 September; Neil Puffett, 2018j, 'Initiative to Help Youth Services Raise Commercial Income Launches', *CYPN*, 5 September.
24. Neil Puffett, 2018k, 'Violence Strategy "Provides Little" to Help Council Efforts, Children's Leaders Warn', *CYPN*, 11 April.

25. Unison, 2016, *The Damage: A Future at Risk—Cuts in Youth Services*, London, Unison; Robert Booth, 2018, 'Tories Plan to Enlist Disadvantaged Children as Guides and Scouts', *Guardian*, 10 September.
26. Tristan Donovan, 2018d, 'Give Youth Work Remit Back to DfE, Children's Services Leaders Urge', *CYPN*, 2 July.
27. Joe Lepper, 2017a, 'Union Calls for Creation of Cabinet-Level Youth Affairs Role', *CYPN*, 22 September.
28. Joe Lepper, 2018d, 'MPs Urge Creation of New Department for Children', *CYPN*, 25 June.
29. Adam Offord, 2016, 'Government to Publish Three-Year Youth Strategy', *CYPN*, 8 November.
30. Gabriella Jozwiak, 2017, 'Sector Leaders Assured Youth Strategy will Continue', *CYPN*, 23 June.
31. Sophie Eminson, 2017, 'Government "Dragging Heels" on New Youth Policy', *CYPN*, 27 October.
32. Neil Puffett, 2017b, 'Government Ditches Youth Policy Statement', *CYPN*, 17 November.
33. Joe Lepper, 2017b, 'Councils Warn of Lack of Government Vision for Youth Services', *CYPN*, 6 December.
34. Patrick Butler, 2018a, 'Council Cuts Leave Vulnerable People at Risk, Says Tory Peer', *Guardian*, 3 July.
35. Institute of Fiscal Studies, 2017, *UK Health Spending*, Nuffield Foundation, https://www.ifs.org.uk/uploads/publications/bns/BN201.pdf; Kailash Chand, 2017, op. cit., https://www.theguardian.com/healthcare-network/2017/jan/04/2016-was-the-worst-year-in-nhs-history-we-must-fight-for-its-survival.
36. Alice Ross, 2017, 'Schools Cutting Mental Health Services to Plug Funding Gaps, Warn MPs', *Guardian*, 2 May.
37. Sally Weale, 2017, 'Schools Fear Impact of Budget Cuts Amid Girls' Mental Health Crisis', *Guardian*, 23 September.
38. Joe Lepper, 2018e, 'MPs Criticise "Unambitious" Children's Mental Health Green Paper', *CYPN*, 9 May.
39. Neil Puffett, 2018l, 'Third of Children Referred by Schools Denied Mental Health Treatment', *CYPN*, 14 May.
40. Neil Puffett, 2018m, 'DfE "Examining Children's Services Funding", Zahawi Reveals', *CYPN*, 14 March.
41. Neil Puffett, 2018n, 'Timpson Warns of "Crossing the Line" on Children's Services Funding', *CYPN*, 26 June.

42. Neil Puffett, 2018p, 'Children's Services Spending to Increase by £542m', *CYPN*, 29 June.

43. Joe Lepper, 2018f, 'Struggling Council Outlines Major Cuts to Early Help and Youth Services', *CYPN*, 4 September.

44. Tristan Donovan, 2018e, 'DfE "Misguided and Shortsighted" on Children's Services Spending', *CYPN*, 21 June; Neil Puffett, 2018q, 'ADCS Conference: "No Fat Left to Trim for Children's Services, Gallimore Warns"', *CYPN*, 5 July.

45. Neil Puffett, 2018n, op. cit.

46. Patrick Butler, 2018b, 'Tory Ex-minister Blames Cuts for Crisis in Child Protection', *Guardian*, 11 July.

47. Darren Hayes, 2018, 'DfE Warns of Uphill Struggle to Secure Children's Services Funding', *CYPN*, 9 July.

48. Kailash Chand, 2017, '2016 Was the Worst Year in NHS History—We Must Fight for Survival', *Guardian*, 4 January.

49. Mark Townsend, 2018, 'Some Children Reach the Brink of Suicide Before Getting Help with Mental Health, Charity Warns', *Guardian*, 5 May.

50. Caroline Davies, 2018, 'Mental Health Services for the Young Is NHS's "silent catastrophe"', *Guardian*, 25 June.

51. Joe Lepper, 2018e, op. cit.

52. David Lammy, 2017, 'The Bias in Our Justice System Is a Social Timebomb', *Guardian*, 8 September.

53. NCVYS, *Youth Report 2013*, p. 2.

54. Patrick Butler, 2017, 'UK Survey Finds Huge Support for Ending "Austerity"', *Guardian*, 28 June.

55. Nick Bostock, 2018, '£20 bn NHS Funding Boost by 2023 "Still Falls Short", GPs Warn', 18 June, https://www.gponline.com/20bn-nhs-funding-boost-2023-still-falls-short-gps-warn/article/1485253.

56. Nick Triggle, 2018, 'NHS Funding: Theresa May Announces £20b Boost', BBC, 17 June, https://www.bbc.co.uk/news/health-44495598.

57. Laura McCardle, 2014, 'Youth Minister Rob Wilson Rejects Statutory Services Motion', *CYPN*, 4 December.

58. Joe Lepper, 2018g, 'Crouch Dismisses Calls for NCS to Be Evaluated Against Traditional Youth Services', *CYPN*, 26 January.

59. Robert Booth, 2018, op. cit.

60. Neil Puffett and Joe Lepper, 2017, 'Political Parties Urged to Make Youth Services Statutory', *CYPN*, 11 May.
61. Darren Hayes, 2017, 'Institute for Youth Work "Seeks Assurances" Over Government's Commitment to Young People', *CYPN*, 20 November.
62. Tristan Donovan, 2018e, 'op. cit.'; Joe Lepper, 2018h, 'MPs Launch Inquiry into Role of Youth work', *CYPN3*, 29 May; Joe Lepper, 2018j, 'NYA Calls for Civil Society to Include "youth covenant"', *CYPN*, 30 May.
63. Neil Puffett, 2018r, 'Labour to Establish National Youth Service Body with Protected Funding', *CYPN*, 31 July; Peter Walker, 2018, 'Labour Vows to Make Provision of Youth Services Compulsory', *Guardian*, 31 July.
64. HM Government, 2018, *Civil Society Strategy: Building a Society That Works for Everyone*, pp. 41–42
65. Joe Lepper, 2018f, op. cit.
66. Janaki Mahadevan, 2011, 'Somerset Youth Centres Face Closure as Council Cuts Youth Service by 75 per cent', *CYPN*, 4 February.

# Further Reading

Batsleer, Janet. 2010. 'Youth Work Prospects: Back to the Future?', in Batsleer, Janet and Davies, Bernard (eds), *What Is Youth Work?* Exeter: Learning Matters, pp. 153–165.

Davies, Bernard. 2017. 'Beyond the Local Authority Youth Service', *Youth and Policy*. No. 116. May, pp. 24–44.

de St. Croix, Tania. 2016, *Grassroots Youth Work: Policy, Passion and Resistance in Practice*. Bristol: Policy Press.

Farthing, Rys. 2012. 'Why Youth Participation? Justifications and Critiques of Youth Participation Using New Labour's Policies as a Case Study'. *Youth and Policy*. No. 109. September, pp. 71–97.

Goodman, Peter S. 2018. 'Britain's Big Freeze: In Britain, Austerity Is Changing Everything'. *New York Times*. 28 May.

HM Government. 2018. *Civil Society Strategy: Building a Society That Works for Everyone*. August.

Jeffs, Tony. 2015. 'What Sort of Future?', in Stanton, Naomi (ed), *Innovation in Youth Work: Thinking in Practice*. London: George Williams College, pp. 11–17 (Extended version at *Youth and Policy*. No. 114. May 2015, pp. 75–95).

Labour Party. 2018. 'Labour Party Consultation 2018: Building a Statutory Youth Service'. August. https://www.policyforum.labour.org.uk/commissions/education/youth-services.

Lanchester, John. 2010. *Whoops! Why Everyone Owes Everyone and No One Can Pay*. London: Penguin Books.

Lanchester, John. 2018. 'After the Fall'. *London Review of Books*. Vol. 40, No. 13. 5 July, pp. 3–8.

London Youth. 2013. *Hunch: A Vision for Youth in Post Austerity Britain* (2nd ed.). London: London Youth, https://issuu.com/londonyouth/docs/hunch__february_2013_.

Ord, Jon. 2016. *Youth Work Process, Product and Practice: Creating an Authentic Curriculum in Work with Young People*. London: Routledge, Chapter 15.

Taylor, Tony, et al. 2018. 'The Impact of Neo-Liberalism on the Character and Purpose of English Youth Work and Beyond', in Alldred, Pam, et al., (eds), *The Sage Handbook of Youth Work Practice*. London: Sage, pp. 84–97.

# Index

A

A4E 70

Accountability in youth work 13, 78, 111, 151, 190. *See also* Impacts/outcomes

Accreditation of Prior Learning 283

Action Plan 24

ADCS 157, 257, 356, 359, 361

'Adolescent brain development' 161

Adult-imposed labels 11

Ages of students recruited 308

*Aiming High for Young People* 25, 29, 39

Albemarle Report 12

Alinsky, Saul 110

Allen, Graham 116

All Party Parliamentary Group. *See* APPG

Ambition 129, 238, 258–262, 264, 265, 269, 270, 310, 357

merger with UK Youth 129, 260–262

and social impact bonds 146, 163, 248

take-over of NCVYS 259, 260, 269, 270

Ancillary contributor 169

Anti-social behaviour orders (ASBOs) 24, 57, 241, 247, 328

AO.com 240

APPG 240

Fit and Healthy Childhood - 2018 357

Youth Affairs – 2018 361

Applied Quantitative Research consultancy 166

Apprenticeships (modern) 284, 293. *See also* Training for youth workers

© The Editor(s) (if applicable) and The Author(s), under exclusive license to Springer Nature Switzerland AG, part of Springer Nature 2019
B. Davies, *Austerity, Youth Policy and the Deconstruction of the Youth Service in England*, https://doi.org/10.1007/978-3-030-03886-1

Apprenticeship schemes 162
APYCO 57, 58, 305
AQR International consultancy 175,
    269
Area Based Grant scheme 51, 256
Armed services and young recruits
    221
ASDA 189
Association for Young People's
    Health 131
Association of Chief Executives of
    Voluntary Organisations
    (ACEVO) 111
Association of Child Psychotherapists
    360
Association of Directors of Children's
    Services. *See* ADCS
Association of Principal Youth and
    Community Officers. *See*
    APYCO
Audit Commission 71, 114
Austerity 4, 7, 53, 67, 75, 77, 89,
    97, 112, 204, 238, 255,
    305, 306, 332, 343, 353,
    357, 358, 361, 363, 364
'Austerity' cuts 77
'Austerity' policies 4


BA degree (Community and Youth
    Work) 285, 293, 306
Balls, Ed 24, 182
BAME 355, 360. *See also* Young
    people, BAME/BME
Banking crisis (2007-2008) 1, 29,
    67, 160, 209, 336, 353
Banking system 1

Bank of England 5
Barclays Bank 98
Barking and Dagenham, London
    Borough of 249
Barnardo's 263, 360
Barnet 37
Behaviour modification 36, 336
Berry, Sian 91, 101, 346
Best Value Statutory Guidance paper
    257, 272
Bexley, London Borough of 76
Big Lottery Fund. *See* BLF
Big Music project 270
Big Society 109, 110, 112–114, 116,
    135, 186, 255
    Bank/Capital 110, 112, 113, 117,
        264
    Big Society Fund 113, 329
    community organisers 110, 112,
        114
    Network 112
Big Society Blueprint Programme
    264
'Bonfire of the quangos' 291
Birmingham 200, 220, 221, 255
Birmingham City Council 75, 76
Birmingham St Paul's Community
    Trust 255
Birmingham University 303
    Jubilee Centre for Character and
        Virtues 127, 136
Birmingham Youth Action Network
    255
Bite the Ballot 265
Black, Asian and Minority Ethnic
    (young people). *See* BAME/
    BME
Blacke, Fiona 56, 74, 146, 310

Blair, Tony 23, 25, 26, 31, 33–35, 45, 51
BLF 224, 249
  'Reaching communities' programme 95
Blunkett, David 182
BMA 359
BME 13, 264, 293, 360. *See also* Young people, BAME/BME
Bolton Lads and Girls Club 54, 90, 239
Boys' Brigade 217, 219, 220
Bracey, Michael 337
Bracknell Forest Borough Council 76, 305
Bradford/Bradford Youth Service 91, 133, 327
Bradford College 305
Brexit 265, 361
Brighton/Brighton and Hove City Council 75, 331
British Chamber of Commerce 97
British Medical Association. *See* BMA
British social attitudes survey 2017 361
British Youth Council. *See* BYC
'Broken society' 185
Brown, Gordon 23, 24, 28, 29, 33–35, 37, 51, 182
Bubb, Steve 111
Buckinghamshire/Buckinghamshire County Council 32, 90
Business/businesses. *See* Private sector/businesses
Business in the Community 99, 183
Business models 13, 260, 268
BYC 259, 264, 265, 328, 334, 344

C
Cabinet Office 73, 74, 78, 85, 93, 113, 128, 142, 158, 163, 188, 192, 197, 198, 200, 203, 204, 223, 244–247, 253, 268
  Outcomes Framework 2014 78
Cadet Forces/Bursary scheme vi, 166, 217, 219, 221
Calderdale Gay and Lesbian Youth 257
Camden, London Borough of 75
Cameron, David 3, 5, 68–70, 75, 109–112, 114, 116, 118, 128–130, 132, 135, 182–186, 189–191, 195, 207, 212, 255, 265, 329
CAMHS 311, 354, 358, 359
Cantle report 35, 114
Capabilities and character 168
Capita 93, 101, 115
Carillion 5
Carnegie trust 263
Case studies 24, 162, 164, 169, 217, 222, 328
Casey, Louise 133, 138
Casey report 133
  and concentration on Muslims 133
  and 'integration' 133
  and 'social cohesion' 133
Catalyst consortium 78, 152, 267, 339
Catch 22 187, 188, 192, 263
Centre for Ageing Better 111
Centre for Crime and Justice Studies 119

Centre for Social Justice 116, 123, 185

Centre for Youth Impact. *See* CYI

CETYCW 282, 283, 288

Challenge, The 185–188

Changing the Trajectory - Charting a New Course for Youth Services 259, 266

'Character Awards' scheme 128

'Character'/character training 3, 127, 135, 160, 182, 221

Charitable status 342

Charities 3, 69, 75, 96, 99, 110, 111, 113, 117, 145, 185, 189, 196, 206, 223–226, 237, 239, 248, 249, 256, 263, 313, 331, 356, 360, 362

Chelsea and Kensington, London Borough of 93, 94, 282

Cheshire County Council 333

Chichester, University of 306

Child and Adolescent Mental Health Service. *See* CAMHS

Child care v

Child protection v, 29, 134, 359, 362. *See also* Children (and Young People) services prevention 31 safeguarding 73

Children Acts 27

*Children and Young People Now. See* CYPN

Children and Young People's Plans 28

Children (and Young People) services 24, 26, 28, 31, 46, 57, 74, 77, 134, 148, 257, 287, 358, 359

Children and Young People's Workforce Strategy 289

Children's Improvement Board 291

Children's Plan 2007 25

Children's Services Network. *See* CSN

Children's trusts 28, 51, 289

Children's Workforce Development Council. *See* CWDC

ChooseYouth 259, 289, 332, 334, 335, 347
First AGM 334
Manifesto 334

Chorley Borough Council 240

Chorley Onside centre 240

CHYPS 58, 72, 76, 146, 171, 242, 244, 257, 261, 264, 267, 295, 308, 310, 336

City and Guilds London Institute 283

City Gear 226

'City Pitch' 96

Civil liberties 28

Civil society organisations. *See* Voluntary (youth) sector/ organisations

Civil society policy statement 357

Civil Society Strategy 2018 361, 362, 368

Class 3, 111, 225, 354

Cleverdon, Julia 183, 191, 222

Climbè, Victoria 29

Clothworkers' Foundation 96

Clubs for Young People 264, 275

Coalition (Government) vi, 4, 7, 8, 28, 67, 70, 72–74, 77, 92, 98, 113, 116, 118, 131, 133, 141, 157, 166, 171, 182, 183, 239, 243, 247,

255, 264, 267, 292, 305,
332, 337
Collaboration 2, 4, 24, 97, 113, 207,
258, 260, 261, 284, 309,
318, 362. *See also* Voluntary
(youth) sector/organisations
Collectivism - collective organisation
3, 227
collective campaigning 183
Commissioning/commissioners 4,
31–33, 51, 52, 68–70, 77,
78, 142, 143, 145–147,
157, 162, 163, 166–169,
218, 243, 244, 246, 247,
264, 267, 295. *See also*
Privatisation
'bid-candy' 69
Community and voluntary sector.
*See* Voluntary (youth)
sector/organisations
Community and youth Workers'
Union. *See* CYWU/Unite
Community cohesion 34, 35, 114,
205, 247
Community organisers. *See* Big
Society
Community safety teams 24
Community service 11, 52, 181, 182
Community, Youth and Playworkers
section (CYPW) 318
'Competence'/'competencies'
281–283, 285–287, 292,
296, 305, 317
Composition of the student body
308
Compulsion 223
Compulsory 'national service' 182
Confederation of British Industry
(CBI) 282

Confederation of Heads of Young
People's Services. *See*
CHYPS
Conferences and seminars 337
Conflicting aims 27
Connexions Service 25–29, 45, 90
Conservative Party 109, 112, 120,
130, 133, 182, 183, 185,
189, 191, 221, 266, 293
*Constructive activities* 50
ContactPoint 28
'Contest' strategy 34
Contracting Out 32, 68, 331
Co-operatives. *See* Mutuals
Co-op Foundation 224, 356
'Cornerstones' 336
Corporate Citizenship consultancy
183
Coulson, Andy 195
Council for Education and Training
of Youth and Community
Workers. *See* CETYCW
Counter-Terrorism and Security Act
132
Course placements 197, 311
accredited placement centres 313
Coventry/Coventry City Council
333
Creative Collisions 258, 273
Criminal justice system 360
Crouch, Tracey 158, 190, 356, 357,
361
Croydon, London Borough of 118,
240
CSN 246, 247
Cumbria County Council 32
Cuts to youth service. *See* Youth
Service (local authority)
'Cutting the Cake' briefing paper 52

CWDC 288–292, 297–300, 319, 320, 339
CYI 79, 259, 260, 262, 265, 273, 337
*CYPN* vii, 17, 40, 58, 61, 63, 73, 75, 84, 95, 97, 256–258, 342, 349
CYWU 286, 288, 289, 304, 339, 357
CYWU/Unite 289, 332–334, 337, 339
Community, Youth and Playworkers section 318
*The Future of Youth Work* 333, 346

D

D2N2 Youth Work Alliance 327
DCLG 35, 36, 117–119, 124, 125, 245, 257, 272
DCMS 158, 199, 203, 269, 357
DCSF 24, 25, 39, 41, 48, 52, 55, 56, 58, 62
DDYP 176, 245–247, 253
Defending youth work/Youth Service 327, 343. *See also* ChooseYouth; CYWU/ Unite; Green Party; IDYW; IYW; Labour Party; Liberal Democrats; Plaid Cymru; Unison; Young people, activism, campaigning
Delivering Differently for Young People. *See* DDYP
Deloitte consultancy 115, 122, 185
*Demonstrable outcomes* 60
De Montfort University 313
  Youth Service enquiry 59
Demos think tank 128

Department for Culture, Media and Sport. *See* DCMS
Department for Education and Science. *See* DES
Department for Education. *See* DfE
Department for Education and Science (DfES) 31, 38, 50, 58, 61, 175
Department of Children, Schools and Families. *See* DCSF
Department of Communities and Local Government. *See* DCLG
Department of Health. *See* DoH
Department of Housing, Communities and Local Government 358
Department of Work and Pensions. *See* DWP
Derby, University of 312, 322
DES 40, 175, 190, 285, 288
de St Croix, Tania 192, 208, 210, 214, 297, 300, 343
Detached youth work/youth workers 26, 28, 40, 72, 209, 336
Devon 94
Devon County Council 330, 331
DfE 72, 82, 98, 127, 128, 134, 137, 138, 144, 163, 173, 175, 199, 238, 252, 257, 261, 269, 291, 292, 298, 300, 335, 341, 356, 357, 359
DfEE 284
Dip HE (Community and Youth Work) 285, 307
Disability 26, 55, 111, 135, 217, 306, 330. *See also* Young people, disabled
DoH 117

'Doing more for less' 69
Dormant bank/building society
    accounts 249, 356
Dorset Youth Association 310
Drifting 'missions' 262
Duke of Edinburgh Award Scheme
    184
Duncan-Smith, Iain 116
Durham, University of 304
DWP 117, 247
DYS Space Ltd 94

E
Ealing, London Borough of 90
Early Day Motion. *See* EDM
Early help 92, 172
Early intervention 92, 116, 161,
    249, 329, 358
    early intervention foundation
    117, 118
    early intervention funding 118
    Foundation. *See* EIF
    Parenting Early Intervention
    Programme 116
    Youth Fund 355
Early Intervention Grant 68, 118,
    151, 165
Easterhouse estate 116, 123
East London, University of 306
Easy cuts option 158
ECM 27–29, 31, 37, 39, 48–50, 59,
    77, 287
EDM 91, 114, 335
Education Act 1944 12
Educational policies/provision. *See*
    Schools/schooling
Educational principles and purposes
    59, 296

Education and Inspections
    Act - 2006 33, 130
    Statutory Youth Service base/
    guidance 34
Education and Training Sub-
    committee. *See* ETS
Education Maintenance Allowance.
    *See* EMA
EIF 117, 118
EMA 8, 266, 269
Employers 128, 182, 281, 283,
    284, 286–288, 291, 292,
    309–311, 313–315, 342
Empowering Young People pro-
    gramme 51, 161
Ending Gang and Youth Violence
    team 161
Endorsing youth work methods 34
Engage4Life 205
Equality Act 2010 330
Essex 90
Essex Boys and Girls Clubs 248
Ethnicity/Ethnic minority young
    people 3, 135. *See also*
    BAME/BME; Young
    people, BAME/BME
ETS 293, 294, 313, 314, 317, 318,
    341
Europe 337
European Union (EU, referendum)
    5, 6, 265
Evaluation processes 363
Every Child Matter 51
    outcomes 51
Extremism 7, 35, 131
    and childcare 132
    and higher education 132
    and schools 132

and Youth offending teams
(YOTs) 132
extremism taskforce 132
right wing extremism 132

F
Fairbridge 261
Faith sector 171
Fallon, Michael 221
Family/families 7, 23, 54, 116–120,
129, 135, 148, 150, 159,
160, 166, 168, 195, 224,
241, 288, 310, 312, 329, 358
and Coalition youth policies 247
and New Labour youth policies
52, 53, 59, 60
Feinstein, Leon 41, 48, 50, 53, 61,
62, 144
Ferguson, Rosie 128, 137
Financial crisis 2007 1, 29, 67, 160,
209
First AGM 334
'Five outcomes' 28, 48, 77
FMP 93
For-profit businesses. See Private
sector/businesses
Foundation degrees, modern. See
Training for youth workers
'Framework for ethical practice' 341
Free schools 4, 51, 200, 243
Freire, Paulo 110
Further education 132, 161

G
G4S 70, 115
Gangs/gang members 90, 96, 117,
248

Gender/gender differences 3, 12, 26,
111, 135, 218, 354
General Election Manifesto 2010
109, 183
General elections
2010 159
2015 6, 332, 335
2017 5, 6, 134, 328, 338, 357,
361
General Federation of Trade Unions
334
General Youth Work Council 339
George Williams College 173, 290,
312
Germany - Youth Volunteering pro-
gramme 187
'Gesture' policies 249, 355
'Gig economy' 8
Girlguiding 99, 100, 217, 218, 227,
229, 263, 265
Girls Brigade 217
Globalisation 5
Gloucestershire County Council 32
Glover, Jeremy 238
Gove, Michael 158, 185, 265, 268
Government funding 54, 68, 75, 77,
117, 119, 165, 239, 256,
257
Government spending 68, 117, 118,
208
Government targets 287
Greene, Stephen 189
Green Party 91, 333
Greenwich, London Borough of 256

H
Hackney, London Borough of 32

Hammersmith and Fulham, London
    Borough of 93
Hampshire County Council 76
'Hands-off' government policies 116,
    158, 327
Haringey, London Borough of 220
Harsh financial climate 59
HE 296, 303, 306, 309, 311, 314,
    316
HE/HE courses. *See* Training for
    youth workers
Health, education, social care 69
Health policies/services iv, v, 4, 30,
    69, 131, 357
Health trusts 30
Hetherington, Peter 114, 121
Higher education (HE). *See* Training
    for youth workers
Hill, Charlotte 97, 207, 224
Hilling, Julie 332
Hodge, Margaret 48, 50
Holliday, Steve 226, 228, 234
Homelessness. *See* Young people
Home Office 24, 52, 129, 131, 132,
    134, 249, 269
Hope Not Hate 265
Hope, Phil 48
Horsham District Council 90
'Hotspots' 162
House of Commons Briefing paper
    2018
    definition of young people 10
House of Commons Communities
    and Local Government
    Select Committee - 2010 36
House of Commons Communities
    and Local Government
    Select Committee - 2011
    115

House of Commons Education
    Select Committee/report
    2010–11 141, 158, 164,
    169, 205, 290, 292, 294,
    305
    definition of youth work 288
    first report 116
    NCS 187
    payment by results 78
    remit 141
    second committee report 141
    second government's response 141
House of Commons Public Accounts
    Select Committee - 2017
    119
House of Commons Select
    Committee (Health,
    Education) 358
    second joint report - 2018 358,
    360
House of Commons Select
    Education Committee.
    2010-11 293
House of Lords 334
House of Lords Select Committee
    226
Howells, Kim 26, 33, 47
Hughes, Beverly 38, 50, 51, 54, 57,
    58, 62, 63
Hunt, Aaron 330, 333
Hurd, Nick 142, 158, 163, 164,
    171, 188, 196, 222

IDYW 100, 193, 208, 259, 270,
    276, 334, 336–338, 348
    'Is the Tide Turning?' 338, 339
    Open Letter 336, 338

IMF 68
Impacts/outcomes 4, 11, 32, 53, 55,
    60, 77, 135, 136, 161, 166,
    167, 170, 221, 246, 269,
    284, 305, 336, 337. *See also*
    CYI; Measuring; Metrics;
    Monetised evidence; Social
    (investment/impact) bonds;
    Youth Service (local author-
    ity), performance measures/
    outcomes
    Cabinet Office outcomes frame-
        work 78
    evaluation processes 363
    measuring 32, 147, 170
    metrics 248
    'monetised' 78
In Defence of Youth Work. *See*
    IDYW
Independence 222
Index on happiness 130
Individuals/individualism/indi-
    vidual qualities 3, 23, 29,
    35, 54, 59, 69, 110, 114,
    132, 135, 144, 160, 161,
    167, 168, 249, 257. *See
    also* 'Character'/character
    training
    and defining problems 134
    individualistic traits 135
    'risks' 310
Informal education 11, 29, 49, 120,
    168, 209, 237, 266, 316,
    341, 360
'Information, advice and guidance'
    49, 55, 89, 152, 285, 292
    drop-in facilities 49
    One-stop shops 49

Information technology. *See* Social
    media
Inspire cards 228
Institute for Youth work. *See* IYW
Integrated children's services 27
Integrated youth support 30, 309,
    313
International Monetary Fund. *See*
    IMF
*Involving Young People in
    Commissioning* - NYA guide
    146
'Is the Tide Turning?' 338
IYW 190, 259, 265, 339–343, 350,
    351, 361
    charitable status 342
    code of conduct 341
    strategic plan 342

Jack, Linda 332, 346
Jarman, Rod 218, 220
Javid, Sajid 134
Jeffs, Tony 173, 300, 311, 319, 321
Jewish Lads' Brigade 220
JNC 94, 283, 286, 290, 293, 295,
    306, 307, 312, 314–316,
    318, 339. *See also* Youth
    workers, salaries/conditions
    of service
JNC conditions 295
JNC under pressure 314–316
Johnson, Boris 90, 111, 219
Joint Negotiating Committee. *See*
    JNC
Jordan, Amanda 183, 191, 222
Joseph Rowntrees Foundation 71

K

Kensington and Chelsea 247
Khan, Sadiq 90, 100, 355
Kids Company 257
Kings' Fund 131
Knife crime 90, 162, 355, 360, 362
Knowsley, Metropolitan Borough of
93, 94, 243, 247

L

Labour Party 73, 93, 131, 133, 190,
205, 206, 226, 291, 331,
332, 334, 338, 356, 361,
362
Labour Party/Labour governments
1997-2010 28
'Modernising' public services 53
Lambeth, London Borough of 32,
94, 256
Lammy, David 360, 367
Lancashire County Council 240
Lanchester, John 353, 364
Leamington Town Council 90
Learning Business, The 283
Learning South West 290
Leeds Beckett University 307
Leeds Metropolitan University 306
Legal obligation to provide a Youth
Service 74
Lent, Matt 270, 277, 312
Lewisham, London Borough of 94,
240
LGA 58, 71, 81, 163, 207, 242, 245,
265, 314, 315, 357–359
strategy paper 357
LGBT. See Young people
LGBT young people 257
LGiU 171, 176, 246

Liberal democrats 73, 183, 206, 332
Friends of the Youth Service 334
Licence to practice 334, 340–342
Life Chances fund 249, 355
Lifelong Learning UK. See LLUK
Liverpool 112, 186
Liverpool City Council 115
Liverpool John Moores University
306
Lloyds Banking Group 98
LLUK 288, 291
Lobbying Act 263
Local authorities 5, 12, 13, 24–30,
33, 35, 37, 46, 47, 51,
58, 71–75, 89, 92, 94,
100, 118, 119, 127, 130,
143–148, 150–152, 157,
158, 164, 165, 169, 171,
172, 181, 187, 190, 200,
207, 237, 239–247, 259,
265, 269, 283, 289, 290,
292, 295, 305, 308, 314,
332, 333, 356, 357, 359,
361, 362. See also Youth
Service (local authority);
Young people, homelessness
children services 24, 26, 28, 74,
358
conservative 73, 75
revenue support grant 68
spending cuts 207
Local authority youth service.
See Youth Service (local
authority)
Local Government Association. See
LGA
Local Government Information
Unit. See LGiU
Localism Act 244

Localism/Localism Bill vi, 114–117, 135, 150, 159, 171, 243, 258
and youth workers 114
Locality 31, 110
Local Safeguarding Children Boards 28
Local Young People's Foundations 362
London Play and Youth Work Campaign 327
London terror attack 134
London Youth 96, 128, 207, 259, 264, 275, 361
Loughton 130, 143, 157, 159, 161, 163, 164, 166, 185, 239, 243, 257
Loughton, Tim 99, 113, 142, 158, 160, 238, 267, 268, 359
Lynas, Michael 189, 203


M
Madrassah Citizenship Programme 37
Managerialism (new) 3, 336
Manchester 220, 241, 243, 337
Manchester City Council 97
Manchester Metropolitan University 306
Manchester 'terror attack' - 2017 134
Manchester, University of 304, 321
'Manifesto' 334
Market (The)/Market freedoms/ Marketisation of services 2, 4, 161
Market economy 268
*Market Provision of Positive Activities for Young People* 50, 61

Maude, Francis 93
May, Theresa 6, 113, 195, 248, 249, 355
Mayor of London 90, 219, 223, 264. *See also* Khan, Sadiq; Johnson, Boris
(Development) Fund 111
Mckinsey (Management consultancy) 185
'Measurable' societal outcomes 167
'Measured' outcomes 77
'Measure' their impacts 4
Measuring. *See* Impacts/outcomes impacts and outcomes 77, 144, 145
Mental Health Foundation 131
Mental health/services v, 9, 131, 159, 160, 195, 208, 218, 269, 355, 356, 358–360. *See also* Young people, mental health problems
2017 Green Paper 360
and youth work approaches 131
Meritocracy 248
Metrics. *See* Impacts/outcomes
Microsoft 98
Military option 182
Milliband, Ed 133, 335
Ministerial scepticism 165
Ministers' expressions of doubt 47
Ministry of Defence 219, 222
Ministry of Education 339
Ministry of Justice (MoJ) 247, 355
Modern apprenticeships. *See* Apprenticeships (modern); Training for youth workers
Monetised evidence. *See* Impacts/ outcomes
Moral panic 360

Morgan, Nicky 127, 128, 136
Mudie, George 47
Muirhead, Adam 342
Muslim/Muslims 35–38, 132, 221
  youth workers 38
  'social mobility challenge' for 135
Muslim (young people) 7, 34, 46,
    132–134, 195. *See also*
    'Prevent' strategy
  'Radicalisation' 35, 52, 195
Muslim Council of Britain 262
  mutuals support programme 93
Mutuals 69, 92–94, 166, 237, 245,
    247, 362
MyPlace/youth zones 30, 53, 54, 56,
    57, 97, 166, 237, 239, 243
  aims, provision and impacts 241
  funding 238
  and youth work 242


NAO 198, 199, 203–205
NatCen Social Research 128
National Association of Boys Clubs
    129
The National Association of Mixed
    Clubs 129, 262
National Audit Office. *See* NAO
National Children's Bureau. *See*
    NCB
National Citizen Service. *See* NCS
National Council for Vocational
    Qualifications. *See* NCVQ
National Council for Voluntary
    Organisations. *See* NCVO
National Council for Voluntary
    Youth Organisations. *See*
    NCVYS

National Occupational Standards -
    Youth work 284, 285, 291,
    341
National Service 184, 186
National Society for the Prevention
    of Cruelty to Children. *See*
    NSPCC
National Union of Students. *See*
    NUS
National Vocational Qualifications.
    *See* NVQs
National Youth Agency. *See* NYA
Nazarene Theological College 293
NCB 128, 258
NCS 5, 79, 112, 141, 142, 166,
    183, 185, 187, 228–230,
    239, 265, 269, 313, 332,
    337, 343, 355, 361
  age range 197
  aims (short-term; long-term) 185,
    186, 195, 198, 200, 203,
    208
  community projects 186, 201
  contracts 186, 188, 205
  critiques 205
  funding/costs 5, 187–190, 198,
    204, 205, 208, 343
  impacts/outcomes 200–203, 207,
    209
  long-term cultural change
    184–186, 189, 198, 200
  marketing 198, 204
  NAO report 200, 206
  National Youth Board 189
  origins 183–185
  participant recruitment/recruit-
    ment 199
  participant recruitment/retention
    197–199

pilots/piloting 184–186, 196, 197
policy group 185
process and task 208
programmes 98, 166, 185, 187,
    188, 208, 209, 229, 230,
    314
Public Accounts Select
    Committee report - 2017
    204, 205, 207
social 'mixing' 200, 201, 208
staffing 196, 197, 206, 209
statutory base 188, 199, 204, 333,
    361
transition to adulthood 201
and youth service 187, 188, 190,
    200, 205, 207, 229, 250,
    361
and youth work 197, 206
NCVO 225
NCVQ 282
NCVYS 76, 78, 84, 89, 100, 113,
    122, 145, 148, 152, 223,
    255, 257–259, 261, 262,
    264, 265, 267, 268, 271,
    272, 275, 276, 290, 337,
    340, 341, 349, 350, 367
'Not in my name' campaign 268
Youth Report 2013 78
NEET 27, 241, 247–249, 256, 264
NEF Consulting 78
Neo liberal 54, 69, 109, 134, 182,
    291, 335, 336
Neo liberalism 2, 3, 5, 7, 13, 67
    defined 1, 77, 92, 136
    Objective 67
Network of Regional Youth Work
    Units 208, 327
Newcastle 337

New Labour 26, 31, 34, 37, 50, 54,
    57, 58, 69, 77, 116, 143,
    237, 288, 294
Newman University, Birmingham
    304
New model of public services vi, 25
New Philanthropy Capital 'wellbeing
    index' 145
New Policy Institute (NPI) 8
New Public Management. See
    Managerialism (new)
New universities 303
Nichols, Doug 335
Norfolk 244
Northamptonshire County Council
    5, 32, 71
North Somerset Council 330, 333
    court case 330
'Not in Education, Employment or
    Training'. See NEET
Nottinghamshire County Council
    89, 100
Nottingham Trent University 327
NSPCC 358
NUS 259, 334
NUT 315
NVQs 282, 283, 285, 289, 303, 317
    Level 2 283, 286
    Level 3 283, 290, 293
    Level 4 285, 286, 293, 317
    Level 5 317
NYA 32, 40, 41, 51, 52, 55, 56,
    58, 74, 83, 97, 98, 114,
    122, 125, 130, 141, 146,
    155, 188, 207, 221, 223,
    224, 242, 247, 259, 261,
    264, 265, 267, 269, 276,
    282–284, 290, 293, 300,

305–307, 309–311, 313,
314, 317, 320, 322, 334,
337, 339–341, 349, 350,
361

O

O2 189, 207, 309
Oasis College of Education 293
OCS 111
Office for Civil Society. *See* OCS
Office for National Statistics. *See*
ONS
Office for Standards in Education.
*See* OFSTED
Office of the Third Sector 111
OFSTED 29, 30, 32, 40, 41, 47,
48, 60, 148, 281–283, 286,
288, 296–298, 305
Oginsky, Paul 3, 128, 185
Oldham 241, 243
ONS 130, 354, 359
OnSide 97, 239–242, 333
evaluation 241
impacts 241
and youth work 242
youth zones 97, 239
'Open Drive' programme 57, 58. *See
also* Open for the Weekend
'Open for the Weekend' 57, 58
positive activities briefing paper
58
Open Letter 208, 336, 338, 343. *See
also* IDYW
Open University 287
Osborne, George 8, 68, 112, 329
Oswestry Town Council 90
Outcomes. *See* Impacts/outcomes

'Outsourcing' 31, 68. *See also*
Commissioning/commis-
sioners; Privatisation
Oxfordshire 75, 118, 329, 333
Oxfordshire Association of Youth
Clubs 95, 113
Oxfordshire County Council 95,
113

P

Parliamentary Roundtable event 335
Partnership for Young London 258
Partnerships/partnership working 4,
98, 99, 152, 157, 224, 246,
257, 261, 262, 267, 290,
362
Paul Hamlyn Trust 131
PAULO consortium 284
Payment by results 78, 95, 119, 142,
145–147, 163, 237, 248,
267. *See also* Social (invest-
ment/impact) bonds
PAYP 30, 50, 57
Performance measures. *See* Impacts/
outcomes
Personal advisors. *See* Connexions
Service
Personal and social skills 149, 160, 165
Personal Development Point consul-
tancy 128
Personal privacy. *See* ContactPoint
Philanthropic bodies 4
Philanthropy/Philanthropic organ-
isations 4, 54, 75, 76, 96,
189, 240. *See also* Charities;
Voluntary (youth) sector/
organisations

Pickles, Eric 115, 118, 124, 219, 220
Plaid Cymru 134
Plymouth MarJon University 79
Police/police forces 24, 38, 57, 133,
    162, 204, 219, 220, 329,
    340, 353
Polytechnics 303
Positive activities 30–32, 34, 50–53,
    55–58, 89, 96, 143, 152,
    172, 246, 292
    accessing 51
    strong supportive adults 53
    support from skilled adults 52
    transport guidance 51
Positive Activities for Young People.
    *See* PAYP
Positive for Youth 79, 98, 265, 291,
    337, 356
    discussion papers 161, 165
    'narrative for youth work' 166
    progress report 163, 169
*Positive for Youth* policy vi, 98
Poundland 185
Poverty 116, 228, 354. *See also*
    Young people, poverty/new
    precariat
Power balances 1, 281
Powerlessness 5, 6
Precariat/precarity. *See* Young people,
    poverty/new precariat
Pre-history 2, 339
Preston 240
'Prevent' strategy 34–38, 52,
    131–134
    channel programme 131
    and communities cohesion 34,
        35, 205, 247
    critiques 135

impacts on (Muslim) young peo-
    ple 34, 36
introduction/definitions/aims 172
and positive activities 52
and right-wing groups/organisa-
    tions 36
stigmatising muslims 134
and youth work methods 133
youth workers' role/involvement
    46, 132, 134
'Preventative' youth work 30, 51, 59
PriceWaterhouseCoopers 31, 50
Primarolo, Dawn 25
Prince Charles 218, 219, 222, 223
Prince's Trust 9, 76, 78, 184, 187,
    248, 261
Private companies 70, 99
Private sector/businesses 32, 54, 68,
    69, 73, 93, 97–99, 142,
    145, 147, 157, 162, 164,
    223, 237, 238, 249, 260,
    262, 263, 289
    private companies 70
    'socially responsible' businesses
        70, 97, 98
Private sector investment 145
Private sector methods of manage-
    ment and delivery 25
Privatisation 245, 333. *See
    also* Commissioning/
    commissioners
Pro Bono Economics consultancy
    226
Procurement 32. *See also*
    Commissioning/
    commissioners
Professional/professionalism 38,
    46, 93, 110, 168, 209,

286–289, 291–294, 304,
315, 334, 339–342
Professional Association of Lecturers
in Youth and Community
Work. *See* TAG
Professional qualifications 196,
285–290, 292–296, 303,
306, 307, 309, 316–318.
*See also* Training for youth
workers
Protection framework 25
Protect Services' petition 335
Public Health England 131
Public service jobs 68, 109, 110
Public Services (Social Value) Act
2012 69
Public transport 51, 55


Q

QAA 304, 319
Qualification 292
Quality Assurance Agency for Higher
Education. *See* QAA
Queen's Trust 240


R

Race on the Agenda 115
Radicalised/radicalisation 35, 133
RAF Benevolent Fund 96
RAMPs 286
Reading, University of 304
*Reconstruction* 361
Redbridge, London Borough of 32
Reed, Steve 206
Reformulation of the distinctive
values 263

Refugees/asylum seekers 90, 220,
248, 266
Regional Accreditation and
Monitoring Panels. *See*
RAMPs
Register of qualified youth workers
339, 340, 342
Registration 342
Resistance to deconstruction 327,
333. *See also* Young people,
activism, campaigning
campaigning through the unions
333
local campaigns 328
political defence 332
*Resourcing Excellent Youth Services
(REYS)* 46, 47, 77
'Respect' Agenda/Action Plan 24
Respublica 268
Revenue Support Grant 67, 165
Rigby, Lee 132, 133
Rio Ferdinand Foundation 327
Rio Tinto 185
RockCorps 189
Rose, Martyn 185
Rotherham/Rotherham Borough
Council 91, 134, 340
child sexual abuse 170
Royal Masonic Trust for Girls and
Boys 96
Rudd, Amber 355
Runnymede Trust 115
Ruskin College 305


S

Safer communities 52
Salisbury, Lord 96

Salmon Youth Centre 54, 238
Santander Foundation 96
Schools/schooling 9, 24, 33, 37, 38,
    50, 71, 95, 119, 127, 128,
    133, 141, 148, 159–161,
    166, 169, 184, 185, 190,
    195, 197, 198, 219,
    221–223, 226, 229, 238,
    241, 243, 267, 269, 308,
    310, 312, 329, 332, 355,
    357, 358
  character 128
  pastoral care 358
Scout Association/scouting 75, 96,
    103, 207, 217, 229, 265
Sector Skills Council for Care and
    Development 291
Sefton 74
Serco 70, 98, 115, 188
Serious violence strategy 249, 355, 356
Sexual orientation 111. See also
    LGBT
Shaftesbury Partnership 192
Sheffield Children and Young People
    Empowerment Project 257
Sheffield City Council 355
Sheffield futures 248
Smee, Anna 259, 260, 262, 275
Smith, Cat 335
'Social action' 7, 92, 112, 113,
    183, 186, 196, 208, 209,
    218, 221–228, 249, 260,
    269, 355, 357. See also
    Volunteering – young
    people
  social action fund 207
Social care 69

Social enterprises 4, 13, 69, 92, 94,
    110, 113, 146, 157, 189,
    223, 237, 246, 248, 312,
    331, 356
Social enterprise UK 70, 267
Social finance 70, 146, 267
Social impact bonds 78. See also
    Impacts/outcomes
Social media 9, 10, 52, 162, 337,
    342. See also Young people,
    and social media
Social Pedagogy 312
Social Value/Social Value Act 69, 94,
    241
'Socially responsible' business. See
    Private sector/businesses
'So far as reasonably practicable' 33
Somerset/Somerset County Council
    76, 359, 362
Southampton, University of 304
Spence, Jean 63, 250, 285, 297, 298,
    300, 311, 316, 321, 323
Spending on services for young
    people. See 'Youth services',
    budgets/funding
Spending reductions 246
Sport England 224
Sports activities and young people 52
Spurway, Kelly 331
Starbucks 98, 224
Starting from Strengths 281, 282, 296
State as public service provider 182,
    189
Statutory Youth Service base/guid-
    ance 5, 12, 33, 74, 114,
    130, 132, 143, 169, 171,
    330, 332, 333, 335, 343,

361. *See also* Youth Service
(local authority)
On the Education and Inspection
Act – 2006 52
'So far as reasonably practicable' 33
and 'youth work methods 34
Step Up To Serve 217, 223–225,
228, 234, 249, 334, 355
and youth work 224
impacts/outcomes 225
St Johns Ambulance Brigade 220
Stoke City Council 241
Stop-and-search 162
Story-telling workshops 338. *See also*
IDYW; *This is Youth Work:
Stories from Practice*
Structural factors/inequalities 3, 23,
128, 130, 135, 159
Sunderland 94
Sunderland City Council 240
*The Sun* 218
*Sun* newspaper 198
Support workers. *See* Youth workers,
as 'support workers'
Surrey 200


Targeted youth work/support/inter-
ventions 24, 25, 30, 38,
74, 89, 92, 94, 95, 135,
141–143, 161, 162, 169,
170, 218, 220, 242, 243,
246, 315, 329, 331
Teach First 197
Teaching agency 291
Teenage parents 248
Teenage pregnancies 72, 89, 131,
149, 152, 162, 247, 270

Ten Minute Rule Bill 332
Thatcher, Margaret 2, 160
Third Sector. *See* Voluntary (youth)
sector/organisations
*This is Youth Work: Stories from
Practice* 338
Thurrock Borough Council 94
Timpson, Edward 128, 163, 164,
359
Torbay Council 94
Trade union 73, 259, 333
CYWU/Unite, Unite, Unison 3
Training Agencies Group (TAG)
295, 304, 306–308, 311,
313, 317, 318, 323, 334
Training for youth workers 281, 285,
288, 289, 295, 317. *See also*
HE/HE courses
accreditation routes 308
aims
occupational/vocationalism
287, 290, 296
personal/professional development 256, 288, 291, 293,
307, 311, 317
apprenticeships 162, 285, 294,
317
degree 294, 317
modern 293
composition of the student body
308
course curricula/modularisation
309, 311, 312, 316
course placements 197, 306,
311–313
accredited placement centres
313
courses: number of 306, 307, 318
course targets/intakes 307, 309

degree: BA/postgraduate 285,
    293, 306, 307
Dip HE 285
employment-based routes 285
ethic balance 308
for part-timers and voluntary
    workers 281, 282, 286
foundation degrees 285–287,
    289, 294, 306
    foundation degree forward 294
    foundation degrees, modern
    284
functional analysis 283
gender balance 308
modern 284
on-the-job training 290
portfolios 282, 283
privatisation of courses 240,
    282–284
Professional Qualification
    Guidelines 318
    review 318
student numbers 307
students
    age ranges 26, 308
    employment prospects 309
    ethnic balance 12
    funding 308
    gender balance 26
    sponsored 305
subject benchmarks 311
teaching methods 306, 308
towards a new strategy 316
*Transforming Youth Work* 45–48, 336
'Transitions' 6, 165, 201, 228
Treasury 119
    discussion paper 2007 24, 46
    Revenue Support Grant 67, 68
    Spending Review 2010 68, 359

'Troubled Families' Programme/Unit
    92, 118, 133, 161
    targets 119
Trowbridge 76


U

UKCES 291
UK Commission for Employment
    and Skills. *See* UKCES
UK Youth 97, 223, 224, 238, 257,
    259–262, 265, 267, 269,
    270, 334, 337, 361
    Big Music Project 270
    and business funding/sponsor-
        ship/partnerships 97
    and character development 129
    conception/definition of youth
        work 288
    and government's youth policies/
        strategy 1
    IT Hubs 270
    merger with ambition 238
    money management programmes
        for young people 98
    and NCS 98, 207, 259, 260
    Social Development Journey 260,
        270
    Youth Action programme 98
    Youth Sector Collaboration
        Project 259, 269
    and youth volunteering 224
    and youth work training 288
UK Youth Parliament 328
UK Youth Voice 328
Unclaimed assets in bank accounts
    30, 54, 55
Uniformed youth organisations 217,
    218, 356

militarism/anti-militarism 219,
222
Uniformed Youth Social Action
Fund. *See* UYSAF
Unison 73, 315, 333, 334, 337, 338
Unite 264, 308–311, 314, 315, 318,
330, 338. *See also* CYWU/
Unite
United futures 98, 99
United States Peace Corps 184
Universal services 141, 142
Universities 306. *See also* Training for
youth workers
assessing 'excellence' 303
New 303
Russell Group 303, 306
University and College Union 315
UYSAF 220, 221
Impacts/outcomes 221


V

Vinspired 182, 187, 188, 224, 228,
259
'Violent extremist' 7, 35
Virgin Money Foundation 224, 240
Vocational training 303
Voluntary, Community and Social
Enterprise (VCSE) 127, 246
Voluntary (youth) sector/organisa-
tions 57, 93, 110, 111, 142,
163–165, 171, 181, 182,
184, 335, 340
and the big society 110, 111
collaboration and alliances 258
collective impact project 261
drifting 'missions' 262
filling services gaps 4, 75, 96

funding
cuts 68, 77, 95, 111, 255, 258
sources 57, 89, 92, 96, 239,
256
independence – threats to 3, 59,
222, 267
and managerialism 3, 263
mergers 238, 261, 262
mission/values/role 262, 263
'marketisation'/partnerships with
business 157, 264, 267
Volunteering England 219
Volunteering – young people 7,
113, 182, 184, 189, 217,
221–223, 226, 227
compulsion 182, 223
and 'disadvantage' 182, 224
full-time 226
impacts 226
Military option 182
professionalised/bureaucratised/
commodified 228
purposes
individual or shared/collective?
227
in whose interests? 227
'rebadged' 183
and youth work 229
Volunteers - adult 110, 111, 220,
291, 293, 340, 341
ethnicity 282
face-to-face workers 282
training 290
Voting age 6, 328


W

Wandsworth, London Borough of 94

Warwickshire 118, 328
Warwickshire Association of Youth
    Clubs 256
Warwick, University of 284
Wei, Lord 185
Welfare benefits/system 79, 204,
    266, 267
Wellbeing 129, 130, 135
    and 'happiness' 129
    Health and Wellbeing Boards 130
    National Wellbeing Programme
        130
    objectives 130
Wellcome Trust 258
Westhill College of Education 303
Westhoughton Town Council 90
West Sussex County Council 76, 90
White, Chris 69
Whizz Kidz 129
Wigan/Wigan Metropolitan
    Borough Council 74, 240,
    241, 243
#iwill 223, 249, 355
Williams, Becky 328
Williamson, Howard 224, 233
Wilson, Rob 114, 116, 158, 171,
    197, 207, 225, 246, 249,
    361
Wiltshire County Council 58
Windsor and Maidenhead Borough
    Council 94
Wings South West, Devon 257
Wishart, Nicky 329
Wolverhampton 243
Wolverhampton City Council 241
Woodcraft Folk 220, 259, 266, 276,
    334
Woolwich 133

Workforce Development
    Implementation Group
    284, 290, 305, 339
Working class/working class boys
    6, 9
World Health Organisation 9
Wright, Ian 171
Wylie, Tom 141

Y
YAT 184, 185
YCF 30, 49, 54, 55, 57, 72
YMCA 73, 99, 133, 266, 276, 290,
    361
YMCA Derbyshire 95
YOF 7, 30, 49, 54
Yorkshire and Humber region 313
Young Adult Trust. See YAT
Young Cumbria 95
Young Foundation 166, 169, 267
    Framework of outcomes for young
        people 77, 166
Young Men's Christian Association.
    See YMCA
Young people 11
    activism, campaigning 218, 328
    age discrimination 135
    balances of power 11
    BAME/BME 13, 222, 264, 354,
        355, 360
    bus travel 51
    deficit model of 24, 29, 182, 185
    defined 1, 7, 10, 29, 46
    disabled 13, 220, 222, 241, 257,
        354
    election turnout 6
    homelessness 162, 248, 354, 355,
        358

housing benefit 6, 266, 269
individual qualities/self-reliance/
    resilience 24, 38, 149, 167,
    219
lesbian, gay, bisexual and trans-
    gender 3, 13, 218, 257, 354
levels of life satisfaction 9, 227
mental health problems 9, 131,
    266, 354
Muslim 7, 34, 46, 52, 132–134
offending/offenders 50, 89, 95,
    129, 195, 247, 248, 256
peers 11
poverty/new precariat 7, 159,
    264, 267, 354, 360
rural 264
and social media 1, 10, 162
'Transitions' 6, 165, 201, 228
unemployed/'NEET' 6, 27, 78,
    181, 247, 249, 256, 355
'voice'/participation/'empower-
    ment' 5, 7, 30, 32, 36, 46,
    55, 67, 93, 144, 146, 163,
    169, 170, 223, 224, 246,
    259, 291, 312
and 'violent extremism'/'radicali-
    sation' 36, 37, 132, 133
and volunteering 142, 166
volunteering. See Volunteering –
    young people; 'Social action'
voting age 6, 328
working class (white) 9, 134
young carers 359
Young People's Workforce Reform
    Programme 285
Young women 9, 13, 218, 264, 266
Young Women's Christian
    Association. See YWCA
Young Women's Trust 266

Youth affairs minister 357
Youth Capital Fund 30, 256. See also
    YCF
Youth Contract 161
Youth Engagement Fund 247
Youth Inclusion Programmes 38
Youth Innovation Zones 243, 244
Youth Investment Fund 248, 355
    aims 249
Youth Justice Board 132
Youth justice v, 285
Youth Matters 29, 48, 49, 50
Youth Matters: Next Steps 46, 48, 49
Youth offending teams (YOTs) 30,
    35, 132, 312
Youth Opportunities Fund 30. See
    also YOF
Youth Opportunity Card 50
Youth policies v, vi, vii, 1, 2, 6, 11,
    13, 23, 25, 26, 37, 50, 59,
    60, 67, 116, 118, 127, 142,
    149, 158, 159, 164, 182,
    183, 223, 239, 250, 265,
    268, 281, 284, 327, 335,
    339, 343, 353, 356, 357,
    361, 364
    child-saving 59
    non-interventionist approach 162
    objectives 181
Youth Professional Standards 289
Youth Sector Collaboration
    Consultation 259, 269
Youth sector market 267
Youth Service (local authority) 12,
    24, 26, 28, 29, 32, 34, 37,
    46, 57, 59, 68, 74, 89, 109,
    114, 116, 136, 164, 243,
    289, 360
    absences 24

accredited/recorded outcomes 47
and Coalition government 4
  curriculum statement 47
  outsourcing 32
and 'deprivation' 24
buildings 363
bureaucracy/management structure 158, 363
decision-making structures and
  procedures 13, 363
deconstruction – steps towards
  181, 332, 360
funding
  cuts 143
history/definition 12, 142
legislative/statutory base. *See*
  Statutory Youth Service base/
  guidance
local offer 169, 172
Ministers' expressions of doubt 47
and MyPlace/youth zones 56, 238,
  240, 362
and NCS 5, 187, 200, 207
and New Labour 23, 45, 47, 53,
  60, 74, 164, 171
'patchy and unsatisfactory' 33
performance measures/outcomes.
  *See* Impacts/outcomes
and *Positive for Youth* 165, 167,
  171
staff(ing)
  ethnicity 26
state funding/budget cuts 71–73,
  79, 89, 91, 93, 94, 116,
  118, 147, 158, 165, 171,
  243, 246, 250, 266, 289,
  328–331, 333
'unreformed and unco-operative'
  165

youth services 73
'Youth services' 163, 165
  budgets/funding 74
  cuts/effects 68, 71, 72, 146,
    148, 151, 242, 246, 247,
    258
  and child protection 74, 161
  defined 13
  joined-up/integrated/seamless 26,
    27, 30, 51, 120, 162, 169,
    287, 289, 309, 313
  and New Labour
    joined-up/integrated/seamless
    26, 27, 30, 51, 120, 162
  and 'marginal' young people
    52, 265
  'modernisation'/reforms 26
  multi-agency working 31
  outsourcing 4, 5
  *Positive for Youth* 74, 148, 162,
    163, 166, 167, 243
  staffing 74
  targeting/targets 162, 168
Youth Service Bills 335
Youth Service Development Council
  181
Youth Social Action Fund 223
Youth Social Action Journey Fund
  223
Youth Task Force 25
Youth Taskforce Action Plan 24, 52
Youth United Foundation. *See* YUF
'Youth Voice' 5, 7, 169, 259
'Youth volunteering' 7, 182, 217,
  222, 223, 226, 227
Youth work
  accredited outcomes 59
  alternative organisational
    structures. *See* Mutuals/

co-operatives; Social
enterprises
appendage to other services/prac-
tices 169
as child-saving 120, 312
and community cohesion 36
detached/outreach 12, 26
digital 10
as 'early intervention' 169, 314
education-focused 31
history/definitions 11, 142, 167,
288, 336, 341
informal approaches 55
as informal education 49
as a 'learning process' 45
and MyPlace/youth zones 56
and NCS 113
and New Labour 33, 45, 47, 287
New Labour spending 46
on the wing 59
'open access' 11, 47, 53, 59, 60,
74, 79, 89, 94, 95, 100, 142,
144, 145, 147, 151, 152,
167, 168, 207, 208, 230,
269, 313, 338, 360, 363,
364
outcome and impacts. *See*
Impacts/outcomes
and positive activities 49, 51
and *Positive for Youth* 167
as prevention 310, 311
and Prevent strategy 46, 134
process 52, 167
professional 286
senior members 295
targeted 13, 246, 310

training and qualifications. *See*
Training for youth workers;
HE/HE courses
'unstructured' youth clubs' 34
voluntary engagement/self-chosen
49, 142, 167, 284
voluntary sector/organisations. *See*
Voluntary (youth) sector/
organisations
and 'work with young people' 14,
246
young people's views on 170, 328
youth leadership 12
as youth volunteering 229
Youth workers 24, 36, 37, 46, 48, 56
career routes 295
digital practice 10
ethnicity 12, 26, 111, 293, 305
for part-timers and voluntary
workers 290, 291
gender balance 12, 26, 293, 305
marginal roles 26, 46
part-time 240, 281–283, 286, 295
'Protected' title 339
qualified - replaced by volunteers
258, 264
recruitment/retention 305, 306,
309
salaries/conditions of service 94,
314
skills 120, 281
as social care workers, etc 294, 310
strikes 333
as support workers 292, 293, 309
training/qualifications 49, 363
Youth Work Expert Group 264

Youth Work Foundation 309
Youth Work Narrative 166, 168
Youth work training 281, 285, 288,
    295. *See also* HE/HE courses
  for part-timers and voluntary
    workers 281, 286, 290
  towards a new strategy 316

YUF 218–221, 231, 232
YWCA 266

Z

Zahawi, Nadhim 358
Zero hours work 8, 98, 228

Lightning Source UK Ltd.
Milton Keynes UK
UKHW021317051219
354675UK00017B/705/P